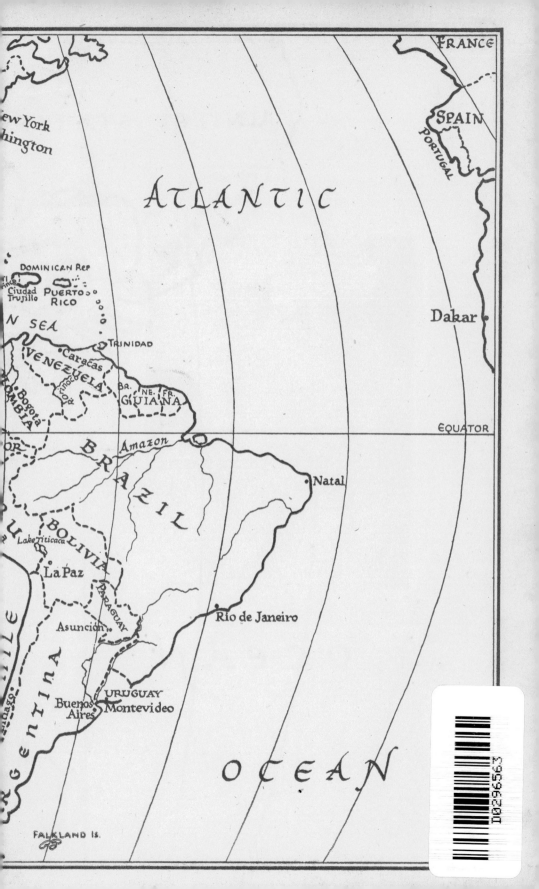

FRANCE

SPAIN

PORTUGAL

ATLANTIC

ew York
hington

DOMINICAN REP

Ciudad
Trujillo

PUERTO
RICO

Dakar

N SEA

Caracas

TRINIDAD

VENEZUELA

BR. NE. FR.
GUIANA

OMBIA

Bogota

Orinoco

OR

Amazon

EQUATOR

BRAZIL

Natal

OR

BOLIVIA

Lake Titicaca

La Paz

PARAGUAY

Rio de Janeiro

Asunción

GENTINA

URUGUAY

Buenos
Aires

Montevideo

OCEAN

FALKLAND IS.

BY THE SAME AUTHOR

AND SO TO WAR

Good Neighbors

ARGENTINA
BRAZIL
CHILE

& Seventeen Other Countries

BY HUBERT HERRING

NEW HAVEN · YALE UNIVERSITY PRESS

LONDON · HUMPHREY MILFORD · OXFORD UNIVERSITY PRESS

COPYRIGHT 1941 BY YALE UNIVERSITY PRESS

Printed in the United States of America

First published, July, 1941
Second printing, August, 1941
Third printing, September, 1941
Fourth printing, November, 1941
Fifth printing, April, 1942
Sixth printing, October, 1942
Seventh printing, June, 1943
Eighth printing, April, 1944
Ninth printing, December, 1944

FOREWORD

THESE pages were chiefly written in the hills about Córdoba and under the long shadows of the Chilean cordillera. They are written in affection for thousands of Latin Americans who have received me in friendship during my fifteen years' wanderings in their homelands. They are written in candor, in an effort to escape the romanticism which so readily besets Northern wanderers in lands where summer is winter and the language of Cervantes takes the place of the idiom of Milton. They are written in urgency, for the Americas face their gravest threat. They are written in hope for the free and loyal alliance of the 260 millions of the twenty-one republics of the Western World.

There is a certain presumption in any outsider who essays to write of others' lands. If my Latin-American friends take offense at my candor, I answer, we of the United States can take as well as give. We, too, entertain guests who presume to hold the mirror to our life, to tell us where democracy falters, where racial bigotry stains, where economic inequities condemn millions to poverty. I have written of the laggard constitutionalism of Latin America, of the biting misery of the masses, of the threat offered by unteachable conservatives, fanatical radicals, and alien disrupters. Any Latin-American visitor can write of our Boss Hagues, our ruthless lobbies which block public will, of hungry share croppers and hounded itinerant workers, of our city slums and country tenements. I have sought to be fair, but I have undoubtedly made mistakes in emphasis and interpretation. Latin Americans will write books about the United States, they will seek to be fair, they also will make mistakes. The cause of inter-American understanding is served by a mutual frankness which risks mistakes.

This book is chiefly devoted to Argentina, Brazil, and Chile; not that other lands are less important in the teamwork of the Americas, or of less interest, or have people less worth cultivation. I have chosen to give more attention to three important countries rather than spread my attention and that of the reader over twenty nations.

It is high time the people of the United States discover the other Americans. Our world closes in upon us. American solidarity, once regarded as a pleasant elective, has become an imperious necessity. The United States needs Latin America for the goods she can sell, and as security against attack. The Latin Americans need the United States if their sovereignty is to be assured. The United States might conceivably travel alone, but no Latin-American nation can do so. The United States, inviting an all-American front, offers as much as it asks.

I am indebted to hundreds whose names do not appear—public officials, textile workers, scholars, bartenders, bootblacks, priests, schoolteachers, shopkeepers, and boys on the street. I cannot list all of their names, I therefore list none. Many spoke in confidence, and their names could not fairly be given. My debt to writers of books is indicated in the bibliography.

I thank Eugene Davidson and his staff of the Yale University Press, whose labors are never perfunctory. I appreciate the permission of the editors of *Harper's Magazine* and *The Yale Review* to reprint material which first appeared in their columns. I acknowledge my chief debt to my wife, Helen Baldwin Herring, for months of delving, sharing with me the gathering of material and the preparation of the manuscript. My daughter Virginia Herring has given me weeks of intelligent help.

HUBERT HERRING

New York, May 1, 1941.

CONTENTS

PART II. BRAZIL

PART III. CHILE

PART IV. SEVENTEEN OTHER COUNTRIES

ILLUSTRATIONS

MAPS

Maps by Helen Baldwin Herring and Robert Galvin

A PROLOGUE FOR AMERICANS

THERE have always been two Americas . . .

America North . . . the America of the Anglo-Saxon who settled Massachusetts and Virginia, established town meetings, and believed in the Word.

America South . . . from Mexico to Patagonia . . . the America of the Iberians, seekers after gold, builders of cities and cathedrals . . . peoples who lived by the sword and swore by the Cross.

The Americans North and the Americans South have gone their separate ways, four hundred years South, three hundred North . . . killing their Indians, importing their black slaves, breeding and intermingling . . . welcoming boatloads of Poles, Greeks, Italians, Germans, Swedes, Spaniards, Turks, Russians, to tend looms in Massachusetts, to dig tin in Bolivia, to raise wheat in Minnesota, to pick cotton in Alabama, to gather coffee in Brazil, to chop coal in Pennsylvania.

The Americans have found no common tongue, there has been little traffic in ideas between them . . . their peoples have not understood each other or cared whether they understood each other . . . Americans North have viewed Americans South as pleasant but impractical neighbors, always late for dinner, not to be trusted in business deals, knowing nothing of law or government . . . Americans South have viewed Americans North as ill-mannered fellows who do not shake hands, *mal-educados* intent upon closing a deal and without taste for the more leisurely gifts of the spirit.

Americans North and Americans South cut their cords with Europe . . . in 1776, in 1810, and in the years which followed . . . Americans North created a state with thirteen colonies which forthwith leaped the Alleghenies and the Mississippi and the Rockies . . . Americans South divided into twenty states, from pocket republics in Central America to the sprawling empire of Brazil . . . each with its flag, constitution, congress, presi-

dent, courts, army . . . each a free sovereign independent republic, a democracy with the people supreme . . . so the pre-
amble of each separate constitution affirmed.

There was still no traffic, North and South

. . . save for a few traders who swapped rum, plows, carpet
tacks, muslin for coffee, cotton, sugar, bananas

. . . and a few missionaries who carried the Gospel . . . to the
continuing annoyance of the Americans South who thought they
already had the gospel

. . . and a few marines, dispatched by Americans North for
the redemption of near-by Americans South . . . taking half of
Mexico's ill-policed territory . . . conferring the blessing of free
elections upon Nicaraguans, of hygienic cookery upon Haitians,
of a speculative independence upon Panamanians . . . and upon
all the privilege of making uninterrupted payments to the National City or some other bank.

Then some bankers took the savings of college professors and
of country doctors in Elgin and Elyria and thrust crowded handfuls of it upon Brazil, Chile, Peru, Bolivia . . . excellent interest,
plus commission, minus security . . . the investors can see the
docks and the palaces which their money built in Rio, Lima, and
Valparaiso.

But there was still no tie between America North and America
South . . . boats sailed east and west, Buenos Aires to Liverpool,
Rio to Southampton, Montevideo to Naples . . . carrying goods
and ideas . . . some sailed north carrying goods . . . Americans
North continued to view with ill-disguised contempt all Americans South who had not learned the orderly fashions of government prevailing in Chicago, Jersey City, and other centers of
light and learning . . . Americans South continued to find Paris
more interesting than New York, and it became the fashion to
speak of the materialism of the North.

And then the Americans North invented Pan-Americanism
and began to call conferences in Washington, Rio de Janeiro,
Buenos Aires, Santiago, Mexico, Havana, and Montevideo . . .
where the beauties of brotherhood were periodically pledged in

Moet et Chandon . . . with conventions, agreements, and peace pacts aplenty, few of which were ratified by any sizable list of the twenty-one sovereign republics . . . Andrew Carnegie built a palace in Washington for the Pan-American Union where the orations on Bolívar, Washington, Lincoln, and San Martín might have a suitable background of potted palms . . . Americans North thought it delightful . . . Americans South translated it into careful Spanish which said Pan-Americanism means Buy from the United States.

And then came the era of the good neighbor . . . Americans North were washed in the Blood of the Lamb, forswore their ancient ways, vowed repentance and a change of heart and life . . . this really began with dour Coolidge who sent Dwight Morrow to Mexico . . . continued under honest Hoover who got the marines out of Port-au-Prince and Managua . . . found fulfillment in the reign of the gentleman farmer from Hyde Park, who went all the way to Buenos Aires on a battleship to proclaim the Doctrine of the Good Neighbor, to preach the beauties of brotherhood, righteousness, the good life, democracy, and peaceableness . . . calling upon all Americans everywhere to abjure evils elsewhere prevailing . . . the Americans South were almost persuaded, a few continued to wonder . . .

And still there was no living Pan-Americanism, no sense of a commanding unity binding Americans in defense of democracy against disturbers of our Western peace

. . . no Pan-Americanism in the United States . . . Iowans seldom saw Argentina, Argentines never visited Iowa . . . Iowans continued to have no idea about Argentines . . . save that Argentine beef and wheat and corn should be kept out . . . no slightest conception of what manner of men lived in Argentina, suspecting only that they were not so good as they should be, something like the French perhaps, or Negroes, or Turks

. . . no Pan-Americanism in the South . . . Mexicans, Nicaraguans, Dominicans, and Haitians wondered when we would annex them . . . Colombians remembered Panama . . . Argentina kept talking about the beef we did not buy . . . the younger

intellectuals recited words about the Champs Élysées, and referred to the sordid North.

Meanwhile what little democracy there was in the South was
ebbing . . . constitutional governments were overturned in
Brazil, Bolivia, Uruguay, Paraguay . . . dictators ruled without
benefit of courts or congresses . . . Vargas in Brazil, Benavides in
Peru, Trujillo in Santo Domingo . . . self-conscious little Na-
poleons . . . dispatching their critics to jail or to eternal glory.

But the *savoir-faire* of the Good Neighbor was not to be disturbed . . . Mr. Roosevelt continued to address his "great and
good friend," General Trujillo of the Dominicans, and he
stopped in Rio de Janeiro to embrace the "co-author of the New
Deal" Dr. Getulio Vargas . . . meanwhile using words which
when translated into Japanese, German, and Italian sounded
like "skunk" to describe the gentlemen who rule in Tokyo, Berlin, and Rome . . . these courtesies seemed lost on the rulers of
the Americans South . . . rumors spread that Benavides was
playing with Mussolini, that Vargas loved German ways overmuch.

And then came Adolf Hitler . . . creator of the first authentic
Pan-Americanism to flourish in this Western World . . . under
the whip of fear the Americas suddenly felt such flush of mutual
affection as to upset all previous calculations . . . the Washington Congress voted $500,000,000 to the Export-Import Bank, and
Warren Lee Pierson, its president, crammed the money into his
wallet and flew from airport to airport, seeking out ways in
which to give the money away.

And the Americans South are bewildered by this sudden evidence of neighborly affection . . . wondering whether it is love
for love's sweet sake or whether there is a dowry in the offing
. . . not quite sure whether to welcome the visiting cruisers and
destroyers with hosannas or with hisses . . . curious as to what
strings are tied to the gifts which they are about to receive . . .
which reveals the Latin Americans as eminently practical men
despite their own disclaimers.

And Franklin Delano Roosevelt, President of the Americans

North and chief hero of millions of Americans South, avers that we must defend the Hemisphere against all comers.

And Americans North want to know exactly who are these good neighbors for whom we are about to bare our breasts and armor plate . . . what they eat, think, and propose to do . . . what sort of men rule over them . . . whether they plan to play with us or with the foe . . . when and if that foe appears.

That is what this book is about.

PART ONE: ARGENTINA

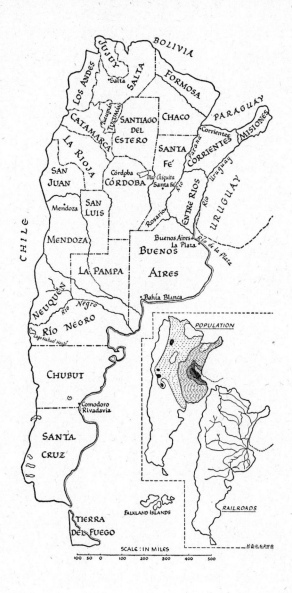

ARGENTINA

A IS for Argentina in that South American tripartite ABC, of which diplomats speak when about to provoke a war or promote a peace. Not that Argentina is the most populous or the largest or the most exciting of the republics to the south. It is not.

Why then should we write of Argentina? Why indeed should anyone read of Argentina? There is scant glamour there. If you would have exotic colors, strange plants and birds, you will turn to Ecuador or Brazil. If you seek sixteenth-century churches with groaning buttresses and chipped saints you will find a half-hundred of them in one square mile of Guatemala Antigua. If you have a taste for Mayan and Incan mounds, buried cities and carved temples, you will go to Mexico and Peru. If you would paint Indians in strange attire, then Bolivia will serve you better. If you look for snow-crowned mountains piled by the sides of lakes, you will turn to Chile. If you search for strange tribal ways, you will not find them in Argentina, for her ways are about as strange as those of Back Bay, Oak Park, and Pasadena.

Then why bother with Argentina?

There are two excellent reasons.

The first is pique. The reading of Argentine gibes at the United States excites curiosity as to what there is in us which churns up such tempests in Argentine breasts. Much of the written output of Argentina, all the way from Manuel Ugarte's thrusts to *La Nación's* column from New York, suggests that the dwellers by the Río de la Plata are annoyed with us. Their chronic distaste invites inspection.

The second is prudence. South America has overnight become important to us. It may remain the one friendly spot in which we can collect postcards and sell our curling irons. American solidarity, long regarded as a pleasant elective, has become a clamorous necessity. There will be no Pan-Americanism which does not reckon with Argentina, the most mature, alert, and enterprising of our American neighbors. Furthermore, Argentina is a nation, which is more than may faithfully be reported of some political divisions south of Key West.

There are other excellent reasons for cultivating Argentina, but pique and prudence will serve as starting points.

CHAPTER I

THE LAND AND THE PEOPLE

ARGENTINA'S 13 millions occupy an area somewhat in excess of 1 million square miles—an area roughly equivalent to that of the United States east of the Mississippi, plus Louisiana and Texas. Argentina reaches north and south 2,285 miles, with a maximum width of 930 miles and a coast line of over 1,600 miles. South, it touches the 55th degree of latitude in the Antarctic; north, the 21st degree in the foothills of the Bolivian Andes. If you would think in northern terms, it corresponds to the span from the southern shores of Hudson Bay to the central plateau of Mexico. It is a big country—bigger than Britain, France, Germany, Spain, Portugal, Italy, Switzerland, Belgium, Yugoslavia, and Denmark put together.

Three fourths of all Argentines live in one quarter of the country: a half-circle inscribed with Buenos Aires as the center, swinging some 300 miles north, west, and south—a rich-soiled, well-watered, treeless, and temperate plain. This one quarter furnishes more than three fourths of the resources of the nation. Here are the chief cities, most of the industries, the cattle, the sheep, the grain.

South, west, and north the country spreads out. The south, Patagonia, is dry and cold, chiefly useful for the sparse grazing of sheep. The central-western zone is semiarid, productive only when irrigated. The subtropical plains, swamps, and forests of the north yield cotton, sugar, yerba maté, tobacco, rice, and quebracho. On the western and northern fringes is the high cordillera, with snow-banked Aconcagua, Incahuasi, Veladeres, and Famatina standing guard 20,000 feet above the sea.

This was once an Indian land. The Guaranís, no one knows how many, held the north. The Patagonians (i.e., "the large-footed," Magellan's name for the Tehuelches) ranged the south.

These Indians refused to come to terms with the Spanish invader, and were steadily pushed back as European settlement expanded. There was free mingling of blood in the north, where many Argentines speak a Spanish with the lilt of Indian America, and have eyes betraying their more ancient lineage. The Argentine way with the Indian was also the American way—outright extermination, or exile to the dry lands where he could starve in peace. The device has worked. While the United States reduced its Indian population by one half in the nineteenth century, Argentina was even more successful: of the estimated 1,000,000 in 1825, some 20,000 to 30,000 pure Indians survive today. Argentina is a "white man's country."

Modern Argentina is the creature of European immigration. *Gobernar es poblar* (to govern is to populate) was the formula prescribed by Juan Bautista Alberdi, author of the Constitution of 1853. Argentina's stock is white European and presents a different face from that of Indian Mexico, Peru, Bolivia, and Ecuador. The immigrant tide began in the 1850's, was in full flow by 1870, and continued to the eve of the first World War. As migrants arrived by every boat, the Indian was forced to make way. In 1877 General Julio Roca cleared Patagonia of the last obstinate first-Americans and released 70 million acres for national expansion.

News of this open frontier spread. Between 1858 and 1928, 5,740,000 settlers entered Argentina, 79.6 % of them from Spain and Italy. Since 1910 some 1,200,000 Spaniards and 1,000,000 Italians found homes there. The population of Argentina breaks down in some such fashion as this: European origin 77.4 %, European by birth 19.5 %, those with some Indian blood 3.1 %.[1] There are few Negroes, as slavery was never important and was abolished in 1825. Argentina and Uruguay, whose racial pattern is almost identical, may be set down as the *whitest* American republics—not excluding the United States, with its 10 % of Negro citizens.

---

1. These are Alejandro E. Bunge's figures for 1939. Their decimalized exactness raises the question of their source. The last census was taken in 1914.

Argentines divide into two unequal parts: the *porteños,* or
"port dwellers," the 3½ millions of Greater Buenos Aires; and
the 9½ million *provinciales.* A gulf is fixed between them. The
tumults of the nineteenth century were rooted in their antagonism. It still serves as a decisive factor.

First the *puerto* and the *porteños.* Buenos Aires offers few sur-
prises to those who know Chicago. The two cities have the same
noises, the same smells, the same flatness, the same politicians,
the same bad habits, the same saving graces. There is more smoke
in Chicago, there are more trees in Buenos Aires. Buenos Aires
has the best subway in the Americas, Chicago has the worst "El."
Chicago's skyscrapers are higher, Buenos Aires has more room to
breathe. Buenos Aires, like Chicago, deserves credit for doing
so much with so little help from Nature. She has what passes as
a river, the Río de la Plata, named the "River of Silver" by Juan
Díaz de Solís. This river is an arm of the sea into which the
Paraná and the Uruguay pour the sifted topsoil of four nations
and churn it with sea water to produce a mustard emulsion which
only the very drunk or the very-much-in-love or those-who-have-
never-seen-the-Hudson could possibly call silver. The builders of
Buenos Aires made a city on the mudbanks of the Río de la Plata.
Its highest hills would hardly reach the knees of Grant's Tomb.
They laid out miles of tree-lined streets and generous boulevards,
scattered good and bad statues about, built houses and office
buildings picked at random from the Rue de Rivoli, the Strand,
Friedrichstrasse, and the Calle de Alcalá, and then as an afterthought added a thousand apartment houses copied after German and American modernists. Streets are lively, flower stalls
surprise you at every turn, shops invite, and there are the nicest
confiterías with the most lacy curtains in the world. So, as cities
go, Buenos Aires is one of the most enlivening.

The porteño who lives in this City of Good Airs by the River
of Silver may be a lawyer or a clerk, a student or a waiter, a taxi
driver or a justice of the supreme court, but he shows typical
markings. He speaks Spanish with the vigor of a pile driver, a
Spanish which has neither the caress of the Mexican nor the

cadence of the Colombian. He works hard, idles feverishly. He has little of the leisurely grace of the Brazilian, and does not know how to waste words with the profligacy of a Peruvian. He is alternately maddeningly suave and harshly abrupt. Migrants fresh from Brazil or Chile incline to think him discourteous. If there are grounds for this gratuitous description, perhaps the bleakness of Nature may be saddled with the blame. Perhaps Nature's slight upon Argentina explains the typical music, the tango, which seems to mirror the sadness and the monotony of the pampas that lie at the end of every city pavement—the mood of the lone horseman of the plains rather than the notes of birds in pleasant valleys. There is a determined sophistication in the cultural life of the capital, as though its contrivers were fiercely intent upon forgetting something and upon seeking escape in other worlds. Argentine painting, with notable but scant exceptions, is synthetic French. Argentine music is almost altogether borrowed. Argentine writing, with exceptions again, is diluted Proust, Molière, and Racine. The porteño fancies himself as a cosmopolitan. He dresses the part. I get the impression of more well-dressed men on Buenos Aires streets than in any city in the world. If he aspires to culture, he reads in French and plans another journey to Paris. He turns his back as though in shame upon the pampas which give him life, and reckons himself a citizen of a world which lies east. The porteño, no matter how tiny his business or practice, knows himself cut off by ponderable barriers from his uninitiated countrymen.

The *provincial,* citizen of colonial Córdoba, Salta, Tucumán, Santa Fé, dweller in the hinterland of the pampas, delights in his apartness from the capital. Buenos Aires, he tells you, is not Argentina. (Nor, swears Iowa, is New York the United States.) The provincial knows himself as belonging to the authentic stream of Argentine life. In his veins flows conquerors' blood. His father's fathers carried Spanish civilization from Sevilla to Lima, from Lima to High Peru, they crossed the cordillera to found the colonies of the Río de la Plata. He claims as his own the hero saga of the land, the gaucho legend, the living embodiment of the frontier spirit. The gaucho was the horseman, the frontiersman, the true creator of the New World, the man in whom Spanish and Indian blood mixed for the production of a prouder race. As he disdained the life of the city, so does the dweller in Córdoba and Salta of today despise the perfumed life of the capital, with its aping of alien ways. The provincial distrusts the city's faithlessness and clings to the traditions of church and family, the folkways of a Spanish civilization which tend to lose their hold on the capital.

Which of these is Argentina? Feverish, ambitious, proud, somewhat mad Buenos Aires? Or is it Córdoba, where the viceroy still seems to live, and where men and women abide by the eternal verities of correctness and firm faith?

The answer is, both.

You can never understand Argentina without knowing both the porteño and the provincial.

You can understand neither without remembering Spain.

CHAPTER II

THE LONG ARM OF SPAIN

WHAT would have been the fate of America," muses a Latin-American friend, "had the Spanish landed in Massachusetts Bay, and the English at Vera Cruz?"

There *was* a difference. New England was settled by men who asked work, homes, freedom. New Spain—all Spanish America —was first opened by men who asked gold, quick profit, a speedy return to the homeland. Settlers came later.

There *is* a difference. Modern Argentina in particular, all Hispanic America in general, must be understood in terms of Hapsburg-Bourbon Spain. Spain's arm is long. Her fingerprints are clear on the Argentine flesh.

First, there is the Spanish imponderable *dignidad.* It cannot

quite be translated. "Dignity" does not cover it. Dignidad implies class feeling, a set of attitudes which go with graded ranks.
It carries definite implications as to the baseness of manual labor.
I remember the injured spirits of my Córdoba friend when I
carried a suitcase through the streets. The proper Cordobesa may
carry a little package tied with string from the confitería, but a
shoebox, never. I also recall fifteen years' fruitless search for a
Latin-American friend who really enjoys swinging an axe or
wielding a hoe. Dignidad creates an aura in which men trade,
negotiate, associate. It perhaps accounts for a certain indirection
which so often marks international dealings, and explains why a
Cordell Hull will never understand a José María Cantilo.

Second, Spain imparted the passion for latifundia ("broad
farms," in literal Latin). Just as the first families of Sevilla joined
league to league until there was no room for the *rotos,* "the
broken ones," so did the first families of Santa Fé and Buenos
Aires plot out their feudal realms. This colonial habit persisted
into the days of independence. Today, two thousand families
own one fifth of all the land, a much larger share of the best
land, and gather the major toll of field and pasture.

Third, Spain taught Argentina the lessons of bad government.
The Spanish empire prospered long as the raider of the seas
rather than as the cultivator of her gardens. When Spain opened
America, the dominant aim was to fix outposts for the collection
of profits rather than to settle ambitious sons. (In fairness, it must
be noted that the English were no less avid for profit, no less
willing to exploit.) Spain systematically denied her colonists the
catharsis of self-rule. A grudged measure of municipal self-
government was permitted under the *cabildo* (the "town council"), a severely limited liberty at best, usually dominated by the
priests. Membership in the cabildo was often bought and sold,
knocked down to the highest bidder, and in some cases was
hereditary. All the higher offices in colonial government, the
bulk of the lower, were preëmpted by favored sons of the ruling
families of Spain. Even these favored sons were not trusted, but
were frequently displaced by new appointees from Spain in or-

der to assure the subserviency of this shifting officialdom. Spanish colonial rule was a feudal cheat. The Crown pressed the viceroys for profit; the viceroys bore down upon the cabildos and the *estancieros*[1] and the mine operators; the foremen worked their Indians from "sun to sun." Then the process turned upon itself. Slaves swindled the bosses, the bosses cheated the tax collectors, the tax collectors held out on the viceroys, and the viceroys took their full toll before remitting to the king. The leaven of corruption worked from top to bottom, from bottom to top. In this school of politics Argentina (and all Latin America) was shaped.

Fourth, Spain gave the Church to America. The Spanish Church had already become something of a problem at home, with its expensive hierarchy of impressive princes, its army of priests and friars, its Inquisition, and its distaste for new ideas. The Church moved into America in full force, with a glittering parade to be supported by the tithes of the new-found faithful, with demands for stone cathedrals and convents to be built by the forced labor of Indians. The Church fixed upon the land of the Río de la Plata, as upon all Hispanic America, its distinctive pattern of piety and conformity. With the Church also came rare spirits who softened the asperity of conquest, held soldiers and looters in check, and protected the Indians as they could. Much of the less lovely in the Church's record may be balanced off by citing the devoted service of the Jesuits in their lonely missions among the Guaranís. If there were grasping priests in Hispanic America, there was also Bartolomé de las Casas, author of the *Law of the Indies of 1542,* the uncompromising albeit defeated protagonist of the Indian.

There has never been such open clash between Church and state in Argentina as marks the history of Mexico and, to a lesser degree, Chile. Nevertheless, there has been a steady loosening of the Church's hold. The men who created Argentina—the Rivadavias, Mitres, and Sarmientos—were officially Catholics but they had been caught by the fervor of the liberalism of the

1. *Estancia,* Argentine for the more common Spanish word *hacienda,* large farm, ranch, plantation. The *estanciero* is the owner.

times and took for granted that a free nation could not live under
the domination of the Church. From 1820 on through the century there was curtailment of the special privileges of the clergy,
the secularizing of the schools, the placing of limits on church
property. As early as 1826 Rivadavia proposed the creation of a
national Church, guaranteeing freedom of thought. The Argentine's way with his Church has resembled English fashions. The
wise Briton views his Church as a slightly wrinkled symbol of
his own respectability, the guardian of sacred property, the token
that all is well. He expects his children to be baptized and married under her forms, and he himself to be buried with the
proper words. But an intelligent Englishman would be miffed
if accused of really listening to the Archbishop of Canterbury.
So it is with the intelligent Argentine. He expects the women and
children to go to Mass; his wife will faithfully aid the pious chari-
ties which all good women share, and he will appear upon proper
occasion to make the gestures which custom dictates. But the
leaders in the business and professional and intellectual life of
Argentina no longer accept the claims of the Church with any
seriousness.

However, the hold of the Church upon Argentina cannot be
so lightly dismissed. Two groups maintain their fidelity. The
first includes the old families of the provinces, those of the best
names and the most land and the fine houses. For them the
Church is an instrument of regularity, discipline, conservatism.
No matter how much intellectual dissent may stir their minds,
they know that life is safer in a nation where the priest prevails.
Then there is the second group of the inconspicuous faithful, the
chief support of the Church in every land. You see them on the
streets of Salta, Tucumán, Santa Fé, and Córdoba—the women
in black leading docile children into the church on the plaza.

The lively struggle between religion and secularism must be
reckoned in any appraisal of Argentine life. Take the provincial
capital of Córdoba as an example. A city of 200,000, it has always
been dominated by its bishops, its priests, its Catholic families.
The hierarchy has its own newspaper, Los Principios—its critics

call it "the organ of the sacristy"—which daily makes known the will of God for the faithful, continues the battle for Franco's Spain, clamors for Catholic schools. "Who can deny," it argues editorially, "that only the Catholic school is in accordance with Argentine tradition?" This paper is on the breakfast tables in the fine houses and in the homes of the dutiful poor. But *Córdoba,* liberal, able, merrily anticlerical, goes on jabbing at stuffy *Principios,* and *Córdoba* has some 35,000 subscribers as against the Catholic journal's 32,000—this in the Church's stronghold in Argentina.

Fifth, Spain granted America the doubtful boon of supporting the mother country. Spain was beggared by its battalions of spendthrift nobles, by its immense ecclesiastical establishment, by its disastrous concentration of land which effectually barred the rank and file from fruitful enterprise. "In 1723," says J. F. Rippy, "one Spaniard out of every three was an ecclesiastic, a noble or a servant." Sixteenth-century Spain lived from tribute, not toil. When the tribute sufficed, Spain indulged in fresh wars with France and England, and was further impoverished.

For three centuries the Spanish colonies, chiefly Peru and Mexico, kept the aged mother in rather better style than that to which she was accustomed. The mines of America—Zacatecas and Guanajuato in Mexico, Potosí and Huancavélica in Upper Peru —served their purpose. Silver, gold, and quicksilver flowed in a steady stream to Sevilla, some 7 million pesos annually by the close of the sixteenth century. This flow continued on through the seventeenth and eighteenth centuries. The records of the profitable year 1747 listed 4 million pesos in gold, 30 million in silver, 30 million more in precious stones, hides, wool, quinine, sugar, indigo, tobacco. Impatient settlers who asked that a more considerable share of this wealth be spent in developing the New World were silenced. Spain had hungry princes who needed castles, priests who could not forego silver altars, soldiers who would have one more war.

Spanish colonial rule blocked fruitful enterprise. The royal heart did not leap with joy over the news of wheat and corn and cattle from the farms of La Plata; that pulsing organ found solace in gold and silver from the mines of the cordillera. But the thrifty court saw to it that the pampas rendered toll. The devices adopted were simple. First, La Plata was attached to Lima, and all trade was required to pass through the Peruvian port. Second, all American trade must finally be cleared through La Casa de Contratación (Board of Trade) of Sevilla. This clumsy and highly uneconomic system effectively throttled La Plata. The colonists must load their wares on the backs of mules for the 3,000-mile journey over the high mountains to Lima, there to be shipped by sea to Panama, then transshipped by mule pack to Cartagena, and finally loaded on galleons for Spain. Finished goods and supplies for the colonists returned by the same labored course. The price of goods increased six times along the way. This wasteful system was gradually relaxed and was ended by the close of the eighteenth century. But we have records from the middle of the eighteenth century which tell of cotton and wool shipped to Cádiz (which had taken the place of Sevilla as the trading center), from there shipped to England for manufacture into cloth, then back to Spain, and from Spain sold to the colonists of La Plata. This system left scant margin of profit to the producer and removed all inducement to enterprise or to colonization. The rich pampas remained little worked and sparsely populated. The colonists learned to cheat the law. Cut off from legitimate trade, smuggling became the most profitable business of the citizens of Buenos Aires.

The long arm of Spain still touches Argentina and all Hispanic America. Its markings still appear in an undisciplined feudalism, in exaggerated pride based on class distinctions, in contempt for physical labor, in the persistence of the latifundia, in the corruption of government, in the strong hold of a laggard Church, and in an economic system too greatly dependent upon the sale of raw materials. In varying degrees, the peoples of Spanish America make their escape. Argentina shows the greatest emancipation. She is learning to smile at her priests, to take education into her own hands, and to deal critically with the sacred opinions of

yesterday. She is beginning to criticize the land system in which
the few own so much. Most important, she knows that a secure
nation must be more than a granary and a pasture for the world,
the seller of raw materials, the buyer of finished goods.

The hold of Spain's feudal arm is loosening.

CHAPTER III

THE MAKING OF THE ARGENTINE NATION

FAITHFUL Argentines honor the name of José de San
Martín, post his name on plazas and avenidas, erect statues
to him where streets converge, and render homage to him
as the father of Argentine independence. They err. The real
father was the little corporal of Corsica. Napoleon Bonaparte set
the stage for the freedom of all the colonies of Spain (save only
Cuba, Puerto Rico, and the Philippines).

The events of 1810, when Hispanic Americans from Mexico to
Buenos Aires first struck against Spanish rule, must be understood in the light of the European struggle. In 1810 the Spanish
throne was occupied by Joseph, the puppet of his troublemaking
brother. The deposed Bourbon king, Ferdinand VII, a frivolous
erratic fellow, held his rump court in Sevilla. When the revolutionary junta of Buenos Aires, with Belgrano and Moreno as its
ablest leaders, seized the government of the port and organized
an army, it was Napoleon rather than Ferdinand whom they
fought. La Plata was faithful to imperial Spain.

However, the colonists had their grievances. They had not forgotten Spain's trade exactions, even though a more liberal policy
had finally been granted. There were seeds of secession in the
lively dislike between old and new Spaniards. The old Spaniards,
the creoles, the sons and grandsons of Spanish settlers, while
holding to their Spanish citizenship, felt themselves builders of
a new world. The new Spaniards were the officials sent by Ma-

drid to rule the colony. Madrid, out of fear that long absence would breed forgetfulness, changed them constantly so as to assure their primary loyalty to the royal court. This shifting army of bureaucrats held the great and little posts, collected the salaries and perquisites, and enjoyed the honor of position. The old Spaniards hated the new Spaniards on economic grounds. The new Spaniard was the tax collector and the tax spender. Furthermore, the new Spaniard was viewed as an interloper, an upstart. Time and the free air of America had worked its metamorphosis in the soul of the creole. He had the pride of the frontiersman. He had land and leisure. He had read widely and was the intellectual of the New World. In his isolation, he had felt from afar the sweep of the flames which swept over the Bastille. He had read Montesquieu and learned to scoff at the politician; he had read Voltaire, but had not learned to scoff at the priest. He had caught something of the intellectual rapture of the encyclopedists. To be sure, the radicalism of the French Revolution found no deep roots in the Argentine creole. His enthusiasm was cultural, emotional, intellectual. He was the aristocrat playing with new ideas. He hated the Spanish officials who arrived on every boat, not because they were reactionaries, but because they were soft shiftless fellows who did not know how to read a book.

The Argentine revolt of 1810 was a halfhearted affair. The first acts of independence were timorous. The colonists did not really want to break with Spain, they simply wanted to punish Napoleon for unseating the Bourbons. When Napoleon retired to Elba in 1814, and Ferdinand was propped on his battered throne, Argentine patriots were troubled. They had a constitution, a flag, and they had declared themselves a free nation—but many would still cling to Ferdinand. In the debate which ensued San Martín pled for a complete break. We have a letter written by him to a hesitant delegate of the second congress in Tucumán in 1816:

How long shall we wait to declare our independence? Is it not slightly ridiculous for us to coin money, to have a flag and a national cockade and to wage war against a government upon which we still admit ourselves dependent? Let us say what we mean. What does it profit us to behave like pupils, to be treated as rebels, supinely accepting the role of vassals? No one will help us in such a plight. Our position will be immeasurably strengthened if we take our stand. Take heart, achievement is reserved for men of valor. See clearly, my friend, what failure to declare our independence means. It nullifies all the acts of this Congress. These acts, with their assumption of sovereignty, are measures of usurpation so long as the Congress accepts the sovereignty of little Ferdinand.

The Argentine break with Spain, formally declared in 1816, was lacking in zest. Economic advantage prevailed over loyalty: there was profit in separation, so they separated. The well-born and wealthy settlers of La Plata sought no revolution in ideas. They were faithful to the Bourbons in 1810—and their great-grandsons were equally faithful, 125 years later, to the spiritual son of the Bourbons, Francisco Franco. But that is another story.

If, then, Napoleon was the catalytic agent who provoked Argentina to independent life, it remained for José de San Martín to compel the Spanish garrisons to quit the soil of La Plata. This "Saint of the Sword," as Ricardo Rojas describes him, was a son of the Argentine frontier, born in Yapeyú, a Jesuit outpost among the Guaraní Indians. The liberator of Argentina, Paraguay, Uruguay, Bolivia, Chile, and Peru (sharing honors with Simón Bolívar of the north) had his roots in America. His boyhood and youth were spent in Spain, where he learned soldiering. He fought in the Moorish wars, in the campaign against Napoleon, and then returned at the age of thirty-four to offer his services to the self-appointed Buenos Aires junta. In 1814 he was assigned command of the expeditionary force against the Spanish garrisons of Upper Peru (present-day Bolivia). Convinced of the futility of that effort, persuaded that the first strategy was to drive the Spaniards from Chile and then to carry the attack north upon Lima, he begged appointment as governor of the province of Cuyo on the Chilean frontier, established himself at Mendoza under the shadow of the Andes, and from that base prepared for the campaign against Chile. He led his army of some three thousand infantry and one thousand cavalry, including many Chilean recruits, over the high passes and freed Chile by the victories of Chacabuco (1817) and of the River Maipo (1818). He turned north, entered Lima in 1821, and assumed the office of Protector of free Peru. He had not won peace. The Spanish garrisons still held the interior, Buenos Aires was lukewarm in support, rival generals conspired in jealousy. He returned to Buenos Aires, was received with chill regard, and retired to Europe, there to live in poverty until his death in 1850. His only request from the Argentine Government had been for a piece of land worth $200 upon which he might retire, and that was refused. Honors came only with death.

The freedom of Spanish America was assured by the battle of Ayacucho in Peru in 1824. The peoples of the viceroyalty of La Plata forthwith split into four nations—Paraguay, Bolivia, Uruguay, and Argentina.

Argentina, free now, still had to struggle for unity. The provinces were mutually suspicious. The hinterland imputed base motives to Buenos Aires, while the porteños were loud in contempt for the provinciales.

The first years of independence were frantic. The ill-fated junta of 1810 was followed by two ineffective triumvirates before 1814, then a feeble directorate until 1820, and then nine years of the shifting rule of the governors of Buenos Aires until 1829.

One luminous name emerges from this confused period— Bernardino Rivadavia, the one considerable statesman of Argentina's first half-century of separate life. He served in the triumvirate, then carried Argentina's appeals for recognition to the courts of France and England, returned to serve in the cabinet of the vacillating General Rodríguez in 1821, and was elected in 1826 as the first constitutional President of Argentina.

Rivadavia was the businessman in politics. He was unimposing, well fed, a pompous, roundheaded and round-bellied little man, proud that he was neither a general nor a lawyer, but clinging to his ceremonial sword. He had the good businessman's contempt for bad housekeeping, devoted himself to the organization of Argentina's life, laid the foundation of the nation's legal system, wrote the first law for the naturalization of foreigners, and bade them come. He ended the importation of slaves, abolished discrimination against foreigners in trade, created a uniform currency system, established the national treasury. He argued for but did not win "a law of forgetfulness," as his proposed law of amnesty was phrased. He organized the post office and the police force, established a Bureau of Statistics. He organized an agricultural school, founded the University of Buenos Aires, and made a beginning at the creation of secondary schools. He appealed successfully to the women of Buenos Aires for the creation of La Sociedad de Beneficencia, the first organized charity in South America, and holds the record as the first Argentine to recognize the place of women in public life. He attacked the accepted privileges of the Church, stopped direct state allowances to priests, abolished the Church's tithe and seized some church property.

Rivadavia, concerned for national unity under a central government, convened the Congress of 1825, urging its members to "give form to the union of the Republic." The provincial delegates blocked his efforts and he was forced to seek safety in Europe while Congress was still in session. Congress continued to wrangle, failed to agree on a constitution, but instead provoked a war with Brazil over the status of Uruguay. By early 1826 the quarrelsome delegates belatedly recognized their impotence and recalled Rivadavia to the office of President. Rivadavia forthwith made Buenos Aires the federal capital—a step resisted by the provinces for fifty years. He cajoled Congress into framing a constitution which that body duly adopted in December 1826, and which was as duly rejected by the provincial caudillos. He pushed the war with Brazil to a successful conclusion, freeing Uruguay. But the provincial politicians were more than a match for him, and Rivadavia retired in July 1827 after a year and five months in office. That ended Argentina's first experiment in constitutional government.

The "boss of Buenos Aires," Juan Manuel de Rosas, who ruled

Argentina for twenty-four years (1829–52), is the prototype of the Latin-American dictator. His model has since been copied and improved upon. He was cruel and thorough. He had arguments with Bolivia and Uruguay, a set-to with the French who blockaded Buenos Aires, and with the British who seized the Falkland Islands. He compelled the provinces to accept the leadership of Buenos Aires. Rosas is charitably summarized by F. García Calderón:

His authoritative character of a Spanish patrician made him the paterfamilias of the Argentine democracy. . . . Rosas made federal unity a reality. . . . He defended the country against the territorial aggression of foreign coalitions, and his own power against conspiracy and revolt; he dominated the capital city and moderated provincialism; he painfully founded the Confederation. . . . His cruelty was effectual, his barbarism patriotic.

Argentina's turn toward constitutionalism dates from 1852. Governor Urquiza, the despotic governor of Entre Ríos, with the help of Uruguayan and Brazilian forces, finally dislodged Dictator Rosas and sent him into retirement. Urquiza called a national assembly, but was blocked by the porteños who would not yield to any provincial's bidding. Whereupon Urquiza set up one government in Paraná, while Buenos Aires seceded and for seven years maintained a government of its own. In 1853 a constituent assembly of the provinces met at Santa Fé, adopted the constitution largely written by Juan Bautista Alberdi, and elected Urquiza President. Finally in 1862 the election of Bartolomé Mitre was accepted by both the provinces and the capital, and Argentina was well launched on its modern life.

Argentina's constitutional course from 1862 to the outbreak of the first World War in 1914 was marked by increasing orderliness and legality. There were at least four Presidents of stature —Bartolomé Mitre (1862–68), Domingo Faustino Sarmiento (1868–74), Nicolás Avellaneda (1874–80), and Roque Sáenz Peña (1910–14). Others were less able. A few were corrupt. Argentine political life during that period suffered few of the relapses which mark the records of Bolivia, Peru, Colombia, and many of the other republics. The nation was knit together, population increased, frontiers were opened, economic life flourished.

The economic dislocations of the first World War shook Argentina and brought new elements into the political arena. The Conservatives were opposed by the growing strength of the Unión Cívica Radical, a mildly liberal party organized in 1890. The Radicals carried the election of 1916, naming Hipólito Irigoyen to the presidency. Irigoyen was an egotist convinced that he knew what was best for the country. He was honest, independent, tactless, fearless, nationalistic, violently hostile to the United States and to Europe. He successfully resisted all efforts to involve Argentina in war. He was the *personalista* in politics—the continuing scourge of Argentina and all Latin America—who knew that only his friends were fit for office, and when the supply ran out left the offices vacant. "I well know," he announced, "that I am no routine ruler, for no human power could have prevailed upon me to assume office as such a ruler. . . . I am entrusted with the highest mandate of the nation, which has bidden me fulfill the just and genuine aspirations of the Argentine people." In twenty instances he intervened in provincial affairs, setting aside the elected governors and imposing his own men. In international affairs the United States was the chief object of his distrust. He was convinced of our imperialism. His anti-Americanism was quite honest and it was good politics as well.

In 1922 the election went to Marcelo T. de Alvear, leader of the antipersonalistas of Irigoyen's Radical party. Alvear's six-year term was marked by various digressions in social legislation. In 1928 Irigoyen returned to office with an overwhelming electoral majority, and with a boisterous *personalismo* which even his followers could not stomach. His highhandedness and the gathering force of the world depression finally defeated him. In 1930 General Uriburu, with the army at his back, seized the office. Uriburu served two years, and yielded the presidency to Agustín P. Justo in 1932.

Justo's regime (1932–38) marked a retrogression from the

democratic ideal. His election had been clearly fraudulent and his crushing of political opposition continued without regard to legal niceties. Nevertheless, Justo won much respect for the intelligence of his rule. It was a period of building and of prosperity. Reviving world trade favored him. His finance minister Hueyo was astute, and the nation prospered. Justo was something of a dictator, but not crass. He was no Rosas.

The election of 1938 went to the Conservatives' Roberto M. Ortiz. The press and public opinion conceded that the Radical candidate Alvear had the votes, but the Conservatives had the money and the electoral machinery. However, Ortiz has disappointed those who elected him as another "strong man" who would rule for the sake of the few and without regard to the many. He has consistently stood for honest elections, and is regarded as a firm protagonist of democratic practice. The first weeks of 1941 find him in semiretirement, a sick man, and with Argentina wondering what will happen if Vice-President Ramón S. Castillo must take his place. We will return in a later chapter to a more detailed discussion of current events.

The political life of Argentina matures. The people of Argentina give every evidence of seeking an orderly constitutionalism. Sectional disputes grow less bitter. National unity steadily crowds out lesser loyalty. Argentina comes of age.

CHAPTER IV

THE ARGENTINE BALANCE SHEET

A S rich as an Argentine" has long been a magic phrase for bellhops and headwaiters in the hotels of Cannes, Nice, Juan les Pins. Argentine wanderers have had plenty to spend, for behind them are flat black acres, corn, wheat, cattle.

Rich Argentina. For seventy-five years she has known the joy of expanding frontiers, increasing production, enlarging trade.

Proud Argentina. Some seventy years ago, when railroads were being built, the Argentine Senate debated a proposal to vote 10 million pesos for a line to the foothills of the Andes. President Sarmiento urged the appropriation. There was protest from the opposition. "Preposterous," they called it, "suicidal." "How," cried Sarmiento, "can you be afraid of a mere 10 millions in additional debt? I tell you that this nation can carry a debt of 100 millions." The President was interrupted by a ripple of laughter. "No," he added, "I shall say, 1 billion." Again there was laughter, redoubled, and Sarmiento turned to the stenographer and said, "Put that laughter into the record, so that posterity may know with what kind of fools we had to work."

Let us look at the balance sheet.

The Wealth of the Soil

DRIVE west or south of Buenos Aires into the pampas which are as flat as the world of Moses. Handle the soil, sift it through your fingers. There are no pebbles in it, no rocks to clear, nothing but black black soil in which the plow cuts clean furrows which are black all the way through, the soil piled deep by the rains and the rivers which robbed the heart of a continent to make rich Argentina.

This is the primary wealth of Argentina. The world's chief exporter of beef, furnishing two thirds of the world's trade in beef and veal; first also as a seller of corn; chief producer of the world's linseed; second world exporter of wheat, lamb and mutton, wool; possessed of almost a monopoly in quebracho; producer of hides, cotton, sugar, tobacco, wines.

It is a sizable land, 690 million acres altogether. One tenth (10.7 %) of this area is now under cultivation, 44.4 % of it is in pasture lands (much of them the best in the world), a total of over 55 % of the national area is used for agriculture and grazing. Argentina's agricultural experts estimate that the area now used for the raising of grains may be increased (by providing irrigation, drainage, and transportation) from 10.7 % to 28.68 %, still leaving about 39 % for pasturage, showing a total of about 67 % of all Argentine area as usable for agriculture and grazing.

They calculate that after further allowance for 17.9 % of forest
lands—much of it economically valuable—there remains in Argentina but 14.3 % of the area which is completely unproductive
from the point of view of the agriculturalist.

The more intensive use of the land for grains has reduced pastoral industry. There were 43,882,728 sheep in Argentina in 1937
—a drop of 41 % since 1895. There were 33,207,287 cattle—a drop
of 10.4 % since 1922. On the other hand, swine multiplied six
times between 1895 and 1937. But pastoral industry has steadily
yielded to cereals as Argentina's cash crop. In the period 1872–80,
about 95 % of Argentina's exports were animal products; in
1890, 60 %; in 1938, 46 %.

It is upon the yield of these grainfields and these herds of cattle
and flocks of sheep that Argentina depends for the food of her
people and for the cash exports which make possible the purchase of foreign goods. In 1939 her sales to the world aggregated
$425,543,000, and of these exports about 97 % were in agricul-
tural goods. Items on this selling list: 99 million dollars' worth of
meat, 60 millions of wheat, 56 millions of linseed, 56 millions of
corn, 48 millions of wool, 31 millions of hides and skins. Her
buyers, and the shares which they took, stood in 1939 as follows:

United Kingdom	35.9 %
United States	12.0 %
Germany	5.7 %
France	4.8 %
Italy	2.1 %
Japan	0.7 %

Wealth-under-the-Soil

HERE Argentina faces a debit. Nature, generous to Peru, Chile,
and Brazil, seems to have forgotten Argentina.

There is no coal, and no iron. Argentina hopefully dreams of
opening the veins in her mountains on the Bolivian and Chilean
borders. But the existence of mineral wealth which can be economically exploited remains unproved. To be sure, Argentina

produces some lead, tin, zinc, manganese, and tungsten. She mines such prosaic items as sand, lime, and building stone. But her entire production from the subsoil, not including petroleum, aggregated about $29,000,000 in 1939.

There is petroleum, and Argentina has established a national trust, YPF, Yacimientos Petrolíferos Fiscales, which is designed gradually to displace foreign operators, including Standard Oil, and fields are being developed near Comodoro Rivadavia, the province of Mendoza, and in other scattered spots. Plans are maturing for tying up Argentine oil production with the undeveloped oil fields of Bolivia which the Bolivian Government seized from Standard of New Jersey. Argentine production is still small, in 1939 furnishing 56.8 % of the petroleum requirements of the nation.

The lack of coal is a part of the general fuel shortage, and explains the high cost of power and heat and light for home and industry. Almost half the nation's petroleum must be imported. Electric power is produced thermetically. There is little water power developed or likely to be developed, due to the distances between potential power sites and the centers of population. Much wood and carbon are used for home consumption and in some industries. In 1938, of the total fuels used in home and industry 41 % were produced nationally, 59 % imported. This imposed an import charge of $50,768,000 in 1938.

The Forests

THERE are some 123 millions of acres of forests in Argentina, with a great variety of hardwoods and trees yielding dyes, tannin, and medicinal extracts; but much of this forest wealth is inaccessible and unused. Argentina does not even produce the lumber required for her own use, and in 1938 imported a total valued at more than $16,000,000.

On the asset side, Argentine forests of the north produce the bulk of the world's quebracho, the source of tannin for the leather trade. In 1939 this accounted for over $10,000,000 of her exports.

The Industrialization of Argentina

THE Buenos Aires town booster, kin to those of Chicago and Oskaloosa, talks of industry. He will tell you of Argentina's future as one of the great industrial nations. He will show you packing plants, flour mills, textile mills, tire factories, shoe factories, motor-assembly plants. He will cite figures to prove that Argentina's industrialization has proceeded at a faster pace than even that of the United States during recent years. He will tell you that Argentina packs her own foodstuffs, makes her own wine and beer, manufactures her own tobacco, makes her own cement, soap, furniture, glassware, shoes, and finished clothing; that she turns out one third of her cotton cloth, two thirds of her finished linen, over three fourths of her woolens, and most of her own silk and rayon. He will paint the future for you and quote figures which are touched with the blue of the skies. He makes a good case. You may question some of his figures, as you would those of town boosters anywhere, but you are convinced that Argentine industry is on the march.

But—there are some things which must be said to the Argentine enthusiast for industry:

First, that there is no coal, no iron, not enough petroleum, and little cheap electric power.

Second, that the natural wealth of Argentina is in her wheat, corn, beef, mutton, hides, linseed, wool, quebracho.

Third, that she consumes about 63 % of her domestic production, and that the balance must be used in the world market to buy those items in which she is deficient—coal, iron, petroleum, sundry metals, heavy machinery, and scores of other items.

Fourth, that the industrial nations of the world which have coal, iron, and machinery to sell may take their pick of many markets in which to buy wheat, corn, meat, and wool. They will buy where they get the best bargain. They will buy from Argentina only as they can sell to Argentina.

Fifth, that Argentine development of her industry to the point where she could stop buying typewriters, cameras, adding machines, tractors, and automobiles would kill many of her markets for corn, wheat, beef, hides, and wool.

The facts suggest caution. Argentina is rich in agriculture, poor in the natural elements of industry. An overreaching and uneconomic industrialism would threaten the market for her basic wealth.

A further warning. The industry so prized by Argentines is but one half Argentine in ownership and control. Railroads, for example—25 % of them are owned by the state, while the balance belongs to the British with an investment of more than a billion dollars. Petroleum—the imports are furnished chiefly by Standard of New Jersey, Socony-Vacuum, Texas, and Shell. Quebracho—half of it is processed by an English company. Cement production—an American firm predominates. Automobile tires —the factories are Goodyear, Firestone, Michelin, Dunlap. Meat packing—the American firms of Swift, Armour, and Wilson; the British firms of Anglo, Smithfield, and Argentine. Chemicals—Du Pont's and Imperial Chemical. Public utilities—American, Swiss, German, Belgian capital. Telephones—about half of them are in the hands of the American I.T. and T. Streetcars and subways in Buenos Aires—chiefly British-owned. Automobile-assembly plants—Ford and General Motors.

On the other side of the picture, Argentine capital increasingly turns to industry. Bunge and Born, the largest Argentine investors, concentrate on industry. Argentine capital dominates flour milling, textiles, paper production, glass production, shoes, and many lesser lines.

The industrial census of 1935 reported a total industrial investment of about $1,435,000,000. A little less than 50 % of this investment was foreign capital, directed by foreign technicians and foreign managers, with the best positions reserved for foreigners. This means that some half of the profits are drained off to England, the United States, and until lately to Belgium and Switzerland. Every peso of exported interest or dividend is a call upon so many pounds of Argentine beef or wheat in the international market.

The Buenos Aires town booster may well be proud of Argentine industry. He may quote the industrial score of 1939, and tell you of

> 49,381 industrial establishments, using
> 2,880,831,418 pesos' worth of raw materials, with
> 4,709,089,883 pesos' worth of goods produced, and
> 663,906 workers employed.

But the planter or the stockman can still point out that the real wealth of Argentina is in its farms and flocks, that agriculture in 1939 represented a total investment six or seven times that of industry—and that agriculture is almost 100 % a domestic investment.

Is industry then on the asset or debit side of the Argentine ledger?

An asset, certainly, is Argentina's increasing capacity to process its meat, its cotton, its wool, its quebracho, its leather; an asset, Argentina's lessening dependence upon foreign markets for glassware, medicines, shoes, cotton goods, woolen cloth, paper, silk, flour, finished rubber goods, small machinery. All this means increased national use of her own raw materials, increased employment, increased national buying power. And there is still room for expansion. Argentina buys a long list of items which might be more logically and cheaply manufactured at home. I pick at random from the list of Argentina's imports—paper cartons, common glass, tiles, wrapping paper, newsprint—the raw materials for all of these are in Argentina.

But there is danger of a debit, also. Argentine industrialists talk of the day when they will make automobiles, trucks, heavy machinery. They must face two questions. Can this be done economically—with imported iron, steel, copper, coal, petroleum? And, even though it could be done, what would such industrialization do to their British, German, and other markets for beef and wheat?

Argentine industry is an asset—so far. It may still be expanded with profit, especially if Argentine, rather than foreign, capital does the expanding. The danger line—the point at which uneconomical home industry kills off profitable exports of raw materials—must be found by experience and by the technicians.

A Record of Recovery

ARGENTINA's economic record during the decade of the 1930's deserves mention. She staged a recovery from the postwar depression which stands out in brilliant contrast to the experience of other South American countries, testimony not only to her economic resources but to the skill and energy of her leaders.

The depression which began in 1929 struck Argentina with full force. Dependent upon her agricultural exports, overextended in her capital investment in roads, railroads, and industrial plant, with land prices artificially high and with a heavy mortgage burden, she was subject to the same forces which precipitated the panic of 1929 in the United States. The dropping of prices in the world market for her exportable goods, the disastrous drought in Argentina in that same year, meant that her heavy commitments for imports—agricultural machinery, automobiles, and other finished goods from the United States and elsewhere—had to be paid for by the withdrawal of Argentina's gold supply. The results were swift. Argentine exchange was demoralized, prices of land fell, mortgages were in default. In 1930 the economic crisis brought the overthrow of Irigoyen. But the economic convulsion, whose main lines resembled those of the United States, was more quickly resolved. Argentina, unlike the United States, had no such army of industrial workers to be rescued. A vigorous control of the exchanges, sharp economies in government, and relief legislation for the mortgaged farmers had by 1932 yielded substantial improvement. The national budget of 1932 almost balanced. The record from 1932 to the outbreak of war in 1939 has been steady and brilliant. She has not defaulted on her federal bonds. External dollar loans were reduced by more than $100,000,000, with many issues rewritten on better terms. Over two thousand miles of British-owned railroads were acquired by the state. Many foreign-owned industrial enterprises were brought under Argentine ownership. A favorable start was made at developing a national petroleum business.

The devices employed for working this economic recovery were various:

Taxes were increased. A moderate income tax, hitherto unknown in Argentina, was imposed.

Rigid exchange control was instituted. While in 1927 Argentina had had a favorable trade balance of 336 million pesos, in 1928 another favorable balance of 132 million, 1929 saw the swift drop of agricultural prices, her exports declined, her imports increased, and she was confronted with an unfavorable trade balance of 375 million pesos. Her peso dropped rapidly in relation to the pound and the dollar, and she went off the gold standard in December 1929. By October 1931 the Argentine peso stood at about 60 % of its 1929 value. Argentina took drastic action. The peso was pegged at 15 to the pound. All imports were placed upon a permit system. The importer of automobiles from the United States, for example, must now obtain a prior permit to purchase the required exchange. In this way Argentina has sought to hold imports in line with exports and has largely succeeded. But there has been more to the plan. Trade with each foreign country has been treated as a unit. Those who buy more than they sell in Argentina are favored, those who sell more than they buy are penalized. The penalty has been in the difference of rate of exchange and, more recently, in quota restrictions. Britain, which buys grains and meats in exchange for machinery and other finished products, has occupied a favored position. The United States, with plenty of automobiles and tractors and machinery to sell, has no national appetite for buying corn, wheat, beef—and has therefore been penalized. This penalty varied in the course of the decade. Restrictions were loosened or tightened as trade demand fluctuated. Luxuries were often effectively barred by application of the higher penalties. In 1935, for example, 35 % of American imports were admitted at the lower official rate, 65 % paid the penalty rate, about 20 % higher. In 1936, 46 % of American imports were favored, 54 % paid the penalty. Out of these regulations came heated arguments with the United States, and considerable bad blood. Argentina could always counter: We are simply spending the dollars you send us. Send more, and we will gladly buy more from you.

The gains for Argentina were indubitable. She has been able to keep imports in line with exports, thereby protecting her gold reserves. She has collected a steady profit out of commissions on exchange. She has collected further profit out of penalties imposed, with the United States serving as the chief contributor. While this may not have made for international comity, it has made for Argentine economic security. We will return to the United States' arguments with Argentina in a later chapter.

There is a footnote to be added to the record of Argentine recovery from the first World War. It definitely records her escape from colonial economy. The World War, the boom years, and the inevitable depression which followed taught Argentina that it is unsafe to rely upon the sale of raw materials, leaving the processing and finishing to other nations. The panic of 1929 brought Argentina to her feet. For thirty years she had enjoyed favorable trade balances, but now she knew that she must make more shoes, spin more cotton, and process more foodstuffs. Argentina dealt with panic and fear and came out victor in the decade of the 'thirties.

The breaking of the second world war in September 1939 confronted Argentina with conditions made familiar by the earlier war. England, her chief customer, still bought, but her communications faltered and she found it increasingly difficult to pay in gold or in goods. Argentina turned to the United States for credits with which to finance her sales to England. She took fresh account of her government costs and made drastic cuts. She planned public works to meet the growing unemployment. She watched, with anxiety, her piling surpluses of wheat and corn and meat. She waited, as other nations waited, to see how her national economy would fare in a world at war.

CHAPTER V

HOW FARE THE ARGENTINE PEOPLE?

W E have dwelt upon the wealth of Argentina. We have listed in millions and billions the wheat, corn, linseed, hogs, cattle, and sheep.

But what do Argentines eat, with what are they clothed, what comfort and security attend them? How many are rich, how many are comfortable, how many are poor? The answer to that question cannot be given with the exactness for which an economist begs. Argentine statistics incline to sketchiness. Our conclusions are reached by comparison of government and private figures, by the testimony of numerous Argentines.

There are 13 million people in Argentina, according to the official estimators (the last census, taken in 1914, put the figure at 7,885,237). These 13 millions may be divided into the rich, the comfortable, and the poor. (This, of course, is a classification which would be denounced as a pious evasion by any careful social scientist—but let him find a better classification if he can, and we will happily quote his figures when he gets them.) How many are there in these three classes, and how do they fare?

First, there are the rich. These are the people who own the land, the forests, the banks, the trading houses, and the industries. These are the people who once bought first-class passages to Europe, brought joy to the best hotels of Paris and the Riviera, returned with jewels and fine dresses to live in the best houses in Buenos Aires, Córdoba, and Rosario, and to spend a few weeks each year on their estancias. These are the people described by the phrase "as rich as an Argentine."

How shall they be counted?

Many devices suggest themselves, but there is one criterion which seems sound. In Argentina, wealth and social position are chiefly measured in terms of land. If you own an estancia, you count. The estancia's generous reaches prove your capacity, economically and socially. We can therefore turn to the figures on the great holdings of land as an index to the Argentine rich. The *Censo Agropecuario* of 1937 furnishes figures:

In 1937 there were 2,072 holdings, each in excess of 10,000 *hectareas*—24,710 acres. These 2,072 holdings aggregated 134,316,095 acres, and averaged 64,824 acres each. The total area of Argentina is 690,097,920 acres. The conclusions are clear. Some 2,072 families owned one fifth (19.46 %) of all Argentina. Therefore we may infer that there are at least 2,072 "rich" Argentine families.

But wait a moment. We must do a little scrutinizing of that figure.

Certain items might increase the number of those families. A given "family" may be two, three, four, or more families—father, married sons, and daughters. Or a given holding is sometimes owned by a corporation with a number of stockholders. Other items might decrease that figure. There are families which own several "holdings." There are partnerships and corporations which own multiple units in different parts of the country. Balancing these items against each other, we may guess that they more or less cancel each other off. No one knows.

There are further considerations which complicate the reckoning. Which of these holdings comprise the best land, which the worst? Which pay, which are a drag? For example, it proves little to cite the fact that there are, in the southernmost territory of Tierra del Fuego, forty-four holdings which include more than half of its area: that is poor dry land, and bitterly cold, fit only for sheep, and my Argentine sheep-raising friends assure me that one acre of that land will care for just about one fifth of one sheep.

More meaning is to be gathered from the figures on the province of Buenos Aires, the richest and most productive of all the political divisions of Argentina. In 1939 its estimated population was 3,453,561 (the province does not include the capital city). Its total area is 27,495,664 acres, almost all of it highly productive land, as good as there is in the world. Out of those 3½ million people, 230 holders owned in 1937 an aggregate of 10,624,062 acres, an average of 46,191 acres each. So we find 38.63 % of the land of the most prosperous and populous province owned by just 230 families (with such deductions and additions as we have already suggested).

Argentina is not unaware of the social unwisdom of such concentration of land. The government since 1933 has made a determined effort to encourage the smaller landholder. The Banco de la Nación Argentina and the Banco Hipotecario (the mortgage bank) have increased loans to the *chacarero,* or small farmer, to carry him through bad seasons, to finance the handling of crops, to provide for improvements. This has served to discourage the enlargement of the great estancias through forced sales of smaller farms. The government seeks to stop the drift toward the cities by improvements in rural housing, by increased electrification, and by encouraging colonization. A law sponsored by President Ortiz looks toward the gradual division of the larger holdings, with operations financed by government banks. But factors which hasten the division of great estates in England and the United States—high real-estate taxes, steeply graded income and inheritance taxes, and high labor costs—do not exist in Argentina. Taxes are low. Labor is cheap. Furthermore, the government is still dominated by the growers of grain and the producers of stock, who have hung out a sign which may be clearly read by all troublemakers: DON'T TOUCH AGRICULTURE.

How many are there of the rich, those with enough for comforts and luxuries and investments? The answer must be a guess. Take the figure for the chief owners of land, and add those who have made substantial success in commerce, banking, and industry (most of them already counted as landowners). Then multiply—or divide—according to taste. Call it 3,000 families, and you probably have the roll of those who enjoy the major profits of Argentine wealth.

Second, there are the comfortable. These are kin to the shopkeepers, doctors, lawyers, brokers, traders, swappers, and profit collectors who make enough to buy a house with a garden in Evanston, Scarsdale, or Riverside; who have a new car in the garage, a good radio, some life insurance, a savings account, and

know how to read a book. How many are there in Argentina? I
found no one who would hazard a guess. This comfortable Argentine middle class is larger than that in any other Latin-
American republic, and appreciably smaller proportionately
than that of the United States. It may also be noted that a large
but not calculated slice of this middle class is more "foreign"
than Argentine.

Third, there are the poor. "Poor," an indefinite word at best, is
here used to cover the nine tenths (more or less) of Argentines
who are neither comfortable nor secure, who are not well housed
or clothed or fed. The description is suggested in diffidence.
There are no convincing figures.

This rough classification includes a range of groups: the lower
middle class of white-collar workers, stenographers, clerks, and
other attachés of industry and business; the 663,000 industrial
workers; the 1 million farm laborers, share croppers, and small
independent farmers. These constitute the bulk of the population.

How do they fare? Let us look at some samples.

Take the lower-paid white-collar workers. The girl selling
notions in the corner store in Tucumán reports a monthly wage
of $16. My grocery clerk in Buenos Aires tells me that he gets
$21. The stenographer who came to type this manuscript seemed
happy with $30 a month. The routine clerk in the bank gets $45.
The woman selling stamps in the post office receives $45.[1]

Turn to industrial wages. There are 663,906 industrial wage
earners in Argentina (1939 figures) who, with their families,

1. American equivalents of Argentine pesos have been reckoned at the quite arbitrary rate of 1 peso = 30 cents U. S. That is a little less than the average rate at
which Argentina sold its exchange for import purchases from 1933 to 1937, and a
little more than the prevailing rate. In January 1941 this rate stood at about 29.7 c.
per peso. On the other hand the "free" market rate was about 23 c. Any satisfactory
adjustment of values is quite impossible. Furthermore, it must be remembered that a
peso will usually buy more commodities than will 30 c. in Akron, Atlanta, or Al-
buquerque. Current prices in Buenos Aires run about as follows: wheat bread, 4 c. a
pound; oatmeal, 10 c.; rice, 6 c.; macaroni, 3½ c.; second-grade beef, 7 c.; lard,
13 c.; potatoes, 2½ c.; sugar, 5 c.; milk, 4½ c. the quart; eggs, 1¼ c. each. On the
other hand, the housing item expressed in dollar terms varies little between Buenos
Aires and Chicago.

account for about one fifth of all Argentina's population. This includes 147,729 railroad workers who get an average of around $52 a month. It includes skilled mechanics who receive an hourly wage of 30 c., printers 38 c., tramway and bus operators 19 c., common labor 14 c., cotton textile workers 13 c., woolen textile workers 28 c. (These are approximate figures for the capital. Workers in the provinces receive from 10 % to 20 % less.) Figures on monthly income reveal that from 125 to 150 pesos (from $37.50 to $45) represent a fair average for semiskilled workers, with the scale dropping to less than 100 pesos ($30) for common labor, and rising above 200 pesos ($60) for an inconsiderable proportion of the skilled.

The Statistical Division of the National Department of Labor (one of the most competent agencies of the government) made a study in 1935 of the case records of 887 typical industrial families. These averaged five members to the family. The average monthly income stood at $38.18 (127.26 pesos). The estimated minimum cost of living was set at $49.25 (164.19 pesos). The average family budget was spent in the following fashion: food 56.9 %; rent 20.54 %; clothing 10.3 %; leaving 12.3 % to cover incidentals, education, culture, recreation, health, and fuel.

These figures on industrial incomes are contested by some who come into intimate contact with family conditions. These realists cite case after case of families whose total monthly income seldom tops $15 or $20.

Argentina has successfully controlled domestic prices, assuring fair stability in the cost of living. Using the base line of 1929 as 100, the 1939 figure was 92, while real wages (figures covering Buenos Aires only) stood at 97. This 1939 figure compared favorably with past years. Still using 1929 as 100, the real wages in Buenos Aires in 1914 stood at 68, in 1918 at 42, and in 1922 at 84.

When we approach the one million or more workers who gain their livelihood from farming and stock raising, we are on even less sure ground. Included in this group are an unreckoned number of the smallest farmers, share croppers, *peones* (wage workers) on the farms and estancias. Some data are available. The *Censo Agropecuario* of 1937 gave data on 113,922 peónes, which

revealed that three fourths of them had monthly wages ranging
from 25 to 100 pesos ($7.50 to $30), with the remaining one
fourth divided between those who received less than 25 or more
than 100 pesos a month. The average was approximately $15 (50
pesos). In addition, they received their housing, often quite inadequate, and their food. The general testimony is that agricultural workers in the more prosperous areas are fairly well fed,
while those in the outlying provinces fare meagerly.

The bitterest economic pills are allotted the agricultural workers in the sugar, cotton, yerba maté, and lumber industries of the
north. Here Argentina repeats the bad habits prevailing in our
American cotton belt, sugar-beet industry, in lumber, grain har-
vesting, and fruit picking. Contract labor involving entire families down to the smallest children, wages paid in company scrip,
company stores with excessive prices, mean housing, inadequate
food, pay of a few cents a day and seldom exceeding fifty American cents—such conditions, according to Juan Antonio Solari,
affect the lives of from 150,000 to 200,000 Argentine workers.
Outright peonage still prevails in some remote areas. More than
one Argentine friend, commenting on John Steinbeck's *Grapes
of Wrath* (which has appeared in Spanish and is widely read)
tells me, "That is the picture of our own North."

A further index to Argentine wealth and poverty is suggested
by the increasing concentration of population in the cities.
Twenty-eight per cent of all Argentines live in Greater Buenos
Aires alone. The aggregate population of the five chief cities
more than doubled between 1914 and 1938. Today 74 % of the
population lives in cities and towns, only 26 % in rural areas.
Here are the figures which indicate the shift since 1869:

	Rural Population	Urban Population
1869	67 %	33 %
1895	58 %	42 %
1914	42 %	58 %
1930	32 %	68 %
1938	26 %	74 %

Such concentration in the cities of an industrialized land would be disastrous enough: in a predominantly agricultural country it means inevitable distress.

The Argentine balance sheet, like that of the United States, tells the story of abundance for some, too little for others. The stature of the common man is not determined, but he is there. If he is an industrial worker, he is making some slight gains. If he is a farm worker, he has made little advance upon his father's status. If he works in cotton and sugar, he is still little more than a slave. The Argentine estanciero holds the best land, crowds the little farmer into the dry corner, and is responsible in part for the piling up of the millions in the cities. Withal, Argentina presents a happier economic face than any other Latin-American nation. And she has leaders of capacity who are demanding a more just and generous spreading of the good things which are Argentina's.

CHAPTER VI

THE FORCES OF DEMOCRACY

THE American neighbors of Argentina make bold to ask, Which way do you take? The way of democracy, to which your Constitution commits you, and in which your chief leaders have guided you? Or the way of repudiation, of return to the creed of the "strong man," in which Rosas schooled you?

A candid Argentine might well reply, We go both ways.

There is a *more* democratic Argentina, and a *less*. Argentina on that point is not unlike the neighbors who put the question.

I essay a listing of some items in Argentine life which indicate fidelity to the constitutional democracy in which Argentina was trained under Mitre, Sarmiento, Avellaneda, and Sáenz Peña, and then an added listing of other items of less democratic flavor.

The More Democratic Argentina

First, the Argentine press is the ablest in South America in editing, news collecting, and mechanical processes. Almost without exception it is firmly prodemocracy, pro-England, increasingly friendly to the United States, and united against fascist influences.

The capital has two notable papers, *La Prensa* and *La Nación,* and others which merit praise—*La Razón, Noticias Gráficas, El Mundo.* Even *Crítica,* emulator of Hearst, does good reporting, and noisily battles all fascists and communists. The provincial cities also have papers of intellectual dignity and journalistic distinction. The newspapers of Argentina, numerous, with wide range of opinion, with large circulations, are the chief uniting force and instrument of democratic education.

La Prensa, founded in 1869 by José C. Paz and now directed by his son Ezequiel, sells over 200,000 copies on weekdays, over 400,000 on Sundays. Able editors, news collectors, and commentators make its columns the most notable in South America and put it on a par with the best in New York and London. Stubbornly independent, beholden neither to advertisers nor to any government, it has never hesitated to rebuke presidents, congresses, or the mighty men of Argentina. When Uriburu seized the presidency by force in 1930, *La Prensa* did not bow. When that dictator threatened to close the paper, its owner, Ezequiel P. Paz, announced that he would move to Paris, continue publication from there, and destroy the credit of the Uriburu government. When Justo was elected in 1932, *La Prensa* denounced the election as fraudulent. Justo's highhanded interventions in the provinces brought continued criticism in its editorial columns. When Ortiz' election in 1938 was marked by irregularities, *La Prensa* did not mince words. The official zest for managed economy, with its threat to good relations with the United States, has been continuously condemned by *La Prensa* as bad economics and unconstitutional. *La Prensa* unflaggingly preaches the doctrine of democracy. "We have never," runs an editorial of October 1940, "entertained doubts concerning the identification of the Argentine people with democratic institutions." Its condemnation of those who would betray the democratic ideal is specific, with the naming of names. Its distaste for the barbarities of fascism, nazism, and communism is explicit. *La Prensa* calls for the closest coöperation with the United States, shows hearty faith in the promises of the New Deal, but can criticize as well as applaud. The reading of *La Prensa* over a period of years leaves one with the firm impression of dignity, honesty, clarity, and democratic conviction.

La Nación, founded in 1870 by Bartolomé Mitre, has a daily circulation of almost 200,000 and a Sunday edition of over 300,000. It is typographically attractive, and covers the world's news in exceptional fashion. *La Nación* is the favorite of the more prosperous, and expresses their point of view with intelligent fidelity. Its tradition, akin to that of the *London Times,* is the support of the government in power. Its democracy is unquestioned, but it is less forthright and critical than *La Prensa*. It cultivates literary perfection, and commands the services of some of the ablest writers of Argentina. Its literary supplements, read throughout Latin America, incline toward the *précieux,* with a daintiness which invites ruffling by the vulgar. *La Nación* often lapses into that querulousness toward the United States which has marked official Argentina during recent years. But read month after month, it leaves one with gratitude for its excellent reporting and its trenchant editorializing. It is a force for democracy in the high places of Argentine life.

The Argentine press is free, freer than that of any other South American country save Colombia and Chile. All attempts to gag the editors meet determined protest from all the newspapers. In August 1940 the provincial government of La Rioja sought to impose a censorship in that lonely corner, but the newspapers of all Argentina made common cause of the issue. Some years ago the government sought to banish the able correspondent of the *New York Times,* but the Buenos Aires papers raised such outcry that the government was blocked. However, in June 1940 the Chamber of Deputies passed a bill muzzling foreign correspondents, despite the protest of the press. There is little if any local censorship. Conservative, liberal, nazi, and fascist papers express their several opinions with fervor and a reckless profusion of newsprint. Any Argentine newsstand serves as eloquent reminder of the freedom and vigor of popular debate.

Second, organized labor is a force for democratic education and control. Collective bargaining and the right to strike prevail in Argentine industry. The trade union, with its constant meetings for discussion and deliberation furnishes an instrument for clarifying public opinion.

There were 663,906 industrial workers in Argentina in 1939. Of these, 436,609, or 65.76 % of the total, were dues-paying members of one or another organized labor group. The Confederación General del Trabajo (CGT) is the largest with 270,320 members. The Unión Sindical Argentina (USA) has 26,980 on its rolls. The Catholic unions (FACE) enroll 18,500. Autonomous unions (including some company unions) number 120,809 members. These organizations differ widely in ideology and method. The USA is a loose assemblage of public employees, maritime workers, telephone workers, with a rough-and-tumble struggle between anarchists and conservatives in its ranks. The Catholic unions consist of women workers in needlework and allied trades, and are not aggressive. The autonomous unions comprise a great variety of local groups in specific industries, with little common program. The CGT—the General Federation of Labor—is the only movement comparable with the labor organizations of England and the United States.

The CGT, with its 270,000 members, is a closely knit and ably led organization akin in temper and method to the American Federation of Labor. The dominant group within the federation is the Union of Railway Workers with 90,000 members. Politically, its leaders incline toward the Socialist party, the rank and file of its members are of the Radical party. Its few Communists play little part—"They are held by a short rope," one of the officers tells me. There is little militancy in the CGT, which is as proper as the A.F. of L., with its leaders choosing to coöperate with the government rather than to fight it. These tactics have won steady if not brilliant gains in social legislation, pensions for railroad men, some improvement in working standards, some laws for the protection of women and children. The federation has made little effort and attained slight success in the organization of agricultural workers—an abstention which explains its relative immunity from attack by Argentina's powerful aristocracy. It is politically safer to make demands on English-operated railroads and American-owned automobile plants than it is to touch with the tip of a camel's-hair brush the most unimportant member of the feudal clan which holds the land.

Third, a growing middle class fortifies democracy. This, the most numerous and vocal middle class in South America, gradually changes the political scene. Its members are the leaders in the Unión Cívica Radical which has captured the numerical lead from the landholding conservatives, and seems assured of electoral triumphs whenever polls are honestly conducted. Schoolteachers, white-collar workers, small businessmen, small-scale industrialists, doctors, and lawyers are a company of a million or more. The books which are printed and sold in generous quantity, the articles which the magazines carry, the newspapers with the large circulations reflect the growing maturity of the tastes of this middle class. The organizations which command middle-class support give evidence of a large awareness of national and international problems. These include committees for aid to Britain, for the rescue of France, for the confirming of democracy. There is Acción Argentina, an enterprising company which unites many thousands for a nationalistic attack on fascism and communism, holds mass meetings in cities and towns, prints its own newspaper, and fixes posters on every wall. It is heartening to come upon a parade of its youth, as they tramp down Calle Florida chanting with tireless fervor, "Democracia! Sí! Argentina! Sí! Fascismo? No!"

Fourth, public education. The public schools reach a greater proportion of the nation's children than those of any other Latin-American republic save Uruguay. Believers in the public school as a force for democracy are heartened to discover that there are

1,977,357 children enrolled in 13,693 primary schools with 74,279 teachers (1939). This satisfaction is heightened by the further discovery that the parochial school plays little part; but 8 % of the primary schools, with 6 % of the children, are under Church control. When to the figures for the primary schools are added those for secondary, normal, commercial, industrial, agricultural, and professional schools, together with the twenty-four university faculties, it appears that there is a total enrollment well over 2,000,000, a teaching force of over 90,000 in more than 14,000 institutions spending annually about 310 million pesos. About 14 % of the federal budget goes into education, in addition to almost 100 million pesos provided by provincial and municipal governments and by private agencies.

Argentina and Uruguay enjoy a favored position among the Latin-American republics in the percentage of literacy. Estimates vary greatly, and none carries much conviction. The *Statesman's Yearbook* for 1936 places the illiteracy figure for Argentina at 25 %, for Uruguay at 20 %. Argentine estimates incline to be more optimistic. Alejandro E. Bunge, for example, puts the figure for 1938 at about 12 %. Whether the rightful figure be 25 or 12—or somewhere between—Argentina is out of the class of Bolivia, Brazil, and Peru, where illiteracy ranges from 65 % to 80 %, or Chile with not less than 50 %.

The quality of the Argentine public school is subject to question. Random visits to schools in Buenos Aires, in the provincial capitals and in the country leave the impression that these schools are still living in the good old days of Duffey's *Readers* and of treadmill reading, writing, and arithmetic. Imitation and memory are stressed, rather than creation. "The school of action" has not yet arrived. Here and there an individual school, with a teacher of imagination, breaks new ground. Argentine criticism of the school system appears with heartening regularity in the editorials of *La Prensa* and elsewhere. These critics roundly condemn the emphasis on "encyclopedic and theoretical education"; plead for "greater participation of the pupils in the learning process . . . less lessons, more practice"; argue for education directed at more practical ends, preparing boys and girls for the actual life they will lead in agriculture and industry. The leading newspapers continue to insist upon the noninterference of the Church.

Despite such reservations, it may be set down that Argentina, by her insistence upon state education and her rapid development of schools in all parts of the republic, is laying a strong basis for democratic institutions. Her schools may lack the imaginativeness of some in Chile and Mexico, but they are far superior to those of Brazil, Peru, and Bolivia.

Fifth, Argentina's robust politics are a force for democracy. Elections are not the sham battles between cliques which pass for political contests in Brazil, Peru, and many another Latin-American state. The average Argentine values his franchise and exercises it to a degree true, among the South Americans, only in Chile, Uruguay, and Colombia. The mill-run Argentine is a democrat, is heartily ashamed of the coup of Uriburu in 1930, of the election frauds of 1932 and 1938, and takes satisfaction in President Ortiz' efforts to restore Argentine elections to the standard which Sáenz Peña established in 1912.

The party alignment is not unlike that of the United States. There are the parties of the Right, now coöperating in the Concordancia, to which all large landholders belong as inevitably as a Pittsburgh steel manufacturer belongs to the G.O.P. There is a party of the Center which occasionally glances to the Left, the Unión Cívica Radical, resembling our Democratic party in its congenital confusions. The Radicals have the support of a strange collection of city machines, mild liberals, middle-class patriots, union labor, people who read newspapers and do not own estancias. But, with occasional digressions, the Radicals stand for honest elections and demand more democratic institutions. The Radicals suffer from their inherited debate between the personalistas and the antipersonalistas, a division rooted in the argument between Hipólito Irigoyen and Marcelo T. de

Alvear. Irigoyen is dead, Alvear is much alive and must be reckoned with by any who would return to dictatorship. The Conservatives and Radicals command the bulk of the Argentine
electorate. The Radicals appear to have the most votes, but the
Conservatives control more ballot boxes—with the result that
more Conservatives are in office.

The Socialists, the one recognized party of the Left, are marked
by a rather attenuated Marxism. They command a devout minority in Buenos Aires and a scattering of votes in the provinces,
and have five members in the national Congress. Their moral
influence outstrips their voting strength, with a dozen leaders
highly regarded for integrity, intelligence, and parliamentary
skill.

Communists and anarchists are few but busy. Not recognized
by the electoral machinery, they must content themselves with
clandestine posting of placards on unguarded walls.

The amenities of electoral refinements are observed with fair
fidelity. The secret ballot was instituted by Sáenz Peña in 1912,
and sporadic measures to abolish it are met with resentment. The
great landholders and employers naturally use their influence to
see that their dependents vote as they should. Charges of vote
buying are freely made by all parties. City machines have been
known to use repeaters, strong-arm squads, and other devices
not unknown to centers of northern culture. The contests are
usually close enough so that some corruption in a few provinces
will defeat the majority. But fair elections unquestionably prevail in most of the country most of the time. Argentine elections
are of a class apart from those of Brazil and Mexico. If they do not
quite measure up to the standard of Madison and Montclair, they
are probably as fair as those of Chicago, and better than those of
Jersey City.

The chief tool of political dictation in Argentina has been the
power of federal intervention. The Constitution gives to the
Executive the power (with the concurrence of his Cabinet) to
intervene in any province where stable government is threatened.

He may oust the elected provincial governor, and appoint an interventor to his place. Irigoyen exercised this right with high-handed frequency, Uriburu and Justo followed his example, Ortiz has made more sparing use of this power. With Irigoyen, intervention was an instrument of pride—he knew best how provinces should behave. With Justo, it was a device for defeating his Radical opponents. Ortiz has resorted to intervention only in cases of malfeasance in office. The latest instance, the appointment of an interventor to the province of Buenos Aires in March 1940, was made necessary by Governor Manuel Fresno's blatant disregard of even the outward amenities of free elections, and by his setting up of a mimic fascist state with its own militia. His removal by President Ortiz was approved by public opinion, by *La Prensa, La Nación,* and other chief newspapers, as a wholesome return to democratic government. The incident prompted former critics of President Ortiz to describe him as a new Sáenz Peña, who would provide a secret ballot and insist upon honest elections even though these worked his defeat.

Friends of Argentine democracy took heart from the outcome of a political crisis which broke in July and August 1940. On July 3 President Ortiz, long a sufferer from diabetes, announced that he would take an indefinite leave, committing the presidential function to Vice-President Ramón S. Castillo. This was disquieting news. Ortiz had evidenced constitutional zeal and democratic faith. Castillo was regarded as an understudy to Justo, overzealous for executive power and highhanded in his attitude toward provincial governments. In August, Socialist members of Congress exposed the "Palermo land deal," charged the government with the purchase of an army airdrome site at a figure five times its value. Members of the Cabinet and of Congress were implicated. The scandal shook Congress and the public. Conservatives, disappointed in Ortiz and considering Castillo more amenable, charged that the scandal proved the "inadequacy of democracy." The Radicals were on the spot, for at least one of their representatives in Congress was implicated and

shot himself. The Senate voted a resolution of censure. Whereupon, on August 22, President Ortiz resigned the presidency:
"I prefer to be a private citizen with dignity rather than a president besmirched," countering the Conservative charge that the
steal proved the failure of democracy with the words, "The desire for dishonest profit is a result of human imperfection and
not a consequence of any political institution." Ortiz' resignation
delighted some Conservative factions. From Rome *Giornale
d'Italia* announced that the resignation of Ortiz would pave the
way for a pro-Axis foreign policy under Castillo. But the more
democratic forces in Congress under the leadership of Marcelo
T. de Alvear of the Radicals rallied to the support of Ortiz. The
Senate, with one dissenting vote, refused to accept the resignation. The keynote speech was delivered by Socialist Senator Alfredo Palacios: "The time has come to demonstrate . . . that
democratic institutions can last indefinitely so long as there is
energy enough to defend them and to protect them. We have
complied with a most painful duty dictated by democracy but
without which democracy cannot live, that of enforcing justice
based on truth." The one vote cast against rejection of the resignation was that of Senator Matías G. Sánchez Sorondo, an outspoken admirer of fascist ways, and named by *Giornale d'Italia*
as the likely appointee to the Ministry of Foreign Affairs. The
crowds who surrounded Congress shouted the issue with substantial accuracy, "Viva Ortiz! Down with Sánchez Sorondo!"

So the crisis passed, and Argentina breathed more freely. Castillo still exercised the presidential office, but Ortiz was President. The new Cabinet was made up of men of democratic convictions, committed to constitutional government. The Minister
of Foreign Affairs was not Sánchez Sorondo but Julio A. Roca,
a man of wisdom and understanding, a lifelong friend of England and favoring a policy of coöperation with the United States.

Argentine politics in early 1941 were in angry confusion. President Ortiz, a sick man, was in the background. Vice-President
Castillo, performing the bulk of executive duties, spoke for the

obdurate Conservatives. Attempts to negotiate a truce between the Radicals and the Concordancia had broken down. The gathering economic distress incident to the war was testing the political structure. Fraudulent elections in the provinces of Mendoza and Santa Fé provoked bitterness. The democratically minded now pinned their hopes on Roberto Ortiz and watched anxiously for the next steps of their opponents.

The Less Democratic Argentina

THIS listing tends to overneatness. There is no man, no company of men who do not betray mixed motives. The believer in democracy may have his lapses; the adherent to the doctrine of the divine right of kings may also be inconsistent. With this caution, I set down some of the *less* democratic forces in Argentine life.

First, the rule of the powerful. We have discussed the strong hold of a little handful upon the wealth of Argentina. These gentlemen of the broad acres constitute a major problem in the democratic leavening of this feudal land. They and their fathers before them have controlled elections and determined policies. In fairness it must also be said that this untitled aristocracy has produced some of the most notable leaders, in whom national loyalty surmounted self-interest. But class interest is powerful, and the owner of an estancia of 100,000 acres does not often care to take chances with the ballot box.

The Argentine conservative has a consuming fear of radicalism. He sees a sword dangling over his head which he calls "communism." He is ready at any time to tell you about the menace from Moscow. It avails naught to remind him that Argentina is singularly free of doctrinaire Leftism. There are a few thousand avowed Stalinists; there may be 100,000 convinced socialists, but they can hardly be described as revolutionists; of wild anarchists, there are a few in the port. The Unión Cívica Radical is about as radical as Charles Evans Hughes. When the Argentine conservative talks of radicalism, he means high income taxes, pressure for division of lands through graded taxes, demands for better wages and living conditions for the peones, and a more scrupulous observance of the laws of free suffrage. These things he cannot abide.

These powerful gentlemen favor a firm hand in the Executive. They welcomed Uriburu who promised to keep order with no nonsense. They went with their peones to vote for Justo in 1932, and for Ortiz in 1938. The landholders of the rich province of Buenos Aires elected Manuel Fresno governor and then resented Ortiz' action in throwing Fresno out for his fascist ways. This does not prove that it takes 25,000 good acres to make a fascist. I have known obdurate die-hards with not enough ground for a pansy bed. (Nor am I forgetting capitalist friends who always vote for Norman Thomas.)

The powerful of Argentina bid fair to be something of a problem. They are spreading word that democracy is an exploded myth, that the strong must rule the weak, lest all perish. That news is abroad in Argentina.

A straw in the wind may be found by going through the pages of the profascist, pronazi, anti-Semitic press—as lurid and violent a press as can be found anywhere in the world. Who supports these journals? Germany, of course, and Italy. But who are the advertisers who help to pay the bills? *La Prensa* asked this question in an editorial on October 17, 1940. Why, it asked, are the journals which fight democracy and applaud fascism given substantial advertisements from government agencies—the National Oil Trust (YPF), the Buenos Aires Municipal Loan Bank, the National Mortgage Bank, the National Postal Savings Bank, and the great Banco de la Nación Argentina? These are government institutions, handled by the chief men of the nation and supported by public funds. "Insolence," *La Prensa* called it.

The answer is only too clear. I can simply repeat charges made in the public press, made in private conversations by responsible men, and generally accepted. The ruling group of Argentina includes many men who despise democracy, believe that its day is done, and that Argentina must adjust herself to a totalitarian world. Many of these men are powerful in industry, business, and government. They are in every ministry. No matter how demo-

cratic and loyal to the Constitution may be the man at the top
(the present government has such men), they have responsible
assistants and heads of departments who look in other directions.
I am told by men worthy of trust that there is scarcely a government office without at least one official who is suspected of dealings with Germany or Italy. This is a serious charge. It cannot
be documented.

Second, many of the "professional intellectuals" must be reckoned among those of doubtful fidelity to democracy. I sought out
the Commission on Intellectual Coöperation and its head, Dr.
Carlos Ibarguren, whose place in Argentine intellectual circles is
attested by his election to the presidency of the Argentine Acad-
emy of Letters. Where does he stand? Perhaps the best answer is
found in his little book on the dictator, Juan Manuel de Rosas.
Ibarguren is one of a little company who seek to salvage Rosas'
reputation, with the implication that Argentina has overdone the
praise of such leaders as Sarmiento and Mitre, and that perhaps
the need of the hour is "another strong man." The emphasis has a
familiar ring.

I turned to the offices of the National Commission of Culture,
state-supported for the encouragement of the arts and for the
appointment of students to fellowships in other lands. The president of this well-financed body is Matías G. Sánchez Sorondo,
the senator who cast the lone vote against President Ortiz in
August 1940, and a eulogist of totalitarian fashions. The secretary
of the commission is Homero M. Guglielmi, who ten years ago
held a Guggenheim fellowship in the United States, wrote some
clever little books of satire with the Americans as bait, and whose
recent utterances have been marked with slight respect for democratic institutions.

The best-selling novelist Hugo Wast turns out a steady stream
of antidemocratic books. His *Oro,* for example, is anti-Semitic.
This is a sample from its pages: "War is a kind of alchemy—it
transmutes the red blood of soldiers into the yellow gold of
Jews." Other names appear, writers who with much show of

erudition plead for alien loyalties. Some of these enjoy high honors, the chief seats on distinguished occasions. All this may be set down as a part of the backwash of feudalism. Trailing along with the Argentine powerful are the pensioners of privilege, the poets laureate of the Crown.

This virus poisons university life. One asks in vain for the names of social scientists in the great and honorable universities of Argentina who are probing deep into the social ills of the nation. Such are not honored with *catedras* (platforms) in academic life. There are men of solid distinction on university faculties, especially in medicine and law, but social ferment is not a qualification for academic honors.

Any account of Argentine intellectual life which consigned all its leaders to fascist ranks would obviously be unfair. Argentina produces men of spiritual and literary power. A sizable group of them are found on the staffs of the better newspapers. A few such have chairs in the universities. Some excellent social scientists win grudged recognition in government offices—agriculture, finance, labor, foreign relations. But the chief seats among the intellectual mighty are reserved for those who do not offend.

Third, the Germans and the Italians are present in Argentina, and are active in the campaign to discredit democracy and to make converts for their new gospels. Their numbers are considerable, their campaign aggressive, and they must be counted among the forces against democracy. Chapter IX deals with these disturbers.

Fourth, the Army and the Navy. Fighters admire the successful of their craft. Germany succeeds. Therefore Germany has many applauders among the men who rule the army and the navy in Argentina, and throughout most of Latin America.

The military men of Argentina have long been courted by Italy and Germany. The army has had many German instructors—the goose step and the steel helmet remain. Detachments of Argentine officers have enjoyed pleasant free trips to Germany in recent years. Their leaders have had their quota of ribbons from the gov-

ernment of the Reich. I am told that one often hears the fascist
hymn of Italy in the barracks of the younger officers.

Where does the army stand today—for democracy or for the
new gospel of Central Europe? I put the question to a great variety of men—three members of Congress, sundry government
officials, professional men. Their answers roughly agree: at least
half of the higher-ranking officers are convinced that democracy
is passing, that Germany will win, that Argentina must proceed
upon those assumptions. One senator had a more reassuring word,
that these same officers would avoid overt acts of treason lest
their pension rights be threatened. Others say that many of the
younger officers and practically all the noncommissioned officers and men are of more democratic conviction. But many Argentines are honestly concerned as to the army's course in any
test between reaction and democracy. They recall that the army
aided Uriburu in 1930.

And the navy? Here more hopeful expressions are heard,
although high naval officials have been courted by Rome and
Berlin.

Fifth, the influence of the Church. Does the Roman Catholic
Church, the official church of the nation, make for democratic
conviction and practice? It is always unfair to say of that Church
in any country or in any period of time that she stands here, or
stands there. The Church works under many flags and must
accommodate herself to diverse political climates.

With some diffidence, as though touching holy vessels with
unwashed hands, I put down the Church as one of the *less* democratic forces in modern Argentina. The Argentine Church shows
that chronic list to the Right which usually marks organized
religion, and it carries the added burden of its Spanish heritage.
Today, in a world divided between protagonists for totalitarianism and democracy, the Church in Argentina finds its reason
clouded by loyalty to Francisco Franco. The defense of the Spanish dictator, devoutly pressed in Argentina, has carried over into
defense of the political ideology of Franco. Argentines fear lest

the Argentine Church may travel too far with that same Franco. It is difficult to place a finger on the spots which mark Catholic influence against democracy. Some hotheads charge Acción Católica, a numerous and active organization of the faithful, with outright fascist propaganda. They probably prove too much. It may more fairly be said that the Church simply continues to be, and with kindled zeal, the handmaiden of Argentina's unhappy feudalism. I question whether the Church would deliberately play Hitler's or Mussolini's game in Argentina. But its deep obeisance to Franco's Spain scarcely makes for increase in democratic sentiment among the faithful poor or the loyal rich.

This citing of the Church of Argentina on the side of the reaction against democracy must be coupled with recognition of the numerous prelates whose work for social justice and democratic institutions has earned them warm respect. Conspicuous among these is Bishop de Andrea of Buenos Aires.

DESPITE all handicaps, Argentina travels toward a greater democracy. The bystander feels her robust strivings as a clean strong wind in the life of the nation. Question the little shopkeeper, the village schoolteacher, the conductor on the railroad, the schoolboy with his bundle of books—get them started on Adolf Hitler, Japan, the shift in the Argentine cabinet, Uruguayan air bases, the cost of living: they have ideas and will express them, they talk as those who build a free nation. Watch the crowds in the movies as the newsreels are thrown on the screen; the great majority of these people are on the side of the more democratic powers. Follow the crowds to the mass meeting in the Plaza de Mayo, catch the words which bring applause, words about honest elections, civil liberties, the sovereignty of Argentina. The people seek a more democratic Argentina and they will have it if they are not betrayed.

The United States invites allies for an all-American front. We do well to cultivate the Argentine people.

CHAPTER VII

ARGENTINA AND HER NEXT-DOOR NEIGHBORS

SOME ten years ago, upon my return from a trip around the South American circle, a moderately literate friend asked, "How is *that country* getting on?" He knew, of course, that there are ten countries, not one, but his question reflected a not uncommon confusion concerning Southern political divisions. The average American citizen seems unaware that the South Americans have fought each other with fervor, that their relations are marked by the same bristling prides and prejudices which adorn boundaries between civilized nations elsewhere. The very phrase "Latin America" is misleading, imputing a unity which does not exist. This conclusion is borne out by a glance at Argentina's dealings with her neighbors.

Argentina has five neighbors—Chile, Brazil, Uruguay, Paraguay, and Bolivia. The relations between these nations and Argentina throw light on current discussion of all-American pacts for defense and profit.

Chile shares with Argentina a border line of some 2,600 miles, which is strung from peak to peak in the high Andes. This boundary was warmly debated during Chile's more prosperous years in the nineteenth century. She defeated Peru and Bolivia in 1879, annexed territory in the north, and came out with the best-trained army in South America. Meanwhile, her nitrate monopoly assured her a constant income. In 1898 Chile served an ultimatum on Argentina, demanding sizable boundary concessions, and war seemed imminent. Calmer counsels prevailed, the issues were submitted to arbitration, the awards were accepted, the two countries swore eternal peace and erected the Christ of the Andes high above Mendoza as a seal to the covenant. This pious gesture was shortly fortified by Chile's declining nitrate trade. Hotheads in both countries would still debate certain lands in the far south, but Argentina has so outrun Chile in economic

strength that trouble seems unlikely. Official relations are entirely amicable, even though the Chileans resent what they pri-
vately describe as the high-flown ways of the Argentines, and the
dwellers of La Plata reciprocate with descriptions no less dis-
paraging. But they do not quarrel. The Chileans admit that they
must go to Argentina for a good steak, but point out that Argentines must go to Chile for a good mountain.[1]

Brazil touches Argentina only in the narrow span between
Uruguay and Paraguay. The rivalry between the two countries is
more psychological than economic. The Argentine inherits the
Spaniard's disdain for the Portuguese, and he does not bother to
conceal it. The race question also intrudes. I have heard entirely
kindly Argentines speak slightingly of "that nigger nation." The
Brazilians profess to find the Argentines rude and uncultured,
and sometimes speak of their crude emphasis upon material possessions. Argentines are disposed to compare figures on crops and
bank clearings to the disparagement of "indolent tropical Brazil." The nationals of both countries have long harbored fears of
each other's imperial ambitions, and neither likes to hear of the
other's arms or gunboats. Fortunately territorial arguments between the two were long since settled by the creation of Uruguay
and Paraguay as buffer states. It is also fortunate that there is little
economic clash between them. Brazil is Argentina's generous
buyer of wheat, and Argentina buys Brazilian oranges and tropical products. Each has meat and hides to sell, but Brazil offers
slight competition. Argentina does not compete with Brazil's
chief exports—coffee, cotton, and cacao. But little love is lost, as
any visitor quickly learns by putting leading questions to stray
acquaintances in Rio de Janeiro or Buenos Aires.

Uruguay, "La Banda Oriental," was contested territory from
the earliest colonial days. Both the Portuguese and the Spaniards
established some settlements there and claimed it for their respective kings. Brazil reached for it in the days when the hold of
Europe was breaking, for the control of the Río de la Plata meant

1. Lest the literal-minded misunderstand, it should be noted that Argentina shares
with Chile the ownership of the cordillera.

safe access to her own hinterland of Matto Grosso. Argentina, equally determined to exclude Brazil, settled the question by the war of 1826 with the help of Britain and France. The creation of Uruguay as a separate state served not only Argentine but British interests, which demanded that the Río de la Plata be kept open as an international river.

Paraguay interests Argentina not only as a retaining wall thrown up against Brazil but as a fruitful field for her own economic expansion. Argentina joined Brazil and Uruguay in the war of the 'sixties against Paraguay's dictator Solano López because that picturesque tyrant disturbed happy trade relations, but there has since been no hint of trouble. Argentina has been Paraguay's zealous friend, faithfully supporting her in the Chaco war and helping her to seize the major gains from the Chaco peace. Argentina (with British backing) has built Paraguayan railroads, developed the steamship lines which connect Buenos Aires and Asunción, and opened up Paraguayan agriculture with Argentine pesos and British pounds.

Bolivia also interests Argentina. Her illiterate population, meager leadership, and economic promise make her a prime object of attention. Chile once had the upper hand in Bolivian affairs, but steadily loses to Argentina. Bolivia has the mineral wealth which Argentina lacks. Argentine cultivation of Bolivian affections suffered a setback in the Chaco war, with Buenos Aires displaying undue interest in the success of Paraguayan arms. But wars are forgotten when economic profit appears. Bolivia's tin and silver and petroleum can be more profitably exported by way of La Plata than over the cordillera to Arica on the Pacific Coast. An Argentine railroad leads through Jujuy to La Paz, and another is projected which will connect Buenos Aires with Santa Cruz on the edge of the Bolivian oil fields. It is common gossip, perhaps a fact, that the oil men of Argentina played more than a passive role in Bolivia's expropriation in 1937 of Standard Oil's fields, and that they view the development of that substantial reservoir as the solution of Argentina's shortage. But the ways of oil operators, as any American can attest, are past human understanding. It may simply be recorded that the Argentine state oil trust, Yacimientos Petrolíferos Fiscales, is an astute agency of whose activities even the Argentines are but dimly aware. Some suggest that the wounds of the Chaco may find healing in Bolivian oil, and that both Bolivia and Paraguay may find refuge in the widening circle of Buenos Aires' beneficent imperialism. Such reflections cause unhappiness to the Brazilians, who have also fixed their hopes on Bolivia. Brazil has built a costly and unprofitable railroad connecting the Amazon system with northeastern Bolivia, and has plans for another line to Santa Cruz. Brazilians see no reason why Bolivian ore and oil should not ride the Amazon. On the face of it, the Argentines seem to make the stronger case.

Spain in the eighteenth century mapped the viceroyalty of La Plata to include what is now Uruguay, Paraguay, Bolivia, and Argentina—with a spot of desert shore on the Pacific for good measure. That seemed a logical economic unit to Charles III who signed the decree in 1776. There are Argentines who today study old maps, cite the unhappiness of weak nations, and suggest that national lines may sometimes be erased for the comfort of all. There are outsiders who ponder the likely course of current history and the strains to which freedom is subjected, and admit that a greater and more self-sufficient Argentina might make for the tranquillity of the Western World. But it would hardly befit a citizen of the United States, long labeled by Argentines the Colossus of the North, to suggest that Argentina should essay the role of Colossus of the South.

CHAPTER VIII

THE BRITISH ON THE "RIVER PLATE"

HIS Britannic Majesty's 50,000 subjects occupy a position of peculiar importance in the land of the Río de la Plata. There is a certain timelessness to British colonists in far lands which is easy to recognize, hard to describe. Whether they stay for one generation or for three, they are still English, speak

Spanish with a British accent, and when they meet a citizen of
the United States inevitably bring in a reference to "your American rugby—so rough you know." (Even the Argentines call it
fútbol.) They have been in Argentina so long that they have imparted their chief national vices—the tea habit and driving on
the wrong side of the road. They also brought their incomparable
gift of translating names into meaningless English—*el campo*
(the country) becomes "the camp," the *Río de la Plata* the "River
Plate."

Argentines have good reasons for liking the British, and they
do. These reasons have tough roots. It was Lord Castlereagh who
decided that England would give her blessing to South American
freedom and take her pay in trade. Canning ratified this decision
and thereby dashed Spanish hopes. James Monroe, in his "Doctrine" of 1823, confirmed a decision made in England.

The Argentine-British compact has paid. British capital built
Argentine railroads, financed the opening of the frontier, furnished agricultural machinery, built packing plants and tan-
neries. Britain continues as Argentina's best customer, buying almost four times as much from her in 1938 as did the United
States. Britain has some $2,200,000,000 invested in Argentina.
There may be something in the remark of the hypothetical
Briton to the hypothetical American, "You may take Canada
from us, but you will never take Argentina."

British advantage in Argentina is easily explained. Great Britain, chiefly industrial, can buy Argentine meats and grains—the
United States cannot. Britain has pressed her advantage. Following the Ottawa Conference of the Dominions in 1932, Britain
concluded the Roca Agreement with Argentina, by the terms of
which Britain agreed not to reduce her purchases of Argentine
meat by more than 10 % of the 1931–32 level: Argentina agreed,
in return, to use all British money thus obtained to purchase British goods (after deducting sufficient funds for service on sterling
loans and dividends on British investments). Some quizzical by-
standers pointed out that England had thereby conferred dominion status upon Argentina. The gains to each party to the com-

pact were obvious. Argentina had an assured market for her beef. British investors in Argentine bonds and railroads were guaranteed larger payments than would otherwise have been feasible. The agreement was followed by an Argentine loan in London, whose proceeds freed blocked funds due British investors. The Roca Agreement was renewed in 1936, and the commercial relations between the two countries suffered no interruption until the outbreak of war in 1939. With England at war, normal trade suffers, England can no longer supply the finished goods with which she paid for beef and wheat, and Argentina casts about for ways in which to collect for the shipments she makes to British buyers.

The British have won and held Argentine respect. Mutually profitable trade and solid investment explain this in part, but the Argentine, in more candid moments, gives other explanations in which he contrasts American and British enterprise. The British investor, he will tell you, moved in with his family and family silver and piano. He came to stay. He built railways, capital plants, banks. He developed the country. The North American came with a suitcase—and a return ticket. He was not a settler but a traveler. He was not a businessman but a gambler. He came to seize quick profits on a deal, and over his coffee talked of getting back to "God's country." This generalization proves too much, but there is enough truth in it to explain the firm place of the Anglo-Argentines in the life of the Río de la Plata, and the lesser influence exerted by the transient representatives of the United States.

The United States has a large bone to pick with the Britons in Argentina. Those hardheaded traders have persistently sought to block all our steps toward Pan-American accord. British trade interest and British diplomacy seemingly move on different tracks. British diplomacy required American aid in 1917, and got it; again in 1939–41, and got it. But the British did not reciprocate when the United States sought Argentine collaboration in the Americas against the gathering storm. Americans, Argentines, and some British in Buenos Aires tell you frankly that British in-

fluence was thrown against the United States at the Conferences
of Montevideo in 1933, Buenos Aires in 1936, Lima in 1938. A
considerable share of Argentine distaste for inter-American action must be charged to British pressure. In 1939, when Washington sought to conclude a trade agreement with Argentina,
there were plenty of whisperings in Buenos Aires that the British
were helping to block the negotiations. One British newspaper in
that capital came out with headlines which suggested, "Now is
the time to talk about beef"—the argument which finally broke
up the party.

The British and the Argentines have remained faithful friends
despite minor arguments. When the war broke in 1939, Argentine public opinion was overwhelmingly pro-British, and it was
still so at the beginning of 1941. Only one argument threatened
to disturb this unity: the old question of the Falkland Islands,
Argentina irredenta.

Every faithful Argentine map, census recital, atlas, or yearbook
includes the Malvinas Islands (as the Argentines call the Falklands) in the list of Argentine territory. But the Falklands (or
the Malvinas) are held by England, and the garrison there has,
since war began, been enlarged by recruits from the British colony in Argentina. This recruiting angers Argentina. Back of
British possession lies a long tale. These islands—more than 100
of them in all—bleak wastelands lying 250 miles off Argentina's
southern shores, were first settled by the French in 1764. The
Spanish acquired them in 1767 and held them (with one brief
British interlude) until Argentine independence was recognized
and the islands passed to the sovereignty of the new republic. Argentina's domestic turmoil led to neglect of the islands, and they
became the hangout of smugglers and pirates. In 1831 a detachment of United States marines ousted the pirates, and turned the
islands over to the British in 1833. Argentines, meditating upon
the Falklands, harbor a double grudge. First, against the United
States, which conveniently forgot the Monroe Doctrine; and second, against England, which hangs on to the islands. There is a
"committee for the reclamation of the Malvinas Islands" with So-

cialist Senator Alfredo Palacios at its head. Some puzzled commentators wonder why Britain does not swap the Falklands for a few herds of cattle, and call it quits. For, after all, you cannot hold dominions in line unless you play with them.

CHAPTER IX

GERMANS, ITALIANS, JAPANESE—A STUDY IN COLUMNS

TRACKING down the fifth column, which became the chief extracurricular activity of all good men and true in the summer of 1940, reached Argentina. Argentines admit that the Axis is very much with them. (Some realists make note that the British and the Americans are also with them.) The Germans are there—some 250,000 or more; the Italians—upward of 2,000,000; and the Japanese—6,000 to 8,000.

First, the Germans

GERMANS have been coming to Argentina for over a hundred years, in search of freedom, homes, opportunity. There are today in Argentina 250,000 to 300,000 first-, second-, third-, and fourth-generation German-Argentines. Some 60,000 of these were born in Germany. They are all Germans, according to official Berlin theory, no matter how many years they have lived on Argentine soil, no matter what intermarriages with non-Germans have been solemnized. Germans justly lay claim to a sizable share in the building of Argentina. They are farmers, traders, industrialists, bankers. Go to Mendoza or Córdoba or Rosario or Bahía Blanca and you will find stores, banks, commission houses, factories with German names. Walk down any prosperous street and read Schumann, Ernst, and Schmidt on brass doorplates. Argentines of German blood built solidly, just as their cousins did in Milwaukee, Cincinnati, Pittsburgh, New York, Chicago.

But there is a difference. In the United States we reckon as a sound American any citizen of German name and blood who says no word and commits no act which belies that claim. In Argentina they are learning to account as German any citizen of German blood and name who does not convincingly forswear his German allegiance. This was not true three years ago. The change has come under Hitler's pressure.

Where do German-Argentines stand today? I put that question to Argentines, to German residents (anti-Hitler Germans, of course), and to Jewish citizens. The answers roughly agree: almost all the German-born are loyal to Hitler; a large minority, perhaps a majority, of the older Germans profess allegiance to New Germany; an overwhelming majority of the young Germans, whether or not they have seen the Fatherland, are fervid in support of Nazi doctrine; 50 to 90 % of German-Argentines stand with the Führer. Those are the guesses of my informants. No one knows.

Hitler's spokesmen are busy in Argentina. Their skill and resources are indisputable. They have made the halfhearted courting of the United States seem the awkward passes of a country bumpkin.

What are German aims? No guesswork is needed. They would unite all German-Argentines, whether born in Germany or in Argentina, whether all-German or part-German, whether citizens of Argentina or not; they seek to make converts among Argentines; they work to discredit England and the United States. All German measures are devised to serve these ends.

Let us examine the German campaign.

First, the German organization is centered in the Embassy, where the ambassador, his counselors, secretaries, attachés, aides, assistants, and clerks do their work. This is the largest foreign mission in the capital. Housed in the same building is the German Beneficent and Cultural Society, an innocent creation which took the place of the Nazi party outlawed in 1939. There are German consular agents throughout Argentina. This is the official organization of Hitler's Germany.

The extraofficial German organization cannot be described with such accuracy. This appears to be a numerous company. Any Argentine official, in confidential mood, can tell you of suspects. Any Jewish resident, with vested interest in keeping watch, can name names. Any anti-Hitler German will report on some of his countrymen: Germans in Argentine public offices, foreign relations, post office, police, army, navy, justice; Germans in schools, banks, business houses, hospitals, city halls; Germans driving buses which cross the lines into Brazil, Paraguay, Uruguay; running rum shops where soldiers pledge their faith, waiting on tables in hotels and restaurants, and listening in five languages. Are these stories all true? Probably not.

The Argentine Government has tacitly recognized the presence of the Gestapo. In August 1940 the government indicted a naturalized Argentine citizen, Arnulf Fuhrmann, conspirator in the Uruguay Nazi plot, charging him with leadership of the Gestapo. Why, inquired *La Prensa* on August 11, does the government refrain from taking drastic action against the Gestapo, now that it admits its presence, knows its street address and its telephone number? A few weeks later Karl Arnold, working from an office in the same building as the German Embassy, was arrested for his alleged Gestapo activities. And down in Punta del Indio the police raided "Buck's Bar" where Argentine flyers congregate, found a list of Gestapo agents in Argentina and a supply of Nazi literature.

Second, German-Argentines are enlisted in Hitler organizations. Persuasion is eloquent: You are German, you have a right to your pride, you belong to a conquering race. Germans who have never seen Germany, Germans with Argentine mothers or wives or children, are convinced. Especially the youth. If persuasion fails, then pressure. A German merchant, dependent upon German imports or sales, obeys or is boycotted. The lukewarm are insulted by old friends. All are taught that one loyalty alone prevails. If pressure fails, there are other ways. If a German resists, his mother or sister or cousin in Germany may go to a concentration camp—authenticated cases are numerous. In some instances outspoken Germans are handled by Gestapo agents in rougher fashion. I know one such German, and have heard the story from his own lips. He is a professional man of irreproachable standing in Buenos Aires. He said what he thought of Hitler and laughed at those who would compel him. One night in June 1940—according to his story to me—he was cornered in a lonely spot by two men whom he knew as Gestapo agents. He moved quicker than they did, and turned them both over to the police. Perhaps he was boasting.

These measures evidently succeed. The majority of German-Argentines are persuaded, or pretend to be persuaded, join the Beneficent and Cultural Society, or any of the hundreds of German clubs which flourish in open or in secret over the republic. Each German helps to pay the costs for this national organization, for its agents, its printing, its hidden ventures of every sort. He is assessed a definite share of his wages, salary, income. This ranges from 10 % up. German firms pay their toll. Argentine firms which enjoy German trade are taxed. The funds are for charity, for *Winterhilfe* in Germany, for food for the German poor in Argentina. No accounting is given. Reports may be exaggerated.

Third, a German mail campaign floods the country with pamphlets, letters, placards. A special weekly air-mail edition of the *Frankfurter Zeitung* is sent by plane to an unreckoned number of first citizens throughout Argentina.

Fourth, the Germans use the press. Some unimportant Argentine papers prove amenable and accept the free services of Hitler's DNB. The Germans have their own press. There are numerous papers in German, the most prominent is the *Deutsche La Plata Zeitung* (published also in a Spanish edition). Germans are alleged to be behind a great variety of newspapers and magazines which flood the country with attacks upon democracy, ridicule of the United States, sabotage of all Pan-American movements, glorification of German and Italian victories. The daily *Pampero* is the chief. Its national circulation is considerable—100,000 is claimed. Newsboys on Buenos Aires streets have the habit of shouting *Pampero* first in listing their wares. I asked one boy why he did it, and he laughed, and shouted again, PAMPERO! *Crítica! Razón!* I found the explanation later—newsboys get an extra commission on sales of *Pampero*. Another is *Crisol,* ostensibly a Catholic journal, but there is no evidence that the Church is behind it. Enrique Oses, publisher of both *Pampero* and *Crisol,* was arrested in July 1940 because of an obscene attack upon Winston Churchill. Another is *Clarinada—Revista anti-comunista y anti-judía,* fifty pages of filthy cartoons, anti-Jewish humor, and general ridicule of democratic institutions. The reading of it carries one back to Julius Streicher's *Der Stürmer.* It carries a three-page black list of *"judío-comunista"* firms, physicians, lawyers, schools, banks, dentists. The only advertisers in the issue which I have before me (September 30, 1940) are the YPF (the National Petroleum Trust), the Municipal Bank of Buenos Aires, the National Postal Savings Bank, the National Mortgage Bank—all government institutions.

Scattered over the hinterland of Argentina are scores of lesser journals of German hue. One of these is *Russland-Deutsche,* published in Lucas Gonzales in the province of Entre Ríos, by the Catholic priest Jacob Riffel. The fascist White Russians have a journal upon whose cover appears a Russian eagle holding a swastika. The Ukrainian nationalists have their pro-Nazi journal. Honorable mention is due *Argentinische Tageblatt,* published at considerable risk to life and limb by an able group of unreconstructed Germans.

Fifth, the Germans use the movies. You come upon UFA news releases in every city and town. These are furnished to movie houses at a fraction of the rates charged for American newsreels. In Buenos Aires two theaters are popularly described as official German ventures, financed and directed from the Embassy. An hour in one of these, the Cineac, made the story credible. The program, aside from Donald Duck and such cultural items, was divided between three newsreels: a short film on the damage in London, a short on the armament program in the United States, and a very long newsreel of Hitler reviewing his troops and mechanized units. The program seems designed to persuade the casual observer that Britain crumbles, that the United States frantically prepares, and that Germany has the greatest army of all time.

Sixth, Germans use the radio. Spanish broadcasts from Germany are widely advertised. Local stations are utilized to some extent. The effectiveness of short-wave broadcasts is generally discounted, for their reception requires costly equipment. Most of the news heard over local Argentine stations is definitely pro-English.

Seventh, German schools are everywhere—twenty-five of them listed as large and influential, and many hundreds of smaller schools scattered over the republic. Many of these claim to be completely Argentine in spirit and control. They are credited with excellent teaching, stiff discipline, and the best of equipment. Germans are not slow to draw contrasts between their excellent schoolhouses and the poor buildings which the national budget affords. The German language is used, with such concession on the use of Spanish as government inspectors can compel. I have in my possession a photostat of a page from the exercises of an Argentine child, seized in a raid in 1940. It is reproduced on the next page.[1]

Eighth, Germany works through her churchmen. The numerous Lutheran churches follow the fashion of their kin in Germany and accept the Hitler rule. Three years ago some German-Argentine Lutherans, inspired by the Niemöller faction in Berlin, resisted Nazi pressure. Few of these are left. There are numerous German Catholic priests, most of whom have found it wise to follow the Hitler line. The Order of the Divine Word, a German Catholic order, operates in northern Argentina, and sev-

---

1. Translation:

On the birthday.

Class work. On April 20, Adolf Hitler has his birthday. He will be 47 years old this year. Adolf Hitler is the Führer of the German people. He loves children and is good to poor people. Therefore we love him, all Germans love him very much. The birthday of Adolf Hitler will also be celebrated by us in Eldorado. . . . The President of Argentina is General Justo, the President of Germany is Adolf Hitler. . . .

Eldorado, 18. 4 1936

Zum Geburtstag.

Gemeinsame Arbeit.

Am 20. April hat Adolf Hitler
seinen Geburtstag. Er wird in
diesem Jahre 47 Jahre alt. Adolf
Hitler ist der Führer des deutschen
Volkes. Er hat die Kinder gern
und ist den armen Leuten
gut. Darum lieben ihn auch
alle Deutschen so sehr. Auch
bei uns in Eldorado wird der
Geburtstag Adolf Hitlers gefeiert

F. 0.   Sch. I.

Merke:

Der Präsident von Argentinien
heißt General Justo, der Präsi=
dent von Deutschland ist Adolf
Hitler.

D D d d Deutschland, D d D d D d.

eral of its members have been indicted by the government for
their Nazi activities.

Ninth, German influence introduces anti-Semitism to a nation
which has never known it. The Jews have been entering Argentina for over seventy-five years until there are some 300,000 today.
Prosperous farming communities of Jewish settlers have flourished for three generations. Many highly regarded citizens are
of Jewish blood. Assimilation of these Jews into Argentine life
has been rapid. Today, the Germans work a cleavage. Not only
must German employers draw the line against Jewish workers,
but pressure is successfully applied on firms which enjoy German
trade. The principal of one of Buenos Aires' best schools tells me
that a Jewish girl has great difficulty in finding a position.

Tenth, the Germans bring pressure upon national leaders. This
pressure ranges all the way from cajolery to bribery. Decorations
to army officers, ribbons for essayists to stick in their coats, free
trips to Germany for generals, academic awards to scientists—
gifts presented with such grace that the word bribery would appear rude. They win support by citing German success, by reiter-
ating the certain victory of Hitler arms, dilating upon the glori-
ous future of Greater Germany—an appealing argument to those
who worship success, as many do in Siam, Kansas, and Argentina. They know the art of bullying. During recent months the
German ambassador has more than once appeared in the Foreign
Office to make statements after this fashion: "When Germany
rules Europe, you will have to play with us. It will pay you to play
with us now."

Eleventh, German air lines thread the country. The German
Condor and its subsidiaries and affiliates reach from Buenos Aires
to the chief cities of the north, and south to the tip of Tierra del
Fuego. They link up with the German air system which covers
all South America. German capital, management, pilots, and
mechanics control. This means a sizable body of aliens in command of a strategic force. Moreover, it affords the Germans a
secure method of communication between their various agents.

The government served notice that all pilots are to be Argentine, but this did not rule out hundreds of trained pilots who are Argentine citizens of German blood. In September 1940 it was ordered that within two years all air lines must be in the hands of Argentine companies, directed and operated by Argentines.

Twelfth, Germans make tacit claims to extraterritoriality. Argentina is aroused over the affront to her sovereignty in the existence of a foreign police force, and in the claim to double citizenship. But more specific charges are being made, one of which was cited by *La Prensa* in an editorial of November 30, 1940. It seems that two Germans of Argentina, one Chilean- and the other Argentine-born (to escape Argentina's stiff divorce laws), applied for a divorce in a German court, forwarding their papers through the German Embassy in Buenos Aires, without notifying Argentine courts. It further appears that this case was heard in the offices of the German Embassy. This seems to suggest, according to *La Prensa,* which unearthed the incident, that "there exists a special sort of justice, Nazi justice, exerting jurisdiction over all the world. . . ."

Thirteenth, the German trade drive on Argentina was in full swing when the war came. It was unadorned barter, payment was made in aski marks which could be spent only on German goods. The drive was meticulously thorough. No possible buyer was overlooked. The salesman of electric engines in the capital followed up his deals. The little German peddler with pills and penknives painstakingly pushed into the smallest village under the shadow of the cordillera. German economic missions arrived in Buenos Aires with regularity, arranging new exchanges in motors and meat. In March 1939 Germany concluded a bargain (never carried out) with the Argentine Government by which railroad equipment for the state railroads was to be traded for 100,000 metric tons of wheat. There has been no lessening of German persuasion although the results seem hardly commensurate with the effort. Here are the figures which show Germany's indifferent success in the Argentine market:

	Argentine Imports from Germany		Argentine Exports to Germany	
1927	11.3		16.5	
1929	11.5	percentages of total Argentine imports	10.0	percentages of total Argentine exports
1936	9.3		5.8	
1938	10.3		11.7	
1939	9.2		5.7	

Argentina is aroused. Official lethargy over the threat of the ill-digested mass of nationals of alien allegiance has been shaken by the demands of press and public. The first alarm came in March 1939. *Noticias Gráficas* published a purported facsimile copy of a letter to the colonial office of the Reich, outlining a maturing plan for adding Patagonia to German territory, with a detailed description of all plans. This was supposedly signed by Embassy Counselor von Schubert and Alfred Müller, chief of the Nazi party in Argentina. This quite fantastic story held the first pages for weeks. Müller was arrested, Nazi offices were raided, Congress ordered an investigation, a few arrests were made. The document was finally described as a forgery, Müller was released, and Foreign Minister Cantilo assured the German ambassador that Argentina would permit no break in the happy relations between their two countries. In the meantime, President Ortiz ordered the dissolution of all political parties which receive orders or support from abroad. The Nazi party complied, and in its stead appeared the Beneficent and Cultural Society.

Early 1941 finds Argentine concern centered on German activities in the northern territories of Misiones, Formosa, and Chaco, and the provinces of Corrientes and Entre Ríos. These face Brazil, Uruguay, and Paraguay. The exposure of Nazi conspiracies in Uruguay in mid-1940 convinced many that Germany has special plans for a new Sudetenland embracing southern Brazil, Uruguay, and northern Argentina. During the spring and summer of 1940 several independent investigations were made of German activities in Misiones—one by the government, at least two by unofficial agencies. The government's findings were published in part. I have seen the results of the two independent investigations but am constrained to give no identification. Here are some of the facts which appear:

Misiones is a frontier territory, an Argentine finger wedged up between Brazil and Paraguay. It has around 300,000 population, with about 80,000 Germans of whom some 30,000 were born in Germany. Germans dominate business and agriculture. The best schools are German, many of them with fine buildings erected in part with Embassy funds, serving as a graphic reminder of the superiority of German culture. In addition to the German population there are many Poles, Swiss, and Scandinavians to whom the Germans are saying: Your homelands are now or soon will be ruled from Berlin. There are a few Jews, leading increasingly troubled lives. Earlier attempts to arouse national public opinion were unavailing. Governor Romaña insisted that all was well. In July 1940 the Federal Government ordered an investigation by the federal *gendarmerie*. Nazi headquarters were raided. Fifty machine guns, 3,500 rifles, and much ammunition were said to have been found and sent to the national arsenal in Buenos Aires. There were unsubstantiated reports of quick smuggling of arms into Paraguay. In Apóstoles, near the capital of Misiones, shots were fired at the commandant of the federal police. Arrests were made. The German ambassador demanded the release of the Germans, denounced the whole affair as a frame-up, charged mistreatment of the prisoners, and denied the story of the ammunition. "The guns were planted," he said. Meanwhile the police uncovered Nazi cells not only in Misiones but in neighboring Corrientes and Entre Ríos. German bus drivers were found operating between Misiones and the Brazilian states of Santa Catharina and Rio Grande do Sul—acting, it was charged, as liaison men between plotters in Brazil and Argentina. German Vice-Consul Winkelmann in Posadas seemed to be the director of these various activities. The post-office authorities in Misiones averred that 95 %, by weight, of all the mail handled in the province was German propaganda. These revelations, and many rumors which went with them, stirred public demand for action. A few people were arrested—among others Kunz, a cell leader in Chacra Aspeci; Sundheim, a physician in Colonia Leibig; Klein, a schoolman; and Hoffmann, a leader of the German labor front in Apostoles.

Argentines have not forgotten that more than a thousand officers and men of the scuttled *Graf Spee* are in Argentina. The internment prescribed was not strict. Some escaped to Chile and were returned. Some were consigned to custody on Isla Martín García, but in August 1940 fifteen of these escaped, creating some question as to the probity of the army guard. Some Argentines admit that the presence of a thousand well-trained German sailors might prove embarrassing in a crisis.

The Italians in Argentina

THERE are about 780,000 Italian-Argentines who were born in Italy, and at least 1 million more whose fathers or grandfathers came from Italy. Perhaps 2 million altogether.

The case of the Italian is quite different from that of the German. The Italians have entered Argentine life. They have proved useful and versatile citizens, as the wanderer over Argentina may attest after seeing their shops in every city and town, their vineyards around Mendoza, their farms. Many Italians have prospered, some of the great names in industry and finance are Italian. It is significant that the present Cabinet includes four Italian names. Not one of these men is viewed as other than a loyal Argentine. The hyphen is out so far as the generality of Italian-Argentines is concerned. Explanation would lead back to comparison between Italy and Germany, between Mussolini and Hitler. Argentine experience indicates that Il Duce holds no such loyalty as does Der Führer. It also suggests that the Mussolini machine is inept compared with Hitler's.

There are disloyal Italian-Argentines, a violent minority who are today coöperating with German-Argentines to discredit democratic institutions and to prepare for the day when Germany and Italy win. But there is no evidence which suggests that these are more than aides to the German machine.

Argentine trade with Italy is not significant. In 1929 her purchases from Italy aggregated 8.8 % of Argentina's import bill; in 1932, 10.7 %; in 1937, 4.7 %; in 1938, 6.1 %; and in 1939, 2.7 %. Italy takes even less: in 1929, 5.8 % of Argentina's exports went to Italy; in 1937, 6.2 %; in 1938, 2.5 %; and in 1939, 2.1 %. This exhibit is significant in view of the steady cultivation by Italian trade missions and the conclusion of a trade pact with barter provisions.

The Japanese in Argentina

THERE are about 2,600 Japanese-Argentines who were born in Japan, and an additional 4,000 to 5,000 Japanese born in Argentina. There has been little or no assimilation. The Japanese live apart and claim a double citizenship. They refuse to register their children with the civil authorities but inscribe them with the Japanese Embassy. Japanese activities in Argentina are largely commercial, but they also make a studied appeal to cultural interest. A visiting Japanese is always available for lectures on Asiatic culture. They maintain their own press, publishing three newspapers in Japanese, each with about 800 circulation. They publish a dainty "crib" of the *Reader's Digest,* almost identical with the American publication in style and design, printing extracts in Spanish from the Japanese magazines. There is no evidence of political activity.

Japan's trade with Argentina is unimportant, although the Japanese have assiduously cultivated this market. In 1929 Japanese sales to Argentina were but 0.5 % of Argentina's imports. Since 1929 Argentine purchases in Japan have increased: in 1936, 4 % of her imports came from Japan; in 1938, 3.7 %; but in 1939 this had fallen to 0.8 %. Argentine sales to Japan have not gained: in 1929 a mere 0.1 % of Argentine exports went to Japan; in 1936, 1.1 %; in 1938, still 1.1 %; and in 1939, 0.7 %. The Japanese are not easily discouraged. In March 1940 (immediately following the failure of the American-Argentine trade negotiations) Japan and Argentina concluded an agreement which promised an increase of $7,000,000 in trade. Argentine beef, wool, and casein were to be exchanged for Japanese textiles, chemicals, iron and steel products. This agreement threatened to cut into British trade, and to eliminate the United States as a market for industrial chemicals—an annual item of almost $1,000,000.

ARGENTINA has her fifth column. The government of Roberto M. Ortiz, increasingly controlled by Vice-President Castillo during the last months of 1940 and the first months of 1941, has been hard pressed to find any answer. Many powerful men seemed indifferent as to which way the battle went, and freely described the activities of German and English propagandists in the same terms. Public opinion, driven by anti-Nazi papers such as *Crítica* and *La Prensa,* demanded action. A few arrests of alleged German agents, a few warnings to the German press resulted. But many sober Argentines, not necessarily pro-Fascist, were unhappily aware that Argentina might have to deal with a victorious Germany, and were loath to take action which might offend the Reich. Vice-President Castillo said nothing. President Ortiz, from his sickroom, gave out a statement in November 1940: "We must win the sense of an American spiritual community . . . and maintain a profound and sincere democratic faith." He called for the protection of Argentina against "ideological invasion . . . a greater danger than physical invasion." Argentina seemed a land of divided counsels.

CHAPTER X

ARGENTINA AND THE UNITED STATES

SOMETHING must be done to clear up the cluttering irritations which accumulate between Argentines and Americans. It is senseless—neither has base designs upon the other. It is wasteful—Argentines are excellent people to cultivate, so are the Americans. It is unsafe—both of us are caught in times which threaten the liberty of men.

There are irritations, and no good end will be served by denial. We are divided by language, history, geography, psychology, and economic interest. Argentine distrust of the United States is chronic and angry. The older leaders of government reveal it at almost every turn. Many younger men share it. The mill run of average citizens, despite long years of anti-United States propaganda, are more and more turning with hope toward the United States (I would divide the credit for this rather evenly between Franklin Roosevelt and Hollywood). The finer spirits among the Argentines, eminent or inconspicuous, do not share that distrust. Americans are not free of the same virus. Many men in diplomacy and in business, who dealt with Argentines during the regimes of Irigoyen, Uriburu, and Justo, incline to lose their temper and to say harsh things about Argentine ways. The average American citizen has no thoughts on Argentina. That land is too far away.

No American who has been admitted to friendship by Argentines in various walks of life can fail to be grieved by the breach between our peoples. He knows the Argentines as generous friends, as able and forthright men and women. He would have his friends of the North and the South know each other. He casts about for the reasons for the traditional and obstinate Argentine distrust.

Three explanations are quickly given—too quickly, perhaps.

First, the Argentine opinion that North American life is materialistic, that we are money-mad, that we lack that sensitivity to spiritual values which is of the essence of Hispanic culture.

Second, that the United States is imperialistic. There are plenty of Argentines, young and old, who do not tire of reciting our record in Mexico, Panama, Nicaragua, Haiti, Santo Domingo, and the Philippines. They will admit that we are now on a different tack, but suggest that ours is the virtue of the sated.

Third, that the United States deals unfairly in trade, that we shut out Argentine beef by a subterfuge.

Then the inquiring American may decide to put these three arguments aside for the moment, and ask for the deeper psychological explanations of the Argentine attitude toward our country. He realizes the presumption of such probing, knows that it would be tonic if both Argentines and Americans would essay such analysis of one another. I shall set down three tentative explanations of Argentine attitudes.

First, there is a dash of envy in it. The typical porteño-about-town admires the same things which the North American-about-town cherishes: two-car garages with cars in them, skyscrapers, fine shops, good neckties, good food, old Scotch, theaters, fine houses, well-dressed women, quiet plumbing, radios—and a bank balance which makes these things possible. The North American seems to have more of these. The Argentine wants more. (So does the North American.)

Second, there is a touch of insecurity in the Argentine attitude. The porteño is proud of his city, but seems to lack an equally justifiable pride in the country which built the city. He is eternally apologizing even while he boasts. He has always tried to create the impression that Buenos Aires is an adjunct of Paris rather than the port of the pampas. Meanwhile, knowing full well that Buenos Aires is not Paris, but having set his pride on Paris, he fails to develop a convincing pride in Argentina. This quandary explains what many observers, Argentines included, put down as "the inferiority complex of Argentina."

Third, there is much national *amour propre* in it, a hangover of feudal dignidad. The Argentine is assured that his country stands high among the nations, and he resents the notion that it must play second fiddle in the American band. This may partly explain official behavior in recent Pan-American conferences, where Argentine statesmen seemed intent upon proving Argentina's importance by administering successive defeats to the United States.

There are, then, two sets of explanations. The Argentines may debate the second list as they will. I shall suggest some American answers to the first set.

North Americans are materialistic—Latin Americans (and including Argentines) give place to things of the spirit. The argument has a familiar cadence. I catch its tones in Manuel Ugarte's *The Destiny of a Continent,* the essays of Navarro Monzó and others who appear in the literary supplement of *La Nación.* This doctrine is supported by some American writers whose affection for the Latin Americans leads them into mystical romancing about the special gifts of the South. Waldo Frank's *America Hispana* is a notable example of this school. Others argue the unique spiritual content of Latin-American culture. Samuel Guy Inman avers that "the intellectuals of Latin America have a broader and a finer culture than those of North America." He finds the average Latin American "a much better judge of the artistic in music and in other arts than is the average North American." He pronounces the Latin Americans "incurably intellectual." He cites the considerable contribution of Latin America "concerning the value of the individual, the place of friendship, the use of leisure, the art of conversation, the attractions of the intellectual, the equality of races, the juridical basis of international life, the place of suffering and of contemplation, the value of the impractical, the importance of people over things and rules."

It is a puzzling argument. Must we decry our own civilization in order to render due mead of praise to the American sons of Spain? The argument no longer interests thoughtful Latin Americans. They know and we know that there are all sorts of people, both North and South. There are idealism, spiritual perception, scholarship, poetry, and music on both sides of the equator. There are base fellows in Buenos Aires, as in New York, who measure success by the cars they drive. The argument should be relegated to the category of such theological niceties as the standing room for angels on the point of a needle.

The United States is imperialistic—that is the second indictment. Here we may be frank and plead guilty. We went through a frightful teething with the first Roosevelt, and did little better under Taft and Wilson. We exercised bad sense and bad morals and bad taste with Mexico, Colombia, Haiti, Nicaragua, and a number of other neighbors. We were pious and opinionated and

ineffectual. Well, you hopeful young Leftist intellectuals of
Buenos Aires, we admit it. We would also point out that we
cleared out of Port-au-Prince and Managua and other way stations, an unwonted action for empire builders. We also add our
conviction that the American people are heartily united in the
determination to stay out of other people's gardens. The United
States learned expensively and unpleasantly that it cannot teach
the Haitians how to cook and the Nicaraguans how to vote, and
it wants no more of it. Does this mean that the United States will
never again land marines in Santo Domingo or Havana? By no
means. We will land marines on the day when—and if—it becomes clear that empire builders from overseas threaten to extend
their political authority on this side of the Atlantic. Furthermore,
just to keep the record straight, when and if that happens, liberty-
loving Argentines will applaud our move.

One further word on imperialism may be said in candor. Argentine outcry against the Colossus of the North has largely sub-
sided, although Argentine Leftists and German-Argentine
agents find it profitable to keep the slogan ringing. Now and
then an echoing of the old alarm serves the ends of lesser Argentine statesmen. Leopoldo Melo, Foreign Minister Cantilo's emis-
sary to Havana in July 1940, found it expedient to plead the rights
of self-determination for the harried natives of Martinique
threatened by prospective American invasion—but the delegates
who knew about Martinique hid their smiles. In past years Argentine politicians made political capital of American invasions
in the Caribbean and Mexico, but I wager that there is more
warm appreciation of Negro Haiti and of Indian Mexico in East
Fifty-Seventh Street than there is in all Argentina. Argentina
knows little of that end of America, and cares less. She dislikes
the blanket phrase "Latin America," for she has no desire to be
bracketed with Indian and Negro lands.

Finally, put it down with all kindness that much Argentine
outcry against the imperialism of the United States may be described as the protest of a rival in territorial expansion. If the

United States must explain Cuba, Argentina must also explain Paraguay.

The third indictment concerns trade. Let us turn to that subject. Peace is finally made in the counting room.

Argentine Trade

First, the economies of Argentina and the United States are competitive, not complementary.

Look at Argentina's selling list. About 96 % of it is agricultural. In the order of value the items are: corn, meats, wheat, linseed, wool, hides, quebracho.

Then turn to the selling list of the United States. Agricultural products are outranked by manufactured goods, but in 1938 we sold in the world market about $100,000,000 worth of wheat, about the same amount of corn, and half that sum in meats and meat products.

Then put the two selling lists side by side. We cannot buy wheat and corn, except in drought years. We can buy small amounts of special meat products—corned beef, for example. There are other items in which we are partly self-sufficient, but of which we can and do buy some—wool and hides, for example. Linseed has long been a heavy American purchase from Argentina. Quebracho, the source of tannin, we must buy.

We compete. There's the rub. Only Rotarians love competitors. We aren't all Rotarians.

Second, the United States steadily buys less and less from Argentina, and invites Argentina to buy more and more. Here are two exhibits:

Exhibit A. In 1929 we spent $89,002,000 in Argentina. In 1939 we spent $51,073,000. Between those years we went as low as $11,278,000 in 1932, and as high as $90,996,000 in 1937. Those 1937 figures prove little, as they represent emergency purchases of corn and wheat in a drought year.

Exhibit B. We have steadily sold Argentina more than we buy from her. Sumner Welles, appealing for a trade agreement in 1939, reported that over a fifteen-year period, 1924–38, this excess totaled $486,900,000—a tidy trade deficit for Argentina, more than she sold altogether in the one year 1939 ($416,355,000).

Argentina has been squeezed in this process. While North American purchases have dropped, there has been steady demand from her own citizens for the goods which the United States can furnish. Argentines prefer to buy Fords, Chevrolets, Cadillacs, Buicks, International Harvester's machinery, Underwoods, National Cash Registers.

Why have the purchases of the United States dropped? Three reasons may be cited:

Reason 1. Before the era of the Good Neighbor we progressively increased our tariff barriers against Argentine goods (and everyone else's). These increased tariffs effectively cut Argentine sales in the United States. Definite instances may be cited.

Look at hides and skins:

Around 1920 Argentina was selling us $44,000,000 worth each year. The 1922 Tariff Act left them duty-free; nevertheless sales dropped to a half by 1929. In 1930 we imposed a 10 % *ad valorem* duty. Since 1933 the average annual sales to us have stood around $5,000,000.

Consider tallow:

We used to buy $2,000,000 to $3,000,000 worth annually. In 1922 we imposed a duty of ½ c. to the pound. In 1936 a special tax of 3 c. a pound was added. By 1938 Argentine tallow sales to the United States had sunk to about $6,000.

Look at quebracho:

Around 1920 we were importing annually from Argentina about $6,000,000 worth. In 1922 we imposed a tariff of 15 %. During the past eight years we have paid Argentina about $2,000,000 a year for quebracho.

Take casein, a milk product:

The figure for 1920 was about $1,900,000. In the years 1923–29 it averaged $2,800,000. In the four years 1933–36 it had fallen to an average of $281,000. In between those figures lies the tariff item of 5½ c. a pound imposed in 1930, and since maintained.

Reason 2. The decline in the dollar value of our imports from Argentina is partly explained by the drop in prices of basic commodities. For example, wool sold in the United States for 53 c. a pound in 1920, for 27 c. in 1930, for 20 c. in 1939. Wheat, $2.33 a bushel in 1920; $1.07 in 1930; 57 c. in 1939. Corn, $1.43 a bushel in 1920; 77 c. in 1930; 45 c. in 1939. Linseed, $2.79 a bushel in 1930; $1.71 a bushel in 1939. The drop in purchases is only partially accounted for by such figures. There has also been a decline in the volume of these imports. The citing of three items will suffice. Wool—the volume dropped from an annual average of 105,000,000 pounds in the years 1919–20 to 46,000,000 pounds in the years 1933–36. Hides and skins—the comparison between the same two periods stands at 161,000,000 and 76,000,000 pounds. Linseed—the figures here for the same years are 17,500,000 bushels and 12,000,000.

Reason 3. American purchases in Argentina have been cut down by increased production in the United States of items hitherto largely bought in Argentina. Linseed is an instance. The United States' annual consumption of linseed during recent years has ranged between 470,000 and 825,000 tons. Argentina has always been our chief supplier. American annual production has averaged during the past ten years about 200,000 tons. The farmers of the Dakotas, Montana, and Minnesota jumped production from 208,000 tons in 1938 to 515,000 tons in 1939, to almost 700,000 tons in 1940. So an item which yielded Argentina $43,101,000 in 1929 and $17,542,000 in 1939 may disappear from the list in 1941 or 1942.

Third, Argentina's chief customers, England and Germany, also closed in upon her. They have imposed rules which restrict her freedom, and they have curtailed their trade.

England, confronted with dominion demands for preferential treatment on purchases of grains and meats, concluded the Ottawa Agreement of 1932. Then, faced with loss of her Argentine market, she signed the Roca Agreement in 1933, Argentina's first excursion in barter trade. This assured Argentina her British trade but tied her hands. Even with these arrangements, British purchases from Argentina declined from $291,889,000 in 1929 to $136,608,000 in 1938, losses partly explained by reduced prices, partly by the increased demands of dominion trade.

Germany, with economic difficulties of her own and with armaments to build, took a leaf from the British book and imposed even stricter barter deals. At that, Germany actually spent in Argentina little more than half as much in 1938 as she did in 1929.

Fourth, Argentina designed her own program in a world where others make the rules.

Argentina awoke to the fact that the producer of raw materials is hard pressed in a world where overproduction (or underconsumption) has become the rule. The builder of a good mousetrap may find a path worn to his door, but the grower of good wheat may have to cut the grass before his own stoop—if others produce enough wheat, and to spare.

Argentina's answer was: England and Germany compel us to use poker chips instead of coins across the counter. All right, then, we are on a poker-chip basis. We will buy from those who buy from us, and we will tally up each separate account. Acting upon this decision, Argentina has concluded pacts with sixteen nations, each marked by some barter features. By January 1, 1941, the United States was the one industrial nation which had no pact with Argentina.

The Argentine system of controls described in Chapter IV means that the nation says what goods, and how much, can be imported from a given country. It is enforced by a system of permits, with the bulk of foreign exchange controlled by government agencies.

Argentines can argue with much show of evidence that the system has paid. Relations with the United States have worsened in the process.

INTERLUDE—WASHINGTON AND BUENOS AIRES DEBATE

TIME OUT, PLEASE. I invite two gentlemen to sit down across the table. One is from the Foreign Office of Argentina, the other from the State Department in Washington. Now, Gentlemen, fight it out, tell us why our respective republics disagree. Please tell the truth, and do not be too polite. Let me put the first question: Exactly what are the issues which divide us in these days when our world is in flames, and when American unity has become so imperative?

Our-fictitious-gentleman-from-Washington: We deplore Argentina's excursion into the never-never-land of manipulated trade. We have sought to keep the roads of the world open, with each buyer free to pick goods where he pleases, with each seller at liberty to seek out the most favorable market, with the trade accounts of the world balancing out around a generous circle as they once did. That was the idea behind Cordell Hull's treaties: two nations at a time sit down together and agree to bring barriers down, and then to spread out such concessions to all most-favored-nation countries. But Argentina follows Runciman, Schacht, Goering in their token trade, each nation seeking to work out exact exchange with the other. That way lies disaster.

Our-also-fictitious-gentleman-from-Buenos Aires: Perhaps. Many of my countrymen are saying the same thing. *La Prensa* editorializes in that fashion about three times a week. But, my North American friend, we are powerless. England and Germany say to us: Here is a Diesel engine, you can have it for so many tons of wheat, so many hundredweight of beef—take it or leave it. What can we do? We want the engine, and we have the beef which no one else will buy. So we make the deal—and swap. These deals fence us in. We must demand similar terms of the United States if we are to survive.

Washington: But that course is artificial, unnatural, and uneconomic . . .

Buenos Aires: Just words, my friend, words which smack of yesterday. "Economic" is what we make it. But, let us suppose for the sake of argument that we agree with you. What can we do? The United States buys less and less from us. To be sure, you were still our third-best customer in 1938, but at that you took only 8½ % of our exports. England took almost 33 %, Germany almost 12 %—the two of them took almost 45 % of all we had to sell. If they did not buy our wheat, corn, and beef we were lost. They could dictate terms to us—and did.

Washington: Maybe. I have a dark suspicion that you did not put up much of a fight. You promptly followed up the Roca Agreement of 1933 with fifteen other arrangements of similar character. Your little circle of managed-trade enthusiasts needed no great coaxing.

Buenos Aires: You may or may not be right. There is one point which I must make: buy from us and we will buy from you. We really want your typewriters, automobiles, farm machinery. But you systematically kill off our trade, item by item. Whenever you see a commodity in which we can make a peso, down comes your tariff ax. You chop off our trade in corn, canned meat, hides, tallow, casein. We still sell you linseed, but not for long—your 65-cents a bushel tariff has set a lot of honest Swedes growing the seed in your northwest. It is a soil-destroying crop for you, but you will have it anyway. We sell you alfalfa seed, which you insist shall be dyed orange, so that your alfalfa lobby can work up popular prejudice against it. I repeat—if you want to sell, you must buy.

Washington: I can only speak for myself. You know how tariff legislation takes form with us. The cattle, sheep, wheat, corn, dairy, linseed lobbies have their high-priced agents (*whores,* in Cordell Hull's whimsical vocabulary) working on our frightened Congressmen. Hull and a lot of other men in Washington know that we cannot sell unless we buy, and are doing their level best to eliminate some of the mistakes in our tariff policy. We are doing the best we can.

Buenos Aires: Exactly. You are doing the best you can, with the obstacles you face. We are also doing the best we can, with our obstacles.

Washington: We have another argument with you. We feel that Argentina has been unfair in her discriminations against the United States in allotting exchange. Even though we grant that you had to keep the trade between Argentina and the United States more or less balanced, why should you lay an additional penalty against purchases from the United States? That is what your system of exchange has done until recently—importers of American goods had to pay from 12 % to 20 % more for their exchange than did purchasers of goods from England, Germany, Italy, and Japan.

Buenos Aires: We knew no other way of discouraging imports from the United States than by making purchasers of your goods pay the higher rate. The tendency was for Argentines to buy your automobiles and machinery, we had to counteract that tendency as we could. Again, we were forced to it by our two chief customers.

Just one other word, before I forget it. The United States should understand Argentine zeal for a trade account which balances, and with a favorable excess in her favor. Your country has had such a favorable balance for so long that you forget how it feels to be in the red. Your worst year was 1936, but even then you had a favorable balance of over 33 million dollars. In the years since 1910 you have had steady trade balances of several hundred million dollars, and in 1938 your balance was over 1,100 millions. Isn't there a trace of self-righteousness in your attitude toward Argentina?

Washington: I'll think about it. But here is a further quarrel. In reckoning her account with the United States, Argentina charges against us all service charges on the dollar indebtedness of Argentina. We must buy that much Argentine produce before we can begin to send you our goods. Would it not be fairer to prorate your total debt service against the trade with all countries? Why penalize the United States for loaning you money?

Buenos Aires: I must simply repeat that our hands are tied. We are compelled to balance our accounts with other nations. We must do the same with the United States. But there is another quarrel between us which has not been mentioned. It is the question of fresh meat. For ten years you have shut our fresh meat from your American markets. You did it by a rider to the Smoot-Hawley Tariff Act of 1930 which banned the importation into the United States of any fresh meat from countries in which *aftosa* (foot-and-mouth disease)[1] exists. We Argentines are convinced that this was a subterfuge to prevent our competition. Let me say frankly, this continued banning

---

1. Aftosa, or aphthous fever, commonly called foot-and-mouth disease, attacks cloven-footed animals. Almost all farm animals are subject to it and poultry are effective carriers. Not so malignant as some other animal diseases, it is perhaps the most contagious of them all. Its toll is less heavy in Argentina, where mild winters and the use of green pastures prevail, than in the United States with its severe winters, frozen ground, and extensive use of hay and dry feed. The United States has effectively fought this scourge, but despite all precautions there were outbreaks in 1914, 1924–25, and 1929, in the course of which more than 400,000 animals were slaughtered at an appraised value of over $11,000,000. For example, the disease was found in Los Angeles County, California, in January 1929; the agents of the Department of Agriculture

of our beef has done more than any other measure to arouse Argentine resentment. We know that our beef is the best in the world. We know that we could sell it in your market if given a fair chance.

Washington: Now we have reached the blistered heel. I have noted that whenever an Argentine and an American sit down to discuss the weather, the relative superiority of bridge and poker, or the immortality of the soul, sooner or later they get around to beef. And I may also say in frankness that I wish we could have Argentine steaks in New York. They are the best in the world. But, my Buenos Aires friend, that is not the real point. The real point is aftosa. Does it exist in Argentina? Can it be carried by fresh meat? Does it constitute a threat to the United States?

Buenos Aires: We know that there has been some aftosa in northern Argentina, but it is lessening, it is not transmissible by fresh-meat exports, it involves no danger to the United States. Look at England —she has been buying about $70,000,000 worth of our meat each year. England knows a good steak and a good joint. Our beef is good enough for her. It should be good enough for the United States.

Washington: Yes—but the British stock industry is unimportant, and there *is* aftosa in Great Britain. This is not a question which can be settled by appeals to Argentine pride, nor by asking the opinion of the Washington cattle lobby—they are alike unreliable. It is a question to be settled in a laboratory, between scientists, not in the halls of a congress between politicians. The nonpolitical scientists in our Department of Agriculture honestly insist that much aftosa clearly exists in northern Argentina, that it is endemic, that Argentina can produce much excellent beef in spite of it, but that the disease is transmissible through fresh meat, and that if it were to be carried to American herds it would break out in virulent form and cost our six-billion-dollar stock industry an incalculable loss.

promptly inspected all farm animals within a wide radius, destroyed 3,591 head valued at $107,539, and there has since been no trace of the disease. Other countries have suffered. An epidemic in Germany and Switzerland in 1920–21 cost about $189,000,000 to eradicate. Great Britain has had outbreaks almost annually since 1918. The British Ministry of Agriculture and Fisheries (Fourth Progress Report of the Foot-and-Mouth Disease Research Committee) reports: "It is clear then that importation of infected meat or offals in a chilled or frozen state is a ready means by which infected material can be conveyed to this country." That same British report notes that the source of the 1929 outbreak in California was found to be meat scraps fed to hogs 57 days after the carcasses had been shipped from South America.

Buenos Aires: I can simply repeat what practically every Argentine, from the most intelligent member of government to the youngest clerk, is saying, that we are convinced that the banning of Argentine beef by the United States is inspired simply by desire to protect your trade, and that the argument on aftosa is a specious invention of your legislators.

Washington: I disagree. But what a fantastic mess we are in. Here is an issue which upsets relations between our nations. It is an issue which should be settled with microscopes; instead we turn it over to writers of headlines in the Argentine press and to the omnivorous cattle lobby in Washington. Instead of arguing, we yell. We have urged Congress to ratify the Sanitary Convention which would lift the ban from areas known to be free of aftosa, Patagonia, for example. . . .

Buenos Aires: Yes, but that convention was initialed by our Ambassador Espil and Secretary Hull in 1935, and it has not yet been reported out of your Senate Committee. We frankly wonder whether you mean business.

Washington: Will you pardon my frankness in saying that you Argentines should be able to understand pigheaded politicians. You have them and we have them. This has become a political football. A handful of "cow senators" have the ball and won't let go. Am I not right that you have similar experiences with stubborn minorities?

Buenos Aires: I admit it.

Washington: I have a suggestion to make. We are confronted with a situation where public opinion is involved. Your public is honestly convinced that the United States works a great injustice against Argentina by a specious subterfuge. Our public is equally convinced that we are taking a legitimate measure to protect our cattle and sheep industry. It is a psychological deadlock. Why not take a new turn at this question? Here is what I suggest: Let the Argentine and American governments each appoint two agricultural experts, empower these four men to pick two other experts from neutral countries, and ask the six of them to make an *ex parte* study of the aftosa question. Let such a commission make its report, saying: Aftosa does or does not exist in Argentina; it is or is not transmissible by shipments of fresh meat; it does or does not carry a threat to the American stock industry. Let them make recommendations as to the admission—none, limited, or full—of Argentine beef into the United

States. Let that report be submitted to the respective governments, and be published in the papers of both countries.

Buenos Aires: But what good ends would be served?

Washington: Chiefly the education of our public opinion. If the quarantine is a great American cheat, as you say it is, then the American people should know it, and they have a way of instructing their senators and representatives. Our American public and press are honest, and will admit the mistake, if there is a mistake. Your press and public are honest, and will admit their error, if error there is. Such a procedure would be democratic and effective.

Buenos Aires: But do nations ever admit that they are wrong?

The Present Deadlock

THE deadlock between the United States and Argentina stands as the chief obstacle to genuine all-American planning. This deadlock is both economic and emotional. It will not be broken by good-will speeches.

On the American side there is the opinion that Argentina has capriciously tripped up almost every step toward hemisphere planning, that she has piled unnecessary and unequitable restrictions against our trade, and that she has used the beef question as a dishonest rabble rouser.

On the Argentine side there is a popular belief that the United States asks everything and concedes nothing, that we obstinately refuse to recognize the realities of world trade, but merrily spin golden fairy tales of a world which once was. Argentina is gloomily aware that she may have to do her trading in a world in which Germany is triumphant, perhaps a world in which the United States could not help her, even if she would. Furthermore, Argentina questions the constancy of the United States, citing our tariff record as evidence, and wonders how long our ardor for continental defense will last. Again, it must be made clear that Argentines take the meat question with all seriousness. It has become more than an item of pride. You may pick up *La Prensa* and read, "Inasmuch as Argentine meat is barred to North American consumers by *unjust sanitary regulations* . . ." When so thoughtful and sober a journal can start off an editorial discussion with these words, we must perforce admit that this is not unconsidered ranting but honestly held opinion.

Two unsuccessful efforts have been made to break the deadlock.

The first was the unratified Sanitary Agreement of 1935, providing that the aftosa quarantine should be applied only to areas where infection exists, not to whole nations. It would permit exportation of Argentine mutton and lamb from Patagonia, which is free from infection, but not from northern Argentina, so long as the disease is adjudged to exist. This agreement would concede a point to Argentina which we have long demanded for ourselves. From 1870 on Washington had successive arguments with Spain, Belgium, Germany, France, and other countries, and by a series of decisions we won assent that it was unfair to ban shipments from a state which was clearly free of all stock diseases simply because another state was infected. The ratification by the Senate of the Convention of 1935 would alter our trade relations with Argentina but little. We can import an inconsiderable amount of lamb and mutton. Its chief value would be as an earnest of our good intentions. Mr. Roosevelt has so far failed to press ratification, probably in fear of storms from the cattle country. The cattlemen will not listen to any measure which opens the way to further concessions. They kept the headlines dancing for months in 1939 after Mr. Roosevelt had dared to approve the Navy's purchase of 48,000 pounds of Argentine corned beef, and had added his opinion that this beef was "cheaper and better."

The second effort to achieve happier relations with Argentina was the ill-fated move for a trade pact. In August 1939 the State Department announced that after four years of preliminary discussions the United States and Argentina would negotiate a trade treaty. It was high time. The United States stood as the one major trader with which Argentina had no modern agreement (save only Japan which signed with Argentina in early 1940). Our Argentine trade was still conducted under an ancient general treaty of friendship, trade, and navigation negotiated in 1857. The Department's announcement assured due protection to

American producers, and genuine concessions to Argentine interests. It listed items in which tariff concessions would be made —casein, quebracho, linseed, tallow, oleo oil, meat extracts, certain types of packed beef and veal, cheese, corn, oranges, pears, some wools, and alfalfa. There was immediate outcry from a dozen Washington lobbies, "Don't touch us." On August 24 the National Coöperative Milk Producers Federation announced that it would fight "every step of the way any concessions on cheese and casein . . . a severe blow to the dairy farmers."

Negotiations continued from August 1939 to January 1940, with hearings in Washington and Buenos Aires. The hands of both sets of negotiators were tied by political considerations. The full tale has not been released by either government. The United States offered to reduce import duties on certain items, notably linseed and canned meats, but limited the amount of the goods which could be imported at such reduced rates. Argentina rejected these proposed quotas, seemingly overlooking the fact that they were larger than American purchases of recent years, and the further fact that such an arrangement would not bar additional purchases at the old tariff rates. The United States offered reductions on one list, and promised to refrain from increased tariffs on a second list of products. It offered the blanket most-favored-nation clause, giving Argentina the benefit of concessions granted others. Washington asked that Argentina reciprocate with a similar most-favored-nation clause, including equality of treatment in the allotment of exchange. The parley broke up. Argentina claimed that the responsibility for the failure rested on Washington, that we wanted everything, conceded nothing. The recurring refrain which echoed in the Argentine press was upon beef. "If the United States will not buy our beef, we cannot play" was the popular reaction in Buenos Aires. The failure of the negotiations was regarded in Argentina as a body blow to the Good Neighbor policy. *Razón* of Buenos Aires suggested that "Washington's stubbornness is a clear contradiction of its repeated declarations in favor of better commercial relations." *Noticias Gráficas* remarked that "the United States negotiators offered no concessions, either large or small." *La Nación* said, "Nothing has been offered Argentina in return for the concessions demanded by the United States." And the unsatisfactory relations between the countries remain as they were before. Argentina, much of it at least, calls us Uncle Shylock.

Two answers may be made to that Uncle Shylock charge.

First, there are some sins which the United States is *not* committing. We have not begun to apply the economic pressures on Argentina which lie within our power, pressures which any first-rate European trader would have used long since. Let me cite one concrete instance—the triangular trade of the United States, Argentina, and Brazil. Look at a few figures. *Item,* we buy the bulk of Brazil's coffee (57 % of her exported coffee in 1938, worth about $75,000,000), and Brazil continues to depend upon coffee for almost one half of her export revenue. *Item,* Brazil buys much wheat from Argentina, $29,597,000 worth in 1938. *Item,* if the United States were as smart as England or Germany, we would dispatch two notes: one to Argentina, "We are about to persuade you to quit discriminating against us on exchange"; the other to Brazil, "We suggest that you buy your wheat from us, or it might prove inconvenient for us to buy our coffee from you." *Item,* there are a number of other odds and ends in which we could practise such tactics, which have become practically office routine with London and Berlin. Some hardheaded Argentines expect us to copy that routine.

Second, the United States gives tangible evidence of her willingness to coöperate with Argentina. During 1940 and early 1941 the Argentine Government negotiated for American loans in order to finance her trade with Britain, to carry over her surpluses, and to safeguard her exchange. By January 1, 1941, total credits of $110,000,000 had been granted. Washington's motives were mixed: the desire to help England, concern for political stability in Argentina, and hope for coöperation in defense plans—these all played a part. The United States is not unaware that Argentina's formula calls for a decrease of purchases from the United States as our increased loans impose their greater load of interest

charges. Nor has Washington forgotten that Argentine discriminations against American trade have often followed such credits.
The loan of $20,000,000 in mid-1940 was immediately followed
by a further restriction on the list of items purchasable from the
United States. *The recent loans to Argentina were made without
any formal agreement on these disputed points.*

Memo for Argentina: Don't call us Uncle Shylock, not just yet.

International Relations Are Personal

THE dealings between Argentina and the United States during
the years of our biting disagreements have not been conducted
by Corporate Entities, but by gentlemen named Cordell Hull,
Carlos Saavedra Lamas, José María Cantilo, Sumner Welles,
Leopoldo Melo. All these gentlemen eat, sleep, suffer occasional
gastric disorders, catch cold, exhibit prejudice, entertain predilec-
tions, love some people, do not like others, and expand under the
warmth of praise. The arrangements concluded between the two
admirable nations called the United States and "La Republica
Argentina" reflect the changing moods of their agents. This simple lesson is sometimes overlooked by the historians—scholars
are often loath to discuss the bile or the glands of their chief
actors.

It will not be amiss to review the record of eight years' diplomatic interchange in the light of such personal factors.

In December 1933 Montevideo entertained the Seventh Pan-
American Conference. The United States and Argentina played
the star roles. In Washington was Franklin Roosevelt, recently
delivered of the Doctrine of the Good Neighbor, as to whose
shapings he was airily indefinite. Roosevelt's chief spokesman in
Montevideo was Cordell Hull, quite guileless in Latin-American
affairs, still smarting under the humiliations of the London economic parley, and obstinately set upon winning an American
victory in the conference. In Buenos Aires, just over the Río de
la Plata, was President Agustín Justo, who was disposed to
leave all international matters to his Foreign Minister, Carlos
Saavedra Lamas. It was freely prophesied that Saavedra, a vain

little man, would wreck the conference for his own glory and the credit of Argentina. But Cordell Hull, one of the ablest horse traders ever to reach trusteeship of the Great Seal, outplayed Saavedra by the simple device of giving him all the glory. Hull saw to it that the Argentine statesman's peace treaty was ratified, assured him first place as the negotiator of the Chaco peace, and later persuaded the Nobel Committee to award him the prize which placed him among the immortals with Nicholas Murray Butler and Charles Gates Dawes. Saavedra's gratitude was immense, and the Montevideo Conference ended on a note of triumph.

In December 1936 the American nations met again, this time in Buenos Aires. Franklin Roosevelt came with a battleship and stole the spotlight, to Mr. Justo's obvious annoyance. Cordell Hull sought an effective expression of all-American solidarity, and again turned to Saavedra Lamas for help. But this was a new Saavedra, in whom the warm glow of appreciation of Hull's contrivings had been swallowed up in the greater joy of election to the presidency of the Council of the League of Nations—perfidious Albion had stolen Saavedra from under Hull's very eyes. Hull could do little with Saavedra. He was checked at every turn. The Buenos Aires Conference said little, and gently.

In December 1938 the Americans assembled for the Eighth Pan-American Conference. Roosevelt still reigned in Washington, and Hull again journeyed south. In Buenos Aires President Justo had yielded his seat to Roberto M. Ortiz. Saavedra Lamas was retired to a privacy which irked him, and his place as Foreign Minister had gone to José María Cantilo who had never been given a Nobel Prize or been elected to the presidency of the world. Cantilo reached Lima the week before the conference was to convene, held the spotlight for a few days, made his speeches, and sailed away to the Chilean lakes as the conference was opening. Latin Americans regarded that exit as a studied affront to the United States. The American Secretary could come all the way from Washington, but the Argentine Minister must fish in Chile. Despite such irritations, Hull sought a common declara-

tion of American unity. Cantilo's lieutenants in Lima could take
no step without cabled permission of their chief. Attempts to
draft an acceptable statement were blocked by Cantilo's delays.
Finally, after two fruitless weeks, Hull threw the decision back
on Cantilo: All right, then, you write the words. When Cantilo's
draft of the Declaration of Lima had been accepted, his final
authorization was again held up for days. The Declaration, finally adopted, was hailed as a triumph of Pan-American diplomacy, but those familiar with its genesis described its carefully
meaningless phrases as another Argentine triumph for innocuity.
The German Ambassador in Buenos Aires warmly congratu-
lated Cantilo upon his success.

In September 1939 representatives of the American foreign
offices met at Panama to consider their course in the light of the
war. Sumner Welles, perhaps the most astute officer of the State
Department, represented Washington. Leopoldo Melo represented Argentina. Argentine demands that the conference stick
to "juridical and economic" matters did not prevent action on
the neutrality zone—wise or unwise as that ambitious scheme
may prove to be.

In July 1940 at the Havana Conference, Cordell Hull was faced
by Leopoldo Melo. Melo, speaking for Cantilo, made it clear that
Argentina would not consider any binding all-American trade
arrangements, or share in joint trusteeship over American colonies threatened with a shift in control. He eloquently condemned
talk of forcing uninvited rule upon Martinique, the Guianas,
Curaçao. These colonies, said Melo, "have the right to decide
their own destinies." But in Buenos Aires Cantilo was hearing
from Ortiz, the press, and the public. They were saying that it
was time for Argentina to play the game. New orders were
cabled to Melo, who quit his speechmaking and signed the Declaration of Havana.

The prospect of happier Argentine-American relations seemed
bright during the early months of 1941. President Roosevelt and
Secretary Hull had warm friends in Argentina, to judge from
editorial comments in the chief papers. The American ambassa-

dor in Argentina, Norman Armour, one of Roosevelt's happiest choices, had won warm regard. President Ortiz and Secretary Julio Roca were regarded in the United States as champions of democracy. The Argentine ambassador in Washington, Felipe Espil, had made a firm place for himself in the respect and affection of Americans. The stage seemed well set for a new epoch in the relations of the two countries. The disquieting news of Cabinet shifts, especially the retirement of Dr. Roca from the Ministry of Foreign Affairs, reminded Americans that foreign policy hangs upon internal politics. Meanwhile, partisans of democratic coöperation in the Americas looked with hope to the continued leadership of President Ortiz. There were signs that the two countries may find common cause as we face times of war. "Men tell me," Julio Roca said to me in September 1940, "that Argentina cannot trust the United States. I do not agree. We can and must trust each other."

PART TWO: BRAZIL

VENEZUELA

COLOMBIA

GUIÁNA

PERU

Rio Negro

Manáos

AMAZONAS

Amazon

Pará

GRÃO PARÁ

ACRE TERRITORY

Rio Madeira

Rio Xingú

Rio Tocantins

Rio Araguaya

MATTO GROSSO

BOLIVIA

GOYAZ

MARANHÃO

PIAUHY

CEARÁ

Fortaleza

RIO GRANDE DO NORTE

PARAHYBA

Pernambuco PERNAMBUCO

ALAGÔAS

SERGIPE

Rio São Francisco

BAHIA

Bahia

Rio

MINAS GERAES

ESPÍRITO SANTO

PARAGUAY

Rio Paraná

SÃO PAULO

São Paulo

Santos

RIO DE JANEIRO

Rio de Janeiro (Federal District)

PARANÁ

ARGENTINA

Rio Uruguay

SANTA CATHARINA

RIO GRANDE DO SUL

Porto Alegre

URUGUAY

POPULATION

SCALE : IN MILES
0 50 100 200 300 400 500

RAILROADS

BRAZIL

THE first view of Rio de Janeiro persuades the son of Adam to forgive the Creator for having consented to Jersey City. This capital of almost two millions, its scattered communities tossed against the mountains and the ocean, its jagged granite shafts of Pão de Açucar and Corcovado jutting up from the street curbs, is laced together by the miles of curving beaches as by a band of silver satin. Tides roll into the harbor and swell the long-fingered inlets of the sea. The islands which rock on the horizon are flecked with gold. Far back is the chipped profile of the Five Fingers of God and Mount Tijuca. This is the City of the River of January which Gonçalo Coelho discovered on New Year's Day, 1502.

And the Brazilians. God bless them, for the most exuberant, impractical, amiable, and exasperating of all the sons of Iberia. Only the impertinent would attempt to describe them. Their world is alien to that of the Anglo-Saxon, and quite apart from the America which was Spain's. These are not North Americans who drive to the point of the argument or the closing of a deal; not Argentines, with that brittle pride which is a sense of inferiority turned inside out. These are children of the sun who have learned the gift of leisure. They were produced in the mingling of Portuguese with Indian and Negro and Italian and many another family of men. Today they are Brazilian and that is enough. They may be lazy or ambitious, courteous or rude, practical or meditative—comparisons and classifications break down. Statisticians and ethnologists should be forever barred, Brazil can improvise her own statistics and theories of race. Reformers should be cast into dungeons at the harbor's mouth for their presumption and their vanity. Brazil should be saved intact for one's old age, when one casts about for an Eden in which nothing is as it seems or as it should be, where one can turn again to the sea and the sun in a land where God is most certainly a gentleman and a Brazilian.

But this is written neither for tourists nor for bankers about to retire. These, each to his taste, may find a map, buy a ticket, and sail into this harbor, stroll up the Avenida Rio Branco the full mile of its length, turn into the narrow Rua Ouvidor with its golden shops, drive over the palm-lined Beira Mar where marble palaces are blanketed with bougainvillaea, and on out to Copacabana where the world stretches in the sun. They will find the roulette tables, night clubs, bars, and trinket shops. If they do not, Cook's will always help them.

This is written for those who ask what manner of land is this, who lives here, what they think, how they are ruled, what they eat and how they get it, and what role they expect to play in a world in which Germany, England, Italy, Japan, and the United States juggle destiny. It is written for those who have heard two things: that this Brazil is the tested friend of the United States and will stand with us against all threats; or that Brazil is off after strange gods, and may not be the good play-fellow of the United States which she is pledged to be. Hope for the first of these, fear of the second, suggest the importance of looking at Brazil.

CHAPTER I

IF YOU WOULD KNOW BRAZIL

I F you would know Brazil, go to the Jockey Club of a Sunday
afternoon, get yourself a seat in the topmost balcony where
you can watch the people from Rio and São Paulo as they
cheer their favorite horses off to a lucky finish. These are Brazilians, these milling thousands of the well-tailored, the perfumed, the manicured. This is the Brazil of those who own Brazil, its cattle ranges, its cotton and coffee *fazendas*,[1] its mines and
forests: representatives of the comfortable company of the secure. They come to Rio to spend the profits of factory and farm,
for Paris and the Riviera are closed. Rio de Janeiro is the brave
front of their empire, in which all are rich, well fed, with plenty
of servants, houses looking out on blue water and purple mountains, gardens with red flowers, and time for love and laughter.
Your afternoon at the Jockey Club persuades you that Brazil is
rich.

Or—

If you would know Brazil, you will leave the Jockey Club,
drive five minutes, take the unpaved road to your right which
sets your 1920 taxi arattling. You will leave your car when the
road ends and walk up the hillside, and you will be in the jungle
of huts of old tin and scrapped boards and caked mud where
Brazilians breed. My friend snapped his camera at a few houses
of tin, some little children with rags over big bellies, but a courteous policeman took him off to the police station where he lost his
film. Brazil asks strangers to be polite, to take pictures of Pão de
Açucar and the lovely ladies at Copacabana, not to look over the
heads of the fine houses to the huts on the mountain sides. I explored side streets and hillside slums. I visited schools where no
camera was required to tell the story of hunger, syphilis, rickets,

---

1. *Fazenda*, equivalent to the Argentine estancia, is a plantation or ranch.

scurvy. I repeated those visits in the back streets of Bahia, Fortaleza, Pará, São Paulo, and in near-by villages. I saw Brazilians,
white and black and all the shadings between, the ragged broken
Brazilians who live behind the marble façade.

CHAPTER II

BIG

LOOK at the map. Brazil sprawls out like the spot of a bottle of
ink on the parlor rug, bigger than any nation save Russia,
Canada, and China. Its 3,275,500 square miles are almost
as big as the United States with an extra Texas to boot. It almost
equals all the rest of South America. It is tossed athwart the equator, stretching from 5° 16' north to 33° 45' south. Fold the map of
Brazil back upon the Northern Hemisphere, and the south tip of
Brazil will touch Atlanta. From northern extremity to southern
limit it has a span of almost 2,700 miles; from the eastern hump
to the foothills of the cordillera is another 2,700 miles. It has as
neighbors all the other nations of South America, with the exception of Chile and Ecuador (although Ecuador still lays claim to a
Brazilian frontier).

Brazil is an empire in which the homeland and the colonies are
gathered under one geographic roof. Its territory breaks down
naturally into five chief divisions. The greatest of these is the valley of the 3,900-mile long Amazon and its more than two hundred tributaries: a hot, lush, and uncharted empire in itself, an
empire of lowland tropical forests and brushlands whose secrets
are still hid. The second, the southern basin of the Río de la Plata
and the River Paraná, is a region of tablelands and rich soil. The
third, the Guiana highlands in the far north, is a region divided
between forests and desert. The fourth, the Brazilian plateau
with its mountain ridges, forests, and plains, contains much of
the population and the wealth. The fifth, the coastal plain, narrow for the most part, spreads out in the far south into generous

grassy plains. Here are the chief cities and towns, much of the cultivated land, especially in the 2,500-mile span from the hump to the southern tip of Rio Grande do Sul.

CHAPTER III

EMPTY

BRAZILIANS live in a small slice of Brazil. Most of their empire is untamed jungle. The 45 million Brazilians have plenty of room.[1] There are about $13\frac{1}{3}$ persons to the square mile—but that is a misleading figure. Three fourths of all Brazilians live in the narrow strip, about 100 miles wide, along the coast. Almost nine tenths (87.5 %) of the population live in the fifteen seaboard states stretching from Ceará to Rio Grande do Sul—and including Minas Geraes which has no sea coast—less than 29 % of the national domain. The rest is quite empty. The inland state of Amazonas, big as three Texases, has about half-a-person to the square mile.

Brazil is one of the few nations with a great untouched frontier. Much of that frontier is forbidding. The hot lands of the Amazon do not appeal to migrants from temperate lands, and the dwellers in other hot lands have neither ambition nor invitation to move. The brushlands and forests of the valley of the Paraná and of Matto Grosso furnish no haven for the soft-handed, and yet there is good land there, abundant rainfall, and an equable climate. Whether Brazil will one day afford homes to a population of 100, 200, or 500 millions, as some predict, is a subject for speculation. The answer hangs upon the further conquests by science of the scourges of the tropics which attack man, beast, and living plant. Highways and roads must also be built.

1. No one knows the population of Brazil. The last census, taken in 1920, reported a total of 30,635,605 for the twenty states, one territory, and the federal district. Current official estimates range from 44 to 47 million. A new census is in progress.

Here is *Lebensraum*. Discount as you will the possible settlement of the Amazon Valley and the unprofitable lands in mountains and deserts, there still remains much land which can be cleared of forests and made to yield a livelihood to men. There are no convincing figures on the use and the usefulness of the Brazilian countryside. The Brazilian Institute of Geography and Statistics estimates that the Brazilian territory breaks down as follows:

Forests, thickets, and brushlands	85.38 %
Seaboard vegetation	1.69 %
Prairies suitable for grazing	9.46 %
Miscellaneous wastelands	3.47 %

No one knows what percentage of the potentially arable land is now in use. The *International Yearbook of Agriculture* estimates that about 1 % of the total area of Brazil is under cultivation (1936). More than one half of all cultivated land is in the three states of São Paulo, Minas Geraes, and Rio Grande do Sul.

Brazil's frontier has called migrants from overpopulated Europe. A few came as early as 1817, a few Swiss, more Portuguese, a scattering from various lands. Midway in the nineteenth century the Italians began to come, and by 1914 some 1,361,000 had entered Brazil. The nineteenth century saw the entrance of Germans and Japanese. There are 800,000 to 900,000 Germans or German-Brazilians, their stronghold in the south. Japanese, perhaps 200,000 in all, have found homes in Brazil. Between 1820 and 1927 a total of 4,269,000 immigrants, two thirds of them Italians and Portuguese, entered the country. The figure for the entire period of Brazilian independence approaches 5,000,000. During that same period more than five times that number migrated to the United States.

The spell of big and empty Brazil has long worked its magic on prospective migrants. That spell still holds in days when aspiring empire builders cast about for new worlds in which to raise their flags. Herein lies the peril for Brazil. There are lands

to be worked, mines to be dug, forests to be felled. The bigness
and the emptiness beckon. Also the wealth—

CHAPTER IV

RICH

BRAZIL has every gift coveted by an empire builder. Her
soil will produce almost every crop known to man. There
is abundant rainfall and an equable climate over much
of her territory. There are deep buried veins of a score of metals.
Everything save coal. Her potential wealth outruns that of any
South American nation. She has wealth denied the United States
—stuffs we must have in peace or war. She has the goods which
Europe needs. Brazil is rich.

Soil

THE rich banked soil is hardly scratched. Brazil, from temperate south to tropical north, yields foods, fabrics, and oils in a
variety to be matched only by combining Minnesota, California,
Alabama, Cuba, and the Dutch East Indies. Millions of fallow
acres await the plow.

Coffee is chief. It is grown in many of the states, but São Paulo
produces three fourths of the crop. Brazil grows almost three
fifths of the world's coffee, and could produce all the coffee the
world uses. In 1937–38 she furnished 52 % of the coffee sold in
the world market. Coffee accounted for 45 % of Brazil's exports
in 1938, a drop from 69 % in 1929.

Cotton, holding second place on Brazil's export list, is the most
sensational of the nation's developments. Production has quad-
rupled since 1930—jumping from a half-million bales to over 2
million. In 1938 some 1 million bales were exported—twelve
times the 1930 figure. In 1938 cotton accounted for 18.5 % of all
Brazil's exports. This swift increase in cotton production is ex-

plained by three factors. First, the coffee business soured in the
years around 1930, due to the stiff competition from other lands,
and the ruinous drop in prices. Coffee lands were put into cotton.
Second, the United States, intent upon raising the levels of life
for its cotton farmers, effectively removed itself as a cheap producer for the world market and gave Brazil her opportunity.
Third, Germany could buy cotton from Brazil. The barter deals
which lifted Germany from third to first place among Brazil's
customers centered on cotton.

Cacao, third among Brazil's cash crops, in 1938 accounted for
4.2 % of all exports. The nation holds second place in world
production.

And other items. Excellent tobacco for cigars, second only to
Cuba's; her own sugar, corn, rice, barley, rye, cassava, potatoes,
yams, and beans; three fourths of the South American supply of
yerba maté; a long list of nuts and oils, babassu, almond, Brazil
nut, coconut, linseed, castor, sesamum, kapok; the insecticide
rotenone from the timbó tree; wax from the palms of Ceará—
these are staples whose production may be increased. She raises
part of her own wheat but imports four fifths of her supply,
chiefly from Argentina. Fruits increase in importance, and
Brazil is now second among world exporters of oranges. Her
agronomists are experimenting with medicinal products. At
their station in Campinas in the state of São Paulo, one of these
men showed me the cinchona trees, source of quinine, given in
1939 by the American Department of Agriculture—a tangible
bit of neighborliness which deserves mention. These agronomists, capable scientists, are doing pioneer work in developing
new products for Brazil, as well as fortifying the coffee and cotton industries through the development of new species. They experiment hopefully with silk culture.

Stock raising expands. The southern plains with their ample
vegetation offer quick rewards to the grazer, but there are generous undeveloped pasture lands in the interior. In colonial days,
Brazil was the chief South American exporter of meat products.
During the past fifty years she has lost this lead to Argentina. In

1938 the sale of hides, skins, and meats accounted for 9 % of
Brazil's exports. In 1935 she had over 41 million head of cattle,
over 13 million sheep, and 5 million goats (that last item might
be endlessly increased if Americans and British would acquire a
taste for *cabrito*).

Forests—about a billion acres of them—are rich in rosewood,
mahogany, pine, eucalyptus, and almost every wood known to
man. These are scarcely touched by the saw and the axe. Over
3 million dollars' worth of lumber was exported in 1938, but
Brazil still buys about two thirds of that amount in wood products from abroad. The chief profit from the forests comes from
nuts and oils.

Rubber. The wild rubber of the Amazon—the first home of
rubber—supplied the world throughout the nineteenth century
and down into the twentieth. Brazilian production jumped from
some 69,128 pounds in 1821 to 46,848,224 pounds in 1897. The
rush began in 1895. Manáos, almost a thousand miles inland,
overnight became a thriving city. Pará at the mouth of the
Amazon became the rubber capital of the world. Fortunes were
made and lost and made again. But these enterprising speculators
failed to reckon with a Briton named Wickham who had smug-
gled some seeds and plants to England in 1876, where he nursed,
guarded, and grafted them. These plants made possible the
plantation rubber industry of the Dutch East Indies and British
Malaya. Meanwhile the Brazilian rubber contractors drove their
gangs into the jungle, gathered rubber, and shipped it with growing carelessness as to quality. The government, scenting profit,
imposed a stiff export tax. The combination of careless processing and shortsighted taxing gave the East Indian producers their
perfect chance. In 1910, 88.2 % of the world's rubber came from
the wild rubber of the Amazon, and but 11.8 % from the plantations in the East. By 1923 wild rubber held but 8.4 % of the world
market, while plantation rubber accounted for 91.6 %. Today
Brazil produces but 1 % of the world's rubber. Nature gave her
the first chance, but she lost it.

Brazilians and Americans watch eagerly as Henry Ford develops his fields in the Amazon. Brazilians look to the recapture of a lost opportunity; Americans to the day when her supply will be more secure. The United States consumes about 80 % of the world's rubber.

Under the Soil

Iron. There are mountains of iron ore, perhaps the greatest reserve in the world, estimated by Brazilian geologists to be 23 % of the world supply. Much of it is high-grade ore, from 63 % to 70 % iron. About one half of this ore is in the state of Minas Geraes (the name means "General Mines"), while the balance is in Matto Grosso and Bahia. Little ore has been mined, but today Brazil plans smelters, refineries, and a steel industry.

Manganese. Brazil shares with Russia and India the chief deposits of this metal required for the making of steel. The Brazilian reserves may be the greatest of all. About a half-billion dollars' worth was exported in 1938, but Brazilians—and Americans—await the day when Brazil can supply the American market, as well as meet her own increasing domestic needs.

Gold and diamonds. Brazilian mines have been producing for two hundred years and are not exhausted. In 1939, $6,300,000 worth of gold was refined.

Other metals. The Brazilian list takes one back to the charts in the chemistry primer—bauxite, chromium, molybdenum, nickel, platinum, tin, tungsten, asbestos, mica, lead, zinc, mercury—Brazil has all of these. The American, heeding the warnings of the Army and Navy Munitions Board, takes note that Brazil has reserves of minerals sorely needed by the United States, notably manganese, chromium, quartz, mercury, mica, nickel, tungsten.

Petroleum. Brazilians tell you of the Labato field in Bahia, where wells are already flowing, and of geologists' glowing reports on widely scattered areas. Meanwhile, Brazil has her National Petroleum Council, a state monopoly, which is exploring and drilling. A refinery is being built in Nictheroy in the state of Rio de Janeiro, and others are planned for São Paulo and

Bahia. But substantial production is still a dream, and Brazil buys her petroleum products from abroad. The bill for these in 1938 exceeded $22,000,000.

Coal. Here is a serious gap in the Brazilian mineral account. There is much low-grade bituminous coal in various out-of-the-way spots such as Matto Grosso, which cannot profitably be developed until communications are improved. Furthermore, it is unfit for smelting. Coal fields in southern Brazil yield a low-grade product which meets about 10 % of national consumption. Brazil imports coal from England and the United States—$15,000,000 worth in 1938.

Water power helps to balance the lack of coal. Brazil's present production of electricity, all hydraulic, is less than a million kw's, but her engineers affirm that Brazil can multiply that production fifty times. Electricity is, as yet, no substitute for coal in the smelting of iron.

Industry

BRAZIL is outgrowing her colonial economy, which made her a seller of cheap raw materials and a buyer of costly finished goods. In 1889, at the end of the empire, there were but 903 industrial establishments in all Brazil. Forty-six years later, in 1935, there were 58,681 factories of various sorts, with a total payroll of almost 700,000 workers, ranging all the way from small enterprises with two or three employees up to great textile mills with several thousand operatives. The greater number of these were for processing foodstuffs. Shoe factories turned out $25,000,000 worth of shoes. The textile industry had expanded to more than 4,000 mills and factories producing more than $100,000,000 worth of goods annually. The state of São Paulo leads in this industrial development, accounting for more than one third of all Brazil's industrial production. In fact, São Paulo is today the chief industrial center of all South America.

Some Brazilian enthusiasts for industry, like their Argentine kin, argue that factories have already crowded the farm into second place. They cite figures which show that industry's production of something more than a half-billion dollars annually exceeds agriculture's somewhat less than half-billion dollars' estimated production. They argue that industrial production is almost twice the average Brazilian export list during recent years ($296,000,000 in 1938). Those figures may prove too much. The fact remains that about three fourths of the Brazilian people derive their livelihood directly from the soil. Many millions live chiefly from their own garden patches: their beans and manioc and potatoes are never reported in the national totals. The industrialists are great men in Brazil, but they will have difficulty in persuading the vagrant visitor that the factory is more important than the farm.

Trade

BRAZIL is second to Argentina among South American traders. Brazil's exports in 1938 aggregated $295,558,000, which represented 16.2 % of the total exports of all Latin America. Brazilian imports in 1938 were valued at $295,389,000 or 19.7 % of all Latin-American imports. In 1940, with the dislocations of war, her exports were about $270,000,000 and her imports a little more.[1] Brazil has enjoyed with few interruptions a favorable balance of trade, but her economy is not well fortified against war conditions. Her coffee and cotton are piling up in warehouses, while her government casts about for loans to carry her through the war.

Brazil's buyers in the world market have tended to shift during recent years, as will appear from this chart:

Brazil's Exports

(percentages taken by countries cited)

	1929	1932	1937	1938	1940*
U.S.A.	42.2	46.3	36.4	34.3	36.4
U.K.	6.5	6.9	9.0	8.8	20.0
Germany	8.8	8.8	17.1	19.1	3.1
Italy	4.7	3.7	2.2	2.1	3.2
Japan	2.0	0.1	4.7	4.6	..

1. Estimated. The final figures are not yet available.

Brazil's sellers in the world market appear in these figures:

Brazil's Imports

(percentages furnished by countries cited)

	1929	1932	1937	1938	1940*
U.S.A.	30.1	30.1	23.1	24.2	36.4
U.K.	19.2	19.3	12.1	10.4	9.6
Germany	12.7	9.0	23.9	25.0	2.4
Italy	3.2	4.1	1.5	1.8	1.5
Japan	0.2	0.3	1.6	1.3	..

* Figures for 1940 incomplete.

The Rich

RICH Brazil and rich Brazilians. Efforts to determine the distribution of the income of the nation yield little more than clues.
The pattern is the familiar one throughout Latin America. A few
collect the major gains. The census of 1920 showed 64,000 owners holding an aggregate of 338 million acres, with an average
holding of 5,281 acres. It may be fairly concluded that those figures mean that less than 1 % of the people own about one sixth
of all the area of the nation. The figures again prove too much
or too little. The holder of 100,000 acres in the jungle may not
be able to pay his taxes, but the ownership of a thousand rich
acres in São Paulo may bring abundant income. The only clear
point is that a few own much. Their profits built hotels, apartment houses, factories, and mills. Fortunes, counted sizable anywhere, have been made from coffee, cotton, and textiles. There
are great names in Brazilian capitalism—the Guinles, Mataraz-
zos, the Crespis—and there is a substantial company of others
who have fine houses and ample surpluses. Amateur statistical
guessers in Brazil tell you that a few score families really reign
and that there may be 25,000 others which are prosperous. These
are the rich.

CHAPTER V

POOR

Havana, unfortunately, was not altogether practical. It met under a dark cloud which hangs over the continent. He who mentions a threat implies a defense against that threat. And defense means cannon. But how can one buy cannon when one does not also sell coffee, cotton, meats, oils, castor beans, cacao, skins, hides and horns? Every activity is stopped. We remove the hides of our cattle and the skins of our sheep and there is no one to sell them to. We suck our own oranges so as not to suck our fingers all the time and so to vary the exercise.

THIS was the comment on the Havana Conference of July 1940 by Assis Chateaubriand in the *Diario de São Paulo*. Such candor comes as a shock to the observer of Brazil's heaped wealth. Facts bear out the Brazilian journalist's description. Brazil's is the familiar Iberian story, in which the loaded board is reserved for the few, while the many snatch for the crumbs.

How fares the common man of Brazil?

First we must look at the listing of the wage earners. The official figures for 1938 were:

Agriculture and stock raising	8,860,000
Commerce, finance, and affiliated concerns	752,000
Industrial workers	731,000
Communications and transports, sea, river, land, and air	365,000
Professions	240,000
Building trades	200,000
Miners	40,000
Common labor, unclassified	700,000
Total of the gainfully occupied	11,888,000

These rough figures suggest the general lines of the divisions of Brazilian life. We can deduce a few general conclusions as to economic groups within Brazil.

First, we can dismiss as a tiny segment the few whose possession of land and other wealth gives them the major toll. To them we can add another small slice of the professional attendants upon the wealthy—their physicians, their lawyers, their managers. (Herein will be reckoned a few thousands out of the 240,000 professional people listed.) We have then a company of 100,000—more or less—families of Brazil which includes the wealthy, the rich, and the comfortable upper-middle class. It includes those with moderate incomes. For example, three *contos* monthly ($150) is considered generous pay for responsible men in government offices, for reasonably successful professional men, and for managers of business. We may safely guess that all of these added together—the reasonably secure and well-fed Brazilians—aggregate not more than 2 % of all the population. That guess is pronounced generous by my Brazilian advisers.

Second, we can group together white-collar workers and low-paid professional people. This group includes 35,000 clerks and bookkeepers in banks, insurance companies, and other financial offices; some half-million white-collar workers in commerce and industry; 70,000 teachers. It includes the majority of those listed under "professions"—few lawyers and physicians attain more than a pittance. It includes the rank and file of white-collar workers for the government, postal clerks, stenographers, and so on. Perhaps a total of 1,000,000 fall into this heterogeneous group— their only ties their "white collars" and their meager income. Here is the way they fare: a village schoolteacher gets about $15 monthly; a teacher in Rio about $21.50; a clerk in São Paulo's best department stores, $32; a postal clerk selling stamps, $25; a reporter on a city newspaper, $30.

The visitor, changing his dollars at the rate of 20 milreis[1] to the

1. Brazilian milreis are here converted into dollars at the arbitrary rate of 1 milreis —5 American cents. (A conto is 1,000 milreis, roughly $50.) This rate is slightly under the official rate now offered for import purchases, slightly higher than the buying rate in the free market. Comparisons of buying power suggest that an American dollar will buy from 50 % to 75 % more in food than in our Midwest, but rents and clothing differ little in dollar terms. Some indication of costs is given by these prices from Rio de Janeiro retail markets: bread 4 c. a pound, rice 4½ c., smoked fish 10 c., lard 12 c., potatoes 2½ c., sugar 2¼ c., beef 12 c., milk 7 c. a quart, eggs 2 c. each.

dollar, has difficulty in understanding what money means to the clerk, the postal employee, the bookkeeper. This was brought home to me one day in July 1940 as I walked down the street in Rio with a Brazilian friend. I asked him to stop with me at the post office, as I had some air-mail letters to post. I bought the stamps, about $2 worth, stuck them on the envelopes. My friend took my letters, went to the window, watched the clerk cancel them, and only then did he let me turn away.

"But why?" I asked.

"Do you realize what all that money looks like to that chap in there? Your $2 worth of stamps is 2½ days' wages to him. Perhaps he has a family short on food, perhaps a child is sick, and there is no money for the doctor—do you see? Don't report that Brazilians are dishonest, but air mail often fails to reach its destination."

Third, there are about 10 million industrial and agricultural workers. These include wage earners and share croppers in the cotton, coffee, cacao, and grain fields; hired hands in the forest and stock industries; operatives in mills and factories; employees on railroads and bus lines. About nine tenths of them are agricultural laborers of various categories. Some figures suggest their lot.

There is an aristocracy of labor. The conductor on a train gets about $15 a month; a fireman or a brakeman about the same; the best-paid textile worker in São Paulo gets $15–$18; the driver of a bus may get as much as $15.

In 1938 the National Ministry of Labor, Industry, and Commerce made a study of rural and urban wages for all Brazil. It reported an average monthly wage of 236 milreis (about $11.80) for all workers in agriculture, commerce, and industry, both rural and urban. Independent analysts suggest that this report failed to include thousands on the economic rag-line—the backwoods of the state of Bahia, the rubber collectors, the forest workers. The average was lifted by the inclusion of the favored industrial workers of São Paulo with more than $15 a month. The average wage in Pernambuco is but little over $5 a month. The government, acting upon this report, ordered a minimum wage of from $4.50 to $12 per month, depending upon the section of the country concerned.

No report gives adequate data on the income and living conditions of agricultural labor. A modified peonage still exists in much of the forest industry, in the gathering of yerba maté, nuts, and wax. The rubber industry remains as it has always been, a rough jungle venture (this does not apply to Henry Ford's plantations, where wages and living conditions are better). Much of the coffee and cotton is cultivated and gathered on the basis still common in our own South: share croppers living on credit, buying in a company store, at the mercy of foremen who overcharge and underweigh. There are great *fazendas* still ruled in the feudal fashion which marked the Mexico of Porfirio Díaz, and which still prevails in Guatemala, Bolivia, Peru, and Ecuador.

"We do nothing well," writes the Brazilian sociologist Afranio Peixoto, "because we are on a diet—a perpetual diet." This gloomy diagnosis is borne out by the studies of other competent Brazilians. Isaias Alves published a study of the Brazilian death rate in 1939. He listed twenty-four countries, and estimated the living inhabitants under fourteen years of age. Brazil stood second on that list. He then listed the same nations on the basis of their living inhabitants between fourteen and fifty-nine years. Brazil stood twenty-second on that list. Where food is inadequate, where medical care and sanitation are lacking, children die. That is the story of Brazil. But no one knows the full details, as there are no comprehensive and authentic statistics on the death rate, the birth rate, and the infant mortality of Brazil.

Other Brazilian sociologists, notably Ruy Coutinho and Josué de Castro, have made studies of the Brazilian diet. They conclude that the great majority of Brazilians do not eat enough and do not eat the right food. The average Brazilian diet majors on manioc flour, black beans, a little jerked beef, corn, and fish. Milk, fruit, and vegetables are conspicuously lacking. This diet may be explained by poverty—they cannot buy as they should, and by ignorance—they have not learned the lesson of a balanced

diet. Rickets, scurvy, and other diseases of malnutrition abound.
Typhoid, dysentery, trachoma, and hookworm—diseases of bad
sanitation—take a great but unreckoned toll.

The League of Nations has assembled the best available figures on the ravages of common diseases in typical cities. These
furnish material for reflection on diet, sanitation, and medical
care. Here are a few comparisons (all figures considered in relation to population). The death score for puerperal fever in Rio is
about two and one half times that of New York. Consider the
deaths of babies under two years from intestinal diseases: Rio's
record is thirty-eight times that of Philadelphia. Deaths from
measles: Rio has twenty-seven times as many as Chicago. Diph-
theria: São Paulo's death rate is eight times that of Baltimore.
Influenza: seven times as many die from that cause as in Boston.
Typhoid: Rio's death record is ten times that of Boston. Infant
mortality: Rio's rate for 1937 was about three and one half times
that of Boston, four times that of New York, despite the fact that
the birth rate for Rio, Boston, and New York differed but
slightly.[2]

We may roughly tally the status of Brazil's workers. The
worker lives in a tenement, a shack on the edge of the city, or in
a country hovel—a house overcrowded, miserably furnished,
without running water or plumbing or electricity. He eats meagerly, and his diet is ill-balanced. His clothing is mean. His medical care is limited to quack doctors, medicine men, vendors of
patent medicines—only in the cities can he occasionally have
medical service at rates he can pay. His children are born too

2. All these figures must be used with caution. They are simply quoted as the best
available. It must be borne in mind that while Philadelphia, Boston, and Baltimore
keep an accurate count of births and deaths, Brazilian cities have neither funds nor
experience for such accuracy. For example: the figure (1937) cited for the birth rate
in Rio de Janeiro is 18.3, for São Paulo 24.8, for New York 13.6, for Boston 19.8, for
Cincinnati 18.2. Any unofficial observer, after wandering through the slums of Rio
and São Paulo, makes a guess that no official tally accurately computes either the births
or the deaths among the poor. This guess is confirmed by those who work among
those poor. Both physicians and funerals cost money, and the poor have their own
short cuts. Only the neighbors know of the children who are born and die.

often and die too young. They have little safe milk, he cannot
pay the price nor does he recognize the need. He and his family
are ill-fortified against disease either by diet or sanitation. They
have little or nothing for amusements, education, or savings. The
future holds no hope. Sons take up the shovel and the pick which
the father lays down. This is the lot Brazil affords her sons.

Who is to blame?

The *fazendeiro,* the millowner, or the contractor who hires
these men? That explanation is too simple. These Brazilian employers compete in a buyers' market where the goods they sell
are overproduced, and where prices are cruelly depressed. Some
make exorbitant profits, but few of them could pay living wages
and survive. These employers are caught, as all are caught, in a
vise not of their own forging.

The Brazilian worker? I hear it said by the well-dressed in
Brazilian clubs and hotel lobbies that the Brazilian worker is
lazy, wasteful, and without ambition, that he spends money on
drink which should buy food. This charge is singularly lacking
in knowledge and imagination. Those who make it so carelessly
should leave their desks and ledgers and take a walk around the
edges of Rio de Janeiro, and out into country roads. For once,
they should look at Brazilians. They will see eyes in which no
light is kindled; skin drawn too tight; backs always bent. These
people are hungry as were the mothers who bore them, and they
are sick. Some dry biologist should say to those brokers and traders: You cannot breed inventiveness and liveliness either into
white rats or into men by starving them. The Brazilian worker
must be fed for at least one generation before judgment can be
fairly rendered.

Or must the government be blamed for this misery? That is
unfair. During much of the last century Brazil's government has
been notable for its social intelligence. Even Vargas, despite his
dubious loyalty to democratic practice, seems moved by genuine
concern for the hard-driven masses. Romanticists give overmuch
credit to Vargas' social measures, but he has at least put better

laws upon the books: a minimum wage, old-age pensions, accident insurance, workers' savings banks, cheap housing, vacations with pay, and the end of child labor—laws which are imperfectly enforced but which represent honest effort.

Brazil is poor—that is the basic fact which explains all else. The federal budget of Brazil, with more territory and one third the population of the United States, stood in 1939 at $204,000,000. New York City, with one sixth Brazil's population, spent almost three times that amount in 1939. Argentina which is one third the size has one third the population: Argentina's federal expenses were half again as much as Brazil's, it spent three times as much on education. Brazil's poverty shows in its international buying and selling. José Jobim estimates that in 1938 Brazil sold $4 worth of goods per capita in the world market, and bought back an equal amount. Denmark, that same year, sold $56.30 worth per capita and bought back $53.30 worth. Argentina sold $20.50 worth of goods, and bought back the same amount.

Why then are Brazilians poor in a land of plenty?

Three answers must be given, each rooted in her history.

First, Brazil's poverty is the backwash of her colonial days. Portuguese and Spanish America suffer the same drag. However, there were sharp contrasts between the economic rule of Portugal and Spain. Portugal was more indulgent with her colonies— or less efficient. Portugal, like Spain, demanded that all trade be routed through the mother country, but enforcement was lax. Despite lesser Portuguese efficiency, the results differed little from those which we have outlined for Argentina, those which marked Peru, Chile, and almost all Hispanic America. Brazil sold raw materials, bought back finished goods, paying toll on every operation. Portugal piled considerable taxes upon her Brazilian colonists, and held a monopoly on salt, Brazil wood, timber for ships, and whaling. Such strangulation did not encourage full use of the soil, the exploitation of the forests, the expansion of industry, or the creation of an imaginative citizenry.

Second, Brazil's poverty is to be explained by more than three centuries of Negro slavery. The Portuguese, sharing the Spanish distaste for manual labor, required slaves. There were few Indians to be impressed into service, so they turned to Africa as did the English in North America. Slavery prevailed in Brazil from the days of the first settlement in 1532 down to abolition in 1888. A total of some 12 million slaves were imported. By the close of the colonial period Brazil was more black than white. Negro slavery fixed bad habits upon Brazil. The white man could not work (nor could he in Alabama). Whites owned the land, blacks worked it, profits were easy and secure. The Portuguese colonists fixed the social tradition which still burdens Brazil. The man who counts disdains menial tasks. The young man's dream is to get by as easily as he can. Employers with whom I have talked tell of their difficulties with young Brazilians fresh from school, of their unwillingness to accept any task which they think demeaning. The ragged whites, if they shirk their tasks, simply copy their betters. It takes generations to unlearn the bad lessons of a slave society, as any candid citizen of Georgia or Louisiana will freely admit.

Third, Brazil's poverty is rooted in her historical overdependence upon one product. Brazil rushed from one enterprise into another, giving major attention to first one and then another product, neglecting balanced development of her economic wealth. The story may be told in the successive dominance of sugar, gold, cotton, cacao, rubber, and coffee. These goods produced wealth. The failure to achieve diversified production made for poverty.

Sugar. Columbus introduced it into the West Indies in 1493. The seed was brought to São Vicente in 1532, and then to Bahia and Pernambuco. By 1600 Brazil's 120 refineries furnished the bulk of Europe's sugar. Brazil held her lead until the eighteenth century, when the West Indies captured the market.

Gold. In 1693 there was a frantic gold rush to Minas Geraes. Many sugar planters, impatient with the slow profits of their fields, moved their slaves to the mines. Brazil's gold mines were generous for almost two hundred years, yielding a total of some 40 million ounces between 1693 and 1875. But each ounce furnished glittering distraction from more creative toil.

Cotton, always grown in Brazil, reigned briefly during the last years of the eighteenth century. Eli Whitney's invention of the gin in 1793 shifted the advantage to the United States. In 1790 Brazil's cotton exports far exceeded those of the United States; in 1800 she furnished but three fourths as much as the Northern republic; by 1807 the United States exported ten times as much as Brazil. Not until the 1930's did Brazil return to cotton as a major reliance.

Cacao, produced throughout Brazil's history, assumed a major place among her exports in the early nineteenth century, but by the beginning of the twentieth century she had lost much of her market to Ecuador, Venezuela, and Colombia.

Rubber was the magic word for Brazil at the opening of the twentieth century. The gold rush of 1693 was matched by the dash to the rubber fields in the 1890's and the 1900's. For fifteen years Brazilians dreamed of quick, rich profit from rubber. Energy which should have been invested in a thousand solid enterprises was dissipated. When the bubble burst it left new poverty behind.

Coffee, which today dominates Brazil's economy, was introduced into the Amazon Valley in 1723, and then spread over the country. By 1820 Brazil was producing 18 % of the world's coffee; by 1860 almost 50 %; by 1900 75 %. Her production has since fluctuated violently. From 1930 on, coffee became Brazil's chief problem although it continued as her chief export. In 1929 coffee bulked as 69 % of her exports; in 1938 it had dropped to 45 %. Prices dropped disastrously. The grade called "Rio No. 7" brought 15¾ c. a pound in 1929; 8¹⁄₁₆ c. in 1932; 8¾ c. in 1937; 5¼ c. in 1938. Competition from Venezuela, Colombia, and the Caribbean area was responsible. The Brazilian Government restricted production, tossed tons of coffee into the sea, burned a half-billion dollars' worth of it during the decade, but to little avail. In 1929 Brazil sold 14,280,815 bags for $333,842,000. In

1937—thanks to the restrictive measures—the exports dropped to
12,176,000 bags, but the money value dropped even further, to
$147,380,000. Alarmed, the government cut export taxes in order
to meet competition, allowed increased production, and in 1938
17,638,000 bags were sold for $134,578,000. Throughout the dec-
ade of the 1930's, as coffee proved an increasingly insecure reliance, Brazil turned again to cotton.

Brazil starves while her lands beg the privilege of supplying
food. It is the immemorial fantasy of want in the midst of plenty.
The answer is found in the heavy drag of the accumulated bad
habits of colonial days—faulty distribution of land, a slave society, dependence upon the sale of cheap raw materials, and the
purchase of costly finished goods. The answer is found in too
great reliance upon coffee and cotton, slave crops the world over.
No nation, not excluding the United States, has found a way of
giving the cotton picker the semblance of a decent life. Brazil's
other crops also depend upon cheap, docile labor.

Brazil seeks escape by increased diversification and by the enlargement of her industrial plant. The promise for the ill-fed
Brazilian is not yet clear. Whether the common man will fare
better in the foundry than on the farm; whether increased national consumption of finished goods will enlarge his comfort
and security; whether extended national profit will lift all incomes, or simply fill the purses of those who are now comfortable
—these are questions to which no answer as yet appears.

CHAPTER VI

DIVIDED

BRAZILIANS have a tradition of state loyalty reminiscent
of earlier days in our Northern union, when men were
Virginians or Pennsylvanians or Yankees rather than
Americans.

The Brazilian you meet on the train, in the hotel lobby, or in the cafe promptly identifies himself as a *paulista* from São Paulo, a *carioca* from the capital city, a *gaucho* from Rio Grande do Sul, or a *mineiro* from Minas Geraes. He is first a citizen of his state, and almost as an afterthought a citizen of Brazil.

Brazil—colony, empire, and republic—has always been divided by lively sectional jealousies. Politics have been state contests, not clashes of ideas between national parties. Economic rivalry between the separate states has been as bitter as any trade war between nations. The individual states, even municipalities, raised tariff walls against each other, collecting custom tolls which sometimes reached one third of the value of the goods exchanged between Pará, Pernambuco, Rio, and Porto Alegre.

Brazil's disunity is rooted in her very bigness and in the inadequate communications connecting her several parts. It is but 1,900 miles, according to the ruler on the map, between Porto Alegre in the south and Manáos on the Amazon. When the traveler makes the trip, he must take a steamer from Porto Alegre to Pará, change to another steamer for the thousand-mile trip up the Amazon, a total journey of eight to ten days. Air lines have helped, but air travel is still expensive.

Portuguese rule laid the basis for this faulty cohesion. Lisbon discouraged trade between the ports of the colony, and the scattered settlers knew little of each other. But Portuguese rule in the colonies was never the compact and centralized rule which Spain imposed through Mexico and Lima.

Regionalism is still dominant, although the spartan rule of Getulio Vargas has imposed outward harmony. The populous and aggressive states of São Paulo and Minas Geraes have long controlled national life. Reluctantly, they learned to respect each other. Then they were persuaded to include Rio Grande do Sul in their reckonings. These three states look upon the rest of Brazil with the same condescension exhibited by starched Britons toward the Sunda Islanders. This attitude ranges from an indulgent imperial pride in the uncharted Amazon empire to ill-concealed shame for black Bahia. They are proud of Matto Grosso's wealth as the English are proud of Tanganyika—both remote from the centers of national life. Good paulistas, mineiros, and gauchos agree that Rio de Janeiro is a pleasant spot for vacations, but suggest that the capital is simply the decorative gate and that they furnish the power of the nation.

The disproportionate distribution of economic power between the states makes for discord. São Paulo esteems herself the most energetic, progressive, and profitable. Although accounting for but one fortieth of the national population, she pays about 65 % of all federal taxes, has more than one fourth the railroads, ships 40 % of the exports, dominates coffee and cotton, and produces more than one third of all industrial goods. Such citations do not quiet the envy of the less fortunate. São Paulo, confident of her superiority, demands control of the national government. She and Minas Geraes named presidents and cabinets with monotonous regularity from the establishment of the republic in 1889 until the advent of gaucho Getulio Vargas in 1930. Her present unhappiness is partly discontent with Vargas' fashions in government, partly resentment that São Paulo no longer rules.

Brazil's inner discord is perpetuated by the paucity of communications. Her scattered peoples are not knit together by those cultural and political forces which make a nation. Let us list some of the items:

Railroads. The railroad system is chiefly confined to the southern part of the country, with a few short lines along the northern coast. There are a total of 20,712 miles of railroad in Brazil. The United States has 236,842 miles. Argentina, one third the size of Brazil, has 24,652 miles. Most of the states of Brazil are not connected by railroads, some of them have not a single mile of railroad track. Brazil has 44,669 freight cars, Argentina 85,000, the United States 1,731,096. About 53 % of Brazilian municipalities have no railroad whatsoever.

Waterways. Brazil's 40,000 miles of navigable streams, the most extraordinary waterway system in the world, partially compensates for the lack of railroads.

Roads. There were in 1938 119,226 miles of roads of all descriptions. The use of automobiles, trucks, and buses increases slowly. There was in 1938 a total of 170,300 such vehicles—a gain of but 3 % over 1928—and 83 % of them were in four states. For Brazil as a whole there was 1 motor vehicle for each 281 inhabitants, as compared with 1 in 4 in the United States, and 1 in 46 in Argentina.

Air lines. Pan American Airways, the German Condor, and various small lines connect the chief cities of the coast and of the interior. Their services are generously used.

Mule pack and oxcart. These remain the standard methods of transport for a large section of the country.

Telephones. There are 241,561 in all Brazil. São Paulo, a city of over a million, has fewer telephones than Harrisburg, Pennsylvania, with 150,000 inhabitants.

Radio. There are about 500,000 receiving sets in Brazil, as compared with 800,000 in Argentina, but they are chiefly in the more populous centers. The cheapest radio costs two months' average wage. Many communities have none at all. The sixty broadcasting stations are chiefly in the south, and do not effectively reach the outlying areas.

Movies. There are 1,300 cinemas in all Brazil, and there are 2,349 towns and cities. But the movies—all foreign—are chiefly American and are more useful in making friends for the United States than in knitting the Brazilian nation.

Education. Some halting progress has been made, but at least 80 % of the children have no schools. President Vargas claims 37,000 schools for 3 million children, and insists that the number be doubled. Brazil spends annually some $15,000,000 (less than 8 % of the federal budget) on education; New York City, with one sixth Brazil's population, spends thirteen times as much. Visits to city and village schools yield a poignant sense of Brazil's helplessness. With few exceptions they are pitifully equipped, and the ill-paid and poorly trained teachers struggle against heavy odds. This impression is deepened by meeting the men who direct the national educational program. While a few show both courage and insight, an hour with Minister of Education Gustavo Capanema left the unhappy feeling that the Brazilian school is the adjunct to an uninspired national government. The illiteracy of Brazil is an unknown quantity. The *Statesmen's Year Book for 1936* quotes a figure of 65 %. Some Brazilian writers claim a better score. Brazil cannot reach national integrity so long as 25 or 30 million of her citizens cannot even read a placard on the wall.

Labor Unions, whose organizations make for national unity in many lands, are no longer permitted free play in Brazil. Official labor organizations have become the appendage of federal power.

The Press. There was once a free and able press in Brazil, with papers of distinction in Rio, São Paulo, Pernambuco, and elsewhere. Today freedom of the press is curbed. Stalwart editors are silenced. Within the proscriptions laid down by government censors, the press serves as a force for unity.

Language. Officially, all Brazilians speak Portuguese. There are still communities where only Indian tongues are used. In the south there are many communities which stick to German and Italian, and Portuguese is seldom heard. In Bahia there are thousands of Negroes who speak a scarcely recognizable patois of Portuguese and African dialects. In early 1939, 500 army conscripts were discovered to speak only German.

Politics. National parties, cutting across state lines and stimulating a national sense, have never been known in Brazil. Today all parties are barred and the government rules by ukase. Getulio Vargas, by vesting all power in himself, and by silencing state rivalries, has brought outward conformity. It remains to be seen whether compulsion can make a nation.

Brazil is still divided by jealous prides. There is little recognition of common possession and purpose. The outsider, clinging to naïve faith in the efficacy of democratic process, concludes that there can be no authentic Brazilian republic until more of the people are given a satisfying share in making national decisions. Brazil's citizens are cut off from each other by ignorance, poverty, and great distances. They are denied the first requisite to true concord, a voice in the life of the nation.

CHAPTER VII

RACE

BRAZILIANS prefer that visitors refrain from discussion of their race question. But how can we consider Brazil without looking at the Brazilians? Brazilians are Portuguese, Italians, Indians, Negroes, Poles, Japanese, Dutch, French, Spaniards, Scandinavians, Germans, Greeks. Brazilians are also a blend of these diverse peoples.

The Indians were here before the white man came. They lived in scattered tribes, some in villages, some as nomads. They had no civilization to be compared with the Aztec empire disrupted by Hernán Cortés in 1519, or with the empire of the Inca which fell before Francisco Pizarro in 1533. Brazil had a scattering of Arawaks, Caribs, Tupuyus, Tupi-Guanarís—some millions of them, perhaps, but no one knows the figure.

The white man came in 1500. The Portuguese navigator Pedro Alvares Cabral, bound for India, by mistake swung too far west and sighted the coast of Bahia. The existence of Brazil had already been conjectured and had been assigned to the Portuguese Crown by the Treaty of Tordesillas in 1493 (following Pope Alexander's attempts to adjust the dispute between his most Catholic subjects in Spain and Portugal). Portugal took little interest in her new domain. She was absorbed in trade with the East. A settlement was made at São Vicente (near Santos) in 1532, and others followed. A few Portuguese came during the sixteenth century, but in no considerable number until the seventeenth.

The black man came with the white. Ships loaded with Africans began to arrive shortly after the first Portuguese settlers. Slaves were the chief import of Brazil throughout the sixteenth, seventeenth, eighteenth, and nineteenth centuries—until slavery was ended in 1888. The total of these involuntary immigrants is estimated to have been 12 millions.

The Indian, the white man, and the black man—these laid the foundation of the Brazilian nation. The Indians, less tractable than the subjects of Moctezuma and the Inca, were not minded to work for the white man. Many were killed, a fashion common to English, Spanish, and Portuguese invaders. The more comely women found their place in the white man's world, and contributed an Indian cast to the faces of many present-day Brazilians. The Indians who escaped murder, resisted baptism and seduction, were pushed back upon the frontier, a few survive to this day. The Negro was given the work the Indian refused. The Negro dug the gold of Minas Geraes, planted and picked cotton, cut sugar cane, tended coffee. His fate was that of his cousins in the English North. He worked patiently in the hot sun, he was treated well or ill, at his master's whim. He lived in a hut under the shadow of the fazendeiro's mansion, had his handful of corn and rice, a few potatoes. His daughters, if they were plain, married their kind; if well-favored, they bore children who inherited the blood of Portugal. There was little social disapproval of such unions. Many of them were solemnized as the years went on. In 1819, according to the historian Villose de Oliveira, Brazil had a population of 4,396,000—of whom 1,000,000 were whites.

European migrants, Portuguese and others, came in the nineteenth century. In 1817, 2,000 Swiss arrived. Pedro II (1840–89) encouraged colonization by Germans, Belgians, Danes, Swedes, Poles, French, Russians. The Italian migration began in 1860; almost 1,500,000 Italians have since settled in Brazil. Over a half-million Germans moved in between 1820 and 1940. Altogether 4,269,000 immigrants entered Brazil between 1820 and 1927, 65 % of them Italians and Portuguese. The Japanese began to arrive in 1920; some 200,000 now live in Brazil, but Japanese immigration has been cut down to a quota of 3,000 annually.

Who are the Brazilians? No adequate study of the racial composition of modern Brazil has been made or can be. According to the estimate of the Museo Nacional do Rio de Janeiro (1922) the Brazilian population may be divided:

White	51 %
White and Negro	22 %
Negro	14 %
White and Indian	11 %
Indian	2 %

Other guesses lower the "white" figure and lift the "Negro." No one knows, no one can know. Race is the exposed nerve of Brazil. Brazilians resent the common taunt of Argentines that "Brazil is a nigger nation." The official Brazilian theory is that the country is being "Aryanized," that the blacks are dying off, that the mingling has stopped, and that the Negro element is less each year. Experts on "Aryanism" from Savannah and Munich would be hard to convince.

Wistful reformers from the United States cite Brazil as a nation without a race problem, where white and black live happily side by side, without prejudice and without discrimination. It is true that no such lines are drawn in Rio de Janeiro and São Paulo as prevail in Atlanta and Chicago. Many Brazilians of pronounced blackness have won recognition in the Church, in government, in the sciences and the arts. The way of the Negro has been immeasurably easier in Brazil than in the United States. But it is also true that throughout Brazilian history a high premium has been placed on *whiteness*. The *hermanidades* (brotherhoods) which flourished in colonial days were often frankly organized on the criterion of white blood. Today, while those of clear Negro pigmentation may win recognition and applause, the scales are loaded against them. It has become more difficult for the blacker Brazilian to get a chance in education, in the government, in business. This appreciable barrier is not, of course, raised against those with some Negro strain. That would be an embarrassing line to draw in Rio de Janeiro, and even more so in the coastal cities of the north.

The presence of an unassimilated minority of many million Negro citizens, illiterate, desperately poor and backward, is an element of weakness for a country which has not yet achieved national stability. Brazilians wonder what can be done with the undigested mass of some 400,000 primitive Africans who live in their communities in the state of Bahia, their leaders the hundreds of priestesses who inherit the magic of the Congo.

If the Negro is a Brazilian problem, so are the other unassimilated alien minorities. Italians, Germans, Poles, and Japanese all have communities in which little Portuguese is heard, and in which absorption into Brazilian life seems far distant. But the process of amalgamation makes headway, especially among the Italians. The Germans offer the greatest difficulty, with sizable islands of German language and culture in the south, of which we will speak in Chapter X. The Japanese make little effort to enter into the life of the nation.

CHAPTER VIII

GOVERNMENT

BRAZIL is the long-time friend of the United States. The Washington government was the first to recognize her independence. Brazilians gave and still give warm applause to the Monroe Doctrine. Rio de Janeiro's spokesmen at the Fourth Pan-American Conference in 1910 proposed a formal all-American recognition of the doctrine's contribution to the peace and security of the hemisphere. When the United States declared war on Germany in 1917, Brazil shouldered her musket. When Washington refused to join the League of Nations, Brazil stood by our side. In all the conferences of the American states, Brazil has been as conspicuous an ally as Argentina has been a nagging critic. We have continued Brazil's best customer. We have told each other that the United States of America and the United States of Brazil were friends whom neither plague nor earthquake could part. But of late days strange reports and sayings come out of Brazil, and we are puzzled by our best friend.

On June 11, 1940, the day after Franklin D. Roosevelt had spoken at Charlottesville, Virginia, and denounced Mussolini's "stab in the back," President Getulio Vargas of Brazil made a speech on a battleship in Rio's harbor:

Virile peoples must follow the line of their aspirations instead of standing still and gazing at a structure which is crumbling down. . . . We are marching toward a future different from all we know in economic, political and social organization, and we feel that old systems and antiquated formulas have entered a decline. It is the beginning of a new era.

The speech prompted the American press to ask: Is Brazil joining the totalitarians? In Buenos Aires, *La Crítica's* headlines warned: "Vargas, with Fascist Language, Justifies the Aggression of the Barbarians." Foreign Minister Oswaldo Aranha quickly explained that the alarm was groundless, that Vargas meant nothing, that he stood shoulder to shoulder with Roosevelt. Vargas cabled Roosevelt that his words did not contradict the Charlottesville speech, that he had not read that speech before making his statement, that of course Brazil would stick by the United States. Cordell Hull assured pressmen that Vargas' words were for internal consumption, without other import.

The incident brought into relief gathering doubts as to Brazil's government. Is Brazil traveling the way of Berlin or the way of democracy? In search of the answer we must trace the development of Brazil's political institutions.

First, modern Brazil must be appraised in the light of her colonial heritage. Portugal ruled from the first settlement in 1532 to the break in 1822. Hers was an indolent rule, with less harshness and thoroughness than Spain devoted to Mexico, Peru, and La Plata.

Portugal's colonial management discouraged unity. The administration of the colony was divided into twelve captaincies, later eighteen, all nominally responsible to a viceroy in Bahia (transferred in 1763 to Rio de Janeiro). But each separate division went its own way, with a succession of rather weak rulers. It was, with the notable exception of the Marquis of Pombal's regime (1750–77), a bungling control. Officials took their toll. Justice was often sold. Colonization lagged. Portuguese contempt for manual labor and dependence upon black slaves blocked inventiveness. The landholders became mighty men with feudal realms and tens of thousands of slaves to whom they dispensed the law and the Gospel as they were minded. Economically, Brazil's colonial experience reveals a marked difference from that of Peru and Mexico. England, from 1642 on, gained increasing dominance over Portugal and opened Brazil to larger trade. "The oldest alliance in the world," writes Ruy Barbosa, "is that between England and Portugal." Portugal's clumsiness in colonial management had its good side for Brazil. She enjoyed that "salutary neglect" upon which Edmund Burke felicitated the thirteen colonies of Great Britain.

When the break with Portugal came, Brazil was unready for self-government. The landowners continued to dominate. Jealous sectionalism persisted. The habits of bad government were not forgotten.

Second, modern republican Brazil inherits the experience of the empire. Brazil broke with Portugal in 1822. It was a fairly amicable family arrangement, with no clash of armies. João VI, who moved the Portuguese court to Rio de Janeiro during the Napoleonic interlude, returned to Lisbon in 1821, leaving his son as regent. Meanwhile the colonists, in part influenced by the example of their Spanish neighbors, were demanding independence. On September 7, 1822 (Brazil's Day of Independence), Pedro declared Brazil an independent empire and assumed rule as Pedro I. He abdicated under pressure in 1831, leaving his throne to his five-year-old son. Regents served in the boy's name until 1840, when his majority was declared, and in 1841 he was crowned Pedro II, Emperor of Brazil. His forty-nine-year reign was one of the longest stretches of constitutional peace enjoyed by any Latin-American state. They were years of expansion and building. Railroads were opened, immigrants welcomed, schools organized, and the offices of government disciplined and extended. Pedro was wise and just, with deep respect for orderly government. His intellectual curiosity served the empire. He visited Europe and the United States, sought out such varied friends as Pasteur, Victor Hugo, Louis Agassiz, Whittier, Longfellow, Alexander Graham Bell, and Ernest Renan, and invited physicians, poets, and astronomers to Brazil. Under Pedro, Brazil was schooled in a generous democracy, in a liberal and critical outlook on education and religion. Scholars, jurists, writers flourished under his eye. Two factors brought the end of Pedro and of the empire in 1889. He angered religionists by insistence that the Church bow to the rule of the state. He angered great landholders by his consent to the freeing of their 700,000 slaves in 1888. The Church and the fazendeiros won. Pedro retired to France. "The only republic in South America is ended, the Empire of Brazil," wrote the President of Venezuela.

Third, republican Brazil dates from 1889. Pedro's schooling in orderly government was not forgotten. For forty years the republic of Brazil observed constitutional amenities with a faithfulness unknown to most of Latin America. Science and education made headway. A notable press exerted powerful influence. Oswaldo Cruz ended yellow fever in the capital. Rio Branco and others led in diplomacy, concluding peaceful settlements of border disputes with Bolivia, Colombia, French and Dutch Guiana. Meanwhile, violent shifts in Brazilian economy brought new political alignments. The sugar industry, major reliance for three centuries, was crippled by West Indian competition. The rubber trade was lost to the plantation growers in the East Indies. Coffee became king. São Paulo, chief producer, took and held the lead in national politics until 1930. By 1930 coffee prices had cracked, Brazil's belt was tightened, rich São Paulo's the most of all. The crisis gave southern Rio Grande do Sul—now rich in herds and grain

—the chance she awaited. In 1930 Rio Grande do Sul came to power in the person of Getulio Vargas.

Fourth, Brazil's government since 1930 is described in terms of Getulio Vargas. Lawyer, soldier, governor of his state, Vargas rode into office in November 1930, with the backing of a cabal of mineiros and gauchos. The election had gone to a paulista, Julio Prestes, but Vargas, with two states behind him and with army support, deposed President Washington Luiz and forestalled Prestes' assumption of office. Vargas, despite his flaunting of orderly processes, was welcomed by liberals as a man after their own heart. His first measures were conciliatory and constructive. In 1932 a formidable uprising in São Paulo almost unseated him. In 1934 Vargas' hand-picked constituent assembly adopted a new constitution and named him president for four years. In 1935 a "communist" uprising led by Luis Carlos Prestes was duly put down. (In reading Brazilian news, bear in mind that all enemies of Vargas are "communists.") Then appeared in full colors the green-shirted Integralistas, led by fanatic-mystic-fascist Plinio Salgado (perhaps with German aid), who with much saluting, marching, and fascist posturing made dramatic appeal to unhappy patriots. By early 1937 observers reported Salgado's large hold on the populace, and freely prophesied that the army would follow him. Whereupon Vargas took Salgado into his camp, promised him ribbons and milreis, executed his own coup d'état on November 10, 1937, sent parliament home, promulgated a new constitution written by Francisco Campos, announced the Novo Estado, and signed an order dissolving the Integralistas. Plinio Salgado is now in Portugal, meditating upon the ingratitude of kings. Vargas has not again been seriously challenged. To be sure, on May 11, 1938, two hundred of Vargas' personal guard and a scattering of allies suddenly closed in upon the Cattete Palace and fired a few shots in the direction of the dictator, but they were held at bay by a handful of faithful servants. The army, after discreetly waiting three hours to learn the outcome of the battle, finally arrived and rescued Vargas. Vargas still rules.

Let us, then, pose the question which nettles. Exactly what is

this Novo Estado of which Mr. Vargas speaks with such affection? Exactly where is Mr. Vargas headed? Exactly what can the
United States expect from Mr. Vargas and his Novo Estado in
the current battle? "Communists" and other rude fellows call it
fascism. Mr. Vargas paints it as "a new kind of democracy."

I can but report as a pilgrim who has wandered over Brazil,
seeing what may be seen, asking questions which were not always answered, talking with the chief actors and with others
whose names mean nothing. Some things are quickly discovered—

Item. There is no Congress. I went to the building where parliament once sat, and was ushered reverently into a dark assembly
hall with heavy furniture. I rubbed an index finger on one desk,
and wiped the dust off on my handkerchief. The building has
been turned over to DIPP—the Department of Information,
Propaganda, and Press. I called on the director of publicity and
saw piles of pamphlets, placards, and posters, each with a lithograph of Getulio Vargas. I was introduced to the head of DIPP,
a little man who brought to mind my last visit to the department
where Mr. Goebbels presides in another Novo Estado.

Item. There are no elections. Mr. Vargas decides everything in
this "new kind of democracy." He picks ministers, judges, and
the interventors who rule the several states.

Item. The executive rules by "decree." The constitution has
markings reminiscent of Rome and Berlin rather than of Independence Hall. The economic life of the nation is directed by a
financial and economic council of great powers, appointed by
the President. The unity of the nation is emphasized, the powers
of the states are stripped. Labor can organize under government
aegis; it cannot strike.

Item. There is no liberty of the press. Mr. Vargas assured me
that only "license" is limited, not "liberty." There are censors in
every newspaper office. No unauthorized dispatch can be sent
out by foreign correspondents. Do not blame American newspapers for the stories which appear with a Brazilian date line.

Correspondents are evicted for a careless word. Spies are every-where.

Item. Brazilian jails hold plenty of political prisoners. Few stay long. This is an amiable dictatorship.

Democracy's precarious tenure may be gauged by numerous incidents. One will suffice:

Consider the case of *O Estado de São Paulo,* for many of its seventy years the most influential newspaper in Brazil, holding a position comparable to that of the *New York Times* in the United States, or of *La Prensa* in Argentina, or of the *Frankfurter Zeitung* in pre-Hitler Germany. Its record has been marked by stubborn independence, democratic zeal, and excellent journalism. The owner and editor, Julio Mesquita Filho, was the grandson of the founder. In 1930 he supported Vargas, believing him the most hopeful leader of the nation. In 1932 he stood by Vargas against his own neighbors in São Paulo. In 1937, when Vargas established his dictatorship with a new constitution, Mesquita denounced the act as apostasy. Whereupon the government stationed two censors in the newspaper's office and bade Mesquita behave. Mesquita did not yield, spent six months in jail, and was then ordered into exile. Meanwhile, the editorial staff exercised such liberty as they could, under repeated threats. In March 1940 police raided the offices, "discovered" a stock of machine guns and ammunition. (Incidentally, this discovery was announced over the government's radio at eight o'clock in the evening, three hours before the raiders reached *Estado's* offices.) Seventeen members of the staff were jailed for two days, then released. The newspaper and its plant, a valuable property, were declared forfeited to the nation, and shortly reopened under the direction of Abner Mourão whose warm sympathy for Italy and Germany is attested by his neighbors in São Paulo. You can find word of this conspiracy in the New York papers of March 28, 1940, dutifully reported as a "communist" plot opportunely nipped in the bud.

Let us turn to the men who rule.

First, the President of the republic, Dr. Getulio Vargas. He seems a friendly man as he welcomes you to the Cattete Palace with a warm clasp of the hand. "Here is the dangerous man you have been writing about," said Dr. Aranha in presenting me. "Does he look dangerous?" I had to confess that this man of not more than five feet, four inches, in a magenta shirt, stirred no fears. Then the President assured us of his deep interest in the United States and of his purpose to work for the closest coöperation between our countries. As he said good-bye, he asked me, "What are you writing now?" "About Brazil," I admitted. But I find it hard to write about Getulio Vargas. He may be variously described. Some say that he is a devoted and able patriot who serves his nation in the only way in which it can be served, by seizing control from the warring state *caudillos,* imposing reforms which could never be won through the clashing factions of representative government, and by compelling national unity through concentration of power in the chief of state. Such descriptions cite his tireless care of all classes, his social legislation, his concern for the education of Brazil's poor. Others cite his faithlessness to Brazil's constitutional tradition, his denial of liberties, his ruthlessness with critics. These depict his New State as a pallid copy of Rome and Berlin.

The sketching of Getulio Vargas must be done in soft crayon, whose lines may be erased or shifted. His ability is clear. He can handle men, else he would not hold this post. He can control the army, first requisite of a Latin-American president. He can double-cross aspiring rivals—Plinio Salgado's is a case in point. He can soothe the rich, giving them chief seats on the powerful Financial and Economic Council. He can satisfy the poor, persuading them that he offers more than pious promises. To critics who question his achievements, he can always argue the difficulty of making a federal budget of $204,000,000 meet the needs of an empire with 44 million people.

Much has been said of Vargas' rough handling of opponents. Fairness suggests recognition that this is a gentle absolutism, as absolutisms go. It lacks the characteristic markings of dictatorships in the Hispanic-American manner. Vargas is no Francia,

Rosas, Machado, or Gómez who hustles critics off to dungeons or firing squads, sends gunmen to catch enemies unaware on lonely roads. When those two hundred palace guards and their accomplices failed in their *opéra bouffe* uprising of 1938, they received no sterner sentence than a stretch in jail. Within a few months those quixotic gentlemen were being released. "Look," said a highly placed government man to me, "the Bank of Brazil is filled with them again. They got their old jobs back without delay." Montevideo, Buenos Aires, and New York have their full quotas of Vargas' political exiles—all quite safe, he let them go. To be sure, he always has a few hundred or a few thousand dissenters in his jails, but their stay is usually short. If Vargas is a disciple of Mussolini or Hitler, he has failed to read the rule books.

Will Getulio play with the United States in the clashes which lie ahead? He tells me so, he tells everyone so. Will he imitate Hitler and Mussolini in destroying all pretense of representative government, fixing a frankly authoritarian rule upon the largest nation of South America? It seems so. Can he play both games? The answer to that is hidden. Perhaps his essays at the education of his two sons afford a hint. He sent one boy to the United States for his schooling, the other to Germany and Italy (that lad came back in a plane with the son of Mussolini). Maybe, argues Getulio Vargas, it were well to have a crown prince in each camp. Perhaps he is right.

Second, the intellectual of the administration, Francisco Campos. The first impulse, upon meeting him, is to hunt for the descriptive word. He is *levantine*—the man who finally wins in any trade. Campos was with Vargas from the beginning, suggesting what should be said, and when. He wrote the Constitution of 1937 and drafted the "decree" edict under which Vargas rules. No one questions his sagacity. In the summer of 1940 he published a book which outlines his philosophy of government. It is called *O Estado Nacional* (the National State), and it was accepted by Brazilians and their neighbors as the authoritative statement of the Vargas position. The argument is a defense of

the "eminently democratic and popular character" of the Vargas
regime. Campos argues that the very completeness of the President's powers constitutes him a trustee for the people. But "the
Brazilian state, while thoroughly democratic, is also totalitarian."
He justifies the use of violence. He views the present as a period of
transition with "democracy stagnant and totalitarianism pro-
gressing rapidly over the entire world." "There is not a country
which is not seeking its man of destiny, no people which is not
clamoring for a Caesar." He describes democracy as a "fantasy
which no longer has a place in the world of today." He describes
democracy as "feminine" in character, today's problems require
"masculine" handling. Campos refers to the presidential campaigns of the United States as "four months of political licen-
tiousness." "Parliamentary institutions in public life," he writes,
"are today so much garbage, destitute of political significance
. . . a parliamentary hall today has about the same influence as
a museum." The only people who question the validity of totalitarianism are those "living in a fairy land of wishful thinking."
He prophesies: "The establishment of totalitarian regimes on a
national basis leads naturally to a merger of national organizations into an international regime, with a consequent reorganization of all humanity along the lines of a community of interest
and objectives." He indicates some of the techniques to be used.

It is necessary to keep the masses in a permanent state of excitement
so that at any moment they can be transformed from a latent state of
violence into an effective force to be used in crushing any attempt to
break down the unity of political command by the Dictator. . . .
This explains why the totalitarian states must divert their internal political tension into international tension.

Other quotations suggest his argument:

There can exist neither discipline nor constructive effort in a system
which subordinates superior people to the inferior, or which subordinates the interests of the state to the competition of political groups.

Democracy is a negative concept of the nineteenth century inadequate to solve the problems created by modern industrial and technical progress.

A century of experience has shown that the principle of individual liberty does not guarantee any rights such as the right to work, the right to an education or the right to social security. Such rights can only be assured by a strong state.

All revolutions of the twentieth century have had the same objectives—to break down the resistance of the democratic machine and to open the way for democratic ideals.

The *New York Times* published an article by John W. White in October 1940, giving the meat of Campos' argument. This brought an answer from Mr. Campos. He described as inaccurate the attempt to paint him "as an enemy of democracy. . . . I do not condemn democracy, although I criticize certain phases of democracy which I consider out of date and unable to cope with modern thought." He averred that Brazilians could accept no other regime than democracy—"not the kind known in the United States, but democracy as the Brazilians know it." He described Franklin Roosevelt as an "authoritarian president."

This Campos riddle was so difficult that I submitted it to a certain ex-president of Chile. He knows Campos well. "You will never understand Campos," said this man to me. "He is really very friendly to the United States, but he is terribly sorry for you, and hopes that you will follow Brazil's example before it is too late."

Third, General Pedro Aurelio Gões Monteiro, chief of staff of the army. Gões Monteiro is accounted the ablest of the army leaders. Where does he stand in the argument between the democrats and the dictators? Residents of Rio de Janeiro recall that during the months before the Vargas *putsch* of November 1937 (days when fear prevailed that Plinio Salgado would capture the army) Gões Monteiro gave almost daily interviews to the press, announcing the imminent end of democratic institutions in Brazil. He has had lavish praise from the Germans. In April 1939 the *New York Times* reported him "drinking a toast to the honor and glory of the German Army." In May 1940 he and his chief, the Minister of War, received decorations from Adolf Hitler for "valued services by Brazil to Germany." His former chief aide, Colonel Gustavo Cordeiro Faria, is now stationed in Berlin. He has been generously courted by Washington. He has been twice entertained in the United States by the American army staff, in 1939 and in 1940. Upon his return to Rio in November 1940 he recalled "happy memories" of his stay in the North, and spoke appreciatively of the "warlike potentialities" of the United States Army. He would like to visit the United States often.

Fourth, Oswaldo Aranha, Vargas' Minister of Foreign Affairs. The chronicler of present-day Brazil is here confronted with a more grateful and more difficult task. Aranha is tall and fair, the handsomest diplomat to grace the forgatherings of American statesmen. He is candid, open, friendly, and affectionate. There is no shiftiness in his eye, no mincing of words in his speech. He is persuasive, as is evidenced by his notable record as ambassador in Washington, and by his later success in talking some 120 millions out of the American Treasury. He never fails to express his confidence in the United States, his desire that the two countries should travel a common road. He is the generous host of visiting journalists. He invariably captivates them ("seduces," say his critics) into a happy coma, and while still drugged they pound out dispatches to their editors saying that Aranha is the true friend of the United States, that Brazil will not betray us. After enjoying his hospitality both in Washington and Brazil on various occasions, I find it difficult to place him in this wonderland called Brazil, where little is ever as it seems. I submit two descriptions of Oswaldo Aranha, one my own and the other a critical Brazilian's, with the suggestion that the reader check them with the record in 1945.

My own description, based on personal observation and checked by the judgment of a score of men who have worked with him in Rio and in Washington, runs after this fashion: Aranha is a capable, versatile, and patriotic Brazilian. He is ambitious, but bides his time. He traveled with Vargas in 1930 and has stayed by him ever since, convinced that Vargas is the best instrument at hand for rescuing Brazil from its unhappy discords. Aranha, unlike Vargas, Campos, and Gões Monteiro, cherishes hope for the return of more democratic days. He is increasingly troubled by developments in Brazil, has little sympathy with the logic of Campos or the cynical opportunism of Gões Monteiro. When Vargas made his "strong man" speech in May 1940, Aranha threatened to resign but was dissuaded by champions of Brazilian-American comity who swore that only he could save Brazil from a completely totalitarian stand. Meanwhile, his influence with Vargas diminishes, and he is cordially detested by the army crowd. A troubled and an unhappy man, he is retained in his post as the "American front" of the Vargas regime. He is assigned the task of quieting the United States and of persuading Roosevelt to continue loaning money, while Gões Monteiro and the generals soothe the ruffled spirits of Italy and Germany. He is watched by the army, and is often blocked.

I give you a second description in the words of a highly placed Brazilian, a man whose name is respected as a long-time symbol of patriotism, sanity, and integrity. He has known the chief actors in Brazil well for many years. I read the forgoing paragraph to this man. His face flushed. He brought down his fist. "Rubbish," he said. "Aranha is hand in glove with Vargas, and always has been. You have been fed on fairy tales. Do you happen to know about Cyro de Freitas Vallo, first cousin of Oswaldo? He was Assistant Minister of Foreign Relations. When war was declared he was appointed ambassador to Berlin. Why? Simply because Aranha is really playing with Germany, and wanted a confidential representative in Berlin. Or do you know about Olavo Egydio do Souza Aranha, another of Oswaldo's first cousins? He is very rich. He controls the firm of Monteiro & Aranha, representatives of Schroeder & Company, who control much of the Brazilian trade in cotton and coffee, and who up to the outbreak of war were the chief agents for German trade. This cousin was educated in Germany and was a friend of Goering. His brother Alfredo was an intimate of Plinio Salgado. That, my friend, is a close-up of Oswaldo Aranha's family connections, and it is a family that sticks closely together. When you tell the Americans that Oswaldo Aranha is their friend and really plans to play with them, that he threatened to resign in protest against Vargas' pro-fascist speech, you are simply fooling them. Rubbish."

I place these two estimates on the record, to be compared at a later day. This much seems clear, that if Oswaldo Aranha is not committed to long-range and intelligent Brazilian coöperation with the United States, then we have no true friend in the administration of Getulio Vargas.

WHAT, then, shall we say of the government of Getulio Vargas as an ally of the United States in the gathering storm? I report as one observer may after talking with Brazilians, Americans, British, Germans, Jews in Pará, Bahia, Pernambuco, Rio, São Paulo, and Porto Alegre, and after shuffling and sorting the diverse opinions gathered. I get a picture of:

A dictatorship for which apologists may find convincing arguments. Vargas has done much to impose order upon a nation torn by wasteful state strife. He has improved official morale, and curbed some of the more flagrant political abuses. He has evinced genuine concern for the poor, has made an honest effort to better their condition.

A dictatorship frankly fashioned after fascist models, and ruled by men who admire fascist ways. It does not follow that Vargas and his lieutenants therefore seek an increase of German or Italian influence in Brazil. On the contrary, no dictator wishes to yield to another dictator. Vargas' attempts to curb the activities of Hitler's agents, largely ineffective as they have been, are gestures toward independence.

A dictatorship in which there is little of the elation and the fire of the stormtroopers of Munich. I know German lads whose eyes dance when they talk of the future they serve. Their strivings have the stuff of crusades. I found no Brazilian whose eye lighted when he spoke of Getulio and the New Brazil.

A dictatorship which is weak. Sectional jealousies persist. São

Paulo, richest state, is angry. The army, meager and ill-equip   149
is filled with intrigue. The government maintains itself in p   ped,
because national disunion prevents effective opposition.   ower

A dictatorship which is, which must be, completely opp   ortun-
istic in its foreign policy. Vargas will wait and see how th   e battle goes. He will side with the winner, with those who of   fer the
best terms.

Such a Brazil offers scant comfort to those who would   defend
the Western Hemisphere. Such a Brazil has its peculia   r appeal
for those who think to extend their imperial lines.

CHAPTER IX

UNDEFENDED

MR. FRANKLIN ROOSEVELT announce
defend the Western Hemisphere, that   s that we will
bors can trust us, that we will not s   our good neigh-
dig his heels into sovereign American soil   ffer any invader to
Birmingham, and Little Valley your   . . . . In Kalamazoo,
bers, and in Washington, the S   ng men are assigned num-
from an urn. . . . They spea'   cretary of War draws pellets
The defense of the Wes   k of these things in Brazil.
ing of each separate ex   tern Hemisphere means effective polic-
by plane along the sea   posed mile of coast line. I recall journeys
the French Guiana   coast of Brazil from the Oyapock River on
Grande do Sul. I r   border to the southern finger tip of Rio
plane, the light or   call the pounding of the sun on the metal
threshing floor (l   the level beaches, the sand bars smooth as a
acres of forest an   nding fields made to order); the millions of
villages and their   brush scarce broken by habitation; the tiny
zon, and the sea   matched roofs; the loose mouth of the Ama-
island of Maraj   de brown by waters from Brazil's heart; the
empty as Greer   et in that river mouth, larger than Belgium,
pinpoints from land, its solitary sentinels the cattle which seem
    he sky. I remember cities, Pará, Fortaleza, Natal,

ter families, are technically competent and well trained. The equipment is meager. The navy presents a similar face.

I asked as to the morale of this fighting force. The testimony roughly agreed: The common soldier is like his kin in any army drawn from the peasant poor. Many officers are able and patriotic soldiers. But there are divisive forces. Many younger men are reported bitterly critical of the Vargas regime. (It must be remembered that the putsch of Luis Carlos Prestes in 1935 had help from the army. Many of those rebels are back in their posts.) Many officers, young and old, have been courted by Germany and Italy, scores of them have enjoyed free trips to Germany. Corruption is also reported, and corruption breeds jealousy. Furthermore, sectional loyalties persist—a paulista is not remade by being appointed a captain. Many officers reveal frank admiration of German arms, conviction of ultimate German victory, pleasure in the prospect. The Brazilian Army and Navy may scarcely be reckoned a democratic force.

Such report is made in diffidence. Documentation is impossible. Names of informants cannot be quoted. Figures mean nothing. It is an opinion, based on other opinions.

I can report as an observer from the curb on the drill of troops in Bahia, Rio, and São Paulo. The officers were smart and alert. The men in each case marched passably well, but with little of the coiled-steel severity of a modern army file. My attention centered on the men themselves, the human material drawn from the slums of Bahia, the coffee fields of São Paulo, and the back streets of Rio de Janeiro. They were white, Negro, and all the shadings between. Their uniforms were shabby. With pathetically few exceptions, these men were slight of frame, hollow chested, with poor carriage, pasty faced. They recalled figures and facts already quoted on the diet of Brazilians, medical care and sanitation, the death rate, the toll of disease. These soldiers are the sons of the hungry poor. Their life record is stamped on skin and hair and eyes.

These are the defenders of Brazil.

CHAPTER X

GERMANS

A CERTAIN Prince Stephan zu Schaumburg Lippe was sailing to Buenos Aires in June 1940. He asked the Brazilian cabin boy, "Do you speak German?" The boy replied "No." The prince remarked, "You had better learn it. You are going to need it." That is the sort of thing Germans are saying in Rio de Janeiro, São Paulo, and Porto Alegre. Wherever one turns, in coffee shop, bar, or hotel lobby, there will be two or three Germans at the next table, discussing the news, making no effort to quiet their exultation. There is also the story (perhaps true) of a group of Brazilians on a Rio ferryboat, arguing the existence of the fifth column in Brazil. A German, listening to the talk, spoke up, "We are *already* here." They liquidated him—permanently.

There are Germans in Brazil. They have been coming for more than a hundred years, settling on farms in Rio Grande do Sul and Santa Catharina, organizing the coffee business of São Paulo, controlling thousands of retail shops in chief cities and outlying towns, practising professions, conducting banks, running cantinas and restaurants, working as enterprising men do everywhere. There are today some 50,000 Germans born in Germany, and 800,000 to 900,000 second-, third-, and fourth-generation German-Brazilians. In Rio the directory of an office building recalls Milwaukee. There are German names on bookshops, department stores, warehouses, factories. In São Paulo more German is heard, and evidence of German diligence appears at every turn. Germans so outnumber British and Americans that a bearer of a northern mien is usually taken for a German. I entered one photo shop. The proprietor addressed me in German. *"No!"* I replied. Whereupon he was all contrition and spoke in English, "Pardon! I hate Hitler, too." In Porto Alegre one picks one's way between close-clipped, fair-haired Aryans speaking German. A skimming of the telephone directory discovers the Carvalhos and the Oliveiras buried in columns of Schmidts and

Försters. A drive into the country brings you to villages reminiscent of Garmisch-Partenkirchen. That is the common picture in Rio Grande do Sul and the neighboring state of Santa Catharina. Preston James of the University of Michigan reported in 1939 on the town of Blumenau in Santa Catharina, where he found 63 % of the population speaking German as their mother tongue, and 33 % Portuguese.

In 1933 I talked with Brazilian friends in these cities, and everywhere I heard praise of the Germans as good citizens, who worked hard and set an excellent example to their neighbors. In 1940 I heard other comments. The Germans are certainly no less industrious, no less successful, no less numerous. But the average Brazilian is talking about the fifth column, and has a new suspicion of his German neighbor. When you argue that many of these Germans want nothing more than to be let alone and to build their homes in America, the Brazilian tells you of dark plots, of drilling in distant fields. The skeptical wayfarer wonders whether this distrust is not inspired as much by envy of German success as by evidence of German perfidy.

Hitler's ways in Brazil are of a piece with those in Argentina, but Brazil offers a more fruitful field. Brazil has three times as many Germans, chiefly concentrated in the south. Brazil has less sense of nationality and assimilation is slower. Furthermore, Brazil's police are less effective than Argentina's, and plotting is easier.

The German campaign in Brazil is directed from the Embassy where Ambassador Kurt Pruefer now presides. He has proved more acceptable than his predecessor, Karl Ritter, who was recalled in 1938 at the request of the Brazilians for his peremptory ways with their foreign office. The German Embassy and consular staffs are the largest any nation maintains in Brazil. The Embassy has its unofficial agents as in every Latin-American country, men in German banks, businesses, factories, as well as the uncounted army of spies. The government makes some efforts to curb their activities. The Gestapo, of course, is there. Everyone talks about it—the stories run a bit wild, perhaps.

The chief German objective is to unite all Germans, German-Brazilians, and Brazilians with German blood into a compact and loyal group. Persuasion, pressure, and coercion are the weapons. Appeals to racial pride win some. Comparison between German skill and Brazilian bungling persuades others. Assurance that German arms will dominate the world is an effective argument. Pressure is used—the threat of the boycott brings many waverers into line. Coercion is the last resort, with threats of concentration camps for relatives in Germany or actual violence against the individual himself.

The German schools are the chief agency for holding German loyalty. They are better schools, in teaching and equipment, than the Brazilian national schools. There were formerly not less than three thousand German schools, chiefly in southern Brazil. President Vargas, after his *golpe de estado* of November 1937, ordered some two thousand closed. Many, if not most, have since reopened, pledged to conduct their classes in Portuguese—a promise rather meagerly fulfilled, according to reliable reports. Government pressure is fitful. A few arrests are made. Bishop João Becker, of Porto Alegre, himself of German descent, in August 1939 instructed all priests to use Portuguese in their churches and parochial schools. In early 1940 Reverend Roland Mieler, Lutheran pastor in the village of Blumenau, was expelled from Brazil for refusal to use Portuguese in his sermons and school. Many German families, in protest against interference with their children's education, were sending boys and girls to Germany before the war began. Two hundred and fifty of them sailed on one ship in April 1939. This official proscription of the German schools, fitful and ineffective as it has been, seems to reflect Vargas' determination to build a national state. He may copy Germany. He has no desire to submit to Germany.

German societies flourish—Germania centers, vereins, athletic associations, and the all-inclusive Cultural Society directed from the Embassy. A Brazilian official recently showed me 175 insignia of various German organizations collected in Rio Grande do Sul. The Vargas government abolished all foreign (as well as domestic) political parties in 1937, prohibited all "shirt" organizations, and the use of foreign flags and salutes. No such law can touch a hiking club of young men or an organization devoted to culture. Even salutes take on new dignity when *verboten*.

There is an active German press, and a steady drive on the Brazilian press. A publisher told me of three offers of increased German advertising, if he would give his news columns a more friendly slant. He named two papers which had acquiesced, and others which had lost heavily because they would not consent. German press services are furnished without charge to all who will use them (recalling the activities of *Havas* in other days).

The movies are used, with the UFA newsreels as the chief bait. The radio brings Portuguese broadcasts from Germany. The mails are used for tons of pamphlets. The special air-mail edition of the *Frankfurter Zeitung* is widely distributed. (It must in fairness be noted that the British propaganda mill is also active.)

German-Brazilians pay the bill for this organizing and propagandizing. Every German individual and firm pays a stipulated percentage of income (10 % and up) into relief funds for Germany. No accounting is made.

The Germans spend their money to good effect. There are German professors in São Paulo and Rio de Janeiro who draw their salaries from the homeland, while the few Americans who teach in Brazil get along as best they can. The Embassy and consulates have money with which to flatter and cajole. Does a Brazilian school need books or costumes for a play? The German consul can provide them. A German musician of reputation lands in Brazil, and can be heard for a few milreis. (When Toscanini came, the tickets were higher than in New York.) A São Paulo intellectual writes a book. The German consul gives a luncheon in his honor and does not scrimp the caviar and champagne. When the American consul makes such fitting gestures, he takes the money from his own pocket.

The piecing together of the German picture in Brazil must remain tentative. Enough appears on the surface to make credible the reports of hidden plottings. Suffice it to say that both responsible Brazilians and observant foreigners agree in believing that Germany has a well-articulated force of trained men ready in southern Brazil, that they have some arms. This conviction was strengthened by the revelations of German conspiracy in Uruguay and northern Argentina in July 1940.

The German aviation network in Brazil seems a part of this military preparation. Condor, the Brazilian subsidiary of Lufthansa, and three smaller German-owned and operated air lines connect the chief cities and the interior. Many of their airports are laid out on a more generous scale than is required for commercial use. This German network seems conducted without regard to profit. In March 1940 Condor secured a license to extend its lines to tiny Oyapock on the far northern boundary of French Guiana. Why? There are few inhabitants in that section and but little trade. The northern route seemed to offer opportunity for checking steamship movements. They made one flight, and the government canceled their charter. But the Germans continue to expand their network. On December 30, 1940, it was announced that Condor was establishing a new service between Fortaleza and Therezina, capital of Piauhy, a scantly populated area.

Brazil has taken measures to control the German companies. In 1939 the law requiring Brazilian pilots was stiffened. In 1940 Condor secured an extension of two years on the provisions of the law. The managers of Condor have their own ways of flattering Brazilian officials. No general or major or third-assistant secretary of public works thinks of paying full, if any, fare on the Condor line. Even a visiting American with a diplomatic passport was offered a 33⅓ % discount as a tribute to his rank. It is difficult to ride on a railroad pass or use a free circus ticket and think harshly of the donor. So it is in Brazil. But Pan American Airways turns a steely eye on the bemedaled Brazilian officer and demands full fare. Despite Condor's concessions and lower rates, it offers little competition to the American company. Inquiry at the Rio de Janeiro office of Condor revealed that I could fly whenever I chose to Buenos Aires, while Pan American regretted that they were booked for three weeks. The American company is favored because of its better safety record.

The heart of the German drive is trade. There has been the same meticulous cultivation of the Brazilian market as in all Latin America—sedulous courting of high officials who place government contracts, and firsthand attention to the smallest town. German traders study the living habits, the buying power of the people, and know the package sizes which sell most readily. They know that the people are poor, that collections are slow, that generous credits make sales. American exporters demand cash in New York, Germans have learned that it pays to wait.

Cotton chiefly explained Germany's prewar success in Brazil. The cotton depression ran ahead of the general world depression. The American farmer, who got 22.7 c. a pound for his cotton in 1925, saw it drop to 18.6 c. in 1928, and to 5.6 c. in 1932 and 1933. The New Deal, thinking to rescue its cotton farmers, lifted the price to 10.3 c. in 1934, and thereby encouraged other nations to compete. Brazil turned much coffee land to cotton. Cotton happened to be a product which Germany could buy. The rapid shift of Germany from third to first place as a seller to Brazil is chiefly explained by the deals in cotton. The first German compensation-agreement with Brazil was signed in October 1934, was renewed in 1936, and was finally discontinued by Brazil December 12, 1939. The terms of the arrangement were never published, but in its main lines it resembled German trade in aski marks which prevailed throughout Latin America. During that period German purchases in Brazil increased some 58 %, while German sales more than doubled. In 1937 Germany took first place as a seller to Brazil, furnishing 23.9 % of Brazil's imports as against 23.1 % for the United States. In 1938 Germany held this lead, selling 25 % of Brazil's imports compared with 24.2 % for the

United States.[1] In 1939 the war restored the United States to first place.

The disruption of German trade by the war has brought no cessation of her sales activity. German traders freely promised during the summer of 1940 that they would be delivering goods by fall. The first weeks of 1941 discover these drummers busily saying to Brazilian traders in cotton, coffee, cacao, hides, and meats: "We will soon dominate Europe and dictate terms. We can then dictate terms to you. If you play our game now, we will play yours later. It is nonsense to talk about a fifth column. We will not need it."

CHAPTER XI

1,600 MILES

BRAZIL, for good or ill, is not our neighbor, but Africa's. It is 4,770 miles from New York to Rio de Janeiro. It is 1,600 miles from Natal on the Brazilian hump to Dakar in French Africa. Africa, unless Hitler's calculations go sadly awry, may become a German-Italian continent. Brazil would be within commuting distance of German bases.

Hermann Rauschning quotes Adolf Hitler on Brazil: "We shall create a new Germany there . . . we shall find everything we need there. . . . The people will need us if they are going to make anything of their country."

Prophecy in the first weeks of 1941 should be left to Herr Goebbels. We can make a few conjectures: If German advance is finally checked, if Italy crumbles, and Germany is forced to sue for peace, with the British retaining their empire and holding mastery of the seas—then Brazil will grope along as she is today, while her German inner-state may wait and plan. But—

1. These figures, according to the Washington Department of Commerce, are to be discounted by 20–25 % because of the artificial valuations incident to dealings in aski marks. Commerce experts, after adjusting the figures, believe that Germany captured but 20.1 % of Brazil's trade in 1937 and 21.6 % in 1938.

If Germany breaks Britain, masters Europe, adds the British-French empire in Africa to the holdings of the Reich, then Brazil stands next in line. All the items herein listed from the human, economic, and political balance sheet of Brazil add up to a prize worthy of imperial attention.

Brazil has everything: empty fertile lands; iron, manganese, and a score of lesser metals; cotton, coffee, and cacao; fruits, oils, tobacco, rubber.

Brazil could not fight a first-class power. Her Portuguese-Negro-Indian population is hungry. Poverty makes weakness. The army could be brushed aside.

The Germans are in Brazil. They have organized, or within a short time could organize, ten thousand trained troops. They may have some arms, and they might seize other supplies from Brazilian arsenals. There might be no fight, for the Germans have learned that it is cheaper to buy generals than to shoot them.

A little too simple? Perhaps.

Then let us set down another and more likely way in which Germany may seek to capture Brazil. We may read some morning in the *New York Times* of a new revolution in Brazil, with a new dictator (possibly the old dictator with a change of linen), a new constitution, a new cabinet—with every name and face Brazilian, with every word in Portuguese, and with no visible trace of alien influence—all bought, paid for, and directed by Hitler's men. This new New State would shout aloud its complete Brazilianism, its devout nationalism, its heartfelt loyalty to the undying democracy of the republic. This new New State would then invite such military advisers as its leaders admired, such financial advisers as could reorganize Brazil's bankrupt house, such schoolteachers as could instruct the people in the faith and morals of the new order in America. If, in the meantime, any rude President of the United States in league with near-by Caribbean presidents should presume to interpose objections, this new and now constitutional Brazilian government would stand upon Brazil's sacred sovereignty and cite the solemn pledges against intervention made in Buenos Aires in 1936 and in Lima in 1939. The Brazilian Department of Information, Press and Propaganda would ship ten tons of purple print to Montevideo, Buenos Aires, Santiago, and Lima, denouncing the imperialistic North which presumes to lay bloody hands upon a free people.

Hitler, some inventive reporter has it, said, "I could take Brazil by telephone."

Maybe.

CHAPTER XII

THE UNITED STATES AND BRAZIL

WASHINGTON and Rio de Janeiro are the Damon and Pythias of the all-American drama. Their fidelity has been pledged and practised for more than a hundred years. If the devotion wants something of the self-abnegation of the Greek, its warmth has become part of protocol. Though Argentina might despitefully use us, Brazil would not leave our side. Though others might play the wanton and appear in curl papers from the Quirinal, we could always count upon the Brazilians—so long as we bought their coffee.

This bilateral tenderness has, of recent years, assumed heroic proportions. In 1936 Franklin Roosevelt called on Getulio Vargas and embraced him as a coauthor of the New Deal. The exchange of courtesies has not abated. Chiefs of staffs, good-will ambassadors, and economic missions have shuttled back and forth. The more Vargas copied Napoleon, the greater waxed our official affection. When he began to lock his critics in the jails, we offered to lend him five shopworn destroyers, but Argentina would not permit us. When we discovered that the Germans were capturing Brazilian trade, we rushed in with a loan of many millions. The Brazilians have but to ask and it shall be given.

Greater love hath no nation. It is all quite new with the United States Government. It has always been generous with advice, but hitherto it never wrapped its counsel with any gift more costly than orchids. Now we speak of battleships and millions.

Why this sudden upsurge of affection? It seems sacrilege to raise such a question when spring is in the air, when American generals are pledging troth with Brazilian chiefs of staff, when the chief democracies of the North and the South are discovering that their several hearts beat as one. Still, the question is asked in Rio de Janeiro, and we might as well ask it here. So let us tell the truth as we see it.

First—the average North American knows as little about Brazil as he does about Bali. He has heard of the Amazon but believes the Mississippi longer. He remembers that the first Roosevelt was very strenuous in the Brazilian jungle. He has read that Henry Ford owns a rubber farm. But the Brazilians—of them he knows little and cares less. It is melancholy, but true.

Second—we are after something, therefore the heart throbs. We will have our way if we can. I would not presume to publish so bald a statement if it were against the public interest, or if it had been told me in strict confidence by the third assistant to the Under Secretary of State, or if the Brazilians did not already know it. We may tell the Brazilians exactly what we want.

1. We want back the money loaned in the days of Coolidge. That debt exceeds $300,000,000. Almost every American widow and orphan has a bond. We want the money. In strict confidence, we may add that we never expect to see it, and that it is frankly the least of our worries.

2. We want Brazil's trade. She has long been a valued customer. She buys our coal, gasoline, automobiles, and machinery. We buy her coffee, cacao, hides, oils, and nuts. Brazil has sound reasons for wanting our trade to continue. Our purchases in Brazil have been overtopping our sales by some 50 millions annually. But trade is not our chief concern.

3. We want Brazil as a safe neighbor. This, our prime desire, has an explicit meaning in this year 1941. We would persuade Brazil that it is wiser to travel with us than with Berlin. We would win her back to more democratic forms if we could. We

have the faith (deemed naïve by Francisco Campos) that a Brazil with elections, a congress, and free speech would prove a better neighbor than a Brazil ruled by decree.

We ask that Brazil play the good neighbor for the safeguarding of the freedom of the Western World. We ask this in good faith. Undeveloped nations have learned by hard experience to distrust the powerful. But the United States harbors no dream of territorial expansion in South America. We have burned our fingers in tropical adventures in the Caribbean and want no more of it.

What is the response?

I am convinced that the generality of Brazilian people look upon the United States with genuine affection—no other word quite fits. The press is pro-United States. The radio has a consistently friendly slant. The applause of crowds in the movies is chiefly for things American and democratic. Why is this? I prodded as I could, and met with reactions which seldom varied: "Brazil and the United States are natural allies. We must travel together. Brazil wants democratic ways, and our best chance lies in league with the Americans."

I found dissenters. One dapper young Brazilian was speaking for others when he informed me that "democracy is worn out. The totalitarians will rule in the future. The United States will come to it."

What does Brazil ask of the United States?

I put that question to Oswaldo Aranha, to businessmen, bankers, common citizens. The answers were almost uniform.

Brazil needs credits to carry her through the war months. Our present unfavorable trade balance—now running $2,000,000 a month against us—will wreck our exchange and imperil our economy. We need arms. If guns do not come from the United States, we must accept them from others. We need help in developing our industries as a bulwark against overdependence upon coffee and cotton. We need assistance in carrying our surpluses, and in developing new cash crops which the United States and others can buy. American coöp-

and Brazil, were called off in 1939. Krupps offered a similar proposition, which was rejected. Japan and Great Britain were rumored to be seeking concessions, but Vargas decided that any steel corporation would be Brazilian. In September 1940 a commission headed by wealthy Guilherme Guinle reached agreement with the Roosevelt administration, and construction is now planned.

Third, the United States proffers coöperation in defense. Military, naval, and air missions help train Brazilian officers. Proposals for the loan of arms, destroyers, and other fighting material are studied.

Fourth, Washington offers technical aid of various sorts. Brazil is making use of such services. Experts on soils, on the handling of surplus commodities, on the eradication of pests— are among those used.

Fifth, the Maritime Commission has worked to improve passenger and freight service between the United States and Brazil. The obstacles are numerous. Even the heavy subsidies granted existing lines do not bring rates down to those offered by competing nations. One example: before the war broke, Brazil could get coal from England and Germany at about $6 a ton, while American coal delivered in Brazilian ports cost $15. Of that $15, freight accounted for about $9.

WHAT, then, may one report on Brazil?

THE botanist is the happy fellow, for he can count the flowers. Or the collector of beetles and butterflies. Or the painter of sunsets. Or the gatherer of old silver. The unhappy task is to contemplate a great helpless people set down in a world denied the boon of time. As the plane whirled south from São Paulo, over coffee lands, grain fields, cattle herds, and villages, one phrase kept recurring to me, *If there were but time.* The very motors seemed to beat it out. Given time, Brazil's millions might find their way. Time might teach them to grow the food which builds bones and solid flesh, to husband their dissipated power, to win freedom through control of their own resources, to create themselves a nation beyond the reach of plotters.

But we are leaving Brazil. The harbor of Rio, the mountains around about Petropolis, the modern city of São Paulo are far behind us, and Paraguay lies ahead. Beneath our plane are the Falls of Iguassú which from the air seem a tiny trinket cut in tinsel and pasted onto the face of the jungle. There is scarcely a hut for a hundred miles. The dense forest is sliced by the Paraná and the Iguassú rivers. Here is time, the time not reckoned in the rotting, sprouting jungle, with only birds and wild animals to punctuate the quietness. But Brazil cannot hide in the jungle, she must face the sea where there are ships and men.

PART THREE: CHILE

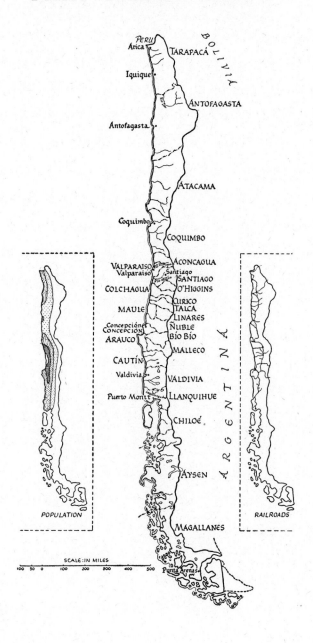

CHILE

THE gods grinned as they chiseled out the land of Chile and stood it on its granite head. Twenty-six hundred miles from tip to tip, seldom more than one hundred miles wide, a string of the earth's high mountains and narrow valleys for the Chilean people. Perhaps the gods were involved in a gigantic Argentine plot to push the Chileans off into the sea.

There is no prosaic approach to Chile. Land at Valparaiso, a gaunt port city clinging to the steep coastal range by its fingernails, its upper levels reached by a series of rattling funiculars. Come by rail from Argentina, and break the journey with a drive over the divide, then by rail down the Aconcagua valley with snowbanks resting on your shoulders. Approach by rail through southern Argentina, then by steamer over Lakes Nahuel Huapí, Todos Los Santos, Llanquihue, with lovely Osorno marking the turn north to Santiago. Take a plane from Buenos Aires, light briefly at Mendoza, then fly for seventy-five minutes over the cordillera, alternately holding your breath and sniffing resolutely at the rubber tube through which Pan American doles out oxygen, while the plane seems to plunge through the clouds straight for Mt. Aconcagua's 23,000 feet of inhospitality, and then drops you on the valley floor of Santiago.

Santiago, city of almost a million, fourth city of South America, home of one fifth of all Chileans, is the heart of Chile. The life of the nation converges here. It is a sprawling city, with mountains as the backdrop for every view. The Mapocho River, tumbling down from the snowbanks, rushes through the city's center. From the heart of Santiago rises Santa Lucía, once the fortress of conquerors, now lined with gardens, sliced by pathways, studded with memorials to other days. High over the city looms Cristóbal, with the statue of the Virgin topping it, reached by a whining car up a steep incline, passengers assured safe delivery by one steel cable and the grace of God. Santiago seizes and holds your affection as no other city in the Americas. You remember it when you have left it, and when you go again the affection has not dimmed, and you stay with it for weeks or months and still love it. You cannot explain your feeling for Santiago. Its streets do not have the beauty of Rio's, nor the trimness of Lima's, nor the flare of Buenos Aires', nor the colonial loveliness of Quito's. It is too wet in winter, too dry in summer. You wander through its streets, talk to its people, idle around its edges. Santiago is weathered and worn, the faces and speech of its people tell of the blood of Spain mingled with that of the Araucanians. There are too many old women begging at church steps, too many pitiful children. The shops are shabby and there is little to buy. The creaking, bucking streetcars are loaded down with people bound for work. The taxis are the oldest in the world, with sketchy brakes, machinery which clanks, and drivers whose performance prompts examination of your soul's account. You will like the Santiago which is down at the heel more than the Santiago of the town boosters, with their new apartment houses, bright suburban homes, and a shiny new hotel which thinks that it looks like the Waldorf as though there were virtue in looking like the Waldorf. The true Santiago is reserved for those who like old hats and old shoes, things lived with and worn.

Chile is a different land from any found on the Atlantic side. The difference is more than geographic. Here is another people, contrived in four centuries of isolation behind the mountain wall. The Chileans speak a different language from the Argentines, a Spanish which has none of the sledge-hammer force of the porteño's, none of those strange sounds which the Argentines acquired from the Italians or invented out of sheer perversity. The Chilean language was molded by Indian nurses, it is chipped and softer and more rapid, to the continuing despair of the outsider.

If excuses are required for writing about Chile, they are easily found.

Sound strategy suggests that we know about Chile. She turns a 2,600-mile front toward Asia. Much of her area is exposed and unoccupied. Her domain includes the Straits of Magellan, one of the two highways between Pacific and Atlantic—important should Panama be closed by well-aimed bombs.

Curiosity will serve—a curiosity which yields to admiration as one sees how excellently these Chileans have managed in the face of Nature's handicaps. The wayfarer learns to appreciate the Chileans as he does the settlers of New England and Vancouver and all pioneers who refused defeat.

Or we write of Chile because we like the land and the people.

Or do we need an excuse?

CHAPTER I

LAND AND PEOPLE

THE Aymarás of the Peruvian highlands called this land by a word which the Spanish soldiers transcribed *Chilli*. It was, the Indians assured Pedro de Valdivia, "the land where the earth ends." Benjamin Subercaseaux writes of *Chile o una loca geografía*—"Chile or a crazy geography"—and understates it.

This is Chile. Look at it. It is a chunk of taffy drawn into a thin ribbon. It is about 2,660 miles from the tip of Cape Horn to the Peruvian border. It briefly reaches a width of 250 miles, most of it is less than 100 miles. Toss it across the United States, it reaches from New York to San Francisco, a slice little wider than the space between New York and Philadelphia. Turn it about, it corresponds to the span between Labrador and Guatemala.

This Chilean ribbon is scalloped on the two edges. On the east, a strip of 50 miles—more or less—is used up by the cordillera of the Andes, stiff young mountains which have not lost their stature, part of the chain which carries through to Alaska. Chile has 300 peaks higher than the United States' highest, and shares Aconcagua, the highest of them all, with Argentina. In Chile one is seldom out of sight of the Andes. Parallel to the cordillera is the low-worn coastal range which rims the Pacific from Antofagasta to Puerto Montt where it slips off into the sea and shows only in the beaded islands of the south.

The rivers of Chile run east to west. They race from the snow-banks, 10, 15, 20 thousand feet above the sea, down across the valleys. Not all reach the Pacific. In the north they are lost in a few tiny oases. In central Chile the waters are all used for irrigation. In the south, where it always rains, the rivers are full and wide. There are some thirty rivers altogether lacing Chile east to west.

There are three Chiles, not one—northern Chile where it never rains, central Chile where it rains in winter, southern Chile where it rains all the year. Northern Chile includes the Atacama Desert which reaches on up to northern Peru, a blistered, treeless, shrubless waste where a raindrop is almost as rare as a meteor in Manhattan, and with infrequent patches of green to advertise a lost river. Central Chile, from the valley of the Aconcagua to Valdivia, a span of 800 miles, with winter rains and summer irrigation, is where the bulk of Chileans live. Southern Chile extends from Valdivia to Cape Horn, with too much rain for some crops and for the tastes of man. Here are the loveliest lakes ever set under the shadow of snow-capped peaks, with generous rivers, forests untouched by fire or axe, unmapped islands, jungle lands never explored, fiords as fine as Norway's, on down to the brush and grazing lands of Tierra del Fuego. Hardy settlers have carved farms out of the nearer forests, but much of southern Chile is virgin. Sheepmen follow their calling in the far south, where the land will pasture about one third of a sheep to the acre, where it is wet and "cold as the heart of a whore," as one stockman solemnly assured me.

The gods who toyed with the granite slabs also arranged a curious ocean current (named after the indefatigable Baron von Humboldt) which swings up from the Antarctic and touches the shore of northern Chile and most of Peru, leveling the extremes of the seasons, catching rain clouds out at sea where their waters cannot serve man, and helping to create the desert.

Chileans celebrate the four-hundredth anniversary of the founding of Santiago in 1941. There were but 150 in that first company of Spaniards, but they kept coming until by the end of colonial days Baron von Humboldt found a population of about 1,000,000. Of this number some 100,000 were unbaptized Araucanians, and the rest were chiefly Spaniards, mixed Spaniards and Indians, and a handful of British, Germans, and other peoples. (The Baron did much guessing first and last, all the way from Mexico to Chile, and his figures can scarcely be classed as statistics.) The Chileans have bred and been added to until now the official figures give Chile a total of some 5,100,000. Of these, there are 30,000 or 40,000 Indians who have resisted the white man's civilization.[1] There are a few hundred thousand migrants, or the sons of migrants, from England, Germany, Ireland, France, Italy, Yugoslavia, Belgium, Holland, Switzerland, Scandinavia, and other lands. Their importance is far greater than their numbers would indicate. They began to come in colonial days, and they have continued to come. They intermarried with the Chileans. One finds excellent German names, umlauts and all, on Chileans who speak no word of the language of Goethe. English names abound, their bearers often speak little or no English. I lived for some months in 1940 on Avenida Lyon, next to Avenida General Körner—both good Chilean names now. The shops, banks, and warehouses bear such names as Balfour, Swinglehurst, MacKenna, Edwards—all Chilean. Braun and Gildermeister are Chilean names in Chile. Nor may it be forgotten that an Irish ex-peddler, Ambrosio O'Higgins, was one of Chile's first revolutionary patriots; his son Bernardo was the first President of the Chilean republic.

The people of Chile present no such diverse face as Argentina or Brazil. There is no Indian as over against white—for the Indian has been largely amalgamated. There is no line of white against Negro—for the Chileans never imported black slaves. There are undigested settlements of Europeans living on Chilean soil, but they are numerically unimportant. Chile is a white country, with Spanish and Indian blended for the creation of a new race. Chile has class divisions, not racial. Chileans have a nationality to a degree not true of Peru, Brazil, and Bolivia.

1. These unassimilated Indians live in isolated communities in the south, and play no appreciable role in the national life.

CHAPTER II

COLONY

THERE are many half-told tales of the builders of America. There is abundant material for any poet, historian, or writer of scenarios. William H. Prescott, almost blind, without setting foot in the lands he pictured, made a living record of Cortés in Mexico, Pizarro in Peru. No writer has put into Spanish or English an adequate recital of the life and loves of Pedro de Valdivia, founder of Nueva Estremadura, today the republic of Chile.

The story of Chile began in the Spanish garrison of Cuzco in Peru. In 1535–37 an expedition under Diego de Almagro had made an unsuccessful sortie to the south, and had returned with reports of gold. That was argument enough. A new company was organized by Pedro de Valdivia, as stout a crusader as ever slit a throat for God and king. There was a heroine, as in every proper plot, named Inés de Suárez, who loved Pedro and reinforced his will. The expedition included 150 Spaniards (one turned out to be a German), 1,000 Indians, pack animals, supplies, guns, and Inés de Suárez. It was a grueling march, as Valdivia reported to his king, and as any wayfarer may vouch after walking his determined mile over the Atacama Desert. For one year this company pushed south along the flanks of the mountains, skirting the desert, struggling from one trickling mountain stream to the next—not knowing how many days or weeks might lie between them—over the sharp rocks and hot sands where it never rains. At last they reached a valley which was wide and green, with a generous river cutting in and out over the valley floor, and Valdivia cried out *"El Valle del Paraíso,"* so Valparaiso got its name, the "valley of paradise." The present-day visitor to the valley of the Aconcagua River, sweating up the mountainside above San Felipe, shares Valdivia's emotion.

In February 1541 this little army reached another river, the Mapocho, which watered a greater valley. In the fork of the river rose a steep hill of stone, which Valdivia called Santa Lucía. Here Valdivia founded the city of Santiago. It offered a natural fortress. Two sides of the hill were protected by forks of the river, on the third they built a wall. They erected an altar by the rock named Huelén, and the first Mass was celebrated. They built rough houses. There was a chapel for Inés, whom Valdivia loved, and who was tireless in preserving the faith of his restless men.

The Araucanians, who had roamed and tilled this valley for uncounted centuries, did not accept Valdivia's decision. They had never been truly conquered. A century before, the Peruvian Inca Tupac Yupanque with 20,000 troops had pushed the Araucanians south to the River Maule, but the Inca forces maintained a tenuous hold. The Araucanians closed in upon Valdivia's garrison—some records recite that 10,000 took part in the siege. The Spaniards' supplies ran low, the men were worn and discouraged, there was brave night foraging for food, and scouts made their way through the Indian lines to carry appeals to distant Peru. Months went by, the ship for which they waited did not appear, mutiny was planned and circumvented, their little settlement was burned. When reinforcements finally came in 1543 it was just in time—there remained but scant handfuls of grain. For ten years Valdivia commanded from Santa Lucía. He led one successful expedition to the south in 1545, established forts and settlements. He retired briefly to Peru in 1547 to take a hand in fraternal strife between rival groups of Spanish kin. In 1551, under orders from the king, he again headed south, for there was still an empire to be subdued. He organized his band, bade farewell to Inés, who must stay behind to quiet the quarrelsome garrison in Santiago. Valdivia and his men fought and hacked their way south through the uncleared forests, forded mountain rivers, beat off the attacks of Indians, and again knew hunger. The Araucanians mustered all their force to stop him. In 1554 Valdivia's force was routed, Pedro himself was killed.

There is a legend (perhaps true) which goes with the story of Valdivia. During the first days of the Spaniards' stay on Santa Lucía the raiding party brought in a spirited thirteen-year-old boy. Valdivia and Inés adopted him as their son and called him Lautaro. They taught him Spanish, the making of bullets, the handling of firearms. He became the chief pride of all the garrison. One day Lautaro disappeared, the conqueror and his mistress mourned his loss, and no reward was rich enough to bring him back. Six years passed . . . Valdivia was the prisoner of the Araucanians, tied to a tree in the forest near Temuco, waiting his fate. Then he heard a voice behind him, speaking in Spanish: "You came for gold. For gold you killed our men, stole our women, destroyed our crops. Now we give you gold." The Indian had a hot fire burning, and over it a little pot of gold. He poured the melted gold down the throat of Pedro de Valdivia. The Indian was Lautaro.

But the Araucanians finally lost, for civilization must be served. They collected in Spanish lives for each league they yielded. Their retreat lasted for two hundred years, and the Araucanians fought each step of the way as they were driven out of the central valley to the far south where their survivors live today. Some Indians gave up the fight and took their place in the white man's world. Some women, by persuasion or compulsion, were taken as wives or mistresses. Some men and boys were captured and impressed as slaves. But the settlers of Chile never had the abundant Indian labor which was the happy lot of the builders of Peru and Mexico. If visible proof of that dearth of docile slaves is sought, compare Santiago with Lima, Quito, Guatemala, and Mexico—the Chilean city has none of those heavy stone churches and convents of the sixteenth and seventeenth centuries which the other cities boast. The Chileans lacked neither stone nor piety, but slaves.

The Araucanians lost. An observer of modern Chile may question the conclusion. Study the face of the Chilean of high or low estate—the mark of the Araucanian is upon him. He may be Spanish, he may have English, German, or other European blood, he is certainly Chilean—and in most instances he is also Indian. Let Chileans tell you of the fierce energy and the biting hatred which easily flare up among the countrymen. Let any owner of generous acres describe the character of the *roto*,[1] of his vindictiveness when aroused, of his carelessness with his own or others' lives. You will be told that life on lonely roads is not safe. I remember one deserted road upon which my friend and I walked one summer day. We saw a man staggering toward us, red with blood from head to feet, a long knife in his hand. We dodged him by a wide detour, and came upon the other party to the encounter, equally bloody, unable to walk. More significant were comments of friends to whom we reported the incident— they saw nothing unusual in it, such things happen. I recalled Lautaro. Perhaps the Araucanian did not lose.

The Spaniard won. There are certain things to remember about the Spaniard in Chile. *First,* assignment to Chile was not esteemed the rich prize that was appointment to Peru. There was gold, but not much. There was soil, but scant. There were few Indian slaves. The favored first sons of chief families elected Peru and Mexico, while the second sons and the less lucky went to Chile. *Second,* Spain's contempt for unprofitable Chile resulted in a wholesome neglect by colonial administrators. Chileans learned to fend for themselves. Some learned to work, a lesson still alien to the best families of Peru. An amateur historian hazards the guess that the Chilean victory over Bolivia and Peru in 1879 was predetermined by the Chileans' earlier pioneer struggle. *Third,* Chile received a larger contingent of northern Spaniards, notably Basques, the toughest and most diligent of all Iberians. These set the Chilean pattern. Alberto Edwards, Chilean historian, notes that "it was not long ago when it was as rare to find a Basque name among the common people as it was to find an English or a German name." Cite any list of the families which now control land and finance, and it will be dotted with names with the telltale *ch's* and double *r's* which indicate their Basque inheritance—Errázuriz, Echazarreta, Echenique, Echeverría, Olavarría, Eyzaguirre, Yrarrazaval, Aguirre.

The Chilean people thus took form out of three centuries of colonial rule. The line between Spaniard and Indian was erased,

1. *Roto,* the "broken one" or the "ragged one," the Chilean name for the poor.

all became Chileans. But the mark of the Araucanian was upon them, on the features and the skins of the people, in the vengeful suspicion and the bitterness of the rebellious masses. The mark of Spain was clear, not only in the faces of men and women, but in the obstinate hold of an unrepentant feudalism. Chile undertook her separate life as a fusion of Indian and Iberian, with the good and the bad of each.

CHAPTER III

REPUBLIC

A TIDAL wave swept over Latin America in 1810. Men marched in Mexico and Argentina. This wave swept south to the least treasured of all Spain's colonies, the Captaincy General of Chile. The Chile of 1810 was a neglected outpost of the Crown, her million people—more or less—chiefly engaged in tilling the soil of the central valley, were divided between a little company of fortunate landholders and the great body of mestizo laborers. There were still some hundred thousand Indians living in angry resistance on the southern frontier. There was also a handful of soldiers of fortune from many lands.

The decision to secede rested with the aristocracy, the landholders, those who owned Chile. Their break with Spain was marked by the same tumult of spirit which afflicted the faithful settlers of La Plata. Good royalists, they had no thought to affront the throne. They might doubt the perspicacity of Ferdinand VII, they had no desire to desert him. But they could not stomach Joseph Bonaparte, and joined forces with Irishman O'Higgins and other queer people not recognized socially, and tipped the Spanish out of office. The republic, thus carelessly launched in 1810, was not easily established. In 1814 the Spaniards recaptured Santiago, and leading rebels fled to Mendoza in Argentina. There they joined José de San Martín, and returned with him to defeat the Spaniards at Chacabuco in 1817 and

Maipo in 1818. The remnants of the Spanish garrisons fled to Valdivia, and Chile embarked upon independent life with Bernardo O'Higgins as "Supreme Dictator."

O'Higgins knew that Chile's independence must be precarious until the Spaniard was expelled from all South America. An expedition was organized under San Martín to rid Peru of her Spanish guards. An English adventurer named Lord Cochrane, lately come to Chile, took charge of the flotilla of four wooden ships which carried the volunteers from Valparaiso in 1820. On a hill above Valparaiso there is a statue to O'Higgins, erected on the spot from which he watched the fleet sail north, and its base bears the legend, *De esas cuatro tablas dependen los destinos de la América*. (On those four planks of timber hangs the destiny of America.) The battle of Ayacucho in Peru in 1824 settled destiny. The Chileans then drove the last Spanish garrison from Valdivia, from Ancud on the Island of Chiloé, and Chile was quit of Spain.

Viva la República! Well and good, but now Chileans must decide who would rule. The aristocracy (dubbed the *pelucones,* "the wigged-ones," because of their formal attire) had welcomed the help of the populace so long as battles were to be fought, but peace was another matter. Out of war had emerged a lot of ordinary people who had been reading about liberty, equality, fraternity, and other foolish conceits—these were called *pipiolos* in derision of their noisiness and innocence. The struggle for mastery was on between the wigged-ones and the foolish-ones. Meanwhile confusions piled up. The bewildering succession of self-appointed juntas which had ruled fitfully from 1810 was followed by the five-year rule of Supreme Dictator O'Higgins 1818–23), who preferred the bright young men. In 1823, a year before the Spanish finally lost at Ayacucho, O'Higgins was pushed out of office and retired to exile and lonely death in Peru. Not until he was long dead did the Chileans recognize that this strange bastard son of an Irish peddler, a fierce idealist who had sat at the feet of Miranda, deserved more gracious treatment. They have since sought to even the score. There is scarcely a

Chilean town without one plaza or broad avenue named after him, and the best-dressed Chileans are happy to spend vacation days in the Hotel Bernardo O'Higgins in Viña del Mar.

O'Higgins' exile settled nothing. Pelucones and pipiolos still wrangled. There was the brief inconclusive dictatorship of Freire, and then in 1830 a quick little civil war gave victory to *la fronda aristocrática,* "the aristocratic branch." Subsequent history chiefly centers on the efforts of the rest of the people to persuade or to coerce that "branch" into sharing the rule of the republic.

The reading of Chilean history excites respect for her hard-headed conservatives. Since 1830 they have either ruled the country or have effectively prevented anyone else from ruling it. Of course they have been a stuffy, obstinate, solemnly clerical company, but it must be said for them that they saved Chile from the braggart dictatorships which cursed Argentina for twenty years, and other nations for longer periods. Chilean government has been marked by seemliness and order. Deserved credit goes to the intellectual father of the conservative party, Diego Portales, the leader in the conservative victory of 1830, chief author of the Constitution of 1833. By 1837, when he was assassinated, Portales had done much to fix the pattern which Chilean conservatism has since followed. The Constitution of 1833, his creation, provided strong centralized government with almost dictatorial powers for the President. That constitution served as the instrument of state until 1925—a quite extraordinary record for Latin America. Portales set himself to create "a strong power, the custodian and the defender of the great interests of society." He sought no office, and stoutly resisted the *personalismo* which is Latin America's dogging curse. Chilean historians of all schools testify to his "sublime disinterestedness." He espoused the "religion of government." He would have an orderly state in which property rights were zealously defended. He would protect the rights of the Church (though his own piety was questioned), for he viewed the Church as a force for stability. He placed Joaquin Prieto in the presidency for the ten years of the 'thirties, and Prieto was succeeded for the ten years of the 'forties by Manuel Bulnes. These were the golden days of conservatism, marked by orderliness, eager protection of property, and exquisite good taste.

Ideas slipped into Chile, despite the conservatives. Sons of first families turned to Europe for their education, and some brought back notions smacking of French liberalism rather than of the policed erudition of the Jesuits. By the middle of the nineteenth century strange talk was being heard in fine houses—talk of representative government, free elections, a free press, lay education. A few began to ridicule the clergy. Out of this churning came the organization of the University of Chile in 1843. The dissenters, an urbane lot, were founders of the Liberales, a party which persists to this day.

The first tilting of spears between conservatives and liberals came during the administration of President Manuel Montt. In 1856 Archbishop Rafael Valentín Valdivieso refused to accept the government's dismissal of the sacristan of the Cathedral—the first state challenge to the Church. The Supreme Court ordered the archbishop into exile, whereupon the pious first ladies of the capital swore that they would cover the streets of the city with their bodies rather than see him go. Montt arranged a tactful compromise, the bishop did not leave, nor did the ladies take to the streets, but "the affair of the sacristan" had brought gentle rebellion into the open—"liberalism" was a force to be reckoned with. It was a mild revolt, for their liberality never shot further than slight distaste for the pope. The liberal break was followed by the first stirrings of another party, the Radicales, recruited from the emerging middle class of enterprising Chileans and newly arrived foreigners. The conservatives continued to rule with Montt (1851–61), with José Joaquín Pérez (1861–71), then jointly with the liberals in the regime of Federico Errázuriz Zañartu (1871–76). In 1876 the liberals elected Aníbal Pinto by their own strength.

Chile came of age with the "War of the Pacific" in 1879. It was a war over nitrates, which Chilean companies were extracting in the Atacama Desert within Bolivian territory, and under a Bolivian pledge that no fresh taxes would be imposed. But Bolivian Dictator Daza needed funds, and in 1876 laid a ten-centavo tax upon each hundredweight of nitrates. In 1879 the Chileans seized the then Bolivian port of Antofagasta, and war was on with both Bolivia and Peru. It was a brilliant little war. The Chileans seized all Bolivia's Pacific coast and Peru's nitrate fields as well. The basis was laid for years of disputes with Peru. Bolivia, cut off from the Pacific, would turn toward the Atlantic and fight Paraguay. Chile was now the first power on the west coast, with a proved army and navy, with a monopoly of the world's natural nitrates which would generously support her government for forty years to come. Chile was now the third power in South America, the C of the ABC.

The war was a victory for the liberals, who proceeded to consolidate their gains. In 1881 they elected Domingo Santa María, who broke off diplomatic relations with the Vatican in a dispute over the appointment of an archbishop. Santa María, with liberal support, took other anticlerical steps long feared by the conservatives—the civil registry of births, marriages, and deaths; state control of cemeteries; reduced state payments to the Church. They liberalized the suffrage, removed property qualifications, granted the ballot to all literate males of twenty-five years, if single—or of twenty-one years, if married. In 1886 the liberals were chiefly responsible for the election of José Manuel Balmaceda. But new forces were at work, minorities were demanding a voice, and the President's powers were being assailed. Balmaceda could not even keep his liberal supporters at peace, and he was obliged to recast his cabinet fourteen times during his first four years. He sought to conciliate the conservatives by a patched-up truce with the Vatican. Crosscurrents were seething. The aristocracy's hold was contested by bankers, miners, business and professional men. Second- and third-generation British, Germans, French, and Italians were contributing to the strength of a new middle class. Teachers increased in numbers and influence. Some landowners saw new light and broke with their feudal brethren. Civil war flared in 1891, and Balmaceda resigned and committed suicide. The year 1891 marks the close of Chile's praetorian peace. For sixty years presidents had ruled with firm hand. On the whole it had been a period of firm constitutionalism, of reasonably honest and always dignified government. But the pipiolos had caught up with the pelucones.

The years 1891–1920 were stormy. Politics became the chief pursuit of the middle class, and politicians learned that politics pay. Nitrates put plenty of money in the treasury. Easy money brought corruption on a scale unknown in the days when conservatives ruled without contest. Vote buying developed into a fine art. The corruption of big and little men became accepted practice. Presidents served one term only—not under legal compulsion, but because they could not control their followers. Coalitions were quickly formed and as quickly broken. Cabinets rose and fell—Errázuriz Echaurren had thirteen between 1896 and 1901, Germán Riesco had sixteen between 1901 and 1906, Pedro Montt had eight between 1906 and 1911, Barros Luco had fourteen between 1911 and 1915, Juan Luis Sanfuentes had sixteen between 1915 and 1920. By 1920 the natural nitrate market of Chile was lost to the artificial nitrate makers of Germany and the United States. Chilean currency sank in the world market, the cost of living skyrocketed, and wages stood still. The nitrate dance was over.

Arturo Alessandri Palma, elected to the presidency in 1920, was the son of an Italian immigrant. His election in 1920 was the first sign of social revolt—the battles of 1810, 1830, and 1891 had been no more than conservative skirmishes for power. Alessandri was elected by an alliance of middle-class Centrists with some of Leftist hue. He had lively human sympathy, liked to walk unescorted in the Alameda on fiesta days, to stop and munch a sandwich with the rotos—to the horror of all proper Chileans. Don Arturo had not yet forgotten that he was a son of the people. When he was elected, the crowds stormed his house and made off with bits of mortar and stone as talismans of devotion. But the ruling aristocracy hated Alessandri in those days, and their majority in Congress blocked him at every turn. The treasury was empty, teachers and soldiers were unpaid, men were without work. The Chilean peso, worth 27 c. in 1919, dropped to 9 c. in 1924. Prices advanced, wages stuck. Alessandri demanded laws improving the wages of the poor, regulating the prices they paid for food. He introduced bills for social insurance, pensions, regulation of hours and wages. His Congress opposed him. Sixteen separate cabinets were formed and fell within four years. He finally won some of his social legislation, and a moderate income tax which enraged the rich. On September 5, 1924, an army cabal forced him to resign, and he sailed for Italy. Seven months later the army and navy men confessed their failure and recalled him. Alessandri summoned a *gran comisión consultiva* to draft a new constitution, which was put in force on October 18, 1925. This constitution conferred large powers on the executive, guaranteed freedom of the press and individual liberties. The President was to be elected for one term of six years, with no immediate reelection. Members of the Congress could not be members of the Cabinet. Church and state were separated, but the Church was assured of a subsidy for five years in which to make her necessary readjustments. Property rights were declared subordinate to the public interest. Elections were placed under the control of a nonpolitical Tribunal Calificador. The common people hailed Alessandri as a savior. Alessandri, wise with experience, decided to retire, and turned over his office to Luis Barros Borgoño.

The seven years from 1925 to 1932 are remembered as the most chaotic in Chile's political life. The election of 1925 went to Figueroa Larraín, but he was burdened with Alessandri's Minister of War—ambitious Carlos Ibáñez del Campo. After a year in office, Figueroa found it expedient to resign, leaving the way clear for a new election which brought Ibáñez to office in May 1927. Ibáñez' four-year rule was an unmasked dictatorship, not lacking in constructive measures, but with complete disregard of the liberties promised by the constitution. Easy loans from the United States created a spurious prosperity. Ibáñez organized a rubber-stamp congress which served as democratic window dressing. A student uprising in July 1931 finally ended his regime, and he retired to Argentina. Then followed fifteen months of *coups d'état* and counter *coups,* including nine months of Juan Esteban Montero and ninety days of Carlos Dávila. General relief, Right and Left, welcomed the reëlection of Alessandri in October 1932.

The second administration of Arturo Alessandri (1932–38) was marked by no more flights to the Left. Older—and, some said, wiser—Alessandri ruled with a firm hand, permitted no troublemakers to interfere, and caused the rich no qualms. He put the government house in order, regularized finances, instituted useful public works, and made possible a fair election in 1938, which brought into power Chile's and South America's first popular front government under the presidency of Pedro Aguirre Cerda.

Chile has enjoyed 110 years of almost unbroken constitutional peace, a record unmatched by any other Latin-American state save Brazil. Presidents, with rare exceptions, have served out their appointed terms and have died in their own beds from natural causes. True, Balmaceda found suicide easier. True, Alessandri found a trip to Italy expedient, and Ibáñez elected the Argentine climate as more salubrious. These were exceptions. Schooled by the honorable conservatives, Chile has shown rare faithfulness to constitutional amenities. To be sure, those same conservatives have long marched their workers to the polls and supervised their votes. It has not been an authentically representative rule. There has been, there is today, much buying and selling of votes. There has been and there is corruption in office. But Chilean political institutions have developed with impressive dignity. The latest test was the peaceful yielding of power by a conservative coalition to a popular front alliance in the autumn of 1938.

Chile's century of political tranquillity is chiefly explained by the refusal to grapple with her fundamental economic ills. Her feudal landowners overcame the rebels in 1830, and they have blocked troublemakers ever since. The turmoil which now tears the country is the old battle between pelucones and pipiolos, between those who own the land and those who have new ideas.

CHAPTER IV

FARM

WHETHER you are an economist asking how people fare, an artist in pursuit of color, or a vagrant intent upon beauty, you cannot resist the Chilean farm. You will go to Limache or San Felipe or Quilpué and take any path which turns up into the mountains, and then out of breath you will rest and trace the lines of trees which mark off green fields, pastures, vineyards, and orchards in the valley of the Aconcagua at your feet. You will leave Santiago and push up the mountainside behind Peñalolén where you can feel the sweep of the central valley. You will see the farms of Chile, the farms which feed 5 millions.

On the face of the figures there seem room enough and soil enough to produce all that 5 million Chileans can eat. Despite her odd configuration, Chile is sizable. Her 285,000 square miles are somewhat more than Texas boasts, although Chile's population falls short of Texas' by over a million souls. When we tally up the figures—count the lands where there is no rain, the lands where there is too much rain, make deductions for mountains which pasture only a few goats—we discover that Chile has farming problems all her own.

Chile, we note, is divided into three parts. When we talk of farms we must immediately count out the unworkable northern desert reaching from Coquimbo to the Peruvian border—over a third (36.1 %) of all Chilean territory. Without rain or water for irrigation, only 0.1 % of its surface can be used for crops or pasture. This Chile yields copper, gold, iron, nitrates. Its population must get its food elsewhere. Nor does southern Chile count in the agricultural calculation. Over one third (37.5 %) of the national domain lies south of Valdivia, an area of uncleared forests, heavy rains, and long winters. "Southern Chile," writes George McCutchen McBride, "has little more weight in national affairs than has Alaska in the United States."

Only Central Chile counts. This is a span comprising the province of Aconcagua south to, and including, the province of Valdivia, little more than one fourth (26.4 %) of all the nation and housing more than four fifths of all the people. Here are the industries, the chief cities, and almost all the farms. Central Chile feeds all Chile. The winter rains replenish the mountain snowbanks feeding the streams which irrigate the valley farms. There is a mild Mediterranean climate, with no extremes of heat or cold, making possible a great variety of crops. Snow seldom falls and there are few frosts.

Central Chile is a scant area in which to produce grains, fruits, and meat for 5 million people. There are but 75,000 square miles here—about equal to the state of New Mexico. Even this area is so piled with mountains east and west that little room is left for field and pasture. Less than 8 % of central Chile is used or is usable for agriculture. There lies the farm problem of Chile. The figures take on life and color for any amateur geographer who tramps country roads and climbs the nearer foothills, who takes a plane and flies across the country, who rides the trains back and forth, drives a car from village to village. Consider two typical cross sections of the central countryside.

Draw a line from the Argentine border high in the cordillera straight west through Santiago to the Pacific coast—the span is about 125 miles. Subtract the Andes which account for about 50 miles of that span. At the foot of the mountains, the valley floor is laid out in farms, with irrigation canals filled from the Mapocho. There are about 50 miles of that watered valley: broad fields of wheat, oats, barley, alfalfa; trimmed orchards of apples, peaches, cherries, pears; miles of grapes; pastures with good Holstein herds; the fields marked off by great eucalyptus trees. The valley ends abruptly with the coastal range, and green fields yield to brown hillsides at the line where irrigation waters fail. There are about 20 miles of coastal range, and then a sudden drop to the sea, with furtive patches of vegetation along the coast.

Or take the journey from Valparaiso on the sea up the valley of the Aconcagua River to San Felipe, up under the chin of Mt.

Aconcagua. There is a rise of 2,250 feet in that 80 miles, and the
river cuts in and out through a narrow valley of watered lands
between bare brown hills. Follow that river valley down through
Calera and Quillota and Limache and Quilpué. The hillsides are
laced with canals which carry river water to the farms below. Go
with the river to the sea and note the last faint stream which is
lost in the sand bar at the ocean's edge.

Eight per cent useful, 92 % waste—that, roughly, is the story
of central Chilean farming lands. McBride gives the figures, as of
1925, for the one province of Santiago. Out of a total area of 5,892
square miles, the actual cultivation was as follows:

Cropped land	228 square miles
Artificial pasture	194
Arboriculture	32
	454 square miles

A total of 454 square miles, or 7.7 % of the lands of the province. Those are the facts with which to silence the perfervid
booster who talks of the day when Chile will house and feed not
5 but 50 millions. The impression deepens that the Chilean farm
will do well to feed the 5 millions.

Farms and Farmers

WE have seen how little useful land there is in Chile. We now
ask how that land is distributed and held. Here we are confronted with the pattern familiar in Brazil and Argentina, the
pattern of latifundia, with a few men owning the great acres
while the many are crowded from the soil. Let us look at the
division of lands in Chile.[1]

In 1936, according to the official figures of that year, there was
a total of 201,997 separate agricultural properties in all Chile.

1. I cite here some figures from the incomplete official tabulation of 1936, but rely
more completely upon the careful analysis of Dr. McBride in his *Chile, Land and Society* based upon the more adequate census of 1925. The picture has shifted consider-
ably in the course of fifteen years. Some fundos have been partitioned. But the older
figures still give the approximate picture of the feudal landholdings of central Chile.

These aggregated 68,282,907 acres. Each holding averaged 338 acres—not a bad showing on the face of it. But we must look further—to the actual division of those lands. Here we can draw out two contrasting sets of figures. First, three fourths of all those properties (150,568 holdings) comprised 4.7 % of all Chilean farmlands, and they averaged 21.3 acres each. Second, there were 626 farm properties (about 0.3 % of all the farms in Chile) which averaged 57,182 acres each, and the holdings of these 626 more fortunate ones aggregated 52.4 % of all the farmlands in all Chile.

These figures may be misleading. Certain reservations are to be noted. Many large farms are owned by several branches of the same family—father, sons, sons-in-law. On the other hand, numerous families own more than one farm. Furthermore, the figures include landholdings throughout Chile, and holdings in the south and the north have little meaning. Also, the citation of large holdings does not necessarily mean the possession of much good land. There are fundos in central Chile which include a few hundred acres of good irrigated land in the valley and many thousands of acres of mountain lands reaching up into the barren cordillera. We must push the analysis further. Here I fall back upon Dr. McBride's analysis of the census figures for 1925.

In 1925 the region of central Chile from Coquimbo to the Bío-Bío River had a total farm area of 28,850,160 acres, which was divided among a total of 82,084 holders. The status of these holdings was as follows:

76,688 holdings averaged 41.8 acres, together these aggregated 11 % of the farming lands of this region. That is, more than nine tenths of the farmers had little more than one tenth of the land.

5,396 holdings, each with more than 494 acres, with an average of 4,752 acres each, comprised 89 % of all these farmlands.

Within this last group, 375 holdings, each with more than 12,355 acres, with an average of 40,165 acres each, made up about 52 % of all the farmlands.

That is the picture of the farms of Chile. The political, eco-

nomic, social pattern of the country cannot be understood without taking into account the powerful company of a few hundred men who have owned the most land and the best land from
the days of the conquest down to the present time.

The Chilean Fundo—a Colonial Survival

THE Chilean fundo with its ten- or a hundred thousand acres,
with stretches of irrigated lands, miles of mountains, generous
pastures, long lines of workers' houses, and its sprawling manor
house set in a flower-decked park, goes back to the Spanish conquest. The fashion in Mexico, Peru, and Chile was the royal grant
of an encomienda to the deserving soldier of the king. The encomienda was not properly a land grant, but the temporary allotment of a specified number of Indians together with the land
they occupied. These allotments were made with vague and generous hand. "From peak to peak," read *cédulas* in Mexico and
Upper Peru. A brave soldier might be entrusted with a million
acres and ten thousand Indians. He was not expected to hold that
land forever, but he found ways to circumvent the law. In Chile,
the despised poor cousin among the colonies, this happy largess
prevailed. In 1544, three years after the founding of Santiago,
Valdivia created sixty encomiendas for his more deserving lieutenants. It proved an empty gesture, for the Araucanians had unhappy facility in running away from the jobs assigned them. Valdivia revised his list, cut it down to thirty-two encomiendas, but
even then there were insufficient Indians. As Valdivia moved
south, he continued his allotment of lands and Indians. Again the
Indians slipped off into the night. Some ungrateful Indians even
murdered their benefactors. The Spaniards were forced back
upon the central valley.

The labor system of the fundo is also a colonial survival. The
enslavement of the Indian never proved the glittering success
that it was in Mexico or Peru. However, by dint of strategy and
persistence, the *encomenderos* built up a rather handsome company of workers. The devices were various. Some Spaniards took
Indian women in legal wedlock, thereby acquiring standing in

the Indian as well as the Spanish world. The more ruthless forced some Indians into slavery. Others conducted raids among the Araucanians, and brought back likely youths who were bribed or beaten into submission. A few Indian slaves were brought from Peru—*yanaconas* they were called. Meanwhile, much extramural breeding was going on, and farmyards swarmed with youngsters who combined the graces of Castilla and Arauco. These mestizos, with no clear place either in the Indian or the white world, laid the foundation for the working population of Chile. Their status differed from the outright slavery of Peru. The Chilean *inquilino,* the worker living on the farm, was theoretically a free man, but actually bound to the land of the patron by economic necessity and by custom stronger than law. He was free—as free as a kitten in a dishpan in the middle of Lake Michigan, free to stay in and starve, or to jump out and drown. That, with some variations, is his state today.

The Fundo Fixed the Social Pattern of Chile

THE possession of land fixes class lines. Those who had lands counted. Those who had no lands were of another breed. The gulf was almost as deep as in the slave society of Peru. It persists to this day.

A quizzical Chilean friend reports a conversation with a landowner acquaintance. My friend had complimented this man upon his fundo, upon the fine houses he had built for his inquilinos. "You really like your inquilinos, don't you?" he said. The man seemed a bit surprised. "Why, yes, I like them. I admire them. They work hard and they are loyal. But, you know, I have a feeling they came from *a different Adam.*"

The fundo became the basic unit of organized life. It was the fief of the Middle Ages, the community centered about the feudal chief. The hacienda house of many rooms took the place of the fortified castle under whose shadow dependents found protection. The fundo community became, and often remains, a self-contained unit with its school and church, its store, its simple amusements. The wise landowner tries to keep his workers at home, safe from the dangerous ideas which towns and cities foster.

This rigid line between master and man is the more remarkable in the light of the common lineage. Both patron and inquilino are Chileans, both share Indian and Spanish blood—although the Indian strain is much more pronounced among the workers. This is not the line drawn between white and black, as in Alabama; or between white and Indian, as in Peru. It is Chilean as over against Chilean.

The Fundo Set the Political Pattern of Independent Chile

WE have outlined the orderly course of Chile's political institutions from 1830 to the present day. That peaceableness is not explained by the democratic zeal of the Chilean people, but rather by the fact that a few hundred men owned the land, and held all other men in firm control. The rich had their own devices for controlling elections.

Government in Chile, until recent disorderly days, was by the "best people"—those who *"tienen fundos, son católicos y conservadores."* The gentleman has land, is a Catholic and a conservative. There was no argument until the rude middle class grew vocal, and until some inquilinos began to read and to demand a vote. ("Communists," "agitators" are words commonly used to describe such.)

The Fundo Fixed the Economic Pattern

THE fundo was a monopoly, and the few hundred chief owners were in gentlemanly agreement. They had the power to hold prices in reasonable accord and to keep wages from rising to absurd heights. The fundos of Chile became a sort of informal national board of trade which settled the questions of national life. Their "trade union," the Sociedad Nacional de Agricultura, has long been the most powerful organization in Chile.

Land was closely held. The possession of land was the proof of social distinction, and the owner was loath to part with it. In earlier times it was the fashion to entail family lands (the *mayo-razgo,* the Spanish called it), and when this was ended in 1857, there was little tendency to subdivide ancestral acres.

The fundos crowded the little man off onto the dry lands. The figures already cited tell their own story. But these things can be seen anywhere in the central valley.

I recall a path in the hills above Limache in the Aconcagua valley. My comrade and I were well above the town, following a large irrigation canal whose waters are drawn from the river some miles up the stream. Below us lay great fundos with fine fields, orchards, and vineyards. For each fundo there were two or three sluice gates fixed in the canal, this water belonged to the fundos. Then we came to a little shack set on a plot of about two acres directly under the canal with its ten-foot flow of brown water. This patch was bare. A few flowers fought the dust, that was all. This family has no share in the canal. One half-inch pipe would give them a garden and fruit and flowers—but they cannot buy the right to insert that half-inch pipe even if they have the money. Water is scarce. The fundos need it. The fundos acquired perpetual rights to stipulated shares in the river water fifty, a hundred and more years ago.

The little fellow is crowded off. If you seek further verification, put yourself in the hands of a hopeful realtor and start out on a bargain hunt for farms in central Chile. I tried this vicarious form of direct research in Santiago, Valparaiso, and Quillota (my belated apologies to the merchants whose time I wasted), and discovered what happens to land values where a few people have too much. You can buy good undeveloped land in the valley of Santiago for about $400 an acre—roughly ten times the price of better land in the Argentine province of Buenos Aires, and two or three times the price of excellent farmlands in Iowa. Such a price seems large when quoted in dollars, but when quoted in Chilean pesos and compared with the earnings of average Chileans, it becomes fantastic. Land ownership has become a luxury available only to prosperous professional and business dabblers.

Chilean farming has become a gentleman's luxury and a highly uneconomic luxury at that. Abundant acres, assured irrigation, and cheap labor enabled the owner to collect a living and a surplus. He did not have to work at his farming. The great fundos of Chile were seldom operated by their owners, nor are they today. The owner spends most of his time in the capital, while an overseer looks after grain and cattle. I spent a day with one hard-hitting owner of a great farm, as he drove me for miles over his property, and explained in precise detail the various operations. "I run this myself," he said in pride. He is an exception. His farm produces. By and large, Chilean farming is wasteful and uneconomic.

The ox team, seen everywhere in Chile slowly pulling the two-wheeled cart or lumbering through the field pulling the plow, is symbolic. The Chilean absentee farmer has but begun to think in modern terms. Labor is still cheap, machinery expensive. The land yields enough for the owner's food and budget, so why worry? There is little pressure to think of scientific fertilization, crop rotation, and the utilization of each idle acre. Furthermore, such cares and skills do not befit a gentleman.

The shadow of the gentleman lies upon the farms of Chile.

CHAPTER V

MINES

ASK the average citizen of the United States what he knows of Chile—he will probably answer, Chile is a long narrow country which produces nitrates and copper. Chile is—and Chile does.

Nature, which endowed Argentina with thick rich soil and withheld mineral wealth, reversed the process in Chile, was niggardly with soil and lavish with metals. From the northern desert (which Chile took from Bolivia and Peru) to the south of

Chile, this land is overlaid and undergirt with mineral deposits—nitrates, copper, iron, coal, and many other substances. Chile's chief gains in the world market come from these minerals, her chief national headaches as well.

If the cordillera cuts off lands which should be green with wheat and corn, it offers in compensation some of the world's richest deposits of copper. If the coastal range is unprofitable for the farmer, it yields iron and gold. And if the northern desert is rainless, that dryness may be thanked for sparing the deposits of nitrate of sodium which furnish fertilizers for worn fields and explosives in peace and war.

The story of Chilean mines is chiefly concerned with nitrates and copper.

Nitrates

IF it rained in the Atacama Desert—if it had ever rained—there would be no thick deposits of nitrates under the dust and sand in the high valley which stretches 450 miles in northern Chile, bulging east to west from 5 to 40 miles. If it had rained, if the nitrates had been dissolved and washed away, there would probably have been no war in 1879 between Chile and Peru and Bolivia. If it had rained, if there had been no war, if Bolivia had not lost its Pacific ports, then there might have been no bloody war over the Chaco on the other side of the cordillera. "If"—that is one way of writing history. The *fact* is Chile's possession of the largest-known natural deposits of nitrate of sodium, a virtual monopoly of the world supply. That fact explains much history.

The war of 1879 gave Chile undisputed possession of the nitrate area. The government's export taxes upon nitrates brought forty years of prosperity, furnishing as high as 70 % of the federal budget. This rush of income relieved the landowners of Chile from the unpleasant duty of taxing themselves, thereby postponing the day of reckoning for feudal agriculture. Politics became lucrative, provoking increase in the company of lawyers devoted to their country's service. This easy money delayed the modernization of agriculture and the promotion of industry, retarding an economy wedded to feudalism. All in all, it may be questioned how well the 100 million tons of nitrates served Chile.

The Allied embargo on Germany during the first World War put an end to Chile's nitrate ecstasy. The munitions makers, their supplies cut off, found ways of snatching nitrogen from the air. Germans led, Americans followed. In 1910, Chile furnished 64.3 % of the world's nitrates; in 1920, 33.6 %; in 1937–38, 7.9 %. During that same period the output of artificial nitrates jumped from 1.4 % to 74.9 % of the world's supply. (The balance of the nitrates of the world came as by-products of other processes.) The loss in volume of Chile's nitrate sales was far less —she sold almost two thirds as much in 1939 as she had in 1910. Chile's loss was chiefly in the lower price received—the price dropped to one fourth of what it had been before the chemists did their experimenting.

The competition of artificial nitrates stirred inventiveness. The older process of extraction (the "Shanks" process) permitted profitable handling of ores with a minimum nitrate content of 15 %. The "Guggenheim" process, since perfected, utilizes ores with but 7 %. There were in 1926 some 150 plants using the older process, but these have been closing down before the competition of the two large plants which use the newer method. In 1939 these two plants turned out 65 % of national production. The Lautaro plant of the Guggenheims cost $30,000,000, a much greater investment than the older plants required. With greater economy of nitrate production has come increased output of the chief by-product, iodine. Chile's annual output averaging about 850 tons of iodine represents about 90 % of the world's supply.

The Chilean Government has since 1933 taken firm control of production and sales. The plants are chiefly owned by foreign interests, notably the Guggenheims, but distribution is controlled by a government agency, the Chilean Nitrate & Iodine Sales Corporation, charged with standardizing the product, fixing quotas for the several plants and supervising distribution. The government takes 25 % of the gross profits of the industry. But nitrates, which yielded three fourths of Chile's export revenue in the period 1900–13, today account for little more than one fifth of that income. Nitrates have fallen from their high estate.

Copper

THE Indians of the Andes dug and refined copper many years before the white man arrived, and its extraction increased during colonial days. Chile was the chief producer of copper for the expanding world market of the nineteenth century. In 1881 the United States took the lead and has held it ever since.

The annual production of copper in Chile has in recent years been well over 300,000 metric tons. In 1939 Chile produced 321,692 metric tons as against the United States' 505,990. Chilean production has steadily climbed during the past forty years, increasing about twelvefold since 1900.

The copper industry is almost completely foreign-owned and controlled. The three chief mines, owned by American capital, produced about 92 % of all Chilean copper in 1938. Two small French companies produced 3.8 %, leaving less than 5 % as the production of several hundred small scattered mines. Practically all the copper is shipped to the United States.

Chilean copper reserves may be the largest in the world. Chuquicamata, owned by Anaconda, is the chief mine—the world's greatest, with an estimated reserve of 1 billion tons of ore, averaging 2 % copper content. Potrerillos, also an Anaconda property, is second. Anaconda's investment in these two properties aggregates about $220,000,000. El Teniente, now the property of the Kennecott interests, represents an investment of $60,000,000, and has about 10 % of the world's reserve of copper and yields over 25 % of Chilean annual production. Prophecies as to how long these reserves will last hang upon the decision of the war makers, the chief copper gluttons.

Copper has steadily assumed a larger place among Chilean exports. During the period 1900–13, copper accounted for but 5 % of her exports; today the figure stands at almost 50 %.

Coal and Iron

CHILE's industrial ambitions are fortified by sizable reserves of coal and iron. Her coal is more accessible and of better quality than Brazil's, but Brazil has more iron.

Coal has been mined in the Bay of Arauco, just south of Concepción, since 1840. These mines are scattered along the shore and reach three miles under the sea. Coal is also found in other spots. This is a semibituminous coal. Chile has long produced about 1,350,000 metric tons annually, but the 1938 production exceeded 2,000,000 tons. Domestic coal meets national needs save for a small margin which must be imported. The chief lack is coking coal.

Iron is found in large deposits along the coast of Coquimbo, Atacama, and Antofagasta. The largest mine is El Tofo in the province of Coquimbo, in which Bethlehem Steel has an investment of some $40,000,000, and from which are shipped about 1,500,000 tons of ore annually. The Chilean Government, intent upon creating a national steel industry, in 1928 financed the Compañía Siderurgica Industrial de Valdivia whose blast furnaces and rolling mills are turning out considerable pig iron and steel. There is sober questioning whether such an enterprise can be made to pay in view of the limited market served, the length of the haul from mine to plant and market, and the lack of coking coal. But steel production is now a matter of national pride.

Nitrates, copper, coal, and iron—these are the major realized assets of Chile's subsoil. There are many other minerals stored away in the ledges of the mountains, with experimental developments under way. Gold and silver are produced in many parts of the country, chiefly as by-products of copper. In 1939 gold valued at $11,455,000 and silver at $450,000 were produced. About 20,000 tons of sulphur are mined annually. There are large reserves of manganese. There are exploitable deposits of cobalt, molybdenum, lead, aluminum, bismuth, mercury, mica, zinc. Petroleum is supposed to exist in various spots, especially in the far south, but production is still only a national hope.

CHAPTER VI

FACTORIES

CHILE was hit by two depressions. The collapse of the nitrate market had all but ruined her when the world's economic tailspin of 1930 came to complete the destruction. Her agony was briefly postponed by the fatuous American loans which bolstered Ibáñez during the last years of the 'twenties. By 1930 it had become clear that she must mend her lines. Two steps were indicated: the recasting of her agriculture so that the people might eat; the creation of an industrial plant which would lessen her dependence upon world markets for finished goods. Agricultural reform was postponed, but the industrial revolution has been in full swing since 1930. The factories of Chile produced 60 % more goods in 1939 than in 1930.

"Fabricación Chilena" is the label most often seen by the shopper, and the loyal Chilean gives preference to goods which bear it. Neckties, kitchenware, matches, cotton goods, shirts, woolens, shoes, furniture, much small machinery, paper, toothpaste, soap, toilet goods, cigarettes and cigars, hats, leather goods, prepared foods—picking at random—are some of the items now made in Chile, which ten years ago came chiefly from England, Germany, and the United States. The 1937 Industrial Census itemized the increased production of key items. Using 1927–29 as the base of 100, industrial production in 1937 was as follows:

Woolen cloth	240
Cotton cloth	762
Paper products	308
Shoes	153
Soap	132
Cement	264
Production of electrical energy	191

The same census reported 19,432 industrial establishments, but one third of these were reported as operated by their owners alone—and another one third as having one to five workers on the payroll. Over one fifth of Chilean workers are in industry. There are some thirty cotton mills of substantial size, over ninety shoe factories, one large and several small paper mills, and a great variety of plants turning out processed foods, matches, glassware, and a hundred other items.

Chilean industrial optimism is boundless. The boosters of Santiago, Valparaiso, and Concepción—the three chief industrial centers—talk blithely of creating new Pittsburghs and Bridgeports. They foresee the day when Chile will make much of her own machinery, most of her finished goods of every sort. This Chilean dream has sounder basis than has the Argentine hope. Chile has iron and coal and abundant water power—Argentina's chief lacks. Chile has already done enough to suggest future possibilities. In the meantime legislation encourages the local producer. High tariffs encourage national producers. Price fixing bolsters up small industry. The regulation of import licenses as a part of the general policy of the government, resembling the Argentine pattern, serves to favor national industry.

Certain danger signals appear. First, capital is scarce. Chile is poor—per capita savings amount to less than $5, as compared with $80 for the United States. Interest rates are high—a stock which does not promise 10 % to 15 % dividends has no ready buyer. Good loans command 8 % interest. Such factors make for high costs. Second, the market is restricted. A thin slice of the 5 million Chileans can buy more than bare necessities. The small middle class is ill-paid. The handful of the prosperous cannot make a market. Nor does it seem likely that Chilean industry can soon compete outside the tariff walls with industrial nations where mass production prevails. Third, Chile's price fixing and protective measures serve to make high prices for her goods. Cursory shopping in Chilean stores lends weight to these warnings.

Consider shoes. The Industrial Census of 1937 reported a total of 156 shoe factories with 8,347 employees. The average Chilean buys less than one pair of shoes per year. The price-fixing and licensing powers of the government are designed to protect the

small and inefficient factories. The international shoe concern of
Bata has made repeated overtures to the Chilean Government,
proposing to develop mass production of Chilean shoes, lifting
quality and lowering prices. The government resists such proposals and protects its uneconomic shoe industry. The results are
obvious. The shoes offered are more costly—item for item—than
shoes in New York.

The same forces operate in other lines. You buy Chilean soap at
12 c. a bar which is decidedly inferior in quality to the ordinary
10 c. brand in the United States. You have little choice in buying
paper, the local product is so well protected that little is imported.
You buy a ream of mediocre bond paper for a figure twice that
asked in New York. In fact, the bargain hunter in Chile soon
gives up. There are few items which cannot be bought in better
quality and at lower prices in any American city. I had this
brought home to me in shopping for a trunk. I found a half-
dozen trunks which bore the Chilean label, made with local
fiber, wood, and national steel, made by Chilean labor. They
were poorly built and cost more than comparable trunks at home.
This observation was borne out by pricing men's shirts, women's
dresses, strawberry jam, and a score of other items. Small production, a meager market, and high costs conspire against effective
Chilean industrialization.

The effective development of Chilean industry might come
through investment of foreign capital, but the foreign capitalist
is uneasy about Chile. The copper companies face the growing
nationalism of Chile, and the threat of a heavy export tax hangs
over their heads.

Prospective investors in Chilean industry also cite the unhappy
adventures of the Electric Bond & Share Company. That concern
(working through American & Foreign Power, which in turn
operates the South American Power Company, which is the majority owner of Compañía Chilena de Electricidad) bought up
most of the electric plants and distributing systems of central
Chile, together with the tramways of Valparaiso and Santiago.
There has been sorrow ever since. In 1935 Finance Minister Gus-

tavo Ross discovered that the utility company was buying dollars
for dividends to American holders in the "bootleg" market, a
practice proscribed by Chilean law. In extenuation the company
argued that many Chilean companies and individuals were
guilty of like practice. The company was faced with confiscatory
fines, its officers with prison terms. The government seemed intent upon nationalization of utilities. The final settlement of the
case provided one united Chilean corporation, with interest rates
on bonds reduced from 8 % to 5 %, with common shares reduced from one English pound to five Chilean pesos (20 c.), with
a board of eleven directors of whom seven must be Chilean, the
government appointing four of these. It was further agreed that
the Chilean company's profits were to be divided as follows:
20 % of the net, before debt service was paid, was to go into a fund
for replacements, improvements, and extensions; the remaining
profits, after meeting service on bonds, were to be divided, one
third to common stockholders and two thirds to the Chilean
Government—one half of the government's share to be used for
lowering rates. The company was also obligated to invest about
$1,200,000 in a new electric plant at Laguna Verde. It was a hard
bargain for the American interests, who felt that the Chilean
Government had effectively confiscated a large share of their investment. Many onlookers, however, both Chilean and foreign,
felt little sympathy for the company whose operations had been a
foolhardy gamble from first to last.

There are Chilean politicians who talk freely of the day when
Chile will follow Mexico's example with oil and take over numerous foreign enterprises. A straw in the wind was the creation
of Copec, a Chilean petroleum corporation, as a check upon British and American operators. Copec has at various times been
granted the right to import its supplies at a lower exchange rate
than that allowed the foreigners. Aside from that, no further
moves have been made. Foreign companies operating in Chile
are aware that their interests might be made the target of any nationalistic movement. That fear effectually discourages further
investment. There are plenty of Chileans who affirm that it is

just as well that their industry should proceed at a slower pace, and escape further commitments to outsiders.

Chile is fully aware that she must free herself from dependence upon other nations for industrial goods. Her struggle toward an increasing measure of self-sufficiency has but begun. She knows at last that her economy cannot safely depend upon the uncertain support of her minerals. She has not yet dared to grapple with her agricultural problem. She has made a brave beginning with her factories. Give us time, is the word of Chilean industrialists.

CHAPTER VII

THE LIFE OF THE CHILEAN

WE have looked at the backdrop of the Chilean scene— snow-capped granite rocks ribbed with copper and gold; green valleys with grain and cattle; modern factories with busy motors. What of the men who drive the oxen, hold the drills, tend the spindles, and shovel the nitrates? We look at the Chilean—his wage, his daily fare.

One out of three Chileans is a wage earner. Their occupations in 1930 were as follows:

Agriculture and Fisheries	506,341	37.8 %
Industries	296,201	22.1
Commerce	147,806	11.0
Domestic servants	96,801	7.2
Mines	77,569	5.8
Communications	54,230	4.0
Administration	48,833	3.7
Professions	27,465	2.1
Defense	20,802	1.6
Navigation	15,550	1.2
Unclassified	46,216	3.5
	1,337,814	100.0 %

With that list as a guide, estimating that each group increased as the population grew 19 % in the decade, we may block in the chief groups of the Chilean population.

First, the rich. These do not appear on the lists of the wage earners. Here are to be counted the 375 owners of fundos each averaging 40,165 acres, which embrace 52 % of the farming lands of central Chile. Add 2,000 or 3,000 others with fundos of more than 5,000 acres. Add those who control factories, banks, independent mines. Add a few hundred foreigners—Germans, Italians, Syrians, Yugoslavs, British—who have built textile mills, organized commercial establishments, banks. There may be 5,000 families with enough for comfort and luxury, with ample homes in country and city, summer homes by the seashore.

Second, the prosperous upper middle class—the lawyers, the traders, the chief shopkeepers, the managers of business. Many of these bear foreign names. Perhaps 5,000 families fall in this group.

Third, the poorly paid white-collar middle class—the teachers, the salaried professional people, office workers in commerce, industry, and government—200,000 or 300,000 perhaps.

Fourth, workers in factory, mine, commerce, transportation— this rough grouping includes women operatives in textile mills, miners of copper and nitrates, makers of shoes, handlers of stock in warehouses, brakemen on trains, stevedores on docks. There are more than 600,000 of these.

Fifth, workers on farms. Here are included the inquilinos and the casual farm laborers. There are over 600,000.

Wages

WE need not pause to consider the economic state of the few thousand rich, and the additional few thousands of the upper middle class. Their "wage" is made reasonably clear by observing the two favored residential districts of Santiago, the seaside city of Viña del Mar, or the few dozen excellent houses in Concepción, Valdivia, Osorno, Puerto Montt. We look rather to other Chileans, and call the roll.

The schoolteacher. There are over 18,000 men and women teaching in public and private schools. The basic salary for the public schoolteacher is $36 per month, $432 per year.[1] At the end of each five years of service this pay is raised 20 %. For service in the far north or south, an extra 30 % is added.

The stenographer. Thirty dollars per month is excellent pay in Santiago, most get less.

White-collar workers in offices, shops, commercial establishments. The Industrial Census of 1937 reports $23.40 as the average monthly pay of 48,000 such workers.

White-collar workers in government offices—clerks in tax offices, stenographers, bookkeepers, postal clerks. Many get as little as $16 a month. Eighty dollars is considered a handsome salary. These jobs are eagerly sought. Eduardo Frei Montalva, in his trenchant *Chile Desconocido* (Unknown Chile) describes the distaste of young Chileans for tasks which they deem beneath them. These consider "a job behind a counter a disgrace . . . but regard it as more dignified to go day after day to some politician or person of influence seeking a little position paying four hundred pesos a month [$16]." Storekeepers in Santiago tell me that they have the greatest difficulty in persuading young Chileans with education to take jobs as clerks, that they must fall back upon the sons and daughters of migrants from Germany, Italy, Yugoslavia.

1. The translation of Chilean pesos into American terms is difficult. The visitor with dollars pays about 3 c. for each peso. There are a variety of other rates for imports, and I have used 4 c. as a fair average for the purposes of comparison. It must be remembered that one peso will buy more of the necessities of life in Chile than 4 c. will buy in New York or Omaha. But the difference is not so great as it was. Rents in Santiago—the smallest apartment with any claim to modernity and comfort rents for 600 or 700 pesos a month ($24 to $28). The tenements and the run-down buildings to which most members of the lower middle class must turn are proportionately expensive. It is not unusual for white-collar workers with some desire for comfort or pretension to spend from 30% to 40% of their income on rent. Clothes—item for item, quality considered—cost as much or more than in New York. Food—pound of bread 4 c., rice 6 c., sugar 5 c., potatoes 1½ c., milk 6 c. a quart, eggs 28 c. a dozen. Transportation—railroad fares are about one half those of the United States. Streetcar fares in Santiago—four fifths of one American cent. Electricity—about 5 c. a kwh. Telephone—about $2 a month for a residence phone. Servants (every middle-class family with a minute income has at least one)—$3 to $4 a month plus room and board.

Miners. In 1938 the average wage of the 19,075 workers in the five chief copper mines was 95.2 c. per day, and they worked an average of 331 days during the year. In 1938, 19,012 nitrate workers had an average daily wage of 71.5 c., and worked an average of 285 days; 12,186 coal miners had an average daily wage of 61 c., and worked an average of 295 days. The living condition of miners, except in some small plants, was materially improved by the provision of houses, free medical service, recreation centers. Some of the larger mines provide company stores which furnish food, clothing, and other items at cost. The large mining companies are generally credited with an intelligent effort to furnish decent living conditions.

Textile workers. In 1938, 14,131 workers in 231 textile mills received an average daily wage of 51 c., with an average of 287 working days.

Industry in general. The Industrial Census of 1937 reported that 146,237 workers in 19,432 industrial establishments (about one third of these were more than tiny private shops) received an average weekly wage of $3.36.

Building trades. Current unofficial figures report wages of masons in Santiago at 7.5 c. per hour, carpenters 12 c., plumbers 8 c., cabinetmakers 10 c.

Agricultural wages. Figures on the wages of the farm workers of Chile are sketchy and inconclusive. The cash wage of the inquilino ranges from 1 to 6 pesos per day. Three pesos (12 c.) may represent a rough average daily wage. I found one inquilino family whose head proudly boasted that his daily wage was 6 pesos (24 c.). But the indirect payments—house, some food, an allotment of land, etc.—represent a sizable addition. The cash wage of the *afuerino,* the itinerant worker, ranges from 10 to 20 pesos (40 c. to 80 c.), depending upon the section of the country, the scarcity of labor, the imminence of harvest.

The Life of the City Worker

Figures on wages and salaries have been quoted. Now we must attempt some description of the life which these wages will provide. Statistics are unreliable and we must fall back upon what we can see, hear, feel.

All tourists visit the golden city of Viña del Mar and some judge Chile by what they see there. There are some 50,000 people, and many miles of neat grass-lined streets with several thousand bright new houses, imitations of something someone saw in Hollywood, Stratford-on-Avon, or the Bois, and they have the loveliest rose gardens in the world.

Valparaiso, with almost 300,000 population, is the chief port and the second industrial city of Chile. The business section is strung along the shore, the living quarters are perched on the mountain sides, reached by a score of funiculars. There is one patch of nice houses. There are miles of sorry tenements. The downtown streets are filled of an evening with as dull-eyed, hopeless men and women as I have ever seen.

Valdivia, Osorno, Puerto Montt, Concepción—the formula varies little. One street, two streets, with a few pretentious houses, a few others which indicate reasonable comfort, and the balance given over to shacks, huts. Antofagasta in the northern desert looks like Leadville, Colorado. You can count the trees in a few minutes. It takes less time to count the comfortable houses.

And look at Santiago—the home of one fifth of all Chileans, the chief industrial center, the head and shoulders of all Chile. If you go beyond the fine streets with gardens, you can walk for miles through streets where the poor live, the people who get 51 c. a day in textile mills, 40 to 60 c. a day for working in the post office, 40 c. a day for working in an office. Tenements built up and back. Corridors reaching from the street with a long row of doors on either side. Jammed, packed. The *carabineros* (federal police) made a survey in 1939, listed 8,627 tenements in Santiago, 67,109 rooms housing 220,412 persons—3.3 persons to each room. Adequate sanitation was found lacking in the great majority.

The Department of Health reports that almost one third of Santiago's citizens are without a safe water supply (that figure goes as high as 80 % in some Chilean cities). Studies made by that same department give details on family budgets, show that the average worker's family spends 80 % of his income on food, 15 % on housing, 1.8 % on clothing, and has 3.2 % left for doctors, education, amusements, savings. Dr. Salvador Allende, Minister of Public Health, reports that Chile annually consumes but one seventh as much milk per capita as does the United States. Dr. Allende tells me that a Chilean common laborer must work six times longer than the American to buy one loaf of bread; almost five times longer for a quart of milk; six times longer for a dozen eggs; ten times longer for one pound of sugar. The Caja de Seguro Obligatario (the Social Security Fund) estimated in 1938 that the minimum living wage for an individual was 16.37 pesos (65½ c.) per day for 365 days of the year, and 45.83 pesos per day ($1.83) for a family of mother, father, and one child. Few families command such an income.

The poverty of Santiago hits the traveler in the face from the moment he steps off the train, and finds an old man eager to carry his trunks and heavy suitcases for 4 c. each to the waiting taxi. There is a death-in-life quality to that poverty unlike any other city in the Americas. It is not New York's misery—where one feels that someone is just about to do something about it all. It is not even Brazil's—for the Brazilian, out of wisdom or contrariness, insists upon being happy. It is not Buenos Aires'—her slums have the rather amiable quality which is New York's. Santiago's poverty is that of men who have given up.

Perhaps the best way to know a people is to catch them on holiday parade. I recall New Year's Eve on the great central Alameda in Santiago. There were gay lights and a mile of booths and side shows. There were thousands of the people who get 30, 40, 50, or 60 c. each working day, who live three or more to the room, who spend 80 % of their pay on food alone, and who have 3.2 % left for education, amusements, doctors, dentists, savings. (Damn the statistics and the statisticians.) I looked for one well-dressed man, of the sort one sees everywhere in Buenos Aires—I did not see him. I looked for one woman having more than a bit of sleazy finery—I did not find her. They were a dull, pasty-faced, driven people, they scarcely laughed. They seemed to say, we are here to enjoy ourselves, and we must—but there was little evidence that they were enjoying themselves. There were merry-go-rounds ("Chicagos," they call them), and the crowds waited patiently for the chance to pay twenty centavos (less than one cent) for a ride. There were side shows, two-headed women, sea monsters, panorama-of-the-nativity, what-every-man-should-see. Three fourths of the concessions were gambling devices—cards, wheelers, rings to be thrown over china dolls—and the crowds thronged about them, to take a fling at a fortune of two-bits. Cheap drinks everywhere, and most of the people had too much. Improvident people, gamblers, drunkards—I am told—people who spend money on lottery tickets and alcohol which should go for milk. These are not attractive people, I reluctantly admitted. Life seems to have passed them on the other side of the street.

The Life of the Farm Laborer

Over one third of all Chileans work on the farms. Some are inquilinos, some work as floating harvest hands.

The inquilino is a distinctive Chilean institution. He is the farm laborer bound to the land of the great fundo or hacienda by tradition stronger than law. Without him the Chilean fundo with its great acres and graceful inefficiency could not have survived. He is not the peon of the Peruvian hacienda, drugged by coca leaves and subject to the will of his master. He is not the serf of Díaz' Mexico who could be whipped or imprisoned or killed if his master willed it. He is legally a free citizen, but economically a slave. He still furnishes the sinews of Chilean farming.

Generalizations on the inquilino are meaningless, there are no figures which tell his story. No government has offered him much more than sympathy. No government has as yet dared to lift more than an admonitory finger toward the three hundred masters of the Chilean farm. (Though any government can safely legislate and bulldoze a foreign textile operator, Anaconda and Kennecott, the Guggenheims, Standard Oil, or Electric Bond & Share.)

The Chilean fundo is outwardly the most gracious survival of colonial life. I recall a visit to one such farm in the central valley. Its 48,000 acres are laid up against the cordillera wall, reaching far up toward the Argentine border. Less than 4,000 acres are considered useful, irrigated land on the valley floor. The approach is a two-mile private road, lined with great eucalyptus trees and spotted on each side with houses of inquilinos. We stopped at one house, talked for a few minutes with the inquilino and his wife, and took photographs of the family. There were four children. The family had two rooms. The house was cane and adobe, unplastered, but this particular house had a tiled floor. It was rather dark inside, but we could see a few old iron beds, a few pieces of broken furniture, and a picture of the Virgin over a burning candle on one wall. There were some bright lithographs, the sort merchants send their country clients. There was no toilet. Water was carried by hand from the irrigation ditch.

A mile down the road between other inquilino houses and eucalyptus trees we came to a lumbering iron gate with granite pillars. Thanks to the generous owner, we were admitted, and found a lovely garden of eight or ten acres, fine fruit trees, flower beds, fountains. The house was typical of those we had seen elsewhere—low, rambling, endless, with hospitable porches, twenty-two bedrooms, a dozen parlors, offices, dining rooms. The owner was glad to tell us of the difficulties of farming in Chile.

There are about nine hundred people living on this fundo, almost two hundred inquilinos and their families. Many of these had fathers and grandfathers born on the farm. Each family receives a house rent-free, and about two acres upon which to raise its food. An irrigation ditch passes each house, which is used by each inquilino for irrigating his plot and filling household needs. No plumbing, no toilets. Each inquilino may pasture one horse, two cows, and a few sheep on the owner's land. Where he shows initiative, he is often given another patch of land—as much as three or four acres—which he works on shares with his *patrón,* the owner furnishing seeds and oxen and machinery, the inquilino doing the work, the produce divided half and half. The worker himself, on work days, is given two meals a day. There is a chapel and a visiting priest every two weeks. There is a school with a teacher furnished by the government, but the owner furnishes the teacher's house. The workday is *sol a sol,* sun to sun— about ten hours in winter, twelve in summer. The wage on this particular fundo is three pesos (12 c.) each working day.

There are no convincing statistics on the economic status of the inquilino. Personal visits to a few fundos, the testimony of other observers, reference to the few studies which have been made yield a diverse picture.

The cash wage ranges from one to six pesos per working day. The houses vary. In some cases, intelligent patrones have taken a personal interest in encouraging improvements, providing material while the inquilinos furnish their labor. In other instances, where better wages are paid, the inquilinos themselves have taken pride in making their homes more attractive. The land provided for the use of the inquilinos varies greatly. I saw plots which seemed to receive no care, others with flourishing gardens. Water for irrigation is usually provided, but not always. Medical care is sometimes supplied, but more often the health of the inquilino family is left to the quacks and vendors of patent medicines. Pasturage for the stock of the inquilino is sometimes allotted. The worker's food allowance varies with the generosity and intelligence of the landlord. Self-interest or honest social concern has prompted an increasing number of farm owners to provide cinemas and other recreation for workers. The holder of the great estate is frankly worried. The organization of *sindicatos* has made progress. Many inquilinos have left the farm to seek employment in cities. The wise farm operator has redoubled his efforts to keep his men on the farm, safe from the distractions of the town.

The inquilinos have the reputation of being the stoutest farm workers in South America. Their Spanish and Araucanian blood has created a wiry and obstinate race. To the casual eye they seem an undersized, ill-fed people. It is the fashion among comfortable Chileans to mourn the degeneration of the inquilino. You hear that he is given to drink, that higher wages would simply go to the cantina; that he is improvident, spending his wages on foolish luxuries instead of food and clothing. One foreman told me of an inquilino who earned a substantial bonus by extra labor and then spent it all on a gaudy doll for his daughter. A landowner told of the alarming increase in subversive ideas among his workers, of the influence of troublemakers. "They are an unruly lot," he said, "I keep several machine guns in the house. It does no harm for them to watch me cut into shreds an oil can on the opposite hill." I could think of no answer to that.

Two Chilean friends contribute stories about the inquilino.

The first comes from a landowner. He was wakened one night by the captain of the federal police: "Señor, one of your best inquilinos, So-and-So, has taken the bad road [*el mal camino*]." One of his men had stolen two sacks of potatoes. The owner dressed, went to the road where the police held the culprit. "Yes, I did it," confessed the inquilino, "and now that I am caught I want to tell you something. For six years, each month I have taken two bags of your potatoes. Each month. You pay me three pesos a day, I have my wife and five children. I could not buy them food. I took your potatoes. Now I am going to prison." This particular story had a happy ending. The man did not go to prison, and he no longer had to steal potatoes.

Another Chilean friend tells a story of a certain inquilino family which he often visited. One day he found them all joyous with drink and extra food. They celebrated the death of their youngest child. "But why," he asked, "can you be happy when your child is gone?" "Ah, but Señor," the father said, "when the child was coming, we kept saying—there are already six children, and we are hungry for there is not enough to eat, and how can another find food? . . . and then the baby came, we loved the baby . . . but the good Lord saw that we did not have enough to eat, and so the good Lord took that baby and she is an angel now, so why should we be sad?"

The second group of agricultural workers, the afuerinos ("outsiders") are casual workers who drift from farm to farm. Their wages range from ten to twenty pesos a day, depending on the region and the urgency of the crop. They are the Chilean counterpart of the seasonal workers in the wheat, lumber, and fruit regions of the United States, and are generally regarded as reckless and irresponsible. Landlords fear them as breeders of trouble among the inquilinos, and use them as little as they can. They may work four or five months a year and then make for Valparaiso or Santiago. They are an angry element in Chilean life.

The Toll of Poverty

THE lot of the Chilean—what is it?

I took the question to thirty-two-year-old Dr. Salvador Allende, Chile's indefatigable Minister of Public Health. For answer he gave me his book, *La Realidad Médico-Social Chilena*, and pointed to the first paragraph: "Chile has the highest infant mortality in the world. For each twenty births, one child is born dead. . . . For each ten children born alive, one dies during the first month; a quarter of them during the first year; and almost one half during their first nine years . . . 27.9 % of our children born alive are illegitimate—the highest figure of any civilized country."

This young doctor told me of the obstacles to social progress and sound building of health. He cited figures and facts in terms of the lives and deaths of people.

Chile's birth rate (1936) was 34.7 to each 1,000 of the population. It about equaled Ceylon's, and was more than double that of the United States, Argentina, Switzerland, Denmark.

Chile's death rate (1936) was 25.3 to each 1,000, as compared with 11.5 for the United States.

Infant mortality. Out of each 1,000 children under one year, 262 died in 1934, 236 in 1938—¼ of all Chilean babies die during their first year. About 4½ times the rate of the United States, more than 2½ times that of Argentina, worse than Egypt's or Malta's.

Dr. Allende shows that Chile's record of deaths from pneu-

monia is 6 times that of the United States, from tuberculosis 7
times. In deaths from typhoid and kindred diseases, Chile's rate
is almost 5 times that of the United States.

THE poverty of the Chilean reflects the poverty of his nation.
The federal budget for 1941 contemplates the expenditure of
$87,776,000—just about the budget of Philadelphia. Philadelphia
has no national government to manage, no army and navy, no
embassies and legations in distant lands, no coast line of 2,660
miles to defend. And her population is less than one half that of
Chile.

The explanation of Chile's poverty is in terms of mines and of
soil. There is wealth under the soil, but ownership and exploitation are in foreign hands, with Chileans collecting only wages
and moderate taxes. There is soil for crops, but not enough—
while Argentina has 6.3 acres of cultivated land per capita, Chile
has but 2.02 acres. Argentina has 2½ head of stock per capita,
Chile $^7\!/_{10}$ of a head. Chile's soil, like Argentina's, is too largely
held in a few hands.

But Chile does not admit defeat. No one can live with the
Chileans without acquiring respect for their pride and courage.
They learn to look frankly at their own weakness. They are experimenting. The bystander, contemplating the vast misery of
this people, can only wish them well.

CHAPTER VIII

THE TUMULT OF DEMOCRACY

THE Chilean air has refreshment for the partisan of democracy. Chileans speak their mind without hindrance.
Despite failure to assure adequate electoral guarantees
there is no curb on free speech. The clash of opinion, expressed
with noisy vigor without policing or surveillance, offers grateful

contrast to practices in Brazil, Panama, Peru, and some other lands. Chile's democracy is something of a tumult, out of which one may pick the voices of diverse contenders in this free forum. We will examine some phases of this debate.

The Press

IF you would hear the rustling of breezes in the Chilean eucalyptus trees, go to the nearest newsstand and buy twenty morning and evening newspapers. A new one is born each Tuesday morning and dies each Thursday afternoon, while a few go on forever. There is a paper for each taste. There is *El Diario Ilustrado,* whose editors view with alarm anything Left of Michael Angelo. *El Imparcial, La Nación, El Mercurio,* and *La Hora*—all sober sheets, *El Mercurio* the best of them, the ablest newspaper in Chile. *Consigna* and *Crítica,* mildly Leftist. *El Siglo,* communist, congenitally befuddled, happily yipping at Yankee imperialism, doggedly trying to keep step with Moscow. Many others. From the side lines wicked little *Topaze* each week viciously prods the great and near-great. There is a sort of censorship, which evokes a fearful howling when trundled out. In January 1941 it was invoked against *El Diario Ilustrado,* clerical conservative, for impoliteness to the President, and against *El Siglo,* communist, for ridiculing Minister Oscar Schnake—but the wayfarer could detect no diminution of impoliteness or ridicule.

Classes

CHILEANS divide into three unequal parts—*clase alta, clase media,* and *clase baja.* Each is as well marked as a steer on the Texas range. They of the "alta" have land, money, names. They of the "media" are making money, buying land, hoping to win names. The rest of the people, short on money and land, are so absorbed with the problem of bread that they have no time to worry over names.

Chilean conservatives, they of the clase alta, make Mr. Roosevelt's economic royalists look like Russians in blue blouses. They have so long saved the nation that they cannot understand those who would displace them.

We found one such on a summer afternoon on an uninvited visit to a great fundo in the central valley. The owner, a little old man of stiff dignity, welcomed us courteously and invited us into the house of forty rooms which his great-grandfather had built. The house is set in a lordly grove with acres of flowers, fruits, vines, and fountains. The rooms are crowded with chairs and tables of all the Louis', the walls with family portraits in the best Parisian pinks and lavenders. This octogenarian owner of 30,000 acres told us in his robust Basque Spanish of the ailings of Chile. He described the communists who ruled the nation, they were taking some of his acres for a hospital. He cited the good days of Chile, when families with Basque names built estates, made the nation rich, gave work to all the people; the days when all had enough to eat, when the lower classes showed deference to their betters, respected morals, family, and the Church. He spoke sadly of the clase media, the upstarts who wreck Chile. "They talk," he said, "of making a national park out of my lands, so that the people of the middle class may come and lie drunken of a Sunday in my groves." An old man, watching his world slip through his yellowed fingers.

I talked with young men who belonged to that same Chile. These agreed that communism and unrest worked Chile's ruin, they mourned the passing of respect for religion, family, property. These men are gracious, intelligent, sensitive, but unreconciled to any change in the nation they love. They explain everything by "communism." When I ventured that each social convulsion is hinged to some social wrong, they were courteous, firm, clearly regretful that I could not understand. When I cited the 24 c. daily wage of girls in match factories to my Chilean friend who had invited me to luncheon in the Gobelin-hung dining room of the Club de la Unión, he gravely admitted: "Yes, Chile has problems, we must crush the communists, or they will destroy our country."

The middle class is a small but diverse company. I recall one robust Santiago lawyer who is exceedingly busy in politics—that chief distraction of Latin-American lawyers. I quoted the ancient conservative's dictum on the middle class. He let out a full-bodied roar. "They don't know what happens to them. Chile is rolling over them, they are flattened out." Then he went on with a rattling account of things done, things about to be done by the popular front government—factories, roads, schools, power plants, colonization schemes. He is a bull on Chile, and on himself. I recall others—lawyers, merchants, doctors, traders—hard-hitting, ambitious men. They like good food, drink much excellent Chilean wine, and will argue until two in the morning. By and large these men evince liking for the United States, hope to visit us soon, do not care for the Nazis, hope Britain will win, are sure of Chile's future.

Clase baja includes most Chileans. Their wage scale permits no more daring extracurricular activities than a cheap movie, a drink in the cantina. Hard-working, ill-served, yet this group contains many a person of dignity. I cite a servant named Brígida, who could not understand and resisted an extra handful of coins at the end of each week. I recall with respect a steward on a Chilean steamer who gravely analyzed the chief political figures with restraint and discrimination.

Chileans live in three worlds, few in any one have more than faint surmises as to the others.

The Church

THE Church, social factor of first importance throughout Latin America, is snugly ensconced on the far Right. Residuary legatee of colonial feudalism, she habitually stands as a bulwark against novelty. The Church is mighty in Chile, firmly supported by the first families who know that religion, morality, and regard for property are synonymous. The devotion of Chilean Catholics is attested by the pride of chief families in furnishing a son to the priesthood—not so true of Argentina, Peru, or Bolivia.

The Church has undergone greater discipline in Chile than in any other Latin-American nation save Mexico. Chile took form as an independent nation with the thoroughly Catholic Constitution of 1833, and the virtual union between Church and state was not dissolved until 1925. By the middle of the century two parties were breaking from the ruling Catholic conservative ranks, the Liberales and the Radicales, both marked by a considerable anticlericalism. Step by step the Church's accustomed privileges were limited or ended—the special legal privileges of the clergy, Church latifundia, control over registration of births and deaths, monopoly of education. French liberalism and freemasonry played a part. Today the middle class inclines to ignore the priest while the Church maintains her hold upon the conservative wealthy and the docile poor.

The Church, blessed with healthy opposition, developed notable leaders. Archbishop Crescente Errázuriz was President Alessandri's warm friend, supported his social legislation (to the horror of the first families), and made possible the peaceable disestablishment of the Church in 1925. His successor, Archbishop J. Horacio Campillo, of different kidney, silenced priests who raised unwelcome questions about the social order. Chile could not stomach Campillo, even staunch conservatives petitioned the Vatican for his recall. I have the story from a brilliant young priest, one of Chile's ablest, who told me of the growing company of younger priests who are troubled by the cruel wages and living conditions of the poor. "Our new archbishop, José María Caro, is with us," he told me in pride. This was confirmed by others who reported the social concern of many churchmen, and described the Church's intelligent social work. I heard, too, that the war in Spain had less unfortunate repercussions in Chile than in Argentina, that fewer Chileans look to Francisco Franco as the spokesman of the Church against the world. They explain this by the preponderant influence of the Basque families, always a more independent breed of Spaniard. The Chilean Church, despite congenital caution, probably stands as the most enlightened arm of Catholicism in Latin America.

The School

CHILE was late starting a national program of public education. Excellent schoolmen worked throughout the nineteenth century, but schools were few and available only in the larger centers. The Church long blocked secular schools. The past fifty years have brought a generous expansion of public education. Illiteracy, estimated to be 95 % in the first years of independence, had fallen to 50 % by 1930. There are today some 3,500 public schools of various categories with a total enrollment of about a half-million. There are still no school desks for 42 % of boys and girls of school age. The present government is doing what it can to multiply schools in cities and rural communities.

The Chilean public school probably stands first among Latin-American schools for the vigor of its program. Scores of schools experiment with newer and freer methods. Educators from all South America turn to Chile for guidance. The credit becomes greater when it is remembered that but $10,000,000 a year is allotted Chilean education.

The Labor Union

THE organized labor movement is a popular movement of force. The CTCh (Confederación de Trabajadores de Chile) enrolls over 50 % of the industrial workers of the country. Syndicates are being formed among the inquilinos. The mining companies are about 60 % unionized. Chilean trade unionism, which has largely taken shape since 1900, lacks the solidity of the Argentine movement. Three elements have shaped its development. First, a powerful minority of communists have fixed upon the CTCh their peculiar habits, a plethora of shouting, and a lack of solid planning. Second, the chief mining companies and some industrial plants have paid wages higher than those prevailing elsewhere, have furnished good housing, medical care, recreation facilities, and have thereby weakened the appeal of union organizers. Third, the government has cut the ground beneath the feet of the unions by some of the most aspiring social legislation in South America. There have been bitter struggles between workers and managers. The general strikes of Valparaiso and Santiago in 1903, of Iquique in 1907 (with a thousand killed in that last strike) will long be remembered.

Social Legislation

THE social legislation imposed by Arturo Alessandri in 1925 represents the most imaginative program of social security yet adopted by any Latin-American country. Other countries, notably Mexico and Brazil, have an abundance of laws, but in neither has enforcement been so effective as in Chile. Critics speak scornfully of the mass of creaking machinery required to administer these laws. They overlook the patent fact that the fault lies not so much with the laws as with the poverty of the nation. The best laws in the world can do little for a country in which industrial workers have an average yearly wage less than $200, and agricultural labor less than $100. There is an elaborate structure of *cajas* (social security funds of various types), into which go stipulated payments from the worker, the employer, and the state for the provision of health benefits, insurance against accidents, old-age pensions, savings funds for the building of homes. These annual contributions range from a total of 8.5 % for workers in industry, 11.5 % in mining, on up to 24.33 % for white-collar employees in certain industrial plants.

Chile makes a brave effort to improve the lot of her humblest workers, the domestic servants, always the most cavalierly exploited in every land. There are some 100,000 domestic workers in Chile, with wages ranging from $2 to $6 a month. We rented a house in Viña del Mar, Chile's fashionable seaside resort. With the house came Carmen, heavily Indian, who looked fifty but admitted thirty years. She had few teeth, could not read a single word or decipher a telephone number, but she could get up at six, work with cheerful tirelessness until ten or eleven at night. Her regular employer paid her $6 per month, but we suggested $8. We asked Carmen her habits on days off, half-days off, whatever the custom was, but she did not understand. It seemed her schedule called for one free evening each week—after dinner. Now, the average Chilean dinner is scheduled for nine or later, which leaves little time for Carmen—after dinner once a week. I was glad to discover that Alessandri had not forgotten domestic servants, that Carmen has a little book into which stamps are pasted each month representing 7 % of her wages and also of the estimated value of her room and meals. Carmen's stamps, bought by her employers, cost about $1.20 each month. The money goes into a caja, is there invested in mortgages and other securities, and stands as a backlog for her. If sick, she goes to a clinic or a sanatorium. There are payments for accidents, and pensions for old age. I remember those stamps for Carmen as eloquent symbols of Chile's good intentions.

Politics

THE casual observer of Latin-American politics easily goes astray. Nothing is ever as it seems—a truism in all politics. The charm of Chile's lies in their prodigious confusion. There is a party to every taste, and where one is lacking, it will be organized tomorrow. No Chilean need be caught in the quandary of the American voter, who must choose between Republicans or Democrats, or climb a tree with Norman Thomas. The Chilean takes his pick among a dozen parties, perhaps with little hope of electing a President, but with fair hope of sending a spokesman to the Senate or the Chamber of Deputies. Chile's system of proportional representation makes that possible.

Labels mean little in the lexicon of Chilean politics. While Conservadores are always conservative, Liberales are never liberal, Radicales are never radical, Democráticos and Democráticas are different creatures, and socialismo means anything from New Dealism to Moscowism and Nazism.

The roll call, as of November 1940, of the National Congress is revealing:

On the Right—

1. The Conservadores with 12 senators and 30 deputies. The party dominant most of the time since 1830, the pelucones, the people who believe in Church, land, family.

2. The Falangistas with 6 deputies. Sons of fine families who have stumbled upon new ideas and propose the redemption of the nation within the arms of religion and conservatism.

3. The Liberales with 10 senators and 35 deputies. The party of conservative professional and businessmen, of some landholders, believers in land, the best people, family, order, but not quite certain about the Church.

4. The Agrarios with 3 deputies. A party of mild dissent among landholders.

5. The Democráticas with 4 senators and 4 deputies. Another party of conservative dissenters.

In the Center—

6. The Radicales with 11 senators and 32 deputies. Party of the middle-class insurrection which began in the 1850's—business and professional people who found the wigged-ones a little stuffy, enlisted many enterprising newcomers from Europe. Represents the city's protest against the latifundia.

7. The Vanguardia Popular Socialista with 3 deputies. Formerly the National Socialists, popularly known as the Nacistas, with trimmings reminiscent of Germany, but with a mind of their own.

8. The Democráticos with 1 senator and 6 deputies. Dissenters with no other place to go and no distinctive program.

On the Left—

9. The Socialistas with 4 senators and 8 deputies. A party of long-standing and chronic dissent.

10. Trabajadores Socialistas with 5 deputies, who think the official Socialists too conservative.

11. The Socialistas Radicales with 5 deputies, a further split.

12. The Comunistas with 1 senator and 7 deputies.

The mysterious workings of Chilean politics may be gauged by scrutiny of the popular front government which came into power in the autumn of 1938. The election that year brought to a head the accumulated confusions of the stormy years since 1920. They had been years of national poverty, with more overturns of government than in all Chilean history, with more ex-Presidents in exile, with more mad shouting and stormy recrimination. Alessandri's second administration (1932–38) had been able, but the common man no longer viewed him as a friend. Democratic guarantees had been forgotten. As the 1938 election approached, two chief alliances appeared: on the Right, a conservative liberal alliance supported Gustavo Ross, a wealthy plunger who had made his money in Europe and as Alessandri's Finance Minister had done much to restore the national credit; on the Left, the Frente Popular united Radicales, various breeds of socialists, and communists in support of Aguirre Cerda. The campaign was bitter, competent prophets conceded victory to the Rightists. Then a wire snapped. September 5—seven weeks before election —a young man named Jorge González von Marées ordered his Nacistas (Vanguardia Popular Socialista) into action, a *coup d'état* to seize the government and place Carlos Ibáñez in the presidency. These well-drilled lads seized one government building while their leader directed operations by radio from the country. At this point, orders arrived from someone—Alessandri perhaps—the carabineros closed in upon the revolutionists, and shot them down. Sixty-one Nacistas were killed, one carabinero. Ibáñez and González von Marées were jailed. The public, until then clearly intent upon electing Ross, turned to Aguirre. From his cell González von Marées ordered the Nacistas to support the popular front. Election Day, October 25, 1938, Pedro Aguirre Cerda was elected President by the precarious margin of 2;111 votes out of a total of 443,525. His first official act was to pardon González von Marées.

The fortunes of the Chilean popular front seem precarious. The President, Pedro Aguirre Cerda, is a petulant man of generous intentions. He comes from the landowning class and is regarded as an apostate by all good conservatives. He has slight influence over Congress, and little has been done in legislation. His own followers in the popular front gradually desert him. Few of his lieutenants regard him with enthusiasm. The Front was an unnatural creation at best, with the paunchy middle-class radicals yoked to the noisy communists. The socialists seem clearest as to what they want, but they have few allies. Minister of Development Oscar Schnake, perhaps the ablest of the socialists, returned from a five months' stay in the United States in late 1940 and announced that he had seen a great light, that Chile must co-operate with the United States. He next headed a campaign de-signed to pitch the communists out of the Front, and then off the electoral rolls. The middle-class radicals leaped to the defense of their communist brothers-in-arms. The Front's unity seemed shattered by early 1941, despite some appearance of victory in the election of March.

The Chilean political Babel offers generous argument to those who despair of democratic institutions in Latin America. Fran-cisco Campos of Brazil, Sánchez Sorondo of Argentina, Oscar Benavides of Peru, Fulgencio Batista of Cuba, or Rafael Leonidas Trujillo of the Dominicans may prove democracy's failure from Chile's riotous politics. The obstinate democrat insists upon find-ing the Chilean scene enlivening and encouraging. There are parties, leaders, issues. There is free talk, sometimes to the point. Out of the mélange, a number of groups command bewildered attention:

The magnificent conservatives. I note the illimitable grace of Senator Miguel Cruchaga Tocornal, whether presiding over a Pan-American conference in Montevideo or addressing the Chil-ean Senate—a perfect symbol of the eternal verities. Or of Senator Maximiliano Errázuriz, whose very name is a seal of greatness, whose wealth in land and favor with the Church assure him place on earth and in heaven. When he rises to speak in the Senate chamber, lesser men crumble. Son of an ambassador to the Vatican, he has the imperturbability of the seasoned European diplomat.

The superb communists, just as authentic sons of Chilean soil as the conservatives themselves. Each has a tradition, a formula, and a Cross by which to live and die. The feudalism which formed a Cruchaga and an Errázuriz must in due season produce a Contreras Labarca. The witch hunters assure you that the com-munists receive aid from Moscow, perhaps from Berlin. Maybe,

maybe not. Communist *El Siglo* dutifully reports the "British-American Imperialist Plot" six times each week, but one suspects that their heart is not in it, that their concern is at home. Chilean communism (which cast 56,000 votes in March 1941) may be explained by reference to Moscow, but it can just as well be explained by the slums of Rancagua, the inquilinos of the central valley, the hunger of the rotos everywhere. Chilean distaste for her communists is explicable, but the naïve surprise at their appearance upon Chilean soil is difficult to comprehend.

The knightly Falangistas. These are a few thousand sons of first families who have broken with their conservative fathers, convinced that Chile must be purged. Devoutly Catholic, these men are faithful to the tradition which produced a Francis of Assisi. Chile cannot lightly disregard Eduardo Frei Montalva in his castigations of the Chilean aristocracy for their preoccupation with European culture, their complete indifference to the misery of Chileans. He tells his peers of the life of the slums, of the thousand homeless children in Iquique, a city of 30,000. He assails the rich for their luxury, while the poor have neither pleasure nor capacity for enjoyment, condemned to seek joy in cheap cinema, cantina, or brothel. "Our dominant class," he says, "is decadent, but it possesses great resources. An inexpert middle class, clamoring for money and position, strikes for power. The people, undermined by subversive propaganda, travel toward revolution."

The marching Nacistas. This company of young men bears watching. There are 15,000 members of the Vanguardia Popular Socialista, according to their leader, González von Marées. Finally responsible for the 1938 victory of the popular front, they remain the chief enigma. Excellent Chileans assure you that these are fanatics, quite insane and unimportant. Professional German hunters tell you darkly that here is the strong arm of Hitler in Chilean life, that these men are directed by Berlin. Perhaps, perhaps not. "Are you in any way related to, responsible to, or financed by the German Embassy?"—I put the question point-blank to González von Marées (who incidentally has a German

mother). "No, in no way whatsoever," was his reply. He is the
sort of man one inclines to believe, no matter how much one may
fear him. Straightforward, intense, clear-eyed, he is the kind who
upsets nations. He would cleanse Chile, fend off all foreign interference, especially from the United States. He seems in earnest
as he talks of Chile's ineffective politics, of the threat of alien imperialism. He would use his power to install a "strong" government. Is it a German or is it a purely Chilean movement? It may
be explained on either hypothesis.

Chile's political course is unpredictable. The elements of violence are clearly present—undisciplined conservatism, bitter misery, economic depression deepened by war.

Chile might revert to the strong-arm dictatorship familiar to
Latin America. An alliance of landlords, army, navy, and city
conservatives might install a strong man of their choice. If their
program promised social reforms, they might win support of
elements which despair of action by the weak-handed popular
front.

Or Chile might be torn by a Leftist revolution, after the Mexican fashion. Anger and hunger are there, but neither money nor
leaders. There are storm clouds, but nothing more at the present.

Or Chile might find leadership in a new popular front reaching a little further Right, taking in moderate conservatives, and
ridding itself of the communists. This seems a pious hope at best.

Or Chile may bungle along, with much talk, with party canceling out party, as they are now doing.

These questions will be answered as Chile moves with other
nations through the haze of war years.

I REMEMBER a great fundo in central Chile where my host, an
intelligent man of old family, received me with warming hospitality. He showed me his fruit trees and flowers, his excellent
grain fields, talked candidly about labor agitators and unrest and
wages, and then drove me down the long road lined with houses
of his inquilinos, houses neither better nor worse than those seen
elsewhere. We turned toward the racing stables, which filled

three sides of a generous rectangle. The buildings were solid, the walls well plastered and painted, the roofs heavy and in good repair—far better than the houses of the inquilinos. He ordered a groom to bring out some of his best horses, amazing creatures with lines of satin and steel, living spirits, evidence of what breeding and infinite pains can produce. "You take good care of them," I suggested. "Yes," he replied, "you have no idea how carefully they must be tended. They must be fed as carefully as babies. And they are."

AN Indian named Emiliano Zapata lived and worked on the hacienda of a certain rich man in the valley of Morelos in Mexico. Emiliano could not read, had no shoes, but knew horses. His master assigned him the care of the racing stables. One day Emiliano had a curious thought: these horses have better houses than my mother and sister, they have more careful treatment when sick, more consideration when old. Emiliano began to ride at night, telling these strange things to the peons in the valleys of Morelos and Guerrero, speaking of *tierra y libertad* to Indians who had neither liberty nor land.

CHAPTER IX

NORTHERN INVADERS

MODERN Chile is chiefly Spanish, with liberal Indian admixture. Her life has also been shaped by the infiltration of the blood of northern Europe. The influence of the English, German, Dutch, Irish, Swiss, and French settlers in Chile is greater than is suggested by the figures of a few thousands who settled there in colonial times, or of the few score thousands who have since made Chile their home. The northern Europeans married into Chilean families of Spanish extraction, and established powerful dynasties.

I sat one evening in the smoking room of a Chilean steamer.

Over our *pisco sours* we discussed family trees. One fine young chap bore a name unmistakably Dutch, his great-grandfather had come from Holland, and one grandmother had been French. His wife's maiden name was clearly English, inherited from a great-grandfather who came to Chile a hundred years ago. Their other forebears were chiefly Basque. The other table companion had a good Castilian name, but his last name (that of his mother) was as German as the Tiergarten. That pattern, familiar in the United States, is frequent in Chile.

The footprints of the British are everywhere. They came while Chile was still a colony, or during the first days of the republic. They invested in banks, established shops, shipping, and manufacturing firms. In 1930 the official estimate of British investment in Chile stood at 50 million pounds, but a much larger stake was held by Anglo-Chileans, Anglican only in name. In 1940 some 7,000 British citizens were living in Chile, but that figure took no account of the larger company with British blood.

Americans (or North Americans, if you prefer the Chilean term) have had little influence. The American investment in Chile is large in dollars, insignificant in men. Some 700 million American dollars have gone into copper, nitrates, public utilities, banking, and government bonds. Few Americans came with the dollars. There is a handful of American residents in Santiago and Valparaiso, almost none in the rest of the country. Out of that handful few have settled down. The Americans in Chile have been salesmen, promoters, organizers, technicians who planned to stay only six months, a year, three years. The American in Chile—in all Latin America—has the air of one about to leave. Ask anyone who knows Santiago how many Americans have bought homes and established themselves. He looks vague, suggests three or four names, stops. The Chilean does not know the American.

And the Germans

No lover of the Bavarian countryside can fail to be moved by southern Chile. There are the same mountains, the same winding

streams, the same farms, barns, houses, and kitchen gardens—
and the same people. There are those unmistakable German
houses with the air of a small boy whose cap has been pulled
down hard over his head; and there are the same German farmers one meets on roads around Eisenach. You are tempted to
pause and call out, *Grüss Gott.*

It is the American who is a stranger here, not the German. The
German came long ago, staked out his farm against the wall of
the forest, built church and school.

The first German on record, a certain Bartolomaus Blumen of
Nuremberg, helped Valdivia found Santiago in February 1541.
He had walked all the way from Peru. Blumen's name proved
difficult to his Spanish companions. "Blumen," said they, "what
does that mean?" *Flores* (flowers) was the answer, so he became
Bartolomé Flores. A notable man, the builder of the first grain
mill in Santiago, he married the daughter of an Indian cacique,
his sons married the daughters of great Spaniards. Proud Chilean
families trace their lineage to the Flores who was first a Blumen.

Germans have been coming to Chile ever since, some during
the seventeenth and eighteenth centuries, more in the first years
of independence, many more after the middle of the last century.
In 1822 the firm of Schutte was established in Valparaiso; in 1824
Johann Stuven of Hamburg set up business in the Chilean port;
in 1840 the first German farmer settled near Valdivia. From
then on the German migrants came in greater numbers. In 1845
nine German families with furniture and cattle established farms
near Valdivia; fifteen more families came in 1847, eighteen in
1848. Those were stormy years in Germany, free Germans sought
liberty in the new world, stout pioneers settled Wisconsin, and
many turned toward Chile. By 1854, 1,929 Germans had settled
in and around Valdivia.

The German settlers in south Chile undertook a task which
few Spaniards would essay. It was a bleak country, and the rain
fell with merciless monotony through long winters. The forest
was solid down to the banks of river and lake. Each inch of soil
had to be ripped from the jungle. The government and people of

Chile did not coöperate. No sooner had colonists cleared land, dragged out stumps, planted crops, than officials came to collect taxes, other officials to debate titles and threaten eviction. Chilean colonists arrived with specious claims seeking to oust the Germans. Under such pressure, the Germans organized for defense. "We will be Chileans," wrote one of their first spokesmen, Karl Anwandter, "as honorable and hardworking as the best. United with the ranks of our new compatriots, we will defend our adopted country against all foreign aggression with the decision and the firmness of the man who defends his native land, his family, and his own interests." The Germans won, and new arrivals filled up the lands around Valdivia, established Puerto Montt, Puerto Varas, Osorno, and the towns around Lake Llanquihue. Other Germans established banks, trading firms, lumber companies. The Gildermeisters invested in mining and a dozen other ventures, as their kin of the same name did in Peru. There are solid German businesses throughout Chile, many of them eighty or ninety years old.

Today there are in Chile some 20,000 Germans, non-Jewish and born in Germany. In addition, there are about 40,000 German-Chileans, born in Chile of one or two German parents. There are about 9,000 German refugees, mostly Jews.[1]

An American sojourner in Chile is torn between respect for the visible German contribution to the life of Chile and premonitions as to their future role. He understands the Chilean's praise for the German migrants. They have built finely and Chile has benefited from them as.has the United States. Go to Valparaiso, the chief port, and walk its streets. Many stores, two banks, strong trading houses bear German names. The best hospital is German. The finest residential section, with spotless houses and watered gardens, is chiefly German. Go to Santiago, examine lists of chief firms in any line of business, walk ten miles through residential streets—there are German names everywhere. Visit

1. There are no official figures. Alarmists, hunting for the fifth column, assure you that there are 300,000 or 400,000 Germans. The figures given here represent the careful estimates of Chilean and foreign agencies concerned with this question.

smaller towns, and see more German names on shops, banks, warehouses.

Southern Chile remains the German stronghold. Go to Valdivia, a city of 35,000 founded in 1552, on the banks of the River Cruces eleven miles from the sea. The country about is laid out in farms of a few hundred acres each, as farms should be—they arouse nostalgia for Saxony or Wisconsin. My cynical train companion remarked, "You can tell a German farmhouse anytime, it is painted." In Valdivia you choose between hotels named Schuster, Pelz, Haussmann, and Schild. You take a German-owned launch for the run down the river to Corral on the sea, the site of the Chilean steel mills, and find a German resort with the *gemütlichkeit* of Munich. You search out the friend-of-a-friend who knows all about the business of Valdivia, and he gives you an itemized list of the seventy-five families who own over 90 % of the chief businesses, of the best land and lumber. You jot down a few names at random: Buschmann von Dessauer, Bentgardt, Klempner, Bittner, Ehrenfeld, Haverbeck, Oelckers; you note their credit standing: $200,000, $320,000, $150,000, $88,000, $500,000. These are the exceptions—most Germans do not boast such rating. There are German clubs—the Deutscher Verein for the portly prosperous, the Club Unión for the less fortunate, the Club de Regatas and the Club Atlético for young men. You engage a talkative taxi driver and cruise the streets, and he tells you the names of the men who own the houses on the best street—almost every name is German. You know the Teutonic lineage of those houses without asking, their architecture is German, 1850—tops do not match bottoms, they bulge strangely, and are painted with clashing ingenuity. "How do you like the Germans?" you ask your chauffeur. "We don't like them," he says. No satisfying reasons are forthcoming. One concludes that envy is not unknown in Valdivia.

It is a trip of some six hours by train from Valdivia to Puerto Montt, passing through La Unión, Osorno, and Puerto Varas, and it is Germany all the way—the farms, the little villages, the people who get on and off trains. Across the aisle was the perfect

German grandmother, of that species which is Germany's chief claim to immortality. Presently we were talking with her, with her German daughter and Chilean son-in-law, with three bouncing German-Chilean granddaughters. Grandmother, it seemed, was born near Valdivia, her parents came from Germany in 1855, she had never been to Germany. I talked to her about Weimar, Dresden, and other spots I know and love, and her eyes shone. She kept falling back into German, which she preferred to Spanish. I carefully avoided the question of the war. Suddenly she asked, "When will North America make war on Hitler?" "Soon," I said. *"Hoffentlich!"* she replied. Then I asked her whether many German-Chileans felt as she did. Yes, some of the older people, not many of the young. Then she told me what I heard so many times in Mexico, Argentina, Peru, Brazil, Colombia—that the young Germans, even though they had never seen the Fatherland, were proud of German victories, coveted a share in German triumph. She tried to tell me the reason for this, she seemed to say that German-Chileans have lost faith in the capacity of the Chilean people to set their house in order, that they saw no hope unless some stronger power lends a hand—but she did not quite say that, for her Chilean son-in-law was sitting with us.

The Germans who picked southern Chile for their homes showed good taste. We had listened skeptically to Chilean friends who described southern Chile as the equal of Switzerland, but we capitulated when the train swung around the side of Lake Llanquihue and into full view of snow-capped Osorno. Here is perfect matching of tree and lake and field and mountain. We left the train, took a car, and rattled over miles of country roads, by fields of potatoes, pastures with heavy Holsteins, trim fences, silos, water tanks, barns, solid dreadful houses, and fussy flower gardens—all unmistakably German. We stopped in the village of Frutillar, in front of the Deutscher Verein, lingered for a few questions. We remembered that town for one Huncke who makes the best jam to be bought in Santiago. We learned that when a new *alcalde*, a Chilean, had recently been elected to office, he discovered that the town's records were in German script, and the new mayor could not discover which dogs had licenses, whose taxes were paid, and when the town's citizens had been born, married, and died.

VALDIVIA (Continuación)

K

Kähler Carlos, casa, Isla Teja	1140
Kähler Carlos 2.o, Chacabuco 802	1136
Kühni Adolfo, casa, Yungay 735	597
» » Oficina Av. Prat 662	904
Kindermann Carlos, casa, General Lagos 1759	1112
Kirch Hellmut, casa, Picarte 1298	1045
Klaasen Teodoro, General Lagos 1608	1091
Klempau Ida B. vda. de, Perez Rosales 787	394
Klempau Juan, Comisionista, Camilo Henríquez 601............	725
» » Particular, Callejón Guarda 295	725
Klempau Ricardo Suc., casa, Picarte 688	1068
Kleinknecht Erwin, Cigarrería «Embajadores», Libertad 199	948
Klett Carlos, Jardinería Canelos, Bueras 169	1007
Knopel G. A., Fundo Ponollanca, ...	R35
Koch e Hijos Suc. Enrique, Fábrica de Jabón, Collico ....-......	837
Koch Max, Fábrica de Jabón, Sta. María 1229	436
Koller Walter, Calzado, Plaza esquina Perez Rosales	834
König Berta A. vda. de, casa, Simpson 398	1005
König Reinaldo, casa, Simpson 550 ...	320
Kunstmann Eduardo, casa, Collico	374
Kunstmann Hermanos y Cía., Oficina Molino Collico	293
y Cía., Oficina Molino Collico	393

FRUTILLAR (Continuación)

Schmidt Ernesto, Punta Larga	39
Siebald Adolfo, Punta Larga...	41
Strauch Pedro, Playa Maqui	8
Sunkel Guillermo	34
Sunkel Federico...	58
Stemfle Humberto, Cura Párroco ...	60

W

Weil Elisa v. de...	56
Weil Ernesto, Herrería...	46
Weil Germán, Paraguay...	47
Wetzel Adolfo, Punta Larga...	42
Wetzel Suc. Federico, Punta Larga...	33
Wetzel Reinaldo, Punta Larga... ...	43
Winkler Armino...	25
Winkler Edmundo	32
Winkler Erna L. v. de, Zapatoría y Curtiembre	14
Winkler Suc. Reinaldo, Barraca Madera	23
Winkler Otton...	15
Wittwer Suc. Leopoldo	35

PUERTO VARAS (Continuación)

H

Heim Carlos, Empresa de Vapores, Bodega...	56
Hitschfeld Ricardo, Dentista, San José 112	105
Hofmann Suc. Celestino, Pto. Chico ...	20
Hofmann Suc. Edmundo, particular, San Pedro 345	54
Horn Suc. Antonio, Imprenta y Librería, San Francisco...	19

Excerpts from the Telephone Directory of Southern Chile

The town of Puerto Varas is by the side of Lake Llanquihue, and is the stopping point on the way to Argentina. Most of the hotels, the warehouses, the stores, bear German names. The steamers and bus lines linking the town with the Argentine border are all German. We arrived early, listened to German banter, saw a UFA newsreel and a German feature picture. I went into a cigar store, was sold my cigar for "ein-und-zwanzig."

I hunted out a telephone book: 161 telephones were listed—12 were of federal and municipal offices, 15 were of clearly Spanish names, 5 were of doubtful lineage, 129 were indisputably German. That same telephone book tells the story of other cities in southern Chile. Here is the exhibit:

Town	Population 1930	Telephones Total	German names	Per cent of German names
Osorno	16,229	538	259	48.0 %
Valdivia	34,296	578	253	48.8 %
Temuco	35,748	952	168	17.5 %
Traiguen	8,240	68	20	29.4 %
La Unión	4,500	104	33	31.7 %

But where do German-Chileans stand? Telephone directories yield no clues as to what people think about the binomial theorem or the mission of Adolf Hitler. The composite guess at which I arrive is based upon the calculations and hunches of various Chileans, Americans, and Germans. Here it is: First, the great majority of the 20,000 German-born "Aryan" Germans are loyal to Hitler. Second, the refugees are almost altogether against Hitler, reports of spies among them are greatly overdrawn. Third, of the approximately 40,000 German-Chileans born in Chile, a substantial number have intermarried with Chileans; the total group aggregates about 1 % of the total population; about 80 % of them live in south Chile; they hold about 5 % of the total national wealth—and no one has the slightest idea of where they stand in the present world situation.[2]

Guesses, hunches, surmises can be carried further. My clear impression of south Chile is of a lot of simple, hard-working devout Germans who have won their homes by endless patience and labor. My guess is that most of them ask only to be left alone. It may also be noted that German-Chileans have never worked as a unit in national politics. There were prominent Germans on both

2. This summary is based on studies made by a group of competent students, intent upon discovering the extent of German infiltration in Chile. I am not at liberty to identify the source.

sides in the civil war of 1891. There are Germans in every political party, with the exception of the conservatives and the communists. If the Vanguardia of González von Marées is a German
creation as some aver, there is little evidence of popular German
support. Furthermore, the possession of a German name means
nothing. My friend, Congressman Manuel Eduardo Hübner,
may wear an umlaut, but cannot manage three words of German, and is an outspoken foe of Nazi and fascist tactics. Minister
Oscar Schnake has a German father, but he is pro-British, and
pro-American. The National Congress has one senator with a
German name, Carlos Haverbeck of Valdivia, generally regarded as pro-German in sympathy. There are eight congressmen with German names, four of them had Chilean mothers.

What, then, are Hitler-Germans up to?

The German Embassy in Santiago is clearly carrying on the
same sort of campaign already described for Brazil and Argentina. The Santiago Embassy staff numbered about forty persons
in January 1941, as compared with seventeen in the American
Embassy. Toll is levied on German individuals and firms (numerous German distributors of American-made farm machinery
and other wares contribute). Cultural attachés direct the activities of the German clubs which flourish in every community
where German-Chileans live. There are German schools, but
few compared with Brazil and Argentina. German churches are
Nazi centers, although some dissenters raise their voices. (A
community of German monks in the village of Las Casas pub-
lishes a weekly paper critical of Adolf Hitler.) Tons of printed
propaganda cover the country. A German evening paper is
printed each weekday in Santiago. There is some talk but no
proof of German subventions to two or three Chilean newspapers. The German Embassy spends some $120,000 each month
on propaganda—that is the opinion of some Chilean officials.
Tal vez, perhaps, say Chileans.

The average intelligent Chilean entertains slight fear of German interference in Chile. One of these expressed the view which

seemed general in early 1941: "We admire the Germans. They
have set an admirable example of industry and thrift. They have
done work which a Chilean despises. When they farm, they get
up early and work late. They plow every available hectare. They
fertilize correctly, they study soils and seeds, they breed their
animals scientifically. In business they deal fairly. In other words,
the Germans in Chile are like your Germans in the United States.
Why should we get jittery about them because it happens to serve
the mood of American journalists?"

I found others who confessed Chile's failure in assimilating
her German population. These spoke of Chilean clannishness.
The Germans have kept apart because Chile set them apart.

Germans have won a greater respect in Chile than in any other
Latin-American republic. They have made a solid cultural contribution. The schools owe much to German teachers. Second
only to the British, the Germans have influenced the intellectual
life of the country. There is an active German-Chilean Cultural
Institute, of which Senator Cruchaga Tocornal is president.
Señor Cruchaga was long Chilean ambassador to Berlin.

The German trade drive has been persistent. Here, as elsewhere, the German drummer has been resourceful—studying
the market, cutting the goods to fit the market. A thoughtful
young Chilean, quite free of Nazi sympathies, explained German success in marketing: "I have a farm, and I wanted to buy
pumping equipment for my irrigation works. I went to the agent
of the chief American electrical manufacturers. He could give
me no figures, nor draw up specifications. He wrote his home
office, and in two or three weeks, I got his price, a high one, made
without personal inspection of my property. I went to the German firm. The next day a technician visited my farm, spent two
days surveying and measuring. He drew up a precise blueprint,
submitted an estimate of the machinery required, and the cost
was about 30 % under the American bid. He got the contract.
When the machinery was installed, that technician made repeated visits to check up on the work. That explains why we like

to deal with the Germans." That is but one instance. It may prove too much. It tallies with similar stories heard in other South American countries.

The German cultivation of the Chilean market during the Hitler years has assumed the pattern familiar throughout Latin America—barter deals, blocked marks, and infinite patience. German sales to Chile climbed steadily, supplanting Great Britain as second seller in that market, and in 1936 taking first place from the United States. The chief loser was Great Britain. The United States maintained her lead, except in 1936. The figures on Chilean trade testify to the success of the German drive:

Chilean Exports

The percentage sold to key countries

	1929	1932	1936	1938	1940*
United States	25.4	26.4	19.4	15.7	56.0
United Kingdom	13.4	31.5	16.4	21.8	6.5
Germany	8.6	13.8	9.7	10.0	.0
Italy	1.8	4.2	4.4	4.0	0.6
Japan	0.5	0.1	1.5	1.6	2.3

Chilean Imports

The percentage bought from key countries

	1929	1932	1936	1938	1940*
United States	32.2	23.1	25.4	27.8	47.0
United Kingdom	17.7	12.9	13.1	10.2	9.0
Germany	15.4	14.7	28.7	25.8	2.9
Italy	3.2	3.4	1.6	2.7	5.5
Japan	.8	.6	2.9	2.5	5.9

* Estimated.

German salesmen are as active in war days as in times of peace, and spread the word that Germany will shortly control Europe and the lanes of trade, that it will pay all Chilean merchants to deal with the new masters of Europe.

CHAPTER **X**

CHILE AND HER WORLD

THE way of the little nation is henceforth precarious—even though that nation be set where the world ends. Twenty-six hundred miles of exposed sea coast; masses of copper, iron, manganese, nitrates; a hungry proletariat; a people divided by bitter schisms; a disrupted and ill-balanced economy—those are the danger signals for Chile in a world of new imperial ambitions, with old empires threatened with dissolution. Chile is uneasily aware that she must reckon with her next neighbors, with Europe, perhaps with Asia, with the United States.

The Next Neighbors

THESE neighbors are Peru, Bolivia, Argentina. Peru and Bolivia offer no serious threat. The nitrate quarrel is long since quieted, the declining importance of nitrates makes debate unlikely. Peru and Bolivia are weak in man power and military equipment.

Argentina and Chile have long differences, boundary lines in the south are sporadically debated, but the lands involved are of such slight importance as to make serious contest unlikely. The Christ of the Andes stands as a pious symbol of amity between the two lands, but biting distrust remains. Argentina's economic and military power overshadows Chile's. Chile did not sweeten relations with her neighbor by the announcement of November 1940 that her territorial rights included a pie-slice segment of the Antarctic, embracing not only the area below her own borders but that which lies south of Argentina. Many Chileans, including the editor of *Topaze,* received the announcement with hilarity, describing it as comic relief in a cock-eyed world. The Argentines, to the credit of Minister Julio Roca, received the manifesto with discreet solemnity and replied in effect: Yes, this is a serious matter which must be debated endlessly. So will it be.

Meanwhile, candid Chileans are not certain that Argentina is devoid of imperial dreams which include Bolivia and access to the Pacific. This disquieting thought is mentioned when bush-league statesmen get together around Santiago tables.

Europe, Perhaps Asia

CHILEANS seem singularly oblivious to the threats from overseas. A few are aware that Germany and Japan might seek to involve them if the United States goes to war. A few conjecture as to the future of their national economy should Germany win. Chile, they seem to say, is far off the highways of the seas, and we can defend our interests.

The United States, Certainly

MANY Chileans reject the implication that their nation must take account of the United States, arguing that Chile bears no different relation to Washington than she does to Berlin, London, Tokyo. These describe the Monroe Doctrine as American impudence which reasons from accidents of geography rather than world realities. Such arguments are heard from the spokesmen of the irreconcilable Right as well as from the redoubtable Left. Other Chileans, chiefly socialists and middle-class realists, freely admit that Chile will do well to travel with the United States.

Chileans are aware that the United States has more than passive interest in the continuing independence of all Latin America—and of Chile—from domination by Germany or any other power. Some call this imperialism, others good neighborliness.

Chileans are aware that they are in the position to exact a good price for coöperation with Washington. The temptation will be strong to attempt to play the United States for a sucker—random conversations in Chile suggest that such projects are in the minds of some political leaders in Santiago. The confusion of Chilean politics makes these efforts inevitable.

Some Chileans are persuaded that the United States will go far in an honest program of mutual defense free of imperial ambition. There is still room for much persuasion of the leaders of Chile.

The United States has given tangible evidence of its willingness to coöperate. In June 1940 the Export-Import Bank extended a credit of $12,000,000 to be used for buying American industrial and agricultural equipment. This fund is handled by the nonpolitical Corporación de Fomento de Producción. One of its first acts was to import $1,800,000 worth of American tractors and other farm machinery, financing their distribution to farmers through regular trade channels on easy terms. Plans are drawn for a hydroelectric project after the pattern of the TVA. Another venture was the importation of Holstein-Friesian cattle, sold to farmers on long-term instalments.

A second loan was less happy. Oscar Schnake returned from the United States in late 1940 with the promise of a $5,000,000 loan. He and his fellow socialists made political capital out of this. When it was revealed that the money was designed to release frozen credits of American firms, the opposition let out hilarious guffaws. The Nazi and communist press shouted loudly about American imperialism, and the Chilean Ministry of Finance cabled Washington that the loan was not acceptable. Better terms were later offered and the loan was made.

There seems no good reason why Chileans and Americans should not come to firm understanding. We have much in common: a considerable democratic zeal and a pioneer tradition. The mill-run Chilean and his American kin are much the same sort of man—frank, hard-hitting, close-figuring, not obsessed by precedent. Take a delegation from the Akron Chamber of Commerce and set them down in Santiago with the men who manage industry and commerce—they will understand each other. They match each other in healthy realism and saving skepticism.

It is high time that we come to such firm understanding. Chile needs the United States. She is highly vulnerable, economically and militarily. Little of her coast line could be defended by any army and navy she can muster. Her economy will be disorganized if sea lanes are blocked. Furthermore, the United States needs Chile. The control of the Straits of Magellan would become of high importance should Panama be blocked. Chile's problem is the defense of her economy during the years of war, the defense of her territory should others intrude. Her natural ally is the United States. An increasing number of Chileans are aware that the United States is the one adequate ally which can be trusted.

Vale

I WRITE of Chile as the ship sets sail from Valparaiso for the journey north. Each people which permits the wanderer to tarry for a time within its borders, which shares with that wanderer so frankly and so generously as do the Chileans, lays upon him a burden of debt. I, such a wanderer, jot down my blurred acknowledgments. I shall remember the Chile

of the ill-dressed poet who writes passionate blank verse of the misery of the inquilino,

of the ancient aristocrat who mourns decline of piety and respect, and wonders why the poor will not be patient,

of thin-lipped González von Marées who will redeem his land by fire and blood,

of a Jesuit whose heart is sore over the blindness of the rich,

of an inquilino family which gave us cold water and received us as friends,

of a German-Chilean grandmother who waits the end of Hitler,

of Frei Montalva in his pleas to the powerful for a purging of Chilean life,

of Salvador Allende who will not rest until the children have milk,

of dull crowds who would be merry but have never learned,

of Irma Salas and many another teacher with some of the best schools in America,

of Graciela Mandujano whose work for the peasants reminds me of Jane Addams in the slums of Chicago,

of the German farmers around Lake Llanquihue, torn in their loyalties,

of our servant Carmen who was old at thirty,

of as gracious, high-born men and women as one meets in any
land,
of leaden-eyed poor.

THERE are storms ahead for Chile. The world's imperial race
may catch her in its path. Chile's perils are not chiefly without but
within. Chile's inner tumult invites outer attack. Chile denounces
the furious men who cry alarm, unaware that her sickness lies in
the social ills against which those men inveigh. The dangerous
Chilean is not the communist Labarca but the conservative die-
hard who knows the music of the poets but cannot hear the beat
of drums. The communist of Chile may destroy. It is still within
the power of the conservative to rebuild. The wanderer, leaving
Chile with reluctance and deep affection, hazards the guess that
there is not much time.

PART FOUR
SEVENTEEN OTHER COUNTRIES

CHAPTER I

URUGUAY

URUGUAY, smallest of South American states, offers little to the casual tourist, much to the student of government. The first and perhaps the only tourist to be impressed by Uruguay's scenery was Juan Díaz de Solís, who landed there in 1512 and exclaimed "I see a mountain," thereby giving Montevideo its name. Uruguay's excitements are in her governmental experimentation, the stoutness of her democracy, her firm stand against alien intrigue, the intelligence of her citizenry.

Called "La Banda Oriental" (the eastern bank) because of her position on the Río de la Plata, Uruguay is a little larger than the State of Washington (72,153 square miles), has a coast line of 700 miles on the Atlantic and the La Plata, and lies between Brazil and Argentina. Her eastern and southern plains resemble the Argentine pampas, her northern hills look like Connecticut's. The rainfall is dependable, the climate equable, and her generous sea beaches are the favorite summer resort of Argentines and Brazilians.

There are 2,000,000 Uruguayans (2,093,000 was the official estimate in 1937). More than nine out of ten are of European blood —chiefly Spanish, perhaps one-third Italian, with some 16,000 Germans, a considerable number of Portuguese-Brazilians, and a scattering from other countries. Less than one tenth are mestizos, Negroes, Indians. The pattern is much the same as Argentina's. And Uruguayans are like Argentines—a vigorous, dynamic people. One third of them live in Montevideo.

Uruguay lives from her pastures. There are four cattle and nine sheep to each man, woman, and child. Three fourths of the land is used for grazing, more than four fifths (83.9 % in 1938) of her export income comes from animal products. *Frigoríficos* (packing houses) built with British, American, and Uruguayan capital daily handle 4,000 cattle and 7,000 sheep, and the meat

and byproducts are shipped to Europe and the United States.
Only 6 % of the land surface is in crops—wheat, corn, flaxseed,
oats, barley—but Uruguay largely feeds herself, importing tropical products and potatoes, selling a little grain to other nations.

Uruguay, like Argentina, is short on minerals. She has to import her metals, most of her fuels. There is some coal, not yet exploited, but no evidence of petroleum. Hydroelectric development is promising.

Factories are on the increase—almost one fifth of her workers
are in frigoríficos, tire factories, textile mills, furniture shops, machine industries.

Uruguay, thirteenth in population among the twenty Latin-
American nations, is seventh in the volume of her exports. In
1938 the value of her exports was $55,000,000, of her imports
$43,000,000—and she has enjoyed similar favorable balances for
many years, disturbed only by the postwar depression and present-day disruption of trade with Europe. Her exchange regulations and import quotas resemble Argentina's. Her best market
has been Great Britain, to whom she is tied by a long record of
mutually profitable exchange. In 1938 Great Britain bought
26.2 % of her exports, compared with 23 % in 1929. Germany
has usually held second place, taking 23.5 % of her exports in
1938, a large gain over the 14.5 % taken in 1929. The United
States has been a poor customer, taking but 4 % of her exports in
1938, as against 11.9 % in 1929. Uruguay's imports showed the
same trends in 1938: 20.3 % from Great Britain, 16.4 % from
Germany, 11.8 % from the United States. United States trade
with Uruguay is subject to the same handicaps which apply to
Argentina—identity of products and the American quarantine
against fresh meat.

The Politics of a Buffer State

THE flippant description of Uruguay as an "Argentine colony in
Brazilian territory" accurately reflects Brazilian conviction, Argentine ambition, and Uruguayan irritation. She is a buffer state,
created and shaped out of the rivalries of her dominant neighbors.

In 1810, when Buenos Aires broke with Spain, La Banda Oriental was part of the viceroyalty of La Plata, but her 70,000 settlers took no steps against Spain. In 1811 the Uruguayan gaucho, José Gervasio Artigas, began guerrilla attacks upon Spanish garrisons, sought to unite the region of the east bank to the emerging Argentine nation, but abandoned the effort when the Argentines refused the autonomy he asked. For the next seventeen years Uruguay struggled to maintain her independence against the successive attacks of Brazil and Argentina, and in 1828 an Argentine-Brazilian war resulted in the creation of Uruguay as an independent buffer state.

Uruguayan independence, dating from 1828, did not bring tranquillity. For seventy-five years La Banda Oriental reveled in disorder. Two parties soon emerged, and have battled down to the present—Blancos (whites), party of order and religion; Colorados (reds), party of liberalism and anticlericalism. Personalismo rather than principle determined their clashes—the party of order proved consistently disorderly, the party of liberalism was seldom liberal. There are hundreds of yards of yellowing volumes in the Biblioteca Nacional in Montevideo which recite the rival claims of the two parties. The onlooker, scanning this record, wonders what the shouting is about.

Order finally came at the hands of the Colorado leader, José Batlle y Ordóñez, President 1903–07 and 1911–15, dominant in national life from 1903 until his death in 1929. Wise, moderate, and devoutly democratic, Batlle recast the patterns of the state, and his reforms were written into the Constitution of 1917. Liberal but never doctrinaire, he launched projects in state socialism: autonomous state trusts to own and operate packing plants, docks, chemical works, petroleum, banks, insurance, hotels, resorts. The government went into business, competing with but not ending private enterprise. Fuel, alcohol, and cement were made state monopolies. Sensitive to social wrongs, he secured a great variety of legislation protecting the poor, including a program of public works as insurance against unemployment. Batlle, long-time observer of the evils of personal government,

stripped the presidency of its powers; divided executive responsibility between the President and an Administrative Council of
nine; safeguarded the rights of minorities by instituting proportional representation and by granting the chief minority party
one half of Senate seats, one third of Cabinet posts. He lessened
the powers of the Church and pushed secular education with
vigor.

Batlle's success was almost matched by his successor—Baltasar
Brum, President 1919–23. Uruguay was everywhere cited in
proof that a socially intelligent state can be peaceable and prosperous. She might have so continued had not world events inter-
rupted the even flow of Uruguayan beef and mutton.

By 1931, when Gabriel Terra came to the presidency, the country was caught in the world depression. All over South America
constitutional governments were collapsing. Uruguay's imposing structure of state enterprise, with its considerable company of
officials, proved inelastic in days of lessened world demand and
falling prices. Batlle's heritage of divided executive power proved
embarrassing—the Council was at loggerheads with the President. In the emergency Terra assumed dictatorial powers and
ruled in the fashion of Uriburu in Argentina and of Vargas in
Brazil—replacing Council and Congress by a subservient Junta
and Assembly; clamping censorship on the press, suppressing
free speech and political opposition. But Terra could not, probably did not wish to, scrap Batlle's work, and his administration
from 1934–38 evidenced desire to return to democratic institutions. Political activity increased, and the press regained much of
its lost liberty. His Constitution of 1934 is a liberal charter: the
historic powers are restored to the President; the minority party
still has one third of the Cabinet, one half the Senate; suffrage is
universal (including women) and compulsory (the voter must
vote); social legislation covers old-age pensions, child welfare,
state care of mothers, free medical service for the poor, workers'
housing, a minimum wage, the eight-hour day; unions and the
right to collective bargaining are recognized.

In 1938 Terra placed Alfredo Baldomir in the presidency by an election of doubtful legality. The new President, in office until 1942, has shown moderation and increasing faithfulness to democratic principles. His task is complicated by dissidents within his own party, the Colorados, and by the venomous opposition of the Blancos, led by die-hard Luis Alberto Herrera.

Uruguay—Germany, Britain, and the United States

WHERE does Uruguay stand in the present world struggle? The answer is clear, she stands with England. The loyalty has firm roots, the British supported her in 1828, protected her against both Brazilian and Argentine claims, assured her independence. Like Argentina, Uruguay enjoys British investment in packing houses and railroads. Like Argentina, she looks to Britain as her best customer. Going even further than Argentina, she openly sided with Britain during the first World War, and is now expressing her complete sympathy with Britain and distaste for the Axis.

Uruguay is troubled by her 16,000 Germans, too many of whom seem to love Hitler more, Uruguay less. When war broke in 1939, the government of Baldomir, which included Nazi sympathizers in its Cabinet, minimized the danger, and the Herreristas made no bones of their sympathy with the Axis. Some stalwart democrats refused to be quieted; among these young Professor Hugo Fernández Artucio deserves applause. They dug out the facts, pressed the government for action. In May 1940 a document was unearthed which was a military plan to seize Uruguay, to eliminate troublesome citizens, to make the nation an agricultural colony of the Reich. The congressional investigation which followed proved that there was a Nazi party in Uruguay, with branches and agents all over the country; that it collected toll by persuasion and coercion. In June twelve suspects were gathered in, detained a few days, released. The German minister, Otto Langmann, announced the dispersal of the Nazi party and served notice on Foreign Minister Guani that any action against the twelve German-Uruguayans would mean severance of diplomatic relations. The government seemed about to

dismiss the matter, but the Germans forced the issue by persuading the editor of *Fragua,* a pro-Nazi newspaper, to bring a libel
suit against Fernández Artucio for charges made in his book
Nazis en el Uruguay. This stirred widespread public protest.
What does the government mean, it was demanded, by permitting persecution of a patriotic citizen who had exposed traitors?
By September the argument was boiling in the Chamber of
Deputies. Vigorous Pedro Manini Ríos, who had replaced an alleged pro-Nazi as Minister of the Interior, called for prompt
prosecution of the Hitler agents. Under such prodding, the government arrested, tried, and deported eight of the accused men.
Chief among them was Arnulf Fuhrmann, confessed author of
the document outlining the plan for Uruguayan annexation—a
joke, he called it.

Uruguay's obvious weakness makes remarkable her temerity
in braving German anger. She has an exposed coast line, almost
no navy, only 8,000 enlisted men. The performance is explained
by the strong pro-English and prodemocratic sentiments of the
rank and file, the vigor of a few able leaders, and by the tacit (perhaps definite) assurance of United States support. The "good-
will" visit of U. S. cruisers *Wichita* and *Quincy* in June 1940
made Washington's intentions clear.

The question of air and naval bases loomed large in the last
months of 1940, the first months of 1941. The United States
wanted bases, asked for definite leases from Uruguay (so I am
informed by responsible men close to the Baldomir government). Such formal leases would have meant political suicide for
Baldomir, whose own party was split, and who had to deal with
Herrera's Blancos. The President, abetted by his Foreign Minister and Minister of the Interior, took a firm stand for Pan-American bases on Uruguayan soil, made it clear that no obstruction
would be permitted. By January 1941 the issue was settled—
Uruguay would build air and naval bases and put them at the
disposal of American states engaged in defense of the hemisphere. The pledges made by Uruguay and the United States
were not revealed, but Export-Import Bank loans of $7,500,000

during November and December needed no explanation—the United States would back Uruguay to the limit. Comic relief came in December with a visit from some profascist Argentines, led by General Juan B. Molina, to congratulate Luis Alberto Herréra upon his defense of Uruguay's sovereignty. The visit set off a train of anti-Nazi explosions in Montevideo and Buenos Aires. Overseas, *Arriba,* Madrid organ of the Falange, was daily mourning Uruguayan faithlessness and saying that Franklin Roosevelt had become the *"verdadero emperador de la América del Sur, de la América Española"* (the actual emperor of South America, of Spanish America). Observation of the Falange in Spain, and of its conspicuous spokesmen in Uruguay, suggests the peril to American democratic forces from the unteachable clerical partisans of Francisco Franco.

Uruguay furnishes a good case for the usefulness of small nations. Those who have applauded her in other days, then deplored her lapses from constitutional ways, now take heart from her robust stand against interference, her steady increase in democratic practice.

CHAPTER II

PARAGUAY AND BOLIVIA

Paraguay

HERE are partners in misadventure—both isolated in the heart of a continent; both wasted by war; both victims of a century of misrule; both housing illiterate and hungry people.

Paraguay's 175,000 square miles (larger than California) are circumscribed by Brazil, Bolivia, and Argentina. Her capital, Asunción, is 935 miles from Buenos Aires, a steamer journey of two-and-one-half days up the Paraná and Paraguay rivers. Eastern Paraguay's broad low plateaus hold heavy forests, rich soil, and the bulk of her population. Western Paraguay, over against Bolivia, is the region of the Gran Chaco, with grassy plains, thick jungle, many rivers. One fifth of Paraguay's million people live in the four chief cities, 105,000 in Asunción alone. These people are the descendants of Spanish settlers, liberally mixed with the Guaranís whom they supplanted. Many Indians survive, the Guaraní language is still heard. The Paraguayans are a driven, hungry people, who seem but tenants in a land held by outsiders, with millions of acres owned by Argentines and the chief businesses handled by Italians and Germans. Of those with European blood, perhaps 17,000 are Germans, 10,000 Poles, 7,000 Italians.

Paraguay sells little to the world. Her exports for 1938 were valued at $8,251,000—about 85 % meat products, cotton, and quebracho. By that year, the United States and Great Britain had lost their lead in this little market. Her chief buyer was Germany (taking 14.2 % of her exports), and her chief supplier was Japan (furnishing 14.9 % of her imports).

Paraguay's independent history is an amalgam of tragedy and bitter comedy. In 1811 the people of Asunción refused alliance with Buenos Aires and set up their independent nation. The next fifty years were dominated by three bizarre tyrants. The first, José Rodríguez de Francia (1813–40), *El Supremo* by his own designation, was austere, honest, and able. His cruelty, torture, and murder can be explained only by sadism. When he rode through the streets of Asunción, the people hid in terror. He declared himself head of the Church. Seeking to isolate Paraguay, he closed the post offices, maintained almost no diplomatic relations with other nations, seldom permitted anyone to enter or leave the country, and stopped all foreign trade. Francia stands as the first logical and thorough dictator of Latin America. The second, Carlos Antonio López (1841–62), was more moderate but no less capricious. He opened the country to trade, built the most formidable army in South America, picked quarrels with Argentina and Brazil. The third, Francisco Solano López (1862–70), inheriting his father's army and foreign quarrels, possessed a Napoleonic ambition and a famous mistress, Mme. Lynch. The combination was irresistible: he must prove how good a man he was. In 1864 he seized a Brazilian battleship, and by 1865 had Brazil, Argentina, and Uruguay united against him. In the next five years boys of twelve and men of seventy were drafted for the continuous wars; cholera swept the army and civilian population; and when at last in 1870 the corpulent López was driven into a swamp and killed, few able-bodied men remained in Paraguay. Historians claim that the nation lost from one half to two thirds of her people during those five years.

Paraguay, stripped of men, having forfeited territory in the north to Brazil, in the south to Argentina, settled down to an uneasy rest. Women were forced to work the neglected fields, and to this day perform the heaviest tasks. Population slowly rose: not until 1920 did it regain the level of 1860. No new strong men appeared, only a succession of short-lived caudillos. Misery and disorder flourished while the Paraguayans nursed their wrongs. There was still an enemy to be attacked—Bolivia, which held debated territory in the Gran Chaco.

Bolivia

BOLIVIA, a land of some 500,000 square miles, larger than Texas and California combined, is thrown athwart the American cordillera at its highest. About three fourths of the 3,000,000 Bolivians live in that two fifths of the country which is in the Andes—on plateaus ten, twelve, fifteen thousand feet above the sea. The other three fifths of Bolivian territory lies east and north—temperate slopes down to the tropical jungles of the Amazon basin. Almost nine tenths of the people are Indians and mestizos, about one tenth are of European stock, chiefly Spanish. Of the few migrants in recent years perhaps 1,300 have been German, 1,700 Italian.

The great majority of Bolivians live from the soil, with the familiar pattern of a few families owning most of the best land and the bulk of the population living as peons on great haciendas. Agriculture is primitive and wasteful, its produce meagerly feeds the people. The Bolivian Indian is virtually tied to the estate of his master, paid a few cents a day, given scant rations, and worked from "sun to sun." Health and education are neglected: the poor breed, sicken, die—there are no credible figures on infant mortality or the health of this people. Not more than one out of five can sign his name or read a headline.

Mines pay the nation's bills. In 1938, 92 % of Bolivian exports was in minerals, tin alone accounting for 68 %. While there is much tin, the ores are complex and more costly to work than those of Malaya. Bolivia has produced as much as 24 % of the world's supply, but production has fallen during recent years. One explanation is that the Chaco War disrupted labor supply; another is that tin has been controlled by an international cartel (with Simón Patiño as the dominating figure) which takes tin where it is cheapest. Some argue that Bolivia can furnish the bulk of United States tin, but this is debated by geologists.

Bolivian export trade, dependent on metals, has fluctuated between $10,000,000 and $50,000,000 during the past twelve years; the figure stood at $34,613,000 in 1938. Sixty to 80 %, chiefly tin for smelting, went to England before the second world war; much of that tin is now going to smelters in the United States.

The United States has long led in sales to Bolivia—furnishing 25.2 % of her imports in 1938. Of the other sellers to Bolivia, Germany has made slight gains during the past twelve years, England has lost.

The political history of Bolivia, beginning with independence in 1826, is an almost unbroken record of disorder and dictatorship. Despite talk of conservatism and liberalism, her politics have been unrelieved personalismo. Santa Cruz (1829–39) all but carried through the conquest of Peru, but was finally blocked by Chile and Argentina. Thanks to Dictator Daza, Bolivia was plunged into the War of the Pacific (1879–83), lost her Pacific ports and nitrate fields. The tally sheet for the nineteenth century shows lost territory, deaths in futile battles, sixty military coups, ten constitutions, six murdered presidents.

Relief came with the new century, with two presidents of stature—Pando and Montes. The dominant landowners still ruled, but with less tumult. After the dictatorship of President Siles (1926–30), President Salamanca returned to constitutional forms but was discredited by successive defeats in the Chaco. Bolivia, like Paraguay, has since been at the mercy of her war heroes. From 1937 to 1939 a young officer named Germán Busch —son of a German physician—ruled the country and achieved brief fame by his seizure of Standard Oil's 2½ million acres of oil lands, representing an investment of some $17,000,000. In April 1938 Busch set up a totalitarian state, and assumed *la totalidad de los poderes* (the totality of powers). In August of the following year he died mysteriously—suicide was the official story, murder the more common explanation. The country has since been ruled by war heroes Carlos Quintanilla and Enrique Peñaranda de Castillo.

War in the Chaco

THE lowland jungles and swamps of the Gran Chaco lie between Bolivia and Paraguay, the "Green Hell" of Julian Duguid. Debate over its possession has been chief concern of learned men in Asunción and La Paz for a hundred years: tons of volumes have been written to support the rival national claims, men have devoted their lives to the task—*"Doctores en Chaco"* they are facetiously called. Bolivia argued that the colonial Audiencia de Charcas, the legal basis of Bolivian territory, included the Gran Chaco. Paraguay's claim rested upon exploration and some settlement. Meanwhile Argentina received the southern section of this area by President Rutherford Hayes' arbitration award in 1878. Interest in the question was made avid in the 1920's by reports of oil. Furthermore, Bolivia's exclusion from the Pacific had increased her desire for ports on the Upper Paraguay River—to give her an outlet to the Atlantic.

A clash came in 1929, when Paraguayan troops seized some unimportant outposts in the Chaco; war really began in 1932 when further posts were taken. Bolivia, with three times Paraguay's population, with a German-trained army, and with planes, seemed to have the advantage. But Paraguayan soldiers were white citizens fighting for their country, while Bolivian troops were chiefly recruited from Indian farm workers and miners, many of them slaves brought in chains to fight a battle of whose issues they were ignorant. Moreover, the Paraguayans knew the territory, the Bolivians did not, and the Bolivian Indians, accustomed to high altitudes, could not resist the malaria and tropical scourges of the low jungles. After three years in which the Bolivian forces were pushed back to the first slopes of the Andes, both sides were exhausted and agreed to a truce. A Commission of Mediation, composed of representatives of neighboring states plus the United States, worked out a compromise which was accepted in 1938. Both had lost men—a loss proportionately as great as that of France in the first World War. Bolivia had lost territory, thereby fixing another sore spot on the map of America. The sole victor was Argentina, already economically entrenched in Paraguay, now ready to extend her hold over the oil fields of Bolivia.

The Danger

THE threat to the tranquillity of the Hemisphere posed by these two landlocked nations is clear. Both countries are economically weak, politically inept, ruled by little cliques of braggart heroes, and in both the great masses are ignorant, ill-fed, sick. In such a setting democracy is meaningless. Into that scene inject companies of Germans—1,300 in Bolivia, 17,000 in Paraguay—among them are many whose loyalty to the Third Reich outruns desire to create free states in the New World. In each country agents of Hitler are persuading, coercing, buying. Detailed proof is difficult, but two members of the Bolivian Cabinet and at least two in the Paraguayan are reckoned devout supporters of the Axis. The wholesale and retail business of both countries is largely controlled by Germans: to buy certain American automobiles, farm machinery, radios, or bicycles in La Paz you must deal with firms named Gundlach, Zirecks, Elsner. The Germans are responsible for a growing antisemitism, which is directed against the 8,000 Jewish refugees now living in that country. A Bolivian cabinet minister was forced out of office by proof that he had accumulated a substantial fortune by selling visas to Jews.

What are German ambitions in the heart of the continent? One guess will do as well as another. The most common explanation heard on the edge of government circles in Argentina, Uruguay, and Chile is that Bolivia may serve Germany as a useful troublemaking center in the event of American entrance into the war. The Germans might incite Bolivia to attack Chile for reconquest of her Pacific posts, or to fresh attempts in the Chaco—such disturbances might serve to distract the United States. That suggestion, seriously ventured by cautious men, seems the best guess at this writing.

Conjecture is easy. One thing is clear, the account will finally be paid by the people. I remember the strong, proud faces of Asunción women—the workers of that land; and the drugged hopelessness of the mountain Indians. They have been paying for four hundred years, no end is in sight. There is the pity of it.

CHAPTER III

PERU AND ECUADOR

THIS was the land of the Inca. His empire numbered some 10 million Indians who lived in the area now divided between Ecuador, Peru, and Bolivia. His court was in Cuzco ("navel" in the Quechua tongue), his orders were carried by swift runners to *ayllus* (clans) and villages. The Inca was king and priest, he was surrounded by a numerous nobility, and had the power of life and death over the mightiest empire of his time. This empire was highly organized, the interest of no subject was neglected. Production of food was planned and controlled—one third belonged to the state, one third to the grower, one third was stored against disaster. All Incas[1] were united in homage to a Creator-God Viracocha and worshiped the sun with elaborate ritual. They were builders of cities whose walls still stand; their stone bridges are used today, their suspension bridges still copied. They were engineers, devising irrigation systems in the terraces of the high mountains, making use of land which has since lain fallow. They were workers in gold, silver, copper, and clay. They were mathematicians, counting by knots in a rope. Those who would read their story will turn again to William H. Prescott, braving critics who hold that Prescott relied upon his imagination, as though one could write about Incas and Mayas without calling upon his imagination. Or they will read Philip Ainsworth Means's admirable account of *Ancient Civilizations of the Andes*. Or they will visit the dead cities of Chan-Chan, Pachacamac, Pumatampu, and walk through streets where ancient peoples once lived. Or they will visit Don Rafael Larco Herrera's sugar hacienda Chiclín near Trujillo, and see his collection of 20,000 jugs and vases, of exquisite textiles, which picture the daily life of other days.

1. The Inca was the ruler: all subjects came to be known as Incas.

The Inca's fate was sealed when Francisco Pizarro set sail from Panama with 180 men and 27 horses in the year 1528. The story of the conquest of Peru remains the most striking full-length drama of the New World: the founding of San Miguel (modern Piura); marches over desert and mountain; the trapping of Inca Atahualpa and the killing of his followers; the treacherous murder of Atahualpa himself, after a great ransom had been paid; the march to Cuzco; the founding of Lima, the City of the Kings; Pedro de Valdivia's march to Santiago. The conquest of the Incas was made easy by civil war between Atahualpa and his half-brother, Huáscar; and it was followed by wars between the Spaniards themselves. The wanderer, having seen the abandoned cities of the dead empire of the Inca, will turn to the cathedral in Lima to see the bones of dead Pizarro.

But the wanderer over Bolivia, Peru, and Ecuador can never be quite sure who is dead. Certainly not the Indians. On feast days in Huancayo and Cuzco and Quito, Indians dance to the honor of the Blessed Virgin—dance as their fathers danced five hundred years ago. Nor are the Spaniards dead. The sons of the conquistadores live in Lima and Quito, own the great haciendas which blanket the high sierra, work the sons of the Incas in the sugar and cotton fields of Peru, the cacao and coffee fields of Ecuador. Both the Indian and the Spaniard still live in this land of the Inca.

But Peru and Ecuador are two nations today, each with her own personality and her own problems.

Peru

PERU, fourth in extent among the republics of South America, has a 1,400-mile Pacific coast line and an area of about 482,000 square miles. The cordillera creates three Perus. *First,* the coastal plain—less than one tenth of the national domain and housing about one fifth of the population—is a shrubless desert sliced by fifty rivers, few of which reach the sea. *Second,* the sierra— with high plateaus, deep valleys, and topped by peaks of 20,000 feet and more—comprises three fifths of the nation and fur-

nishes homes to almost three fourths of the people. The sierra
is bleak and cold, with the leathery gauntness of an old man who
has spent his years in the wind and the sun. *Third,* the montaña
—the hinterland east of the Andes, a region of heavy rains and
lush forests—accounts for almost three tenths of the total national area but has less than one twentieth of the population.

If you would know these three Perus, select a car with brakes
and a chauffeur who does not know the fear of God. Drive east
from the City of the Kings, pass Chosica and push up to the
15,680-foot divide, drop 3,000 feet to Oroya where Cerro de Pasco's smelters smother the mountains with sulphur fumes, then
on to Tarma and take the road which heads toward the Amazon.
That road is so narrow that police direct traffic east on Tuesdays,
Thursdays, and Saturdays; west on Mondays, Wednesdays, and
Fridays; both ways on Sundays (may Viracocha guard you on
Sundays). *Narrow,* the word scarcely fits—our car did not fit, it
scraped the rocks on the curves. The road is etched into the
mountains, following a little river which becomes a great river
within two hours—the Perené, bound for the Amazon. With the
first dip over the divide the scene changes: gone are the deserts
of the coastal plain and the gritty dryness of the sierra, and now
all is rank and wet, the slopes covered with thick forests. At last
the earth mercifully flattens out in the montaña, you are in the
town of La Merced, and you rest in a hospitable German home
set in a grove of mahogany and rosewood. You have cut across
three Perus between dawn and dusk.

The seven million Peruvians, like the people of Bolivia and
Ecuador, are chiefly Indians and mestizos (*Cholos* in Peruvian
usage). Scarcely 10 % of the population may be set down as
whites. Their precise numbers, their racial pattern, their occupations will be better known when the results of the 1940 census
are tabulated. Some 20,000 work in mines at high wages, 60 c. to
70 c. a day; about 25,000 work in the sugar fields at 25 c. to 30 c. a
day; another 25,000 to 30,000 have been kept busy at road building, the chief enthusiasm of ex-President Benavides and his successor President Prado; some have small farms; the great ma-

jority are *yanacones* (peons) on the great haciendas. The state of the Indian farm laborer has changed but little in four hundred years, though legally freed by Leguía in 1919. The Indian is still in effect bought and sold with each transfer of title to the great estates. He receives a few cents each day, an allotment of food and clothing, and a daily ration of coca leaves with which his cheek is always wadded (a merciful provision, the cocaine dulls his appetite). He stands where the Indians of Mexico stood until they learned the use of power. (But who are the *norteamericanos* to speak of slavery, with men still living who were once sold on the auction block, and with 5 million share croppers whose pattern of life differs little from that of peons?)

Peru's livelihood comes from agriculture, stock raising, oil wells, mines. Over nine tenths of her people live directly from the soil. Some 4 million acres are cultivated—about one seventh of the arable land. About one half of her crops come from irrigated lands. Rare oases on the coastal plain (but 3 % of which is arable) furnish cotton and sugar. The sierra produces wheat, corn, barley, oats, potatoes—Peru was the first home of the potato. The montaña produces sugar, tobacco, and many tropical products. Cotton is the chief agricultural export, accounting for 18 % of export receipts in 1938. Sugar, second but declining in importance, furnished 9 %. Pastoral industry is important, there were about 11 million sheep and almost 2 million cattle in 1929. Peru produces her own meats, exports some wool. The forests of the montaña yield rubber, hardwoods, cinchona (Peru first gave quinine to the world), and many other medicinal plants. Rubber and quinine, once chief exports, are now unimportant on her export list, due to competition from the East Indies. The forest wealth is scarcely tapped.

Mines furnish about two thirds of all exports. Petroleum is first, with annual production fluctuating between 10 and 17 million barrels (13½ millions in 1939), about one fifteenth of the Venezuelan figure. Copper is second, Peru's production is topped in Latin America only by Mexico and Chile. She produces over a third of the world's vanadium supply. In 1939 Peru exported gold worth 9 million dollars, silver worth 7 millions, and smaller quantities of antimony, nickel, tungsten, manganese, and other metals.

Industry, fortified by high tariffs and monopoly concessions, flourishes. Peru makes a large share of her textiles, chemical products, prepared foods, glassware, paper, and other consumer goods.

Peru owes heavy debt to the millions of birds which have been dropping their manure on islands off her coast—within twenty years around the middle of the nineteenth century the Peruvians collected a greater fortune from guano than the Incas ever extracted in gold and silver. This source of fertilizer is still important, although in lesser degree. The birds are not doing so well.

Peruvians live from the soil; their government lives from the taxes on minerals. The soil still produces over twice as much as all mines, oil wells, and industries. Sales to the world during recent years have been about 75 million dollars a year (76 millions in 1938, 72 millions in 1939). Peruvian imports (58 millions in 1938, 48 millions in 1939) have lagged behind exports, leaving a comfortable margin of profit. It is a paper profit, for mines, oil wells, smelters, and refineries are chiefly foreign-owned, with foreign technicians drawing the major salaries, with the lion's share of the final profits siphoned off to foreign holders of stocks and bonds. This is also true of much of the sugar and stock-raising industries. Cotton is the one sizable national enterprise chiefly owned by Peruvian citizens. American capital leads with an investment of about 200 million dollars, British is second with some 150 millions, scattered foreign capital brings the total to about 400 millions. The Americans are represented by International Petroleum (owned by Standard Oil of New Jersey), by Cerro de Pasco which turns out about 95 % of Peru's copper, 75 % of her silver, and 50 % of her gold, and which also does a sizable business in cattle raising; by W. R. Grace and Company, the ubiquitous and able operator of steamships, producer of one fourth of all Peruvian sugar, dabbler in banking and much retail and wholesale business; the Vanadium Corporation which has a monopoly on the Peruvian production of that metal. The British own many of the public utilities, are second to the Americans in production of petroleum, and own textile mills, breweries, flour mills. The chief British enterprise is the 100-million-dollar Peruvian Corporation, which owns over half of Peru's railroads and the steamers on Lake Titicaca. The Italians, of whom there are about 20,000, own farms, mines, utility companies, textile mills, trading firms. The Banco Italiano is a 50-million-dollar institution which controls about one half of the banking business, with strong ramifications throughout the financial life of the nation. The Italians seem well absorbed into the life of Peru, with numerous alliances by marriage with old families. There are about 25,000 Japanese settlers, chiefly farmers and small tradesmen, with a few owners of industrial plants—all thrifty and completely unassimilated. The 3,000 Germans (of whom about 2,000 were born in Germany) are active in every business. The Gildermeisters—kin to the influential family of the same name in Chile —own Casa Grande and the port of Chicama, produce about two fifths of all Peruvian sugar, and are mighty men in national economic life. But the Gildermeisters, like many others with German names in Peru, have been there for two and three generations, have intermarried with Peruvian families, and are generally regarded as good citizens of their adopted land. The foreigner dominates the business life of Peru, owns the major industrial and mining enterprises, exploits some of the best land, holds the best jobs, draws the chief dividends. Peruvians look glumly at the figures on production of petroleum, copper, gold, silver, vanadium, sugar—and reckon that out of each dollar too small a slice stays in Peru to pay wages, to buy materials, to be plowed back into the building of the country; that too large a share goes to the holders of stocks and bonds in New York, London, Cedar Rapids.

Peru became a republic under a serious handicap—her first families had no zest for independence, little desire for democratic life. Independence was imposed by outsiders—by Simón

Bolívar and José de San Martín. While the first families—somewhat less powerful today than in 1824—have become accustomed
to the idea of independence, they have not yet acquired fervor
for democratic institutions.

The political history of independent Peru covers 115 years of
weak and short-lived dictatorships, with military *coups d'état*
following each other in swift disorder. Ramón Castilla's rule in
the 'forties and 'fifties offered grateful exception. Then came loss
of territory and of prestige in the War of the Pacific (1879–82),
followed by more years of political floundering. Augusto Leguía,
President in 1908–12 and again in 1919–30, ruled ruthlessly and
capriciously, but with ability. He gave some relief to the workers,
extended education, tightened up the machinery of government.
The country prospered, thanks in part to a steady stream of easy
loans from the United States. In 1930 Leguía was evicted by
Sánchez Cerro, who renewed the fight with Colombia over
Leticia in the far north, and won the hatred of all classes by his
venality and cruelty. In 1933 Sánchez Cerro was murdered;
Oscar Benavides seized the presidency and held it until 1939,
when he turned over the office to his nominee, Manuel Prado,
who had been chosen by an election of doubtful regularity. Bena-
vides claims credit for measures designed to improve the living
conditions of the masses, and there is some ground for the claim.
He also kept some hundreds of critics in jail and curbed the press.
As dictators go, Benavides was gentle—he seldom killed anyone.
This uninteresting little man is now uneasily in the background,
with rumors rife that he will shortly return from Italy, push
Prado out, and resume control.

Peru is unique among the dictator-ridden republics in having
an authentic opposition party. Such luxuries are effectively
barred in Brazil, Bolivia, and Paraguay. The Peruvian APRA—
Alianza Popular Revolucionaria Americana—is also under official proscription, but all friends and most foes admit that it is the
most numerous party in the country. Víctor Raúl Haya de la
Torre, its founder, is of the breed which makes great leaders. His
quality is attested by fifteen years of exile, imprisonment, and

bludgeoning. Twenty years ago, a student of law in Lima, Haya set about the organization of popular universities for the poor. In 1923 he was banished by Leguía and for eight years wandered in Mexico, the United States, Europe, Russia. In 1931 he returned to Lima, ran for the presidency against Sánchez Cerro, was overwhelmingly beaten at the polls, overwhelmingly elected by the people (so reported impartial Peruvians). Sánchez Cerro threw him into prison; in 1933 he was released by Benavides. Since then he has lived as a fugitive from Peruvian justice in the outskirts of Lima, lived at the sufferance of Benavides and Prado—they dare not touch him for fear of the people. Not even trusted lieutenants can be sure of his hiding place, which changes from week to week. When a friend seeks him, as I have done upon various occasions, he must work through mutual friends who finally arrange a meeting place.

The Apristas and their chief, chastened by adversity, seem to have lost none of their first fervor. Some of their able leaders— Peru's finest—are in prison or in exile. Whenever you meet one of their number in Mexico or Cuba or Chile, or on the campus of some American university, you are given heartening reassurance of the democratic faith of these people. The government of Peru plasters walls with placards, *"Aprismo es comunismo"*—but the Apristas are not communists, they are the most militant democrats in South America. The walls of Lima also proclaim *"Aprismo es ateísmo"*—but atheism is the last charge to be leveled at Haya de la Torre and his friends. This movement is profoundly religious, it has almost evangelical overtones. Nor is it fascist, as some journalists report; its dogged faith in the common man gives the lie to that charge. Some call it socialism, a more accurate description, for Haya has long demanded the recapture of natural resources for the use of the people. But all imported terms fall down—Aprismo is as indigenous as the llama, born and bred of the Peruvian soil.

I last saw Haya de la Torre in February 1941. He was heavier and a bit more grim, but he was no whit less certain that democratic decency will prevail in Peru. He has not forgotten all that

he believed and said in other years of the imperialism of the
North, but is persuaded that the fate of free America rests with
the leaders in Washington. He looks to Franklin Roosevelt with
the confidence which marks so many lovers of liberty in Latin
America. Roosevelt has become the symbol of things hoped for,
not yet achieved, in such exploited lands as Peru and Brazil.

But why does not APRA, with the majority of coherent Peruvians behind it, rise in its power and take over the government?
This is a natural question in the light of the long pattern of
Peruvian politics. The explanation is twofold. First, the temper
of the country: the government controls the army; there are
8,000 federal police well trained by the Italians; the ruling families have money and land; business enterprise is dominated by
British, American, Italian, and German interests which ask nothing but order. The second reason is found in the character of the
movement and the leader: Haya has no taste for bloodletting; he
believes in peace, believes that the just cause will triumph, believes in the virtue of patience. His critics, knowing the strength
of his following, put him down as a fool, never as a weakling.
Many of his friends aver that he has permitted opportunity to
pass by, that he should have seized power before Benavides built
up his army and police. Outsiders who know the man and the
movement look on unhappily, convinced that this could be the
single most potent force for genuine Pan-Americanism, the
best ally of the free forces of all America. Some question how a
government in Washington which proposes to buttress democracy can continue to uphold the caudillo governments of Benavides and Prado, making loans and offering military aid to dictators intent upon crushing the most authentic democratic force
in South America. It is easy to raise such questions, hard to suggest answers.

Peru's role in the world of 1941 is difficult to appraise. Outwardly she offers full coöperation to the United States, accepts a
10-million-dollar loan from the Export-Import Bank, will accept
more; her leaders give proper assurance of adherence to Pan-
American solidarity. Meanwhile, those charged with diplomacy

must be aware that they deal with men elected by fraud, that
Prado and his aides do not speak for the body of Peruvian voters;
aware that neither the politicians nor the first families of Lima
have any heart for increase in democracy; aware of the conspiracies of German agents; and aware that the 25,000 Japanese
might constitute a genuine threat should the United States go to
war. Haya de la Torre expressed the conviction of many Peruvians when he told me in February, "We have the Axis in its
fullness. Each of the three partners has his task assigned. The
German will furnish the brains, the Italian the money, the Japanese will do the fighting." A little too simple? Perhaps—but that
is what Peruvians are saying.

Ecuador

ECUADOR is a little country which has steadily become smaller
with each redrawing of the maps.[2] On Ecuadorian records her
territory touches the Brazilian border. On Peruvian maps she is
a tiny spot on the Pacific seaboard. Peru has been pushing her to
the sea and Ecuador hourly expects another shove. This does not
make for happiness—Ecuadorians nurse as stout nationalism as
any Americans.

Ecuador sits astride the equator—which is, in Spanish, *El
Ecuador*. Her coastal plains are heavy with tropical tangles, with
orchids, snakes, and crimson birds. Her capital, Quito, ancient
seat of the Incas, is 9,800 feet above the sea—center of the Ecuadorian sierra, home of most of the people. Her undefined lands
east of the cordillera are the continuation of the Peruvian montaña. There are chiefly two Ecuadors—that of the hot port Guayaquil, that of cold Quito—and most political struggles of a century sprang from rivalry between them.

No one has ever counted the Ecuadorians, there are no statistics which tell who they are, what they do. There may be anywhere from 2½ to 3½ millions in all; perhaps 10 % of them are
of white European blood, chiefly Spanish; perhaps 90 % of them

2. The Ecuadorian government claims an area of 337,300 square miles. The *Inter-
American Statistical Yearbook* puts the figure at 175,675 square miles.

are Indians and mestizos; perhaps illiteracy tops 80 %. These seem the best current guesses. But what is the point of statistics in a land with the loveliness of Ecuador? Who cares about the size of the lady's foot provided the lady is beautiful? Ecuador offers more excitements to the traveler than all of Argentina plus Kansas and Staten Island. Even Guayaquil, once you forget about yellow fever, has increasing charm. Quito is the perfect colonial city (more perfect than anything in Spain, which invented colonial cities), with churches and old houses which you cannot forget. Drive to Ambato and Riobamba, take a plane to Cuenca, visit Indian markets and fiestas, trace the lines of lost centuries in the clothing and the speech of the people. Stand under the shadow of Chimborazo. You will swear fealty to Ecuador so long as you live.

Poverty attends Ecuador. Her exports seldom exceed $12,000,-000. The great majority of the people live directly from the soil, weave their own cloth, doctor themselves with herbs, never see a movie, never learn to read a book. They raise cacao and coffee (chief export crops), tropical fruits, grains, chickens, hogs. More people have their own plots of land than in Peru; but there are some great estates, and there is peonage of the Peruvian pattern. There is mineral wealth but it is little exploited—a little petroleum and gold are exported. Industries are unimportant, confined to a few consumer goods.

Ecuador separated from Colombia in 1830. Weakest and poorest of the lands freed by Simón Bolívar, Ecuador was at the mercy of hungry soldiers. The recurring struggles which marked her 110 republican years related to the antagonism between Guayaquil and Quito. One President stands out, Gabriel García Moreno (1861–75), gratefully remembered for his uprightness and self-abnegation. García was a devout Catholic, he thought to create a theocratic state in which the state would obey the Church; he committed education to the Jesuits and other orders, and he formally dedicated the republic to the Sacred Heart of Jesus. He invited men of science, opened schools, enforced honest government, built a road linking Quito to the coast. There has since been much argument between conservatives and liberals, and frequent changes of government: the clashes have been between rival caudillos rather than arguments over ideas. President Arroyo del Río, the present incumbent, speaks of leading his country toward more democratic ways, promises full Pan-American coöperation, but he is surrounded by quarreling men, some of whom seem overfond of totalitarian ways.

Ecuador is cut to order for alien troublers. She has natural wealth, an illiterate people, a weak officialdom, and a negligible army. The potential troublemakers are present: some 6,000 Germans, of whom about 1,000 were born in Germany; 1,800 Italians, about 100 of them born in Italy. The Germans and the Italians dominate trade, wholesale and retail, their names are on the chief shops, mills, warehouses in Quito and Guayaquil. The German Embassy in Quito has a force of about 25, the consulate in Guayaquil about 18. (These are unofficial figures reported by curious Ecuadorians.) The German air line SEDTA serves the chief inland towns. Washington asked Ecuador to follow Colombia's example in banishing German operators and pilots, but the Quito government did not accede. Pan American Airways is now extending its lines to parallel each German flight.[3]

Off Ecuador's coast lie the Galapagos Islands, 3,000 square miles of Ecuadorian territory. Washington is negotiating for naval and air bases; Ecuadorians are divided on the issue. Germans in Quito are saying that the United States has bribed Peru to abstain from criticism of the cession of bases on the islands.

Reading of Ludwig Bemelman's *The Donkey Inside* stirs nostalgia for this lovely land, tempts suggestion that all Americans should league together for the creation of an international Eden in Ecuador, reserved for those who would escape Manhattan and Buenos Aires, Hollywood and Viña del Mar. Let a high fence be built around it; prescribe the death penalty for anyone who introduces efficiency or sanitation; insist that Indians cling to their careless ways; demand continuance of dances to the Blessed Vir-

3. As this book goes to press, word comes that American oil companies, which control the gasoline supply, have refused to sell SEDTA more fuel.

gin; make it the last refuge of sanity. The dream dies a-borning. The Germans are killing it. If they do not, the North Americans will. Someone will organize the Ecuadorians one of these days and give them honest elections, cornflakes, and PM. There will probably be neon lights on Chimborazo.

CHAPTER IV

VENEZUELA

NO astute assembler of a twentieth-century empire will overlook Venezuela. Here are the requisite goods of a promising colony—rich soil, empty spaces, oil, gold, iron, coal. Here are the social ingredients which invite conquest—a hungry proletariat, a hapless officialdom, a long record of disorder. If the United States were what some Latin Americans say she is, *El Coloso del Norte,* American marines would long since have occupied La Guaira, established garrisons in Caracas, Maracaibo and Ciudad Bolívar and an American proconsul would sit in the government palace administering finances, signing decrees for the honor and glory of the Stars and Stripes. As it is, Washington is represented by an affable Cleveland surgeon, Francis Patrick Corrigan, whose ambassadorial genius may scarcely be described as proconsular.

Venezuela's unique claim upon American affections is that hers is the land of Simón Bolívar. *El Libertador* was born in Caracas in 1783; at sixteen he was off to Spain for education; at twenty-one he stood in the crowd which witnessed Napoleon's coronation in Paris and was overcome by "the love which an immense populace expressed for their hero . . . the final summit of human aspiration, the supreme desire and the supreme ambition of man." In Paris young Simón met Baron von Humboldt, freshly returned from his American explorings, who told the boy that his native land was ripe for freedom, that only a leader was lacking. Three months later Simón Bolívar fell on his knees on the Aventine Hill in Rome, called God and man to witness that he would not rest his arm or soul until he had broken Spain's chains upon his fatherland. In 1810 he returned to Venezuela to fulfill his pledge. For thirteen years, in defeat and victory, he led his armies through the lands now called Venezuela, Colombia, Ecuador, Peru, and Bolivia. He was variously general, president, protector, dictator. He freed peoples having but half a heart for freedom and laid the basis for five sovereign republics of the New World. The spiritual father of the Pan-Americanism of today, he called the first conference of American states in Panama in 1826. He thought to hold Venezuela, Colombia, and Ecuador together in one great state, but Venezuela seceded in 1829, Ecuador in 1830. He was acclaimed the dictator of Colombia, but his enemies drove him out, set assassins on his trail. Almost alone, almost forgotten, he died near Cartagena in 1830. Hispanic Americans belatedly realized that Bolívar shares with San Martín chief credit for the freedom of their world. Today Venezuelans claim him as their own.

Venezuela and Her People

VENEZUELA'S 352,000 square miles about equal Texas plus Colorado. She has a span of some 900 miles east to west, and a maximum depth south and north of 700 miles. There are four Venezuelas. *First,* the Andean region which is marked by a spur of the cordillera thrust down from the southwest. *Second,* the heart of the country which is marked by the *llanos* (plains) of the Orinoco, one of the three great river systems of South America, whose tributaries drain from the jungles of Colombia and Brazil. This is the land of a hundred swelling rivers and recurring floods, of wild grass and deep soil. *Third,* to the southeast lie the Guiana highlands over against Brazil and British Guiana, plateaus heavy with tropical forests, largely unexplored. Fourth, along the Caribbean lies the coastal plain, spreading out at the west to surround Lake Maracaibo and the oil fields. Venezuela is a land of every climate: steaming heat in the lowlands, temperate comfort in the highlands where the chief cities stand, cold in the high mountains.

Venezuelans are predominantly a mestizo people. Perhaps 70 % of her 3½ millions are a mixture of Spanish and Indian, with some admixture of Negro blood. About 7 % are Indians, 8 % Negroes. The remainder of the population is of more or less pure European stock—many Spaniards, some 15,000 Italians, perhaps 10,000 Germans. There are sharp social cleavages: a handful of the old first families which still hold land and wealth; another handful of aggressive *políticos* who have risen to power from the ranks; a middle class heavily foreign in blood; and the hard-driven workers in oil fields, mines, forests, farms. Less than one third of her people can sign their names or read a newspaper.

Oil Is King

VENEZUELA lives from her petroleum. The hot lands around Lake Maracaibo are dotted with wells, and far out over the lake derricks rise above the water. There are estimated to be not less than 27,000 square miles of exploitable oil fields in the country. Dutch Shell (British and Dutch) and American companies have invested $400,000,000 in Venezuelan oil—Americans furnishing half that amount. Oil accounts for over 90 % of all her exports (93.3 % in 1938).

The Venezuelan petroleum industry was chief beneficiary of the oil wrangles which broke out in Mexico in 1925. When Mexico threatened higher taxation and the expropriation of foreign operators, the latter turned to Venezuela, where the government was conciliatory, where labor was less exacting. In 1917 Venezuela produced 119 thousand barrels of oil; in 1925, 19 million; in 1927, 64 million; in 1934 almost 143 million; in 1936, 155 million. In 1939 she produced 206 million barrels, almost equaling Russia's record (212 million), and was producing about one sixth as much as the United States (1,264 million). She stood third among world producers.

Thanks to oil, Venezuela's government is the most prosperous in South America. It collects royalties of about 12.5 % on all petroleum extracted, further taxes on the properties of foreigners who direct drilling, pumping, and shipping. Her nationals draw wages which return their tithe to the government. Thanks to oil, the federal budget tops $110,000,000—three times the budget of Peru whose population is twice Venezuela's, one half that of Brazil which has twelve times as many people. Thanks also to oil, Venezuela has long owed no money to the outside world—although the exigencies of 1941 compelled her to borrow some $3,600,000 from Washington. Oil has made Venezuela a lone paradise for the capitalist—no income tax, gentle property taxes, no socialistic threats.

Oil's magnificence obscures other Venezuelan assets. The land has reserves of gold, silver, copper, iron, tin, asphalt, asbestos, mica, and sundry other elements. Gold valued at $4,375,000 was produced in 1939. The mineral wealth has scarcely been touched, the developers of Venezuela have been busy with oil.

While oil supports the government, the soil supports the people. The great majority of Venezuelans live from agriculture and pastoral industry. Food products, chiefly consumed at home, range from tropical fruits to temperate grains. Coffee and cacao are exported, coffee furnishing about 3 % of her exports, cacao 1 %.

In 1938, the latest full year of uninterrupted trade, Venezuela's economy seemed unassailable. Selling almost three times as much as she bought—her exports aggregated $279,936,000, her imports but $97,768,000—she enjoyed a more favorable balance of trade than any other nation. Three fourths of her exports (almost entirely petroleum) went to the Netherland West Indies, where foreign operators processed the oil for shipment to Europe and the United States. Her imports, chiefly machinery and manufactured goods, were divided in 1938 between many countries—the United States furnished 56.4 %, the United Kingdom 7 %, Germany 12 %. The United States' lead had long been sustained. Germany's share was 9.2 % in 1929, 15.1 % in 1936, 12 % in 1938.

Venezuela's Government

VENEZUELA's fashions in government must be judged in the light of her history. Her colonial experience resembled that of other Spanish colonies in its rigid controls, its denial of local responsibility, its choking of economic development. Unlike La Plata and Chile, Venezuela was on the ocean highway between Europe, Panama, and the Far East, was visited by Spanish galleons, raided by English freebooters. This was the Spanish Main of fiction and fact. After breaking with Spain, she separated from New Granada (Colombia) in 1830, and entered upon independent life.

Venezuela embarked upon republican life under grievous handicaps. For twenty years she had been the spearhead of the war for freedom. Her creole sons, the intelligent and trained men, had manned the armies which marched into the lands now known as Colombia, Ecuador, Peru, and Bolivia. Civil war between partisans of *patria* and king had laid waste the country. In 1812 an earthquake ravaged La Guaira, Caracas, and other sections of Venezuela—taking a toll of 10,000 lives in Caracas alone. During those twenty years the nation had lost a fifth or more of her population, and a far greater share of her white citizens best fitted for leadership.

That crippled start may largely be blamed for the confusions of Venezuela's 110 years of independence. They have been years of dictatorship and revolution, with 20 different constitutions and over 50 armed revolts. Four great caudillos stand out. The first, José Antonio Páez, dominated the nation off and on from 1830 to 1863. Páez was an illiterate plainsman who had served under Bolívar. He was the most intelligent dictator in Venezuela's history, his rule was marked by dogged honesty and considerable achievement. Himself illiterate, he was indefatigable in promoting education. He organized the national treasury with vigor and reduced the national debt. The second, Antonio Guzmán Blanco, titled "Illustrious American" by his own decree, was dictator—with several interludes—from 1870 to 1889. Guzmán was a skilful administrator and launched numerous public reforms. He enriched himself in the process, ruled capriciously and cruelly, lived profligately. The third, Cipriano Castro, an ignorant Andean mountaineer, captured the presidency in 1899 and held it for nine years. He is chiefly remembered for his personal courage, his brutality with enemies, his prowess with women, his complete venality.

The latest and most spectacular of Venezuelan mighty men

was Juan Vicente Gómez who held the land as his private duchy
for twenty-six years, 1908–35. Gómez was the complete dictator,
logical, thorough, and untiring. He did nothing by halves. As
public administrator he imposed a hitherto unknown efficiency
upon officials. Blessed with expanding oil production, he played
British interests against American, saw to it that the treasury collected generously from each barrel, and wisely retained for the
nation final rights to more than half the fields. He paid off the
last centavo of foreign debt, built roads, public institutions, industries. As trustee of his own fortunes he was equally thorough:
he and his friends collected toll on each operation of government
(while making sure that lesser men were scrupulously honest).
He added farm to farm until he was the chief landholder of the
republic, and his fat cattle were famous at home and abroad. He
and his friends had great houses, with well-paved roads leading
to the capital and to the port. He put his money into factories,
shipping lines, and foreign banks. No reliable estimate of his tak-
ings is possible, but the government confiscated some $25,000,000
of his property when he was dead. As the custodian of order, he
did not flinch. The press printed what he ordered. Prisons were
filled with his critics, often convicted for an idle word, subjected
to horrors recited by Venezuelan refugees all over the world. He
was *El Brujo,* the wizard, to his people. He was magnificent in
his virility, left eighty or a hundred sons and daughters. He never
married. At the last, in his seventy-eighth year, he sought a
woman fit to mother another son.

Such is the political heritage of Bolívar's natal land. When
word of El Brujo's death flashed out in 1935, the people called
him *El Bagre,* the catfish, and looted the houses of his favorites.
But they had no program, no experience in government, no leaders—the politically competent were exiles in New York, Paris,
Mexico, Havana, London. After the first passion was spent, the
crowds turned in relief to Eleazar López Contreras, Gómez' War
Minister, and in 1936 elected him for a full term of seven years by
as fair an election as the country ever enjoyed. López, discreet
and moderate, emptied the prisons of political offenders, invited

exiles home, permitted the press a limited freedom. He reduced
his term of office to five years to conform with older constitutional usage, and sought to reëstablish state governments, to
strengthen the national Congress, to encourage free political
parties. Many of Gómez' former aides were barred from office.
He did something toward improving education and sanitation.
His achievements were modest, he dealt with men reared in the
school of plunder. He proposed "to make effective the principles
of democracy," and gave proof of honest intention by retiring
from office when his term expired in April 1941. His successor,
General Isaias Medina Angarita, was given a fair chance to build
wisely. It remains to be seen how soon democracy can come to
this land of 3½ millions, among whom not more than three out
of ten can read a printed placard and not more than one out of ten
lives in any comfort. In 1804 Baron von Humboldt told Simón
Bolívar that Venezuela was ripe for freedom, that only a leader
was lacking. The judgment still holds.

Venezuela and the United States

ALONSO DE OJEDA visited this land in 1499, found Indians living
in huts perched on stilts above Lake Maracaibo, paddling their
canoes from door to door. He called it Little Venice—Venezuela.
Today the United States has special interest in Little Venice. It is
near the Panama Canal. It has oil which may be the final arbiter
of war. The United States asks that Venezuela travel with her.

Venezuela has reasons for trusting the United States. On two
occasions Washington supported her against European med-
dlers. In 1895–97, when Britain threatened direct action in a dispute over the British Guiana boundary, Secretary of State Richard Olney successfully warded off British intervention. Again in
1902–03, when Germany and England threatened intervention
to collect outstanding claims, the first Roosevelt cited the Monroe
Doctrine and the Allies withdrew. There are statues of George
Washington and Henry Clay in Caracas. There is a statue of
Simón Bolívar in Central Park, New York.

Prospects for Venezuelan-American accord seem bright. President López during his six years in office repeatedly avowed faith in Pan-American coöperation. Even the skeptical credited him with good intentions. Perhaps more important, Venezuelan spokesmen supported Washington's proposals at Lima in 1938, at Panama in 1939, at Havana in 1940. The Export-Import Bank of Washington has advanced $3,600,000 to strengthen Venezuelan economy, and there is still money to be had from that chest. On the American side there is strategic necessity for complete amity. On the Venezuelan side such course seems dictated by common prudence. Thoughtful Venezuelans regard the United States as the one power to be trusted in a world which clamors for oil.

CHAPTER V

COLOMBIA

THE eager American tourist, pursuing romance in southern waters, alights briefly at Buenaventura on the Pacific coast and returns to tell his countrymen of Colombia, a hot, dirty land peopled by Negroes. It is as though a Colombian sailed north to New York harbor, spent three hours in Hoboken, and returned to Bogotá to report all about the United States. Colombia is not hot—nine tenths of her people live in the cool air 4,000 feet or more above the sea. She is not dirty, but rather one of the most sprightly and modern republics in the Western World. She is not a Negro nation, her percentage of Negroes is less than half that of the United States. So much for tourists.

Colombia is a fortress built high in the cordillera, her back turned upon the world, her true life to be found in the interior valleys and on the mountain plateaus. The Andes unknot themselves on her southern border and spread out into three mountain ranges which reach to the north. The life of Colombia flows south to north along the valleys of the Cauca and Magdalena, communications between west and east are blocked by mountains topped by peaks of 18,000 feet. The traditional route to Bogotá from the coast used to mean a week's journey at best—using slow river steamers from Barranquilla on the Caribbean up the Magdalena River, then train to the capital. Now planes make it in less than three hours. The journey from Buenaventura on the Pacific, over two mountain passes, may be made in two days by train and automobile, or in 2½ hours by plane.

Almost nine tenths of the 8,700,000 Colombians live in one third of their 450,000 square miles (Colombia roughly equals the combined area of Arizona, New Mexico, Nevada, and Colorado). Two thirds of the national domain is quite empty: the tropical plains of the Orinoco over against Venezuela, and the uncharted Amazonian jungle facing Brazil to the southeast. The homes, the farms, the pastures of these people are in the fertile valleys and on the high tablelands.

It was, and remains, a Spanish stronghold. Spanish blood predominates, although a scattering of northern Europeans came during and after colonial days, leaving good English, Irish, French, and German names as reminders of their pilgrimage. Traders and slave merchants touched her shores, leaving their motley mark on the sea-coast towns. Bogotá and the interior remained white and Spanish. The official reckoning of 1933 set the figure of "white" population at 35 %. More conservative guessers claim about 20 % pure white, 70 % mixed Spanish and Indian, 5 % Indian, 5 % Negro. There is no social or economic barrier between white and mestizo, both rank as good Colombians. The Indians live in out-of-the-way spots; the Negroes in the hot ports and coastal farmlands—neither have much share in the life of the nation.

Bogotá, capital city with a population of 330,000, is laid up against the mountain wall 8,700 feet above sea level. Founded in 1538, it was the viceroyal center of New Granada after the middle of the eighteenth century, and has been the seat of an archbishop for four centuries. Bogotá prizes the description, "Athens of America," its numerous poets, novelists, essayists, and philosophers support the claim. Some of the best writing in Latin America is done here. There is no abler editorializing in all America than in *El Tiempo,* owned by President Eduardo Santos. Both culture and industry thrive in the bleak air of this mountain capital. The visitor from abroad hugs the lone fireplace in the Hotel Granada and pulls on his red flannels when he goes to dine with Colombian friends; but the chill air is more than balanced by the warm welcome of the Colombians, as forthright, friendly, and able neighbors as this hemisphere affords.

Colombia—unlike Chile, Peru, Venezuela, and Argentina—is not dominated by the capital city. Cali with 102,000 people and Medellín with 168,000 are prosperous and graceful cities in their own right, and because of their lower altitudes afford a more pleasant climate than does Bogotá. Barranquilla, seaport on the

Caribbean, with 152,000 people, is a lively and modern city despite its tropical setting. Near-by Cartagena, founded in 1533 and long a chief port for Spanish galleons, is now a city of almost 100,000 but maintains its colonial lines and colors.

What Colombians Live By

JOURNEYS by plane, rail, and river steamer excite the visitor's curiosity. How can 8 million people make a living in such an inhospitable land of mountains, jungles, and hot coastal lands? But Colombians do well, despite Nature's handicaps.

The soil is rich and well watered in the valleys of the Cauca and Magdalena and on the tablelands above. The crops range from tropical fruits to wheat and corn, for altitude creates variety in climate. The list is varied: oranges, pineapples, bananas, coffee, cacao, sugar, cotton, rice, indigo, temperate grains. Generous herds spot the upland plateaus.

For the ten years ending in 1938, agricultural products accounted for from 68 % to 73 % of her export list. Colombia stands second to Brazil in coffee production, and coffee heads the list of her agricultural exports. The Cauca valley around Medellín yields a mild coffee which has a favored place in the world market. Bananas are her second reliance for export sales. In 1938 coffee represented 60 % of her exports, bananas 6 %.

Colombia's mountains hold reserves of almost every metal, her mines have been worked but little. She is the chief world producer of platinum, selling about $2,000,000 worth each year; her gold production reached $20,000,000 in 1939, and she is the chief exporter of emeralds. Petroleum is her chief mineral export with sales aggregating about 20,000,000 barrels annually. Enlarged oil production awaits investment in wells and pipe lines.

Industrial development has lagged, although Colombia increasingly produces her own processed foodstuffs, textiles, drugs, leather goods, and other small items. Colombia, unlike Chile and Argentina and Brazil, has not approached self-sufficiency in manufacture of consumer goods; despite increased production in many lines, imports of the same articles have also increased. Her

lack of accessible coal is a definite bar to large-scale industrialization.

Colombia's trade has been chiefly subject to the fluctuations in
the price of coffee, petroleum, and bananas. Her exports in 1929
totaled $122,761,000; in 1939, $100,885,000. Her imports in 1929
were valued at $122,281,000; in 1939, $104,536,000. Between those
years, exports fell as low as $64,000,000 in 1932, imports to
$29,000,000. The United States has been consistently her chief
buyer, and the chief seller in her markets. In 1929 the United
States took 74.1 % of her exports, 52.7 % in 1938. In 1929 the
United States furnished 45.9 % of her imports, 51.2 % in 1938.
The United Kingdom, which had long held second place in the
Colombian market, lost her position to Germany by 1936. Germany in 1938 took 14.6 % of Colombia's exports, supplied
17.3 % of her imports.

Colombia's Democracy

THE American, seeking democratic allies among the nations of
Latin America, finds solid comfort in Colombia. Asked to name
the nations with the best modern record for working democracy,
he inevitably falls back upon Colombia and Costa Rica. Pressed
for a rule-of-thumb definition, he offers this: A democratic nation is one which has *elections;* one in which votes are freely
cast and counted with substantial honesty; one in which those
elected are permitted to continue in office until the end of their
terms, then to retire to their own garden patches, ultimately to
die in their own beds from natural causes. Colombia for forty
years has met that test rather better than any other nation in
South America.

Colombia, like Venezuela, was born of the fervor of Simón
Bolívar. Half-saint, half-fanatic, he was "The Liberator" of
Venezuela, Colombia, and Ecuador, and shared credit with
José de San Martín for the freedom of Peru. Son of the equali-
tarian liberalism which had swept Europe, he had deep respect
for ideas and was more democratic in faith than San Martín.
Egoist though he was, he knew that human freedom was more

important than any man's role. When New Granada (as Colombia was called until 1863) was separated from Venezuela and Ecuador in 1830, there were many men in the new republic whose philosophy of life and government had been shaped by Simón Bolívar.

The first century of Colombian independence stood in marked contrast to that of Venezuela, Ecuador, and Peru. To be sure, Colombia had full measure of internal strife—her historian Holquín counts twenty seven civil wars during the first seventy years —but unlike her neighbors, Colombia usually fought over issues rather than over rival personalities. It was a running battle between conservatives and liberals, with the issue of states' rights an incidental concern. The conservatives, like all their Latin-American kin, were the rich, the well-born, the cautious, the devout. The liberals, while led by sons of first families inspired by French liberalism, also included in their ranks some of the less privileged. They were theoretical lovers of revolution, dabblers in new ideas, strongly anticlerical.

Throughout the nineteenth century there were bloody tussles between the ins and the outs. Liberals held power from 1849 to 1880, with Tomás Mosquera as their most conspicuous leader. They disestablished the Church and made marriage a civil contract in the 'fifties; nationalized much church property and limited the rights of priests in the 'sixties and 'seventies. In 1880 conservatives captured power, which they held until 1930. They resumed relations with the Vatican in 1888, and restored churchmen's privileges.

At the turn of the century two blows brought the nation to her senses, and ended the chronic strife. *First,* the three years' war of 1899–1902, a costly contest which brought widespread suffering and the death of 100,000 men in battle. *Second,* the loss of Panama in 1903. The rebuilding of a stricken and humiliated nation was the chief concern of the conservatives, who ruled ably from 1902 to 1930.

The liberals have been at the helm since 1930. In that year Colombia faced a stiff test of her political integrity. Other nations

—Brazil, Uruguay, Argentina, Chile—were overturning their constitutional regimes. Colombia was the one South American exception. An orderly election gave the victory to liberal Olaya Herrera, whose administration was mild but constructive. He was succeeded in 1934 by Leftist Alfonso López. López worked substantial changes: he secured a new constitution with the minimum of bad feeling, barred the Church from control of education, ended official relations with the Holy See, and obtained some excellent social legislation. The election of 1938 brought to power the more moderate wing of the liberal party, headed by Eduardo Santos, a man of character, ability, and firm democratic conviction.

The present political atmosphere of Colombia reminds the visitor of Chile. There is the same tempestuous debate in the press, the same violent utterance by party chieftains. The press is entirely unshackled: *El Siglo,* organ of conservative Laureano Gómez, lays the lash on all liberals and especially on Alfonso López, who covets a second election in 1942. Gómez' editorials during the winter of 1940–41 suggested everything short of murder for that ex-President.

The chief issue dividing liberal from conservative, and splitting the liberal party as well, is Colombia's policy toward the United States. President Santos stands for complete Pan-American coöperation, offers Colombian aid to the United States for protection of the Panama Canal, and has proved his zeal by ending German control of Colombian air lines. Another faction of liberals, headed by Alfonso López, condemns Santos' affection for Washington. However, those who know López have no fear that he will play with Washington's potential enemies.

The conservatives, led by Laureano Gómez, ridicule talk of German threats and demand that Colombia refuse coöperation with the United States and assume a more self-reliant attitude. Gómez, a devout Catholic, is a fervid apologist for Francisco Franco, and is regarded as sympathetic with Germany and Italy. His contempt for the United States is vigorous. The conservatives hope that the widening split between Alfonso López and

Eduardo Santos will so weaken the liberals that the conservatives can capture the presidency in 1942.

Colombia and the United States

COLOMBIA has an obstinate grudge against the United States. She has not forgotten Theodore Roosevelt ("I took Panama," he boasted). No matter what history books may say, all good Colombians are convinced that Roosevelt took their territory by trickery—arranging the Panamanian revolt and financing its chief actors. Even the belated $25,000,000 payment did not still that memory. Whether or not their recital is accurate, Colombians owe the first Roosevelt a lasting debt—his "taking" of Panama helped to unite the Colombian nation.

Despite Panama, Colombian-American relations have steadily bettered. At Lima in 1939 Colombia made common cause with the United States for Pan-American solidarity. President Santos has lost no opportunity to affirm his faith in Washington and the American people. In his message to Congress in 1940 he said: "American solidarity has its moral and spiritual foundation in the identity of our democratic convictions, and the determination to make this new world the guardian of those free and just ideas which rightfully adhere to human personality." Colombia has actively coöperated by ousting the German aviation company, SCADTA, whose lines joined her chief cities. First compelling SCADTA to sell a large stock interest to Pan American Airways, she later forced complete German withdrawal, and sent the German pilots and ground crews home to the fatherland in 1940. Pan American Airways holds 64 % of the stock of the reorganized company, Colombian nationals the balance (Colombians can buy a controlling share whenever they wish). This was Colombia's substantial contribution toward the defense of the Panama Canal—no longer are there German air fields within two or three hours of the Gatun locks.

What lies ahead in the relations between these two countries? Economic realism suggests that Colombia play with the United States, her best market. Her security is linked with the United

States because of her proximity to the Panama Canal, which she knows will be protected at any cost. Psychologically she is close to the United States: the energetic middle-class Colombian seems thoroughly at home in the United States, as does the American professional or businessman in Bogotá.

However, there are plenty of Colombians who would drive a wedge between Colombia and the United States—chiefly the conservatives of Laureano Gómez' school, feudal survivors such as may be found in every Latin-American country. Then there are in Colombia some 15,000 or 16,000 Germans (about 1,000 were born in Germany); some of these are busily working as good Hitler-Germans work throughout Latin America. They have money and brains, many are powerful in coffee, cotton, trade, industry. Furthermore, they have potential allies in such die-hards as Laureano Gómez. They hold a threat for Colombia, and for the United States.

THE Isthmus of Panama still lies north, the lost province of Colombia, reminder of old wrongs. Parenthetically, one may ponder our fairer fortune had the elder Roosevelt exercised a little patience and dug the Canal with Colombian coöperation. One might even think that the interest of all would be served should the Colombian Navy steam into Panama's harbor and take that country away from President Arnulfo Arias and his coterie of strange friends. It would be simple. All that the second Roosevelt need do would be to order the American marines in Balboa to look the other way for an hour or two. It would be a delightful surprise for Colombia.[1] It also offers attractive opportunity for the dominant Roosevelts (sometimes called "mavericks" by the other branch) to settle all scores with their kinsmen. But such things happen only in books.

1. A distinguished Colombian official, after reading this paragraph, retorts "No, it wouldn't be a 'delightful surprise.' We have troubles enough, thank you."

CHAPTER VI

MIDDLE AMERICA

FIFTEEN flags fly over Middle America, the America of the Caribbean. The flags of Britain, France, Holland, and the United States find their place with those of eleven sovereign Latin-American nations. We have already dealt with Venezuela and Colombia and will not concern ourselves here with the colonies of European powers, important as they are in the defense plans of the hemisphere; nor with Puerto Rico, an American colonial outpost. We now turn our attention to the three island republics—Cuba, Haiti, and the Dominican Republic—and the six Central American countries.

Middle America is shaped by the mountain ranges which swing north and south. The Andean range carries through Central America, its buckled spine connecting Panama, Costa Rica, Nicaragua, Honduras, Salvador, Guatemala, and Mexico with the Rockies of the United States. There is a second range to the east—the continuation of the Guianan and Brazilian highlands, which loses itself in the Atlantic, appears in the thousand islands of the Antilles, and finally emerges as the Appalachian range of the eastern United States. The eastern and western ranges create Central America, the speckled Antilles, and the Caribbean Sea. That sea, key to the defense of Panama, is well enclosed, with no open passage over 120 miles in width. The American flag flies over Puerto Rico and the Virgin Islands, and over five bases leased by Great Britain.

America had its beginnings in the Caribbean world. Columbus came here in 1492, 1493, and 1498. He established the first European settlement in America on La Isla Española (corrupted to Hispaniola by the English), now the home of the Haitians and the Dominicans. Cuba and Española were long the headquarters of soldiers who raised the Spanish flag from California to Patagonia. Balboa pushed over the Isthmus and founded the city of

Panama in 1519; Hernán Cortés subjugated Mexico in 1519–21; Pizarro sailed from Panama to capture Peru in 1528. A score of others explored the coasts of Florida, Mexico, Central America, the Spanish Main, and charted the islands of the Caribbean. This became a Spanish world—with fitful settlements of British, French, and Dutch. Here came 3 millions of black slaves from Africa, until much of Middle America was more black than white. It became the highway for trade between Europe and the East: galleons put into Cartagena, transshipped to Panama, thence to the Philippines. Traders of every nation and race rested here, and left their signature on the faces of the people living in Kingston, Colón, La Guaira, Port-au-Prince, Santo Domingo. The eyes and profiles and skins of these people bespeak their varied heritage—Oriental, Indian, African, North European, and Mediterranean.

In the background stands the Indian. The Nahuas settled the plateau of Mexico and reached down into Central America. The Mayas lived in Yucatan and what is now Honduras and Guatemala, leaving great cities and temples: Copán, Quiriguá, Tikal, Palenque, Uxmal, and Chichen Itzá. Arawaks and Caribs inhabited the islands. Columbus reported to his king the trustfulness of these native peoples, their affectionate kindliness. Within fifty years these gentle Indians were largely dead, their place taken by chained slaves. Guatemala remains the only predominantly Indian land of Middle America.

Independence did not come to Central America until 1821. The wealthy creoles were loath to break with the Crown, they feared the half-breeds and Negroes in the coastal cities. In 1821 a common soldier named Gainza led a popular revolt against Spanish rule in Guatemala, set up an independent government, and unsuccessfully sought union with Mexico. "The United Provinces of the Center of America" emerged in 1823, a republic with five provinces which shortly broke up into five separate nations.

Puerto Rico and Cuba, having neither will nor power to secede, remained in Spanish hands until the close of the nineteenth century. Haiti and Santo Domingo, under French rule since 1795, were the first to revolt. Haiti ended French rule in 1803, held the entire island until 1843, when the Dominicans split off. Panama became a separate state in 1903.

Cuba

THE island of Cuba is the long-time object of foreign affection, first Spain's and then the United States'. Spain collected tribute of sugar and tobacco for four hundred years; the United States coveted the island from the first days of her independence. Jefferson and Adams talked of annexation. Clay warned France in 1825 against any attempt to change Cuba's status. Polk debated her purchase in the 'forties and Buchanan her seizure in the 'fifties. Seward found her "very attractive to the American people" in the 'sixties. Intervention seemed imminent during the Cuban rebellion of 1868–78, and in 1898 the Spanish-American War brought Cuba into the orbit of American power with a limited freedom.

Cuba, 750 miles from west to east, with an area equal to that of Pennsylvania, is a land of many troubles. She was the center of Spanish slave trade and today one third of her $4\frac{1}{3}$ millions are Negro. (An Alabama judge would set the percentage higher.) When other colonies were driving out Spanish garrisons, Cuba's white families were restrained by memories of the Negroes' butchery of the French in Haiti. The first attempt at freedom (1868–78) brought death to thousands of Cuba's sons, and produced the chief heroes of her history: Carlos Manuel de Céspedes, Máximo Gómez, the mulatto Antonio Maceo, Estrada Palma (destined to be the first President), and José Martí—inspired pamphleteer of free Cuba.

Cuba's independence years have been heavy. The American occupation under Leonard Wood was wise and moderate—order was restored, schools established, yellow fever eliminated. The future seemed auspicious when Estrada Palma assumed the presidency in 1902 and ruled constructively for four years. The subsequent record was less happy, with official venality and tyranny

alternating with American intervention. Cubans had no experience in self-rule, only a long schooling under corrupt colonial
governors. The unhappiest period was the eight-year rule of
Gerardo Machado (1925–33), whose peculations, extravagances,
and cruelties place him among the least pleasant of Latin-American dictators. His flight in August 1933 precipitated a period of
looting and murdering, shortly followed by the *coup d'état* of an
army cabal headed by astute Sergeant Fulgencio Batista. Batista
has ruled since 1933—first as the head of the army through a succession of presidents whom he dominated, and then since 1940 as
the duly elected President of the republic. Batista's rule has been
a moderated dictatorship, with some show of democratic forms.
As commander in chief, he concentrated control of the schools,
the customhouses, and other governmental functions in the
hands of the army—this proved profitable to the little group of
officers he commanded. When Batista became President, his successor in the army, José Pedraza, mistakenly concluded that he
had inherited the perquisites; but Batista, now directly responsible for balancing the national budget, took the customhouses
away from the army. Whereupon Pedraza organized a revolt. In
February 1941 Batista made a quick visit to army headquarters at
Camp Colombia, successfully appealed to the loyalty of the officers, placed Pedraza in a plane for Miami. The Chief of the Navy,
Angel González, followed him. Batista now rules without debate. Cuba has had worse rulers.

Sugar, Cuba's chief reliance, accounts for about three fourths
of her exports and she furnishes about one fourth of the world's
export sugar. Her production fell from an annual average of almost 6 million tons in 1928–29 to little over 3 millions during the
five years 1936–40. The fluctuating price of sugar decides Cuba's
national economic health: in 1920 sugar touched 22½ c. a pound
in New York (without duty); by 1932 it had dropped to 0.93 c. a
pound; in 1939 the average price was 1.96 c. Cuba's total exports
reached an all-time high of 722 million dollars in 1920, sank to 80
millions in 1932, were 142 millions in 1938—a record chiefly explained by the fluctuations of sugar trade. Cuba's sugar ties her

to the United States. American interests dominate the industry. Cuban sugar enjoys a preferential tariff in the American market —never less than 20 %, now 52 %; it has a preferred place on the American quota, in force since 1934. By the terms of this quota, the United States and its insular possessions (chiefly Hawaii and Puerto Rico) are allotted 55.59 % of estimated American consumption, the Philippines 15.41 %, Cuba 28.60 %, all others 0.40 %. Cuba usually sells about 30 % of the sugar consumed in the United States.

Cuba's soil produces the world's best cigar tobacco—her second export—and a variety of other crops. She has belatedly learned to diversify her agriculture and to grow her own foodstuffs, but over one quarter of her imports are still grains, meats, vegetables. The Cuban people, chiefly dependent upon agriculture, are caught in a vise: working on the lands of others, drawing wages which seldom reach $1 a day, with long periods of seasonal unemployment; buying their foodstuffs and finished goods in a market artificially high because of dependence upon imports. The major gains are allotted to owners of land, chiefly aliens, and to the more energetic recent comers of Spanish and other European bloods who control chief businesses and industries. The fortunate ones are those who draw steady pay from the army, those who hold the numerous governmental posts.

Cuba has mineral wealth: large reserves of manganese, iron, gold, copper, chromium, asphalt, silver, mercury. In 1938 she shipped 218,000 tons of manganese ore to the United States.

Cuba bears an undeniable colonial status. The Platt Amendment of 1902 gave Washington the right to intervene "for the preservation of Cuban independence, the maintenance of a government adequate for the protection of life, property and individual liberty"—the legal basis of a thinly disguised colonial rule, repeatedly exercised as such. In 1934 that Amendment was abrogated, to the joy of Cubans and to the credit of Sumner Welles. Many Cubans applaud Washington for commendable restraint during recent years. Harry Guggenheim, Hoover's ambassador, was heartily damned for not unseating Machado, but critics overlooked the fact that Washington was making an honest effort to let Cuba clean its own house. Sumner Welles and Jefferson Caffery were damned for refusal to recognize Grau San Martín in 1933. Some guardians of liberty would have Washington enforce more democratic procedures upon Batista. The way of American diplomats in Cuba is a rocky one, and Washington is fortunate in the formidable George Messersmith who now dispenses the gospel of the Good Neighbor in the Pearl of the Antilles. The Roosevelt administration is as eager as any Cuban that the island republic should shape her own destiny without meddling from the North.

Economically, American investment in Cuba stands at 700 million dollars—about one fourth of our total direct investment in all Latin America. (In 1929 the figure for Cuba exceeded 1 billion dollars.) This investment is in sugar, utilities, railroads, mines.

La Isla Española

THE visitor to the lovely island home of the Haitians and the Dominicans understands the extravagant emotions which swelled the breast of Columbus. Today 3 million Haitians hold the western third, 1½ million Dominicans the eastern two thirds of this island about the size of South Carolina. This mountainous land has furnished the setting for more tragedy and tragicomedy than any other spot in the Western World. For over four hundred years it has been fought over by Indians, Spaniards, French, Negroes, British. When other enemies are lacking, the Dominicans and the Haitians fight each other.

The Indians discovered by Columbus were soon dead of European disease and bullets; their place was taken by Negro slaves. In the early sixteen hundreds French buccaneers settled the western end of the island, and the French colony of Saint Domingue (Haiti) was recognized by Spain in 1697. Throughout the seventeenth and eighteenth centuries this French colony was one of the richest spots on earth. Some 35,000 French colonists commanded a half-million slaves, produced half of Europe's sugar, much of its coffee, cotton, tobacco. Meanwhile, the eastern end of the island continued as a sluggish Spanish colony, with a few Spaniards and their 16,000 slaves leading an unproductive life. In 1795 the entire island passed to the sovereignty of France.

Partisans of liberty remind us that the first Latin Americans to take up the slogan of *liberté, égalité, fraternité* were black slaves in the mountain valleys of Española. In 1779 Comte d'Estaing stopped in Haiti on his way to join Lafayette in America, and 800 black volunteers sailed with him, forgotten heroes of the battle of Savannah. By 1791 black rebels—with some white help —rose against French garrisons. In 1793 British and Spanish troops occupied the island. The revolt then became a clear-cut issue, blacks against whites. The leader was a fifty-year-old slave, Toussaint l'Ouverture, "first of the blacks," one of the authentic liberators of America. He raised an army of 4,000, killed the Spaniards, outplayed the French, outwitted his rivals among the blacks. By 1801 he held the city of Santo Domingo, controlled the entire island, notified France that he accepted French sovereignty, and appointed himself governor for life. Napoleon, preferring to name his own governors, dispatched his brother-in-law Leclerc with 12,000 men, under orders first to crush the Haitians and then to join the garrison at New Orleans—that last barrier against the advancing ambitions of Thomas Jefferson. Toussaint was captured and sent to France to die in prison, his army was routed. Then yellow fever killed Leclerc and much of his army. (Dwellers in the Mississippi valley may thank Toussaint for detaining and yellow fever for ending Leclerc, thereby speeding the Louisiana purchase.) That ended French rule in Haiti. In 1803 Dessalines, the most savage of Toussaint's lieutenants, proclaimed the independence of Haiti and crowned himself emperor. Three years later Dessalines was killed by critics who objected to his tortures, and the rule was divided between Henri Cristophe in the north and Petión in the south. Both finally fell and the rule of the entire island passed to Boyer. In 1843 the island split into two nations: French-speaking Haiti and the Spanish-speaking República Dominicana.

The Dominican Republic

THE Dominicans seem born for sorrow. The Spaniards neglected them and the French bullied them for three hundred years, the Haitians harried them for forty more. Independent in 1843, they suffered a varied misrule, a return of Spanish occupation in 1861–65, the angrily resented control of American marines in 1916–24, and finally the most complete dictatorship of their history under Rafael Leonidas Trujillo. The American marines must accept credit for ·the generalissimo; they taught him to shoot during their tenancy. Trujillo has ruled with unflagging consistency. Citizens have learned to speak no idle word, to think no unhallowed thought; those who have not learned find themselves in exile, jail, or eternal glory. Only a man of Napoleonic mold could have renamed after himself the ancient city of Santo Domingo—the seat of the oldest university in the Americas and the resting place of the bones of Columbus (San Marcos of Lima debates the first claim, Sevilla the second). But Trujillo has proved a good housekeeper, the country is cleaner and more prosperous, there are more schools. It must also be reported that Trujillo has given 75,000 acres for a colony of 1,300 European refugees, that 1,000 more are expected. Such items lead some to overlook the signs in every restaurant "Discussion of politics forbidden," and the neon sign over the ex-Vice-President's house, "For God and Trujillo." Meanwhile Washington has proved its good neighborliness by loaning Trujillo $3,000,000 with which to build a hotel in Santo Domingo (pardon, Ciudad Trujillo) and to buy road-building machinery from the United States.

Sugar and cacao represent four fifths of the Dominicans' exports, other crops feed the people.

The 1½ million Dominicans—more or less—are chiefly a mulatto people, with a few of predominantly white blood in the capital city's 71,297 population. The country has produced notable leaders in the arts and letters, names well known over Latin America. The professional class in the capital are an intelligent and attractive company.

Haiti

THE history of independent Haiti during the period 1843–1915 records twenty-two presidents of whom two served out their appointed term, several were murdered, others found safety in flight. It may be said for Haiti that few if any aliens have been killed in local broils since her independence was won; she has not imposed her disorders upon outsiders—the outsiders have imposed themselves on her.

The story of American intervention in Haiti began in 1914 when an American battleship sailed into the harbor of Port-au-Prince, removed a half-million dollars in gold from the vaults of the Banque d'Haiti, carried it to New York for safekeeping, and for the protection of bondholders who considered their interests imperiled. In 1915 President Guillaume Sam executed 167 political prisoners at one time, then sought refuge in the French legation, was dragged out by his outraged townsmen, and was cut up into small pieces. At this point another American battleship steamed into the harbor and the marines landed for a stay of eighteen years. There are two ways of telling the story of marine rule in Haiti. American apologists cite the record of sanitation, road building, education, reorganization of finance, training of the army, improvement of agriculture—to prove that the occupation was constructive. Haitians describe it as invasion of a friendly people's territory, say that the gifts bestowed were of dubious use, and recall that the Haitians paid for these blessings whether they would or not. Several points are pertinent: the occupiers were honorable men but often short on comprehension; they were uninvited white men in a Negro nation; they sometimes forgot their manners, overlooked the fact that the chief Haitian families included people of personal and intellectual distinction. The officers introduced the color line, decreed separate beaches and golf clubs for whites and blacks, and their wives often forgot to return calls made by Haitian women. The marine officers made other unhappy mistakes. When the *cacos* (mountain peasants) refused forced labor on the roads, there was some shooting. The eighteen years were quite unhappy for both marines and Haitians.

I sometimes hear brave patriots in Long Island and Evanston exclaim that what we must do, by God, is to go into all of these nearby nations and clean 'em up. I recall the city of Port-au-Prince during the years of rule by marines. I remember the gentle courtesy of intelligent men and women who told me of the humiliations imposed upon them. I remember the sailors (Join the Marines and See the World) compelled to serve out their time, who milled around the town and were noisy in their distaste for the whole performance. I remember them in water-front bars, as they worked at the problem of making their little pay cover one more drink or another game of penny ante, bantering the hours away with French-Negro-Spanish-Chinese ladies of the evening who were so happy with the Americans. Meanwhile Washington was tiring of this venture in making Haiti safe for bondholders, and began to take the boys home. The policy of the Good Neighbor, which really began under Coolidge and Hoover, took on more solid flesh when the last marine was out of Port-au-Prince.

Haiti's progress toward democratic institutions must inevitably be slow. The great masses of her 3 million people—crowded 300 to each square mile, of almost completely Negro blood, speaking a patois of mixed French and African dialects—make a frugal living. A little handful of the élite, many of them with liberal admixture of French blood, well-educated and priding themselves on their precise French of the *Académie,* own much of the best land and hold the chief posts in government and business. There is a deep gulf between the élite and the masses, one which the well-born make little effort to bridge—they would prevent recurrence of disorder by holding the power firmly in their own hands. Stenio Vincent, President since 1930, has ruled with such vigor that he has not only successfully excluded the masses from authentic political activity but has also won the enmity of many of the more privileged. The press is muzzled and dissidents find silence expedient. Meanwhile the nation is orderly and collects 7 or 8 million dollars annually from its exported coffee and sugar.

The moral for the United States is reasonably clear. It takes a long time for any people to learn the art of perfect government (Cook County for example). No nation can successfully teach another how to keep house and mind its babies—Theodore Roosevelt and Woodrow Wilson notwithstanding.

Central America

THE six republics of Central America reach from the Colombian border to Mexico—a span of 1,000 miles following the spine of the cordillera. A land of coastal plains, lakes, and mountain plateaus, it furnishes homes to about 7¾ millions—Indians, Negroes, mixtures of many races. It is an area where soil is rich, rainfall is plentiful, and life is easy. Coffee hangs heavy in the shade of old groves, bananas grow like weeds, the soil yields foods with little argument. It is a world which lives in the sun, where man finds it easy to relax.

The Central Americans first thought to unite with Mexico, but strutting Emperor Iturbide muffed his opportunity. They then arranged the elaborate federal union of 1823 which did not work, for communications between the states were scant, religious arguments were bitter, ambitious caudillos ruled over each section. In 1838 the federation split into the separate nations of Guatemala, Honduras, Costa Rica, Salvador, and Nicaragua.

Guatemala, the most populous with some 3 million people, is a little larger than Pennsylvania. This is an Indian land in which few can decipher a headline, where the majority live as did their forefathers centuries ago. Privileged people of European blood own land and coffee groves, while the Indians are effectively tied to the land and work long hours each day for a few cents. Tourists may drive over the mountains to Lake Atitlán and Chichicastenango's market, while Indian women in homespun cotton look on with solemn eyes. Civilizations meet in Guatemala, they do not seem to mingle. The 5,000 Germans own many businesses and coffee *fincas;* the mestizos hold offices and run politics; the 2 million Indians toil, breed, and die.

Nowhere in the Americas, save perhaps in Ecuador, have the Indians clung more successfully to their primitive dress and ritual. Spain's churches dominate the village square, but the Indian has carried his more ancient rites to the very altar of Our Lady, and his dances find a place in the temple enclosure.

Guatemala is a land cut to the heart's desire of a dictator, and she has known no other sort of ruler. Conservative clerical Carrera ruled 1839–65; anticlerical Barrios 1873–85; cutthroat Cabrera 1898–1920. The current dictator, General Jorge Ubico, is more urbane. He faithfully follows Washington's slightest suggestion, quiets all agitators, permits no criticism, and gives the country a carefully policed peace.

Salvador, smallest of all, about the size of Maryland, lies completely on the Pacific side and lives from coffee which constitutes about 90 % of her exports. Her 1¾ million people, crowded more than a hundred to the square mile, are divided between a small ruling class of predominant Spanish blood and more than a million workers on the soil—a mixture of Indian, Negro, Spanish, and other bloods. There are a score of families with great houses and many acres, whose control of the country has suffered few setbacks for the past century. The incumbent of the presidential office since 1931 has been Maximiliano Martínez, who satisfies his friends, keeps workers in their place, and gives no hint of early retirement.

Honduras, somewhat larger than Virginia, has a population of about 1 million, exports bananas, gold, silver, and coffee. A small ruling class of whites and mestizos; many workers of Indian, Negro, and Spanish blood; politics of alternate confusion and dictatorship—Honduras fits the current Central American pattern.

Nicaragua is about the size of the State of New York and has the largest lake between Titicaca and Michigan. She shares with Panama the boon of a deep depression in the cordillera, affording easy crossing by way of Lake Nicaragua. The California gold rush of the 'forties brought many pilgrims this way, and stirred British and American ambition to build a trans-Isthmian Canal. In the wake of the gold seekers came the American filibuster Walker who made himself president of Nicaragua in 1855; restored slavery; won substantial support from Southern partisans of slavery; sought to persuade Washington to annex the state; and was finally evicted by Costa Rica with the help of her neighbors. The disorderliness of the balance of the century was capped by the regime of dictator Zelaya (1893–1909), whose sixteen-year rule was arbitrary and brutal but brought marked improvements in education and material prosperity. The United States ousted him in 1909, and from then until 1933 American marines were in and out of Nicaragua—policing elections; maintaining governments in power; pursuing but never catching the rebel band of Sandino (patriots, many Nicaraguans called them); winning the praise of the presidents they protected, and the scorn of almost everyone else. Anastasio Somoza, the genial dictator who now curbs the liberty of the people for their own good, revels in the friendship of Washington. The doctrine of the Good Neighbor has enjoyed no more pleasant vindication than was afforded by the spontaneous ovation offered Somoza when he visited Washington in 1939. He was met at Union Station by President Roosevelt and members of the Cabinet, the proper guns were fired, the military bands played glad music, and the streets along the line of march were lined by tens of thousands of government employees granted three hours of liberty to express their unstudied welcome. Mr. Somoza's happiness was complete when the Export-Import Bank pressed 2½ millions upon him.

Meanwhile the million Nicaraguans of Spanish, Indian, and Negro mixtures are divided by occupation and economic privilege as are the other people of Central America. Bananas and coffee furnish the bulk of the exports which total from $5,000,000 to $7,000,000 annually. Economically and politically the country is tied to the United States. From 60 % to 70 % of her two-way trade is with the United States. The army is American-trained, and the government loses no opportunity to affirm its solidarity with Washington.

Costa Rica is unique among the Central American states in the whiteness of her population, the honesty and constitutional orderliness of her political life, the intelligence of her citizenry. Her 600,000 people, in a country about the size of West Virginia, are in large part of pure Spanish extraction, especially in the heavily populated area around the capital city of San José. Mixed bloods, Indians, and Negroes live in the coastal towns and remote mountain valleys. For eighty years, with few interludes, political life has been tranquil, and Costa Rican elections are exemplary. Presidents serve out their appointed terms, handle the nation's business frugally and honestly, and peacefully yield to their elected successors. The school system is the best in Central America: Costa Ricans boast more schoolteachers than soldiers. It is a country of moderate-sized farms whose chief export crops are coffee, bananas, and cacao. Despite the persuasions of German agents, Costa Rica is a firm ally of the United States, which buys more than half her exports.

The Banana Empire is the title assigned to Central America by authors Kepner and Soothill in their careful study. The United Fruit Company must be reckoned an extra government in the Central American pattern. That facile company has flourished for forty years—buying out competitors, acquiring some 4 million acres of land along the Central American coast, building 1,500 miles of railroads, and operating a handsome fleet of ships which carry tourists, traders, and bananas. This whole area chiefly lives by grace of United Fruit, buys from it, sells to it. The company has built ports, fought tropical fevers, erected hospitals. It is the chief employer of labor, and if its average daily wage of about $1 seems small by American standards, it is high compared with prevailing pay in Central America. Dana G. Munro of Princeton has described the hold of this company upon the economic and political life of these nations, their powerlessness before the company's superior weight. The company's agents have long been charged with making and unmaking presidents.

Today observers are generally agreed that the cruder tactics of earlier days yield to fairer practice, but United Fruit is still mighty in banana land.

Panama is the latest addition to the Central American constellation. Freed from Colombia by the one-act skit of 1903, in which title roles were played by Theodore Roosevelt and sundry French, Panamanian, and American promoters, Panama was embarked upon independent life. Her half-million people, occupying an area the size of Maine, are a mixture of Spanish, Indian, Negro, and many other families of men. The two port cities, Panama and Colón, are generously international. A walk through their main streets reveals the names of the merchants—they are Arabian, Czech, Egyptian, French, German, Greek, Italian, Japanese, Yugoslav, Polish, Spanish.

The people and their government live from the Canal. Washington's annual payment of $250,000 has now been raised to $430,000. There are jobs for all comers in the Canal Zone, and the pay is higher than elsewhere in Middle America. Almost one half the population lives directly or indirectly from the Canal— workers in the zone, domestic servants in the homes of Americans, vendors of goods to travelers on the boats which pass through (5,903 in 1939). The rest of the people live in the backland valleys and raise bananas, cacao, coconuts, coffee, and sugar.

Panama is dominated by a little coterie of professional politicians. The creation of an authentic national life is blocked by the poverty and illiteracy of the masses, the presence of a large unassimilated body of West Indian Negroes and of other aliens. Government since 1903 has been by grace of Washington, a situation which galls patriotic Panamanians. There have been a few notable and able patriots, among whom ex-President Ricardo Alfaro deserves grateful mention. The overshadowing power of the United States and the assurance of secure income from the Washington treasury make for servility and venality in public officials. In 1939 Washington ratified a new treaty with Panama, canceling the earlier guarantee of independence (which, like the Platt Amendment in Cuba, was regarded as an abridgment of sovereignty), and welcomed Panama as a "joint partner in defense of the Canal."

The latest round in the political arena was the election of 1940. Ricardo Alfaro ran against Arnulfo Arias, and Arias emerged with most of the votes. The new President, fresh from European travel, seems overimpressed with totalitarian fashions, his right-hand man is a ubiquitous pro-Nazi editor named Antonio Isaza. One of his first acts was the promulgation of a new constitution, promptly approved by a plebiscite of the people, which installed a quasi-totalitarian regime. Arias takes steps to eliminate foreigners from business—a measure which worries American nationals. He clamped a censorship upon the press and evicted Edward W. Scott, editor of the *Panama-American,* a paper owned by ex-President Harmodio Arias, his brother and bitter foe. Dark stories circulated through the winter of 1940–41 concerning the pro-Hitler opinions of the new President—reports variously explained as fiction and fact. Meanwhile, Washington negotiated for new protective bases, was repeatedly delayed by Arias' demands for better terms. This proves Arias an excellent realtor.

Panama presents her peculiar puzzle to the United States. Officially, we cherish the myth of Panama's sovereignty, it yields a comforting sense of national virtue, and we hope it persuades all Latin Americans of our immaculateness. We raise our mission in Panama to the rank of an Embassy, treating this Isthmian Republic on a par with Great Britain and Soviet Russia. We pay what they ask—Panama is our only creditor who is paid in old gold dollars. Our ambassadors are patiently correct. But we know, the Panamanians know, everyone knows that the military stake of Washington in the ten-mile Canal corridor will be protected no matter what it costs in dollars, in hurt pride.

Meanwhile Panama becomes robustly nationalistic. The President has assured his people that no change will be made in the national flag or the national anthem. The national motto is being revised. The old motto, *"Pro Mundi Beneficio,"* adopted by the founding fathers of 1903, must go. A nationwide contest was held in January 1941, and the prize of $100 went to the author of the slogan "Only God Above Us," but the National Assembly finally decided upon a tactful compromise: "Honor, Justice, Liberty."

CHAPTER VII

MEXICO

THERE are some things which any American knows about all Mexicans: Mexicans are bandits, they carry guns, they make love by moonlight, they eat food which is too hot, and drink drink which is too strong, they are lazy, they are communists, they are atheists, they live in mud houses and play the guitar all day. And there is one more thing which every American knows: that he is superior to every Mexican. Aside from these items the atmosphere between Mexico and the United States is mild and friendly.

Of course we think the Mexican picturesque. He makes little jugs and paints flowers on them. He wears *huaraches* instead of shoes, a *sarape* instead of a coat, and an oversized hat. His women carry their babies on their backs, tightly wrapped in blue *rebozos*. We like the Mexican's villages, outlined with cactus hedges, spotted with houses of sun-baked adobe, enlivened with communal washing centers where women scrub and talk and sing. We delight in the village market lined by neat geometric piles of carrots and peppers and onions and more peppers, the tall *ahuehuetes* in their spare magnificence and massive vines of bougainvillaea topping the scene with purple blaze—all dominated by the lacy grace of a sixteenth-century church pock-marked by the sun and the rain and the wind and the spent bullets of dead revolutionists. This Mexico invites the eager curious from Kansas, Oregon, and Maine: the tourists who crowd trains, planes, steamers, and automobiles bound for Mexico, filling hotels and pensions, jamming restaurants, buying painted pigs, gaudy sarapes, and jaunty straw horses as fast as the Mexican can produce them. Mexico becomes a cult. Greenwich Village moves to Taxco. The spell of Mexico is upon painters hunting line and color, schoolteachers pursuing culture and credit, starry-eyed wayfarers seeking vicarious atonement through other people's revolutions. On this restless crowd the Mexican turns a sober eye, ponders the strange ways of man, and raises his prices on painted pigs, lacquered gourds, and *frijoles refritos.*

Discovery and Rediscovery

THIS land of Mexico bulks 764,000 square miles—one fourth the area of the United States. Her 19 million people make her second in population to Brazil among the Latin-American republics. Mexico's population is largely centered in the upland plateaus which account for three fourths of the country. The capital city, with something over a million people, is the third city of Latin America. This is the land discovered and opened to the world by Hernán Cortés in 1519—the land now being rediscovered by tourist and promoter.

The rediscovery of Mexico is well begun. It has already yielded a few dull books with figures and many bright books with few facts. It has created three separate schools of American thought in regard to Mexico. *First,* the sentimental who find the Mexican quaint and try to copy him. *Second,* the lyrical who find him bold and covet his audacity. *Third,* the dyspeptic who find him dangerous and hope that the United States will annex Mexico and civilize her.

But this rediscovery, no matter how it may be complicated by its discoverers, opens up new meanings and new excitements which lie beneath the kaleidoscopic surface of Mexico. She is a nation thrust up out of the mass of human history, isolated, surprisingly untouched by the forces which have shaped other peoples. Mexico is a conglomerate in which the several elements are bound together by the brittle cement of a common Mexicanism but are not fused. Toltec pyramids are topped but not dominated by Christian churches. Indian Mexico is a nation within a nation, unamalgamated, largely unmoved. Furthermore, Mexico is a land of regions, in each of which life flows in a large measure of self-sufficiency and self-satisfaction. Mexicans say, "I am of Oaxaca," "I am of Yucatan," seldom "I am Mexican."

And Mexico repulses those who would find her. Much of her

life is hidden. There are no highways to ten thousand villages whose patterns of life have changed but little in a thousand years. Even those villages easily reached by train or automobile are not what they seem. Indian Mexico can be looked at, explored, but it looks back from somber eyes, telling nothing, conceding nothing.

The 19 million Mexicans are divided into four unequal parts. There is a little handful of the old aristocracy, a few thousand in all, whose eyes are fixed on the golden days of Porfirio Díaz. These are the survivors of the colonial privileged. They outlasted Iturbide and Santa Anna, hailed Maximilian and mourned his passing, were secure under Díaz. Hundreds of them fled to Paris in 1911, many never to return. The few that remain cling to their houses of hewn stone on the Paseo de la Reforma, but find it difficult to pay their taxes. There is a second handful—and a very small one—of the new plutocracy, the creation of the madder days of modern revolutionary Mexico, the men who made revolution pay. A third and more important segment is the thin layer of the Mexican middle class—a scant 10 % of the population. At the heart of this is the officialdom of government workers, they account for one half of the middle class. The government is almost the sole employer of the technically trained. Grouped with them in the Mexican middle class are doctors, lawyers, small industrialists, shopkeepers, innkeepers, traders, and bargainers. It is in large part of mixed blood—mestizo—although there must be counted in about 100,000 foreigners—including 12,500 Americans, 12,700 British, 7,300 Germans, 5,000 French, and 5,000 Italians (1938 figures). And, fourth, there is Indian Mexico. Of the 19 million Mexicans, 3 million can be classed as practically pure-blooded Indians, to whom may be added those who are largely Indian and whose habits of life relate them to the Indian group: it is safe to say that 15 millions belong to Indian Mexico. This Mexico cultivates corn and tends cattle. According to the census of 1930, Mexicans were divided in their occupations as follows:

Agriculture and other rural industries	77.2 %
Mines and industry	6.3
Trade	5.8
Government employment	4.4
Domestic service	4.0
Communications	2.3

When one surveys this anomalous nation, with its great majority living in isolation, cut off from the main currents of national life by illiteracy, indifference, and lack of communications, it is difficult to place Mexico under any of the accepted political categories. Mexico calls herself a democracy. She has a full complement of the trappings of democracy: elections, universal male suffrage, state and municipal governments cut on the same pattern as those of the United States, a Congress with upper and lower house, a Supreme Court to chaperon the Congress, a constitution, and a President elected by the people. But Mexico's peculiar political genius is not exhausted by such description. The political structure is topped by a quaint institution known as the Party of the Mexican Revolution, tightly controlled by the little group holding national power. The party names candidates for federal and state posts. It presides over the election machinery. It plays a role comparable to that of the Democratic party in Georgia or the Republican party in Vermont. Its candidates are elected with uniformity.

The casual observer concludes that there is no democracy in Mexico. He errs. Mexico has a democracy of her own practical design. She has governments which ultimately yield to the seemingly inert masses of Indian Mexico. The Indian must increasingly be reckoned with. He does not vote, not often at least. He may not hold the chief offices, save in rare instances. But these seemingly inarticulate masses make their will known. Calles fell before their weight in 1935. No president dares ignore them.

The democracy of Mexico—limited and halting as it is—has been hard won. It is the tragedy of Mexico that each new ordering of her national life has been born out of season. In 1519-20 she fell before Cortés and his six hundred men because Tenoch-titlán and Tlaxcala were at odds. In 1810 she followed Hidalgo and Morelos to the creation of a republic, but she was too weak to resist the treachery of Iturbide and of Santa Anna. By the close of the 'forties she had been outstripped by the United States in the race for national maturity, and lost half her territory. In the 'fifties her faith was fired by the emergence of an authentic leader, Benito Juárez, but her national development was inter-rupted by the invasion of Napoleon III's army and the puppet emperor Maximilian. A century of struggle for independence was rounded out by the thirty years' rule of Porfirio Díaz, a rule which left Mexico bound to alien investors invited and encour-aged by Díaz. The years since 1910 have been marked by violent swings between hope and defeat, between leaders and betrayers. With 77 % of her people still living close to the soil, with a con-stantly increasing number caught in the toils of a disturbing new industrialization, Mexico has been hard put to it to make work-able adjustments between tradition and modernity. With a pau-city of technicians, a surplusage of reckless generals and ambi-tious political chiefs, the wonder is not that Mexico has had de-feats, but rather that she has won such considerable victories.

Revolution

MEXICO cannot be understood without reference to the word Revolution. She is a land of fighting men, dedicated to battle.

Mexico fights her colonial past. Nations, no less than individu-als, fight their forebears. When Mexico attacks the *hacendado* and demands land, attacks the Church, insisting that it loose its hold, Mexico is fighting the past.

Mexico fights her betrayers. The 130 years since Father Hi-dalgo declared Mexico free and sovereign are spotted with the names of those betrayers. There were presidents who would be emperors, constitutional leaders who aspired to dictatorial power, and revolutionary leaders intent upon wealth. Mexico has fought them for a century. She fights them today.

Mexico fights the outside world. Tucked by a careless fate under the shadow of the United States, she has an account to settle. There is hurt pride in it, the record of a hundred humiliating years in which the United States and others crowded her, cajoled her, and treated her as an inferior of limited sovereignty and clipped rights. There is the sharp memory of lost territory. There is the sense of her narrowed economic sovereignty, cut by the inroads of foreign capital, and the capture by aliens of mines and oil fields and farm lands.

Men and nations are never calm in reciting their real or fancied wrongs. Mexico fights, and makes mistakes. Fights are never pretty. But it is a winning fight. Mexico is notable in the vitality of her re-creative power. Santa Anna could sell the national birthright and lose even the mess of pottage, but Benito Juárez could write the reform Constitution of 1857, build schoolhouses, attack the holdings of the hacendados and of the Church, and give the nation a glimpse of her certain destiny. Napoleon III could dispatch his men to the gates of Puebla, install his puppet emperor Maximilian, but the men from Oaxaca, Vera Cruz, and San Luis Potosí could block that march, and stand Maximilian against the firing wall in Querétaro. Porfirio Díaz could seize the communal lands of Morelos and allot them to his friends, but Díaz was no match for illiterate Zapata and his barefooted soldiers with machetes. Plutarco Elías Calles, fired with early generous intention, could be corrupted by age and power and wealth, but he went down before Lázaro Cárdenas who spoke persuasively for those who were cut off from their patrimony.

If the journeyer to Mexico detects a lyric note in the Mexican recital he must remember that revolutionists are seldom realists. The word *Revolución* has taken the place of the Blessed Virgin upon the national altar. Watch a barefooted Indian guiding a wooden plow drawn by a team of oxen in a Morelos valley. Perhaps that Indian simply plows and plants, but again it is possible that the furrows he turns are cut in his imagination in the pattern of the revolution. For it is the revolution which gives him the moist comfort of the land; which sends the schoolteacher to his village; which builds roads; furnishes seed corn and credit.

The Mexican Indian begins to know himself as the citizen of no mean country, and to take a timorous hand in determining that country's policy. He gives his Sundays to the building of the village school. He contributes a centavo daily to the salary of Señorita Esperanza, the teacher. On the frequent feast days he joins in singing the *corridos* of the revolution—those curious doggerels of the heroic deeds of Pancho Villa, Emiliano Zapata, and others. He may even vote. He holds his head higher, knows with increasing fervor and insight what he means when he joins his neighbors in shouting "Viva la Revolución, Viva México!"

There are plenty to laugh at him. There are the plush entrepreneurs of the capital, the traders who wear shoes and drive automobiles. There are the dour survivors of old families resentful of lost privileges. But these cannot laugh him down for he feels the revolution in the firm soil under his feet. Nor will he listen to those who ridicule his faith and tell him the revolution has been betrayed. He has the wisdom reserved for seers, the instinct that revolutions are never ended, but simply delayed.

Land

THE Mexican revolution is a pledge of faith, but also an earnest of works. Among these, the division of land comes first.

John Muir had a whimsical explanation of the derivation of the word "saunter." It comes, he said, from the French *sainte terre*. The Mexican understands the meaning of holy earth. His ancient feasts, adopted and renamed by the Church, celebrated planting, harvest, and fertility. Land was the one wealth which the Indian understood. It was his patent of nobility.

Mexico's story can be written in terms of land. The Spaniards found Indians living in communal possession of lands, which were worked jointly. Their title was inalienable. There was neither buying nor selling, borrowing nor foreclosing. The conquerors called these communal villages *ejidos*, and transferred to them some of the rights of the communal units of Spain.

Successive attacks were made upon that communal system,

during four hundred years. The Spaniard rewarded himself by the bestowal of encomiendas, temporary allotments of hundreds or thousands of Indians together with the lands they occupied. These encomiendas laid the basis for haciendas, which later destroyed many ejidos and reduced the Indians to serfdom.

The Church, fellow traveler with the conqueror, also took a hand in the destruction of the ejido. The dying generations of the faithful divided their winnings between their children and the Church. By the middle of the nineteenth century the Church was the chief landholder. Lucas Alamán, a defender of the Church, credited it with ownership of one half the productive property. Other claims ranged from one fourth to three fourths.

The reformers of the 'fifties and 'sixties, dominated by Benito Juárez, broke up the landholdings of the Church, thinking to spread soil ownership among the landless. Their plan went astray. Not only did Church lands pass into the hands of the latifundia class, but many of the remaining ejidos were also stripped of their holdings. "La Reforma," Mexico's first social revolt, left the poor poorer.

It remained for Porfirio Díaz (1876–1911) to complete the destruction of the ejido. Díaz had frank contempt for the Indian. He found the example of the United States admirable, and thought that Mexico's wisest course was to extirpate the Indian and to replace him with European immigrants. Díaz removed the last legal safeguards of the ejido. The free villagers, confronted with the economic power of the ambitious hacendados, were quickly dispossessed. During the thirty years of the Díaz regime, 3 million Indians were reduced to slavery. By 1910 Mexico was a nation divided into great haciendas, with a scant 1 % of the people holding 85 % of the land. One family, the Terrazas, owned 12 million acres in the state of Chihuahua. Three brothers owned the state of Hidalgo. The 12 million Indians worked as slaves upon the lands of their fathers, worked from "sun to sun" at a wage of 25 centavos daily—a little more or less— they were bound to the land by custom and by debt, debt incurred through bitter necessity, debt inherited from generation to generation. They had no recourse save to laws made and administered by their masters. The Indian was a man without rights, without appeal, without hope. But Porfirian Mexico was prosperous. Its credit stood high in the bourses of the world. It had gleaming palaces, proud boulevards, and a substantial gold reserve. Its prosperity was supported by the aching back of the Indian.

In 1910 the Indian struck. It was the centennial of Mexican independence. The octogenarian Díaz made a feast and bade his friends come. There was laughter and much champagne. It was the funeral feast, those about to die did the dancing. The flutes and trombones were suddenly stilled, for men were marching in Morelos, just over the mountains to the south. They had no guns, no shoes, no discipline. But they had the hard muscles and the hard hate of slaves, and they had a leader, Emiliano Zapata, who could not write his name. They burned sugar refineries and the houses of the hacendados. They carried banners bearing the legend—*Tierra y Libertad*. One thing they knew, that land is liberty. It was enough.

For thirty years Mexico has sought to fulfil the promises of Emiliano Zapata. Zapata himself served only as a scourge and left a wilderness where once had been fruitful valleys. His followers seized the lands but could not work them. They had neither experience nor tools nor seed nor credit. The agrarian program was without substance until Calles came to the presidency in 1924.

During the ten years (1924-34) of Calles and of Calles' appointees—Portes Gil, Ortiz Rubio, and Abelardo Rodríguez—more than 20 million acres of land were taken from the haciendas and distributed in small plots or in ejido units to villages. But Calles had meantime lost faith in his own reforms. Lázaro Cárdenas, installed as President in late 1934, returned to land distribution with a vigor which provoked conflict with "the Chief of the Revolution," as Calles was called. In June 1935 Cárdenas broke with Calles, the ex-President was forced into California exile, and the President sliced up great holdings with enthusiasm. Cárdenas spent many months of his six-year term traveling by train, plane, automobile, horseback to distant villages. He listened to complaints, issued orders for division of land, for schoolhouses, and irrigation works. By December 1940 he had distributed over 40 million acres to the villages. Almost half of all Mexicans had been given land. Cárdenas' most ambitious project was the expropriation of "La Laguna," an area of some million acres, about 300,000 of them arable, in the states of Durango and Coahuila. This area had been the property of a dozen families who had invested millions in drainage, irrigation, and equipment. Representatives of the 160,000 farm workers in La Laguna had made unsuccessful appeals to Calles since 1925. In 1936 Cárdenas ordered the dispossession of the former holders, allotted the lands to newly created ejido groups—each a coöperative collective society. The lands thus held cannot be sold or mortgaged. The government, through the Banco Nacional de Crédito Ejidal, finances their operations. The farmer members of these coöperative communities, now vested with land and credit, draw regular wages from the common credit funds; control their joint operations through overseers whom they themselves elect; are given the technical guidance of agricultural experts supplied by the government through the Credit Bank which also serves as their marketing agency; and divide the profits when the harvests are marketed. And, further, the government promises schools, sanitation, and roads.

Criticism of the land program is stormy. The seizures are denounced as flagrant confiscation. Theoretically, each owner is to be paid for his land. Actually, with the Mexican treasury strained to meet the simplest needs and burdened with accumulated debt, there seems little chance that payment will ever be made. The Mexican land program is called communistic. Such charges fall upon deaf ears. Cárdenas and his friends regard that program as the prime instance of the integrity and vitality of the Mexican revolution—proof that a sovereign nation can recapture the lost

patrimony of her most defenseless citizens. Critics reply that
Mexico loses by the land program. They cite figures on the production of corn, Mexico's chief food crop. In 1910, the last year
of Porfirian prosperity, Mexico produced 81,069,000 bushels of
corn. In the three years 1936–38 the average annual production
was less than 65,000,000 bushels. They point up the lesson—20 %
increase in population, 20 % decrease in production of the chief
food of the people. They explain it by wasteful working of land,
by graft and inefficiency. The Indian, they tell us, needs a master. He works better as a slave. The argument is countered by
those who explain that under the old hacienda system the Indian
was fed meagerly, most of the corn was sold in the market; today,
with holdings worked coöperatively, more corn is used by those
who produce it, less of it reaches the market where it may be
counted.

Avila Camacho, President since December 1940, gives no evidence of further attacks upon the haciendas. By April 1941 he
had taken steps to break up the ejidos, and to grant communal
owners their own small farms. He meets angry criticism from
those who argue the superiority of the ejido system, with its
strong roots in Indian tradition.

Oil

MEXICO's petroleum, her chief source of quick wealth, is also her
chief problem. Around 1925 Mexico stood second among world
producers, with an average annual output of over 100 million barrels. She has since slipped to seventh place—producing about 42
million barrels in 1939. Between these years lay a long fight with
the British and American companies which controlled her fields.
This struggle must be understood in the light of the traditional
Spanish and Indian conception of subsoil property. Mexicans cite
the decree of Charles III of Spain in 1783 and the edicts of Benito
Juárez as proving that Mexican law assumes that everything under the soil belongs to the state. This principle was restated in the
Constitution of 1917. Calles, acting upon it, sought to deprive

foreign concessionaires of permanent subsoil rights, but in 1928 reached an agreement with the United States through Ambassador Dwight Morrow, by which Mexico agreed to strip the law of all retroactive force. This truce prevailed until March 1938, when President Cárdenas signed a decree expropriating the properties of seventeen British and American companies with assets variously estimated from 100 to 500 million dollars. This action came as a result of a ten-month labor argument. Seventeen thousand oil workers had struck in May 1937, the dispute had been referred to the board of arbitration and conciliation, a report had been made in August with recommendations for increased wages and enlarged social services. The government argued that these increases would cost the companies 26 million pesos annually; the companies contended that they would aggregate 41 millions, and refused to conform. The two parties to the conflict presented their rival claims. The government charged that the companies made profits of 17.82 % in 1935 while the companies contended that they had made but 7.5 %. The government charged that the companies were paying wages averaging but 30.8 % of those paid by the same companies in the United States. The companies denied this. Many people in Mexico and the United States, with no impartial figures to fall back on, concluded that neither side was telling the entire truth. Meanwhile, the Mexican government, conducting the industry as a national monopoly, had difficulties with production and with marketing. An informal but effective boycott, maintained until 1940, prevented the entrance of much Mexican oil into the United States. A further boycott made it difficult for Mexico to secure oil machinery and parts from the United States. Labor troubles and a shortage of competent technicians made production difficult. By the end of 1940 it was clear that Mexico was tiring of her adventures in petroleum. By March 1941 it seemed clear that President Avila Camacho would shortly conclude an arrangement permitting the American companies to reënter Mexico, and to share in developing and managing the oil industry.

The petroleum adventures of Mexico, no matter what settlement is made, indicate a direction in Mexican life. Policy may
swing Left with Lázaro Cárdenas, or Right with Manuel Avila
Camacho, but the people of Mexico harbor an obstinate notion
that they possess the ultimate right to the wealth of soil and subsoil. Prospective investors in the outer world, sensing this, will
probably be slow to go in with surplus dollars for further excursions in land or mines or oil.

Labor

THE Mexican revolution concerns itself for the industrial workers, a body of about one half million, including 250,000 in manufacturing, 90,000 in mining, 17,000 in petroleum, 80,000 in communications. Article 123 of the Constitution of 1917 is labor's
bill of rights. Its terms are unequivocal. Collective bargaining is
obligatory. Minimum hours and wages are prescribed, compensation insurance is guaranteed. A man cannot be fired without
the payment of three months' wages. When a strike is called, and
officially recognized, the doors of the factory or mill are sealed
until the employer reaches an agreement with the men. No "sit-
down" is needed. The government does the sitting down. Mexico
has had her full quota of labor racketeers. Chicago gangsters
never did a more thorough job at terrorism and exploitation than
did Luis Morones and his aides in the CROM, the Mexican federation of labor, during the Calles regime. Calles gave labor a
free hand for a time, then turned against it. Morones' CROM was
supplanted by Lombardo Toledano's CTM (Confederation of
Mexican Workers) which rode high during the Cárdenas regime. The coming of Avila Camacho to the presidency in 1940
brought a sharp halt to Lombardo's power, and the clear intima-
tion that from now on labor cannot strike against the public
interest.

Mexico's labor policy represents her reaction to earlier experience. Mexican labor was cheap in the Díaz days, and enterprising
foreigners seized their natural advantage. American oil com-

panies, which paid $5 a day for common labor in the oil fields of Pennsylvania and Texas, rejoiced in 50 c. labor in the Tampico fields. Mining companies dug silver with 50 c. labor, cotton mills made cloth with 10 c. labor. Labor unions were crushed, hours were long, conditions of labor intolerable.

American capital's way with Mexican labor excites criticism. Americans, say the Mexicans, come not as businessmen but as gamblers. They are not content to build slowly and solidly, but insist on quick gains. Many American investors admit part of this charge, but insist that the mercurial changes in Mexican legislation force them to seek an immediate profit and a quick getaway. So the argument runs.

Cárdenas threw his weight on the side of the unions, but sought to reassure frightened industrialists. "The workers," he said, "cannot seize factories and other instruments of production because for the present they have neither sufficient technical ability nor the requisite financial experience required for an enterprise of such magnitude. There is no ground for alarm, not even to the employers, in the existence of an advanced social program." Confronted by bitter protests from the organized industrialists of the northern city of Monterrey, Cárdenas warned against any attempt to organize industry against union labor, and specifically against the use of the lockout as a weapon. "Even though the lockout spread and be made national, it will avail nothing. The nation itself will strike." He warned against attempts to make political capital out of antiunion agitation. That way, he said, lies armed struggle. Pressed by the importunities of the Monterrey industrialists, the Mexican President announced, "Employers who grow weary of the social struggle can always hand over their industries to the workers or to the government. That would be a patriotic deed, but the lockout would not be." To employers and to workers Cárdenas laid down the principle implicit in Mexican theory and practice, "The government is the arbitrator and the regulator of social life."

Cárdenas is out, Avila Camacho is in. Labor still has its bill of rights, but the gay days of labor's predominance seem ended for the moment. Avila Camacho busily reassures the foreign investor that Mexico is again safe for wandering dollars.

School

THERE is another cry which rises out of the struggle of revolutionary Mexico—*Tierra y Libros*. Land and books. The demand for schools has been, next to the demand for land, the most insistent note of the revolutionary years.

The Mexican, the barefooted Mexican, had no schools in 1910. The overseer and the occasional priest were his only instructors. He could not sign his name. He did not have the printed word as a link with the outside world. He was isolated by his own ignorance.

Today that Mexican has schools. During the sixteen years since Calles was inaugurated, over ten thousand village schools have been organized. According to official figures, illiteracy has been reduced from over 90 % in 1910 to 60 % in 1940. Critics of the government debate this claim and insist that the improvement is less substantial.

The villager calls his school *La Casa del Pueblo,* the house of the people. That school is the sign of an invincible hope. The wayfarer who visits little villages in isolated valleys, talks with teachers and citizens and children, stands on the edge of school fiestas, shares the hospitality of village homes, becomes aware that these people have poured into their school the dim hopes of defeated years. They who have had little are intent that their children shall have much.

The Mexican school is useful. It is rooted in the community, and the life of the community flows through it. It is the social center, where families meet and learn and sing and play. It is for adults who would learn to write as well as their children. It is the health center in thousands of villages which have neither nurse nor physician. It is often the agricultural training center, with lessons on seeds and fertilizer and the breeding of stock.

The Mexican school program has had fluctuating fortunes. It

reached its finest development under Calles, with Moisés Sáenz as the ablest educator in Mexican history. Cárdenas, with no less zeal for education, permitted the control of the schools to pass into the hands of mediocre men. The momentum of the earlier movement has not been lost, but morale has suffered. The excursions into "socialistic education" under Cárdenas seemed quite unreal, and by 1940 the schools of Mexico had lost much of their earlier distinction. But, after all discounts, the Mexican school still stands as the most imaginative public school in Latin America.

The Church

THE Mexican revolution wages war on the Church. It has always done so, even though the first great leaders of the revolution, Hidalgo and Morelos, were themselves parish priests. Today, under the Mexican law all Church buildings are the property of the nation: the Church uses them as tenant of the state. Clerical education is banned. Priests work under restrictions as to their number and their rights. Priests cannot vote, express their minds on public issues, hold property. Religious orders are banned. For ten years (1925-35) Mexico was torn by the bitterness of this struggle. Politicians often used the issue to their own advantage. Faithful adherents of the Church were grievously wounded in their deepest conviction. There was violence and anger on both sides.

Mexico's war on the Church has been incidental to the larger struggle for social change. For over a hundred years Mexico has fought for her national, political, economic, and social redemption; fought blindly, often unwisely, but fought. The clergy, as is their wont, were usually found on the conservative side. They, and especially the higher clergy, were on the side of Spain against the revolutionists in 1810. They fought civil marriage, birth registration, land reforms, secular education. They accepted dictators Santa Anna and Porfirio Díaz so long as those dictators would stand with the Church. In the 'sixties the clergy sided with the French and Maximilian. Her leaders followed the pattern usually set by organized religionists, whether these are Catholic or Protestant. The determined Congregationalists of Connecticut fought Thomas Jefferson in 1800 with no less fury than the organized Catholics of Jalisco fought Lázaro Cárdenas in 1934. It is the stubborn habit of those who think themselves entrusted with the secrets of the gods.

The tumult is now quieted. The laws governing the Church are still on the books, and the Mexican state still theoretically rules the Church. In practice, the Church is now quite free. This change began under Cárdenas. In February 1937 the police of Vera Cruz broke into a private house where Mass was being celebrated and shot an eighteen-year-old girl in the back. Cárdenas summoned the violently anticlerical governor, ordered an end of such gunplay, and the opening of the churches of the state. From that day, Mexican Catholics have enjoyed liberty denied them by Calles. When Avila Camacho took office in 1940, one of his first statements avowed his personal faith in the tenets of the Church. Churchmen now go about their business without hindrance.

Mexico and the World

THE Mexican revolution turns a proud face toward the outside world. The conduct of Mexican international relations is skilful.

Mexico has won an influential position in inter-American counsels. This was clear at Montevideo in 1933, at Buenos Aires in 1936, and at Lima in 1939. Increasingly Mexico becomes the polarizing center of the northern states of Latin America, as over against Argentina's leadership in the south.

Mexico deems herself the champion of democratic movements in other nations. When, in 1926 and 1927, Nicaragua was torn by strife between Sandino (variously known as bandit and patriot) and the acquiescent leaders picked by Washington, it was Mexico which sent guns and food to Sandino. When, in 1929, Washington was under Latin-American fire for using the weapon of recognition to pick or reject neighboring rulers, it was Mexico, through Foreign Secretary Genaro Estrada, which announced the principle of automatic recognition of *de facto* governments without reference to approval or disapproval. When Machado was busily pillaging Cuba, Mexico furnished a refuge for Machado's foes. When, in 1936, the government of Spain was attacked by Franco and his allies, Mexico was the one American nation which, without argument or apology, shipped food and arms to the loyalists. In 1939 Cárdenas made clear his support of the Allies. In 1940 and 1941 Avila Camacho repeatedly expressed his conviction that Mexico must stand with the "democracies against the dictators."

Mexico turns a proud face toward the United States. She is quick to recite history, and does not forget the record of a hundred years of dealings between the United States and Mexico. Mexicans insist that we took an unfair advantage of their nation in the days of her weakness and youth, to separate Texas, to pick a fight while Mexico was at the mercy of her betrayers, and to appropriate a full half of all her territory. The Mexican has a story to tell of our bludgeoning diplomacy since 1910. The Mexican thinks that Ambassador Henry Lane Wilson's encouragement of Victoriano Huerta led to the murder of Francisco Madero in 1912. He knows that our marines stormed Vera Cruz in 1914. He remembers General Pershing's punitive expedition with its vain pursuit of Pancho Villa. He has not forgiven Washington's bargaining over the recognition of Carranza and Obregón, nor the plethora of notes from Washington when Mexico embarked upon its land and petroleum policies in 1925. He has a lively memory of a certain note, signed by Secretary of State Frank B. Kellogg and delivered to President Calles in 1925, in which Calles was warned "your nation is on trial before the world," and the Mexican delights in remembering the quite universal applause accorded Calles' answer, "If our nation is on trial, so is every nation on trial."

The attitude of Mexico toward the United States is quite unlike the attitude of Cuba which knows she is owned, boots and baggage, by the United States and which entertains no effective hope of freedom. Mexico is aware of the threatening shadow of our economic power, of our political and military power, but she moves as though she were sovereign and, in the process, achieves the sovereignty which she assumes. A change has also come in the attitude of the United States. Ten years ago there was no lack of minor prophets proclaiming that we should set Mexico right, we should discipline her for her own good, and ours. Today, the clamor of outraged oil operators and of William Randolph Hearst is drowned in the chorus of good neighborliness.

The United States' share of credit for the happier state of affairs must be variously distributed. Dwight Morrow deserves a large portion. He patiently taught Washington the implications of sovereignty. His successors in office, J. Reuben Clark and Josephus Daniels, continued to preach the wholesome doctrine that a sovereign nation must be free to make her own laws and to enforce them.

Crowning proof of happier relations was offered at the inauguration of President Avila Camacho on December 1, 1940. Henry A. Wallace, Vice-President-elect, shared honors with the Mexican executive. Avila Camacho pledged allegiance to "the democratic ideal . . . to the Pan-American doctrine" and called for a united front by all Americans against the aggressors. This sentiment was made tangible by continued coöperation with the United States during the winter 1940–41. Negotiations for the use of Mexican bases by American forces, for a friendly settlement of the oil controversy, for cancellation of a Japanese oil contract which Washington deplored, gave evidence that Mexico proposed to travel with the United States. Fears of German activities were expressed, evidence of a busy German propaganda machine was clear, but Washington seemed confident that Mexico would be the Good Neighbor.

The returning pilgrim can never be objective about Mexico. The country is too dazzling, its contours and colors too exciting. The pilgrim may be reminded that there is poverty and meagerness, but he knows that from such soil spring flaming flowers. He may suspect that much of the Mexican revolution is inadequately realized, but he cannot forget the boisterous faith with which Mexico presses on. He cannot dismiss his glimpse of a people whose ardor admits of no defeat.

PART FIVE
—AND THE UNITED STATES

—AND THE UNITED STATES

TWO questions are uppermost—
From the North, Will Latin Americans play with us in this war which engulfs the world?

From the South, Will the United States stand with *us,* during the war, and *after* the war is done?

Affection for Latin Americans has broken out like a speckled rash on the skin of the North American body politic. Club-women read papers on the Humboldt Current, dress up as Aymarás, listen to guitarists strum tunes reputed to come from the Amazon. College presidents substitute courses on the Incas for those on the Age of Pericles. Chambers of Commerce give dinners to visiting Argentine bankers, and keep a set of twenty-one American flags among their props. Schoolgirls cut paper dolls which represent the dwellers by Atitlán. Official Washington takes a half-holiday to welcome itinerant Caribbean dictators. The army entertains Latin-American chiefs of staff, there is no ceiling on expense accounts. The recipient of this sudden devotion is a bit mystified, and the suitor is still a little flushed and tongue-tied, like a boy in his first pair of long pants. Of course, the lady thus ardently pursued has been around for a long time, we did not happen to note her charms before.

There have been three stages in United States–Latin-American relations.

First, that of the *onlooker,* rather bored. This occupied the nineteenth century. The United States, intent upon westward expansion, was only vaguely aware of Brazil and Chile. A few sentimentalists applauded San Martín and Simón Bolívar. The *New York Post* reported the victories of Maipo and Ayacucho. Some perspicacious statesmen, notably Henry Clay, urged recognition of the new republics. Americans looked upon Latin Americans as buyers of rum and carpet tacks or as objects of redemption. To be sure, James Monroe warned Europe against overreaching. True, we fought Mexico in the 'forties and took half of her territory; then debated the annexation of Santo Domingo and Cuba. Neither the Doctrine nor the debates indicated interest or affection. We were in the real estate business.

Second, the era of the *policeman*. Richard Olney sounded the reveille in 1895, warned Britain away from Venezuela, announced, "The United States is practically sovereign on this continent, and its fiat is law upon the subjects to which it confines its interposition." The War of 1898 left us with Puerto Rico, the Philippines—and Theodore Roosevelt, our mightiest policeman. He accepted assignment to keep "all neighboring countries stable, orderly and prosperous"; promised that nations which "act with decency . . . keep order and pay their obligations . . . need fear no interference from the United States"; warned that "brutal wrong-doing, or an impotence which results in a general loosening of the ties of civilized society, may finally require intervention by some civilized nation, and in the Western Hemisphere the United States cannot ignore this duty." This man of "pure act" (Henry Adams' phrase) took Panama, disciplined Santo Domingo, and laid the foundation for a policy continued under Taft and Wilson. It reached fullest ardor under Woodrow Wilson who, while forswearing ambition to win an "additional foot of territory by conquest," proposed "to teach the Latin Americans to elect good men." Marines consecrated to that task were dispatched to Vera Cruz, Port-au-Prince, Santo Domingo, and Corinto.

Third, the dispensation of the Good Neighbor, which began in 1927 when Coolidge sent Dwight Morrow to Mexico, was confirmed by Hoover's first recall of marines, and reached its flowering under Franklin Delano Roosevelt. Pan-Americanism, hitherto defined by Latin Americans as a trade slogan of the United States, took on new vitality at Montevideo in 1933, where Cordell Hull promised the extension of the New Deal to inter-American affairs; at Buenos Aires in 1936, where the United States accepted the ban on intervention by one state in the affairs of another "directly or indirectly, and for whatever reason"; at Lima in 1938 where the American nations pledged their inviolable solidarity; at Panama in 1939; and at Havana in 1940. Meanwhile Washington gave proof of its purged heart by abrogating the Platt Amendment in 1934 and the special guarantees to Panama in 1938; by removing the last detachment of marines from Caribbean ports; by Spartan restraint with Mexico and Bolivia when they seized oil properties belonging to our nationals. The United States was formally committed to the doctrine of the Good Neighbor, a policy of live and let live; a two-way policy recognizing that profit must be reciprocal; a policy which guaranteed the full sovereignty of each separate nation.

The solidarity of the Americas stands pledged as the war sweeps over Europe and Asia; full respect for the sovereign rights of each republic is now the official all-American doctrine. There remain some doubters among the twenty-one Good Neighbors, who eye each other quizzically and ask what will happen if or when alien flares light up the American sky line.

The United States Looks at Latin America

THE candid American, surveying lands and peoples South, reaches some conclusions:

First, Latin America is cut to the order of aspiring empire builders. She has room, millions of empty acres, untouched forests, untapped mines. Her soil and her veins yield or can be made to yield every foodstuff, every product, every mineral needed by an industrialized world. She is the logical prey of troublemakers, with a social pattern of embittering inequalities; her land held by a few men; her mineral wealth largely pledged to outsiders; a colonial economy still prevailing (with exceptions and shadings duly noted). Hungry men listen to Messiahs whether these hail from Moscow or Berlin.

Second, the prevailing Latin-American governments offer scant comfort for an all-American front against the world. The strength derived from the consent of the governed is largely lacking. The United States, seeking allies, is confronted by three separate situations.

The South American dictatorships. The strong men who rule Brazil, Paraguay, Bolivia, and Peru live by the sword and they would fall quickly before the wielder of a sharper sword. Their paraded strength is a screen for weakness. Pacts made with such men offer frail assurance.

The constitutional republics. Chile's popular front government, despite her Communists, would travel with the United States—but the Front might easily snap before a coup of the Right or the Left. Argentina's constitutional government hangs by one frail hair—the health of Roberto Ortiz; his death or ejection by Vice-President Castillo might mean reversion to dictatorship of the Justo pattern. Uruguay's present government of Baldomir is pro-British, committed to inter-American teamwork, increasingly representative, and gives promise of continuing. Colombia, the freest and most faithful democracy, is loyal to American solidarity and seems likely to maintain that stand.

Mexico and Middle America. Mexico has decided to travel with the United States, a decision buttressed by economic advantage. The nine minor republics of the Caribbean area, all dictatorships save Costa Rica, are fated by geography and economic interest to follow Washington's lead. This assurance does not preclude the probability that enemy agents might embarrass us by plottings in this area.

Third, ill winds are blowing in Latin America, threatening all-American solidarity, creating suspicion and hostility toward the United States, blocking the expression of popular will.

Some of these winds hail from Berlin, Rome, Tokyo. The unabsorbed Japanese, 200,000 in Brazil, 25,000 in Peru, scattered colonies elsewhere, cause some anxiety. The 6 or 7 million Italians in all Latin America, chiefly assimilated in the lands of their adoption, include some (few, in the opinion of most observers) who abet German plans. The 1,300,000 Germans scattered over the twenty nations constitute the chief threat to American unity. Not more than 150,000 of that total are first-generation migrants. Over nine tenths of all Germans live in Argentina, Brazil, Chile —their stronghold is southern Brazil and northern Argentina.

Speculation runs wild as to the divided allegiance of these Germans. Lewis Hanke, not to mention men of lesser wisdom, belittles the fifth-column scare, cites a Brazilian major to prove his point.[1] Flitting journalists bring back horrid tales of Gestapo agents in every telephone booth. Any minimum computation of Third Reich activity in Latin America must include the zealous campaigns of persuasion emanating from German embassies, legations, and consulates; the systematic collection of funds and the assiduous organization of loyal Germans; the use of the press, the movies, the radio. The success of this campaign cannot be precisely estimated. My guess, based on careful estimates by others, is that the majority of recent comers from Germany, barring Jews, do Hitler's bidding; that the majority of the second-, third-, and fourth-generation older Germans, having built homes, established farms and businesses, ask only to be let alone; that many, perhaps a majority, of the young men of German extraction, whether they have seen Germany or not, have been drawn into the ranks of Greater Germany. After prudential discounts, it is safe to say that Adolf Hitler has a substantial body of sympathizers which may number from 100,000 to 500,000 scattered over Latin America, their first loyalty to the Reich, who persistently seek to discredit democratic institutions, to poison inter-American relations, to prepare against a Day of whose shapings no one can safely conjecture.

More ominous than the Germans are their unwitting allies among the unreconstructed feudal die-hards. In every nation from Mexico to Argentina there is a little company of men who regard themselves as the residuary legatees of the Crowns of Castille and Portugal. Many of these still hold the best land and the most land. These few thousand men dominate the life of Chile, Argentina, Brazil, Peru; their kin exercise a lesser hold in all the other nations; only Mexico has dispossessed them. Their catholicism—especially in the Hispanic lands—is altogether intransigent, their loyalty to Francisco Franco carries them, often unconsciously, along the road of the Axis. Their consuming

1. "Plain Speaking About Latin America," Harper's. November 1940.

hatred is for all radicalism, they would be willing to block democracy if they thought their vested interest would be served.
They have long been suckled on privilege, they cannot comprehend any challenge to their supremacy. They uphold the strong-
arm rule of dictators, from that of Martínez in Salvador to Vargas in Brazil, for these dictators promise security against the
rabble. Their weight is repeatedly thrown to governments which
seem copied from German models. The Herreras of Uruguay,
the Sánchez Sorondos of Argentina, the Laureano Gómezes of
Colombia, the Miro Quesadas of Peru, while not rightly described as Hitler's agents, are committed to such autocratic policy
as to make them unwitting tools of Fascist agents.

The feudal aristocracy of Latin America is abetted by another
group, the caudillos who hold, or plan to seize, political power.
These are the leaders of the military cliques of Paraguay, Bolivia,
Peru, Ecuador, and other lands. They are not necessarily pro-
German, they certainly have no wish to be gauleiters of the Reich,
but they travel ways which parallel Berlin's. Some of these give
lip service to American solidarity, but offer frail promise for days
of battle.

Fourth, Latin America is undefended. There are about 350,000
enlisted men in the armies of the twenty republics—capable of
increase to 1,800,000. There are 63 war vessels, all but 10 of them
outmoded. Only Brazil, Argentina, and Chile could hope to
patrol their own coast lines, and that but scantily.

There are well-trained soldiers in the armies of Argentina,
Chile, Brazil, and Colombia. The armies of the other nations
range from moderate effectiveness to mediocrity. Equipment of
the stronger nations has been greatly strengthened since 1939, but
it is still meager in comparison with modern armies.

There is much talk, little definite proof, of widespread German and Italian influence among the officers of many armies.
Responsible Argentines, Brazilians, Chileans, and Peruvians say
that high-ranking officers in their forces are avowed partisans of
the totalitarian cause, and they name names. One hears the same
thing in Ecuador, Bolivia, Paraguay, Guatemala.

The outsider tentatively concludes that the defense of the Western Hemisphere will chiefly devolve upon the armed forces of the United States.

Fifth—a more encouraging observation—protagonists of democratic institutions in the Americas find much to hearten them in Latin America.

Political parties with authentic democratic ideology are factors to be considered. Among these we may cite the Radicals and Socialists of Argentina; Radicals, Socialists, and some minor parties in Chile; some factions of the Blancos in Uruguay; the "Bolivarians" of Venezuela; the Liberals of Colombia. There are sporadic political groups which speak their mind in Cuba and other policed lands of Middle America. The only prodemocratic party which has survived persecution under South American dictatorships is the Apra of Peru. There are no authentic opposition parties in Bolivia, Paraguay, Brazil, Ecuador.

The chief newspapers are committed to American solidarity. Constitutional and democratic zeal marks such papers as *La Prensa* and *La Nación* of Buenos Aires; *El Mercurio, La Nación,* and *La Hora* of Santiago; *El Tiempo* of Bogotá. To them may be added a sizable list of lesser sheets in Córdoba, Quito, La Paz, Caracas, San José in Costa Rica, and many others. Less reassuring are the opportunistic *El Comercio* of Lima, the clerical organs of Argentine provincial capitals, the falangista *Diario de la Marina* of Havana, the owlish *El Diario Ilustrado* of Santiago, and scores of papers which beat the drums as they are ordered. The controlled Brazilian press blows warm, blows cold.

Schoolteachers deserve a chief place on the list of democratic allies. Even in lands where schools are meager and ill-financed, you find teachers who preach a more generous doctrine than is practised by chiefs of state. Wherever schools are multiplying and improving, as in Chile, Argentina, Uruguay, Colombia, Venezuela, Costa Rica, and Mexico, they are solid bulwarks for democratic faith.

The small but growing Latin-American middle class—lawyers, physicians, merchants, white-collar workers—looks toward

a released national life. These read the newspapers, the magazines, and the books which are piled high at street corners and
in shops—the quality of the output attests their good taste. They
attend the cinemas, appreciate the best that is offered, and their
applause almost never fails to show them as pro-British and
friendly to the United States.

. The growing body of industrial workers in Latin America
(some 1,800,000 of them are organized in unions) are increasingly conscious partisans of democratic institutions. The labor
union is an effective laboratory for constitutionalism. Many
organized workers, notably in Chile, are reached by Communist
pleas, but greater numbers support such parties as the Socialists
and Radicals of Argentina and Chile, the Liberals of Colombia,
the Apristas of Peru. There are no authentic unions in Brazil.

Any man seeking evidence of democratic zeal in Latin America will be heartened by the popular enthusiasm for the President of the United States. I report upon the conversations of
eight months before, during and after the presidential campaign
of 1940; recall random conversations in hotels, cantinas, railroad
trains; in great cities and small towns, with educated men and
those of little schooling, with prosperous and poor; in countries
scattered all the way from Mexico to Argentina. I remember
what men said, what they applauded as news was thrown on the
screen, the slogans they shouted in mass meetings in city squares.
One great enthusiasm prevails, centering in the person of Franklin Roosevelt. He personifies for millions all that they would have
and would say; he defies Hitler, he upholds Britain, he stands for
the rights of each state, he preaches the doctrine of democracy.
Mr. Roosevelt has won the trust and moral leadership of Latin
America to a degree true of no other American president. They
regard him as their spokesman against forces they fear, for ambitions they cherish.

Latin America Looks at the United States

THE Latin Americans—those in control of parties and governments—turn a quizzical eye upon Washington, regard the pub-

lic and private show of American affection with cold calculation, ask: Exactly what do you want?

Washington replies, in effect: The world's woods are on fire, the fires spread, they may reach American shores, we would prepare by uniting all Americans to fight the flames.

The Latin Americans reply: You overstate the danger, Europe and Asia will have their hands occupied for years to come, we need not worry. This is the substance of the argument of many men who make national decisions in Argentina, Brazil, Chile, Peru, and other lands. Some disagree, admit a possible threat. Thoughtful Latin Americans (if they speak in candor) address other words to their Northern neighbor: You now adhere to the doctrine of the Good Neighbor. Will that doctrine outlast the war? Will we flee German imperialism only to be caught in a new American imperialism?

Latin Americans have studied history, know by rote the record of American expansion, and recall our course in Mexico, Panama, Nicaragua, Haiti, Santo Domingo. They remember our absent-minded tariffs and the havoc wrought upon their profitable trade. They recollect promises not honored—concerning Argentine meat, for example. They like Franklin Roosevelt, but have not forgotten Theodore. They ask: After the Good Neighbor, what? Some impious fellows who have studied American philosophers quote Mister Dooley, "Hands acrost th' sea an' into somewan's pockets."

The Latin Americans, expert politicians, have studied the intricacies of our American politics. Profiting from their own experience, distrusting all politicians, they transfer that distrust to the Washington breed. They recall that our free electorate could give an overwhelming vote to Warren Gamaliel Harding, and they cogitate upon our next choice when at last Franklin Roosevelt must lay aside the purple.

The Latin Americans seem ungrateful for mercies vouched, not quite delicate in looking into the smiling mouths of horses given without price. Meanwhile, gift horses are being trotted South.

The buried gold of Fort Knox is the Good Neighbors' for the asking. The Export-Import Bank was voted a half-billion dollars in the summer of 1940, almost half of it has been appropriated; 20 millions to Brazil; 110 millions to Argentina; 12 millions to Chile; 10 millions to Colombia; 5 millions to Costa Rica; 4 millions to Cuba; 3 millions to the Dominicans; 5 millions to Haiti; 10 millions to Peru; almost 4 millions to Venezuela; 7½ millions to Uruguay; 3½ millions to Paraguay; 4½ millions to Panama; other odd amounts to scattered countries. The general purpose of these loans is to enable governments to maintain their equilibrium under the shocks of war and to strengthen their defenses; specific projects include a steel plant in Brazil, roads in Paraguay, the encouragement to industry in various lands. There is still money to be voted, larger appropriations to be made by Congress.

Military aid is pledged. Our army and navy, growing daily— "the greatest navy the world has ever seen" according to Frank Knox—are at the service of the smallest country of Latin America. We almost loaned five shop-worn destroyers to Brazil but Argentina forbade it. As time and war go on, we will dispatch anything from ship anchors to flying fortresses. Our training missions—military, naval, and aviation—are variously assigned Argentina, Brazil, Chile, Colombia, Ecuador, Guatemala, Haiti, Nicaragua, and Peru—others may have them by mailing a penny postcard to the White House. We ask air and naval bases in return, we hope to get them; we probably will, in one form or another.

Cynical Latin Americans sometimes suggest that these gifts cannot meet the test of the perfect Christmas package—disinterestedness. They intimate that our course is charted by self-interest. The point is well taken, although it seems not amiss to suggest that the self-interest of the United States dovetails into that of Latin America. However, fair-minded Americans can at least appreciate the reticence of Latin Americans in joining the chorus of the new all-American Internationale.

The tale has a simple moral. The lady still needs courting. She has not yet decided to lay her dowry on the altar. The suitor must still patronize the florist and the confectioner.

Washington's Next Turns

WASHINGTON's cultivation of the Latin Americans is a major assignment of every department from Labor to State. The faithful public servant recites lines from Rubén Darío or Gabriela Mistral in place of his paternoster, and appears before chambers of commerce and women's clubs to read papers on the new Pan-Americanism. Nelson Rockefeller has over 3 millions to spend, the State Department's Division of Cultural Relations several hundreds of thousands. Mrs. Roosevelt lectures on cultural relations in chief cities. Henry Wallace rests not, nor is wearied, in taking thought of the Latin Americans whom he genuinely cherishes. Individuals by the thousand, paid and unpaid, give thought to the persuasion of the Latin Americans.

Let base scoffers be warned, whether they speak Spanish, Portuguese, German, or English, that this is serious business. Of course national self-interest predominates. Of course we seek defense of our national lines in a hostile world. Beyond such considerations, there is a growing number of Americans who conclude that our national life will be enriched by reciprocal sharing with the other American peoples. This sudden enthusiasm for Latin America may have its comic side, that is only the feathery frosting on the cake, there is cream and chocolate inside.

There are things to be done.

First, a program of two-way education.

Our own education comes first. It would appear folly to ask the Latin Americans to be intelligent about us while 78.2 % of our qualified electors (a *hunch* statistic) are not sure whether Ecuador is a nation, a mountain, or a tufted parakeet. How shall they learn if they are not taught? How many high schools and colleges give more than careless treatment to the geography, economics, or history of Latin America? Until recent months such courses were as rare as giant pandas, and not so interesting. Under persuasion from Washington, courses are now increased.

textbooks are in preparation, reprints of Latin-American classics are on the press. The American public responds with avidity to its education. The study of Spanish everywhere increases. Latin-American painting and music make new converts. Magazines and newspapers devote more of their columns to material on the lands of the South. Travelers, barred from Europe, turn to Mexico, Peru, Chile, Argentina, and Brazil. This is good, and there should be more of it. Increased funds for scholarships should be forthcoming so that more students and professors may go South. Steamship fares must come down so that travel may be increased in both directions. For it is a two-way traffic which must be encouraged.

Next come projects for educating the Latin Americans about the United States.

The movie barons are falling into line, with Washington pushing. Films on Latin-American subjects are in preparation, other films calculated to arouse confidence in the United States, and to deepen devotion to the principles of Washington and Bolívar, Lincoln and Sarmiento. It is excellent. Charlie Chaplin of the feet is an abler persuader than a dozen ambassadors. His "Great Dictator" told millions (where lesser dictators permitted him to speak) exactly what we would have men hear. "The Mortal Storm" ran for weeks in chief Southern cities, expressing American conviction more effectively than a homily by Cordell Hull. Mr. Nelson Rockefeller can use our tax money to good effect by persuading the masters of Hollywood to turn out their best pictures rapidly, to rush them South on the first plane, to pare costs and profits to the bone, to offer them at low prices to the theaters of every city and town without delay. If the beefy hand of the censor and the propagandist can be warded off, all the better. Hollywood will make mistakes, it is also capable of successes.

The radio fraternity swings into action. Broadcasting companies make contracts for outlets in chief Southern cities, so that the best of American programs can reach the owner of the cheapest instrument. It is hoped that NBC, CBS, and Mutual may spare their Southern listeners their soap dramas and chitchats to the feeble-minded, and that Washington will not compel the use of forthputtings by official propagandists. The best symphonies, operas, news broadcasts will serve better.

Publishers do their part. *Reader's Digest* appears in Spanish and sells enormously. *Life* and some others are cutting export prices so that Latin Americans can buy. *Time* appears on thin paper and is flown South for a mere $10 a year. The team of Farrar and Rinehart and *Redbook Magazine* offer $2,500 for the best unpublished Latin-American novel; Pan-American Union's indefatigable Concha Romero James, together with a jury of John Dos Passos, Blair Niles, and Ernesto Montenegro, awards the prize to Peruvian Ciro Alegría (an Aprista living in Chile for safety's sake); the winning novel and three runners-up will shortly be published. In 1941, seven American newspapers, at the suggestion of Ambassador Claude Bowers, invited Chilean newspapers to send staff members as "guest reporters" in their offices in New York, Baltimore, Washington, and other cities.

Official agencies debate the printing of attractive magazines for wide distribution in Latin America, designed to make friends and influence Latin-American people. The idea has a dismal knell, smacking of professional advertising men taking orders from official propagandists. Such artificial projects seem unnecessary so long as Latin Americans have thousands of newspapers, magazines, and reviews whose columns are open. As a substitute motion, I suggest that Mr. Roosevelt ask some American writers (for example, Louis Adamic, Charles A. Beard, Thornton Wilder, John Dos Passos) to invite an equal number of Latin-American writers (men like Eduardo Mallea of Argentina, Luis Alberto Sánchez of Peru, Gabriela Mistral of Chile, Gilberto Freyre of Brazil, Moisés Sáenz of Mexico) to organize an Inter-American Commission for the Propagation of the Democratic Faith through the Printed Word (use initials, they will feel at home in Washington). Give them a few thousand dollars to hire an office and buy a typewriter. Let them gather excellent articles about people, bridges, parks, soil conservation, coöperatives, schools, industry, dogs, babies, TVA, Brazilian steel, hospitals, tuberculosis—anything which pictures life and progress, North or South. Put the articles into all the languages of the Americas, and shoot them out. Charge for them. Pick names which will be recognized—Pearl Buck, Albert Einstein, Thomas Mann, John Steinbeck, Eleanor Roosevelt, Henry Wallace, Ernest Hemingway—and the best Latin-American names. They will be used from Alaska to Patagonia, provided the job is done intelligently, and not turned over to the eminent advertising firm of Dirk, Dirk, Dirk and Dirk, the specialists on tooth-paste marketing.

The education of the Latin-American public concerning the virtues of the United States presupposes prior study of the audience to be reached. The recurring question thrown at me by forum addicts in Boston, Chicago, and way stations is this: "What do Latin Americans think about us?" to which one can only reply, *"Which* Latin Americans think *what* about *whom?"* There are thirteen different kinds of Chileans, according to my last count—at least thirteen. The contrivers of films, radio programs, books, magazines, articles must study the thirteen varieties and shape their product accordingly. They should not overlook schoolteachers, textile workers, university students, copper miners, farm workers, lawyers, physicians, and housewives.

Skeptical Latin Americans, reading this outline of plans for their education, will murmur, "Just like the Germans." So it is, with one marked difference—in the goods we peddle. Quite a difference, we insist.

We are also embarked on a program of cultural interchange. Some use the phrase as an excuse for a one-way drive on Latin America; others are honestly persuaded that all American life will be enriched by generous sharing of insights. To that latter class belong Charles Thomson and many another in the State Department, Stephen Duggan of long service at the head of the useful Institute of International Education, Henry Wallace, Archibald MacLeish, Waldo Frank, Herbert E. Bolton, Samuel Guy Inman, and other confirmed and long-time admirers of the cultural gifts of the Iberian-American peoples.

The exchange of students and professors is a thriving two-way venture. Everyone lends a hand to promote it: the 15 governments which ratified the cultural convention of Buenos Aires;[2] the Pan-American Union; cultural institutes in a half-dozen Southern countries; the Cultural Relations Division in Washington; the Nelson Rockefeller office; the Guggenheim, Rockefeller, and Carnegie Foundations; the Institute of International Education; scores of colleges and universities, South and North; federations of women's clubs, associations of university women, leagues of women voters; Pan American Airways; the steamship lines, Grace and Moore McCormack. One hundred and nine South Americans spent six weeks at the University of North Carolina in early 1941, visited Washington, New York, and Detroit. Hundreds of American students spend their vacations at summer schools in Mexico City, Lima, and Santiago. During the school year 1940–41, 1,421 Latin Americans studied in the United States, about 600 Americans in various Southern republics. Not every exchange student meets with equal success, he gets what he puts into it, but the two-way stream of students is a happy augury for inter-American understanding.

Mr. Henry Ford, who distrusts charity, might emulate the example of Cecil Rhodes whose 30 million dollars have done much to cement bonds between England and the United States. The investment of an equal sum in scholarships for Latin-American students would make possible the training of thousands of engineers, physicians, and technical men in the universities and research laboratories of the United States.

Second, Washington undertakes economic coöperation with Latin America. The recognition that inter-American relations will be firmly established only on the basis of mutually profitable exchange has gathered force under the steady drilling of Cordell Hull. For eight years Hull persistently sought agreement with individual nations, to negotiate pacts which would lower tariff

2. The governments which have ratified the Convention for the Promotion of Inter-American Cultural Relations, signed at Buenos Aires in 1936, are: Brazil, Chile, Colombia, Costa Rica, the Dominican Republic, Guatemala, Haiti, Honduras, Mexico, Nicaragua, Panama, Paraguay, Peru, the United States, and Venezuela.

barriers and make possible a more generous flow of goods. At home Hull was repeatedly blocked by lobbies of special interests, but agreements were reached with eleven of the twenty nations,[3] with heartening results until war upset all calculations.

The chief problem of the war years is the piling up of surplus commodities in almost all Latin-American republics. This situation became acute in 1941. Argentina has scant markets for her corn and wheat and beef. Brazil has difficulty in selling her coffee, cotton, and cacao. All nations suffer in greater or less degree. June 22, 1940, on the eve of the conference in Havana, President Roosevelt announced a comprehensive plan for the economic defense of the hemisphere, calling for the creation of "an appropriate inter-American organization for dealing with certain basic problems of their trade relations, including an effective system of joint marketing of the important staple products of the American republics." This vague proposal, promptly dubbed a "cartel," was heralded as the new device for a common economic front. The ground had not been well prepared, the Latin Americans had heard nothing of it. The larger nations, notably Argentina, showed little enthusiasm, suggested that such a decision would be interpreted as open defiance of Germany. Meanwhile sharp difference of opinion appeared in Washington. When the conference opened on July 20, Cordell Hull offered more modest recommendations:

1. Strengthening and expansion of the activities of the Inter-American Financial and Economic Advisory Committee as an instrument for continuing consultation with respect to trade matters. . . .

2. Creation of facilities for the temporary handling and orderly marketing of accumulated surpluses of those commodities which are of primary importance to the maintenance of the economic life of the American republics, whenever such action becomes necessary.

3. Development of commodity agreements with a view to as-

3. Cuba, Brazil, Haiti, Colombia, Honduras, Nicaragua, Guatemala, Costa Rica, Salvador, Ecuador, Venezuela.

suring equitable terms of trade for both producers and consumers of the commodities concerned.

4. Consideration of methods for improving the standards of living of the peoples of the Americas.

The program of economic coöperation during 1940–41 chiefly centered on the extension of loans to enable the Latin Americans to carry their surpluses and to stabilize their exchanges. Meanwhile, government agencies studied the development of new products which can be bought by the United States; the purchase of reserves of strategic materials for defense; counseling merchants in the United States and Latin America on possible extensions of trade; encouraging enlarged trade between the Latin Americans themselves.

The United States proposes to concentrate her import buying on Latin America, wherever needed products are available, and to encourage Latin America to turn out other products as she can. This is inspired by sound strategy. In 1940 the Army and Navy Munitions Board listed fourteen strategic materials "for which strict conservation and distribution control measures will be necessary"—antimony, chromium, coconut-shell char, ferro-grade manganese, manila fiber, mercury, mica, nickel, quartz crystal, quinine, rubber, silk, tin, tungsten. These are necessities for defense of which the United States produces little or none. Latin America furnishes a considerable share of our antimony, manganese, mercury, quartz crystal, and tungsten—and could with proper development produce all we require. She also sells us a limited quantity of mica, chromium, and coconut-shell char —she could produce more. Latin America (chiefly Brazil) grows a little rubber; experimental plantations are now at work in Brazil, Panama, and Mexico; it is believed that with time and careful planning Latin America can supply all the rubber we use. Quinine may soon be produced in sufficient quantity in Brazil and Peru to make the United States independent of the East Indies; the same is true of manila fiber. There is tin in Bolivia, smelters are being built in the United States for its refining, and some hope that the United States may free herself from dependence upon Far Eastern sources; this hope is clouded by geologists who find the Bolivian supply inadequate and of poor quality. Silk comes chiefly from Japan; there seems a slight chance that Brazil will one day supply our market; meanwhile, silk substitutes will meet the possible deficiency. There are other items which will be added to the strategic list. Chief among these is bauxite for aluminum, destined to greatly increased use (60 % of a plane's weight is aluminum); it is estimated that the Guianas and various nations of Latin America can supply all we need. Hides and wool, of increased demand in case of war, can be brought from Argentina and Uruguay. Iodine comes from Chile, platinum from Colombia, vanadium from Peru.

The chief sticking point in hemisphere economic planning is Argentina. The assurance of a war-time market for her corn, wheat, and beef is an unsolved economic riddle.

The protagonists of the cartel are quiet, but are still faithful to the ideal. They argue that a German-dominated Europe—a possibility to be reckoned with—will require great stocks of Latin America's metals, grains, meats, coffee, sugar, cotton; that by dealing with each nation separately Germany can impose disastrous terms, capture Latin America's market for industrial goods, and impose control over her economic life. They argue that the safety of Latin America can be assured only by joint all-American bargaining with the outside world. There is no evidence that the South American nations or the United States are ready to consider such a proposal.

The dependence of Latin America upon Europe's trade appears in the figures for 1938—the last full year of peace—when 32.9 % of Latin America's exports went to the United Kingdom, Germany, France, and Italy; 30.6 % to the United States. However, if we look to Argentina we find that she sold 52.4 % of her exports to the European powers, but 8.5 % to the United States. Those figures pose the knottiest problem for those who would build a wall around the economy of the Western Hemisphere. A cartel might work, but only on two conditions; first, the firm support of Argentina; second, the effective military protection by the United States of a highly provocative policy.

Third, the United States belatedly strengthens her diplomatic force in dealing with Latin America. For many years Washington turned over our relations with Latin America to second-best diplomats and deserving politicians. Mr. Roosevelt, in some of his first appointments, carried on that tradition. Today there is a change. In the Department of State, Cordell Hull has won high regard for his firsthand dealings with Latin America; Sumner Welles, able, indefatigable, and with abundant knowledge of the Americas, has moved with precision and skill; Laurence Duggan, wise and penetrating, is a chief designer behind the scenes; Charles Thomson foments cultural relations with tireless affection; George Wythe lives with hopeful plans for enlarged and mutually profitable trade—and there are many others. On the field, we are increasingly represented in Latin America by men of first-line diplomatic skill. Embassy and legation staffs have everywhere been enlarged and strengthened.

This task well begun should be carried further. There is no longer place for ill-equipped men on the staffs of our missions to Latin America. If the people of these several lands are to be persuaded to travel with us, we must send men who are persuasive in personality, knowledge, interests. Dwight Morrow was a great ambassador because he was as completely concerned for Mexico's well-being as for that of the United States—the only kind of diplomacy which will yield moral content to the Good Neighbor doctrine. We require able men not only in chief posts but in the seemingly unimportant consulates. The numbers of our scattered consulates increase, and they should still be greatly multiplied. We should have wise and gracious men in every city of importance south of the Rio Grande. If there are insufficient foreign-service men of the required ability, others should be drafted from business or professional life. Let me state the case in terms of Córdoba, Argentina, a center of business and education. There is a little group of Argentines and foreigners who render distinguished service to inter-American solidarity through the ICANA (Instituto Cultural Argentino Norteamericano). There are many professional men, students, and business people who turn to that Instituto for knowledge of the United States, but few Americans visit Córdoba. I suggest that the State Department borrow some thoughtful American professor of Hispanic-American literature and send him to Córdoba for a year. Give him a clerk to fill out the blanks which are the Department's daily bread; and turn this amateur consul loose to make friends among university professors, labor leaders, lawyers, bricklayers, and schoolteachers. Give him a car so that he can visit all the villages around about, especially Alta Gracia. If we would have friends, we cannot forget the Alta Gracias—the little towns of Latin America. I recall Alta Gracia for the month we spent there, for the schoolteachers and the clerks in stores who wanted to know more of the United States, who had never known an American. We must apply diplomacy by retail as well as whole-sale. There are at least a hundred other spots, such as Córdoba, where a drafted professor or businessman would prove useful for a year. The Germans do that sort of thing, why should they spoil a good idea?

After the Good Neighbor, What?

THIS question is pressed by men in every land from Mexico to Argentina. It is not a captious question, but is inspired by sober reading of a hundred years of history and by examination of the realities of current politics. It is raised by some convinced friends of the United States, by others who suspect our every move.

The current American answer is: The Good Neighbor is here to stay, the policeman is dead. We have reached the mature deci-sion to play the game together. No nation will push another around. The United States will set the example by respecting the sovereignty of her neighbors. We will jointly defend each other's economic stability and territorial integrity. We have pledged our faith, we will keep our word. This answer represents the honest conviction of the men who rule in Washington, the increasing consensus of public opinion in the United States. It does not satisfy doubting Latin Americans who ask the motives behind Washington's fair words. Their incredulity reflects neither upon their honesty nor upon their zeal for a free union of all Americans. These Latin Americans know, as all should know, how suddenly political forces shift, by how narrow a margin a Hughes loses to a Wilson, how readily an electorate swings from a Wilson to a Harding. They know, as we know, that war creates new situations in which pledges are easily forgotten.

The successful application of the principle of American solidarity, which is the continentalization of the Good Neighbor Doctrine, is predicated on two assumptions. *First,* that the United States can and will continue and increase her support of the ruffled economies of weaker neighbors; that she can and will hold the twenty diverse governments of Latin America to some semblance of united action; that she can and will furnish the major instruments of defense. *Second,* that the rulers of Latin America can and will hold their several nations to the line of an honest solidarity; that they will sedulously refrain from giving comfort to the enemy. Many Latin Americans doubt the first assumption, many North Americans the second.

The present pattern of Good Neighborliness is subject to various hazards.

First, the United States, under pressure at home, might tire of increasing financial commitments to Latin America. The efficacy of Santa Claus lies in the promise of another Christmas. The appetite of the borrower tends to become chronic. The Good Neighbor who called a halt to his largess might be damned as a bad neighbor.

Second, the United States, in a crisis, might throw her weight against some government now in control. Washington might conclude that the Apristas of Peru, probably commanding a majority of votes, offer more faithful support to all-American solidarity than the Prado-Benavides combination now in office. Washington might withhold further support from the present government. Our diplomatic representatives in Lima might go so far as indiscreetly to admit that an opposition party exists.[4] Such a move, long urged by Carleton Beals and other honorable protagonists of inter-American comity, might unseat a government in days of increasing economic stress. It might serve the long-time interests of the hemisphere: it would certainly excite fear among the dictatorial hierarchy in other Latin-American lands and be denounced as a fresh instance of American imperialism.

Third, the increased involvement of the United States in the wars of Europe and Asia will create a national atmosphere inimical to orderly inter-American planning. We will be caught by the unreason of panic. Rumors will run wild of Communist plottings in Chile, of German machinations in Bolivia. At home the policeman will become more important than the philosopher, our national mind will be determined by the J. Edgar Hoovers rather than the John Deweys. From Congress, the press, and the sidewalk, demands will arise that we play the sheriff abroad. In panic we might nullify the letter and spirit of the doctrine of the Good Neighbor.

We may readily be confronted by situations which will tax our restraint.

Let us suppose, for example, that our pledged allies fail to cooperate as we think they should. Let us say that we ask Brazil for a base on her eastern hump—and that she refuses. Suppose we ask Ecuador to loan us the Galapagos Islands—and that she refuses. Do we then seize Pernambuco and the Ecuadorian Islands? If we do, the Good Neighbor seems tossed out the window. If we do not, where is our hemispheric defense?

Or assume that our declared enemies incite Bolivia to distract us by an invasion of Paraguay. Or that the Germans stir up their integralista kin to attempt capture of Brazil. These things *could* happen without the visible presence of a single saber-scarred

4. A hypothetical illustration. Our embassy in Lima never admits by word or deed that they have heard of the Apristas. In January 1941 Haya de la Torre sent a representative to the embassy with a message of congratulation for President Roosevelt upon his third inauguration. The envoy was not admitted, the message not accepted for transmission. Ambassador Norweb was meticulously correct.

German or German machine gun. Do we then intervene, even though the clashes are advertised as purely domestic concerns? If we do, where is our pledge of nonintervention? If we do not, how can we prevent a covert drive at the heart of America?

Or imagine that Washington is convinced that President Arnulfo Arias gives but surface support to the defense of the Panama Canal (as some now suspect, fairly or unfairly), that he permits enemy agents to plot on the very edge of the Canal Zone. Do we then take his government from him and install a President nominated by the marines? If we do, what will the Good Neighbors say? If not, what happens to the safety of the Canal?

Or let us dally with further unpleasant possibilities. We may face German victory in Europe, a partial blocking of sea lanes, and a lively contest between the United States and other powers for zones of influence in South America. It will not tax the imagination to foresee a series of *coups d'état,* frankly pro-Axis, or so dominated by anti-United States animus as to preclude a common American front. What shall we do in such event? Shall Washington constitute itself a court of last resort to decide whether a given regime is American or German, friendly or hostile? Shall we then compel coöperation by occupying, as occasion demands, Callao or Valparaiso or Guayaquil or Porto Alegre? If we do, can we persuade the Latin Americans of our faithfulness? If we do not, will the Western Hemisphere be safe from alien intruders?

This line of reasoning, some may counter, is argument by conjecture. These things will not happen. Britain will not fail, Germany will not win. The seas will be policed by American and British navies. Panama will be loyal. Peru and Bolivia and Chile and Argentina and Brazil will play with us. The life of the Americas will proceed as it has, with each big and little nation free to work out her peculiar destiny in her own fashion, with all nations respecting other's rights and coöperating for the well-being of each. To which we answer—this is our hope.

Realism suggests that the war holds no fair promise for American solidarity. If Britain wins, there is room for hope that good neighborliness may prevail in our Western World. If Britain loses, or is permanently crippled, the United States will inevitably be confronted with the competition of a totalitarian Europe in South America. We will seek to hold our southern neighbors in line by continued and enlarged subventions. If economic diplomacy fails, if some nations elect to come to terms with a victorious Germany, there will be frenzied voices demanding that we seize and occupy lands which oppose our will, demands that we go in and clean up the half-civilized countries which show slight regard for inter-American pledges. This argument will be as roomy as Olney's, as pious as McKinley's, as robust as Theodore Roosevelt's, as righteous as Wilson's—it could within a twelvemonth of national panic yield an imperialism which would justify all the warnings of Latin-American prophets. This is more than conjecture, the signs already appear. It is a bale of straws in the wind when Henry R. Luce writes in *Life* of "The American Century," of the "vision of America as a world power," of our duty "to be the Good Samaritan of the entire world." Mr. Luce says what many are thinking, his words release a chorus of happy assent. The implications of his words for our relations in the Americas lead us into stormy zones. The United States cannot be a world power unless she compels obedience in this hemisphere, she cannot be the Good Samaritan to all the world save as she feeds and binds the wounds of fellow Americans who fall among thieves. If the Latin-American victims choose the bandages and broths of Germany, this Good Samaritan will have his hands full. The proponents of "The American Century" prepare us for a day of doubtful glory.

The doctrine of the Good Neighbor, most admirable creation of American diplomacy, now faces the testing ground. Alien broils, feared by Monroe, overtake the Americas. Can twenty-one nations of such disparate cultures and economies find common cause in defense of their several sovereignties? Can twenty-one nations persuade one another to discipline the agents of disruption within their various boundaries? Can wise diplomacy outrun disorder? These questions concern each nation from Salvador to

Brazil. Meanwhile the people of the United States pose a question of equal import: Can we resist the prophets of rosy dawn who would have us assume the role of arbiter of another 130 million Americans? Can we keep our heads when the American Rudyard Kiplings sound the new call to crusade, again offering the white man's burden? The answer is locked in the pages of a history which flows too swiftly for the comfort of mortal man.

BIBLIOGRAPHY

GENERAL BOOKS OF HISTORY AND INTERPRETATION

AIKMAN, DUNCAN. *The All American Front*. New York, 1940.

AKERS, C. E. *A History of South America 1854–1904*. New York, 1912.

ANGELL, HILDEGARDE. *Simon Bolivar*. New York, 1930.

BEALS, CARLETON. *America South*. Philadelphia, 1937.

—— *The Coming Struggle for Latin America*. Philadelphia, 1939.

—— *Pan America*. Boston, 1940.

BEMIS, SAMUEL FLAGG. *A Diplomatic History of the United States*. New York, 1936.

BLACKWELL, ALICE STONE. *Some Spanish American Poets*. New York, 1932.

BRYCE, JAMES. *South America*. New York, 1912.

CARR, KATHERINE. *South American Primer*. New York, 1939.

CLARK, J. REUBEN. *Memorandum on the Monroe Doctrine*. Washington, 1930.

CLEVEN, N. A. N. *Readings in Hispanic American History*. Boston, 1927.

COLUMBIA UNIVERSITY SYMPOSIUM. *Concerning Latin American Culture*. New York, 1940.

DAWSON, T. C. *The South American Republics*. New York, 1904.

EDSCHMID, KASIMIR. *South America, Lights and Shadows*. New York, 1932.

FILES: *Bulletin of the Pan American Union; Christian Science Monitor; Current History; Foreign Affairs; Harper's Magazine; Hispanic American Historical Review; The Nation; The New Republic; New York Times.*

FOREIGN POLICY ASSOCIATION: Reports and Headline Books. New York.

FOREMAN, CLARK, and RAUSHENBUSH, JOAN. *Total Defense*. New York, 1940.

GARCÍA CALDERÓN, F. *Latin America; Its Rise and Progress* (trans.). London, 1913.

GIUDICI, ERNESTO. *Hitler Conquista América*. Buenos Aires, 1938.

HAYA DE LA TORRE, VÍCTOR RAÚL. *Adónde Va Indoamérica?* Santiago, 1936.

INMAN, SAMUEL GUY. *Latin America, Its Place in World Life*. Chicago, 1937.

JAMES, H. G., and MARTIN, P. A. *The Republics of Latin America*. New York, 1923.

KIRKPATRICK, F. A. *Latin America*. New York, 1939.

LATANÉ, J. H. *The United States and Latin America.* New York, 1920.

MACLEISH, FLEMING, and REYNOLDS, CUSHMAN. *Strategy of the Americas.* New York, 1941.

MECHAM, J. L. *Church and State in Latin America.* Chapel Hill, 1934.

MITRE, BARTOLOMÉ. *Historia de San Martín.* Buenos Aires. Various eds.

NERVAL, GASTON. *Autopsy of the Monroe Doctrine.* New York, 1934.

NORMANO, J. F. *The Struggle for South America.* Boston, 1931.

OXFORD INSTITUTE OF INTERNATIONAL AFFAIRS. *The Republics of South America.* Oxford, 1937.

PEREYRA, CARLOS. *Historia de la América Española.* Madrid, 1926.

PERKINS, DEXTER. *Hands Off, a History of the Monroe Doctrine.* Boston, 1941.

POBLETE TRONCOSO, MOISÉS. *Problemas Sociales y Económicas de América Latina.* Santiago, 1936.

RAUSCHNING, HERMANN. *Hitler Speaks.* London, 1939.

RIPPY, J. FRED. *Historical Evolution of Hispanic America.* New York, 1932.

—— *Latin America in World Politics.* New York, 1931.

ROBERTSON, WILLIAM S. *A History of the Latin American Nations.* New York, 1930.

ROJAS, RICARDO. *El Santo de la Espada, Vida de San Martín.* Buenos Aires, 1940.

SÁNCHEZ, LUIS ALBERTO. *Historia de la Literatura Americana.* Santiago, 1940.

SEONE, MANUEL. *Nuestra América y la Guerra.* Santiago, 1940.

SHEPHERD, W. R. *The Hispanic Nations of the New World.* New Haven, 1921.

SIEGFRIED, ANDRÉ. *Impressions of South America.* New York, 1933.

STUART, GRAHAM H. *Latin America and the United States.* New York, 1938.

SWEET, W. W. *A History of Latin America.* New York, 1929.

TANNENBAUM, FRANK. *Whither Latin America?* New York, 1934.

UGARTE, MANUEL. *The Destiny of a Continent* (trans.). New York, 1925.

WERTENBAKER, CHARLES. *A New Doctrine for the Americas.* New York, 1941.

WILGUS, A. CURTIS. *A History of Hispanic America.* Washington, 1931.

WILLIAMS, MARY W. *The Peoples and Politics of Latin America.* Boston, 1930.

YBARRA, T. R. *America Faces South.* New York, 1939.

TRADE, AGRICULTURE, MINERALS, INDUSTRY—GENERAL SOURCES

BAIN, H. F., and READ, T. T. *Mineral Industries of South America.* New York, 1926.

BULLETINS OF THE BUREAU OF FOREIGN AND DOMESTIC COMMERCE, U. S. Department of Commerce.

DIETRICH, ETHEL B. *World Trade*. New York, 1939.

FILES: *Foreign Agriculture,* 1940–41. U. S. Department of Agriculture.

FILES: *Foreign Commerce Weekly,* 1938–41.

Foreign Minerals Quarterly, U. S. Department of the Interior.

INTER-AMERICAN STATISTICAL YEARBOOK (in Spanish, Portuguese, French, and English), Raúl C. Migone, Director. Buenos Aires and New York, 1940.

INTERNATIONAL REFERENCE SERVICE, U. S. Department of Commerce.

MILLER, B. L., and SINGEWALD, J. T. *Mineral Deposits of South America*. New York, 1919.

PARSONS, A. B. *Porphyry Coppers.* American Institute of Mining and Metallurgical Engineers, 1933.

POPPER, DAVID H. *Six Years of American Tariff Bargaining.* Foreign Policy Association, New York.

SOUTH AMERICAN HANDBOOK, 1940. London.

SOUTHARD, FRANK A., JR. *Foreign Exchange Practice and Policy.* New York, 1940.

UNITED STATES TARIFF COMMISSION. A series of monographs on *The Foreign Trade of Latin America.* Washington, 1940–41.

WINKLER, MAX. *Foreign Bonds, An Autopsy.* Philadelphia, 1933.

ZIMMERMANN, ERICH W. *World Resources and Industries.* New York, 1933.

PRECONQUEST, THE CONQUEST, THE COLONIAL PERIOD

(In addition to the more general histories which give greater or less attention to these periods.)

BOURNE, EDWARD G. *Spain in America 1450–1580.* New York, 1904.

DÍAZ DEL CASTILLO, BERNAL. *True History of the Conquest of New Spain* (trans.). Various eds.

FISHER, LILLIAN E. *Viceregal Administration in the Spanish American Colonies.* Berkeley, 1926.

HARING, CLARENCE H. *Trade and Navigation between Spain and the Indies.* Cambridge, 1918.

MEANS, PHILIP A. *Ancient Civilization of the Andes.* New York, 1931.

PRESCOTT, WILLIAM H. *Conquest of Mexico.* Various eds.

—— *Conquest of Peru.* Various eds.

SPINDEN, HERBERT J. *Ancient Civilizations of Mexico and Central America.* New York, 1928.

VALDIVIA, PEDRO DE. *La Conquista de Chile, Cartas al Emperador Carlos V.* Santiago, 1940.

von Humboldt, Alexander. *Political Essay on the Kingdom of New Spain*. Various eds.

ARGENTINA

(In addition to general works cited.)

Alberdi, Juan Bautista. *Bases*. Buenos Aires. Various eds.

Astolfi, J. C., and Migone, Raúl C. *Historía Argentina*. Buenos Aires, 1939.

Borras, Antonio. *Nuestra Cuestión Agraria*. Buenos Aires, 1932.

British Ministry of Agriculture and Fisheries. *Fourth Progress Report of the Foot-and-Mouth Research Committee*. London, 1935.

Bucich Escobar, Ismael. *Historia de los Presidentes Argentinos*. Buenos Aires, 1927.

Bulletins of División de Estadística, Departamento Nacional del Trabajo, Ministerio del Interior. Buenos Aires, 1937–40.

Bulletins of Sociedad Rural Argentina. Buenos Aires, 1940.

Comments, files of the monthly bulletin of the Chamber of Commerce of the U. S. A. in Buenos Aires, 1939–40.

Files: *La Nación, La Prensa, La Crítica*. Buenos Aires. *Córdoba, Principios*. Córdoba.

Files: *Revista de Economía Argentina*. Buenos Aires, 1935–40.

Foot and Mouth Disease, Bulletin No. 666 of U. S. Department of Agriculture; also miscellaneous publication No. 68 on the outbreak in Southern California in 1929.

García-Mata, Rafael, and Llorens, Emilio. *Argentina Economica*. Buenos Aires, 1940.

Hudson, W. H. *Far Away and Long Ago*. London, 1918.

Ibarguren, Carlos. *Juan Manuel de Rosas*. Buenos Aires, 1938.

Ingenieros, José. *La Evolución de las Ideas Argentinas*. Buenos Aires, 1918.

Jefferson, Mark. *Peopling the Argentine Pampas*. American Geographical Society, 1926.

Kirkpatrick, F. A. *A History of the Argentine Republic*. Cambridge, 1931.

Levene, Ricardo. *A History of Argentina* (trans.). Chapel Hill, 1937.

Mitre, Bartolomé. *Ensayos Históricos*. Buenos Aires. Various eds.

Oddone, Jacinto. *La Burguesía Terrateniente Argentina*. Buenos Aires, 1936.

Palacio, Manuel. *Problemas del Campo y del País*. Buenos Aires, 1936.

Phelps, Vernon L. *The International Economic Position of Argentina*. Philadelphia, 1938.

Sánchez Viamonte, Carlos. *Por la Libertad Civil y Política*. Buenos Aires, 1936.

Sarmiento, Domingo Faustino. *Facundo*. Buenos Aires, 1938.

—— *Life in the Argentine Republic in the Days of the Tyrants* (a partial trans. of *Facundo,* with a short biography of Sarmiento by Mrs. Horace Mann). New York, 1868.

Solari, Juan Antonio. *Parias Argentinos*. Buenos Aires, 1940.

—— *Problemas de Misiones*. Buenos Aires, 1940.

—— *Temas de Legislación Obrera*. Buenos Aires, 1939.

Veléz, Mariano. *La Situación Agricola de La Pampa*. Buenos Aires, 1934.

BRAZIL

(*In addition to general works cited.*)

Alves, Isaias. *Educacão e Brasilidade*. Rio de Janeiro, 1939.

Brazil Yearbook and Manual 1940. New York, 1940.

Bulletins of the Ministerio do Trabalho, Industria, e Comercio. April–November, 1939.

Calogeras, João Pandiá. *A History of Brazil* (trans.). Chapel Hill, 1939.

Campos, Francisco. *O Estado Nacional*. Rio de Janeiro, 1940.

Castro, Josué de. *A Alimentação Brasileira á Luz de Geografia Humana*. Porto Alegre, 1937.

Coutinho, Ruy. *Valor Social da Alimentação*. São Paulo, 1937.

Files: O Estado de São Paulo.

Freyre, Gilberto. *Casa Grande e Senzala*. Rio de Janeiro, 1936.

Instituto Brasileiro de Geografia e Estatística. *Sinopse Estatística do Brasil*. Rio de Janeiro, 1938.

—— *Brasil 1938*. Rio de Janeiro, 1938.

James, Herman G. *Brazil after a Century of Independence*. New York, 1928.

Jobim, José. *O Brasil na Economia Mundial*. Rio de Janeiro, 1939.

Magalhaes, Symphronio de. *Contra el Hitlerismo* (trans. into Spanish). Montevideo, 1940.

Motta Lima, Pedro. *El Nazismo en el Brazil*. Buenos Aires, 1938.

Nash, Roy. *Conquest of Brazil*. New York, 1926.

Normano, J. F. *Economic Brazil*. Chapel Hill, 1935.

Oliveira Lima, Manoel de. *The Evolution of Brazil Compared with that of Spanish and Anglo-Saxon America*. Stanford University, 1914.

Simonson, Roberto C. *Historia Economica do Brasil*. São Paulo, 1937.

—— *Brazil's Industrial Revolution*. São Paulo, 1939.

Williams, Mary W. *Dom Pedro the Magnanimous*. Chapel Hill, 1937.

CHILE

(In addition to general works cited.)

ALLENDE, SALVADOR. *La Realidad Médico-Social Chilena.* Santiago, 1939.

BARROS ARANA, DIEGO. *Historia Jeneral de Chile.* Santiago, 1902.

BULLETINS, Departamento de Información Campesina del Ministerio de Agricultura. Santiago, 1940.

DIRECCIÓN GENERAL DE ESTADÍSTICA. *Censo Industrial y Comercial.* Santiago, 1937.

EDWARDS, AGUSTIN. *My Native Land* (trans.). London, 1928.

EDWARDS, ALBERTO. *La Fronda Aristocrática.* Santiago, 1936.

EDWARDS BELLO, JOAQUIN. *El Roto.* Santiago, 1927.

ENCINA, FRANCISCO A. *Portales.* Santiago, 1934.

FILES: *El Mercurio, La Nación, El Diario Ilustrado.* Santiago.

FREI MONTALVA, EDUARDO. *Chile Desconocido.* Santiago, 1937.

GONZÁLES VON MARÉES, JORGE. *El Mal de Chile.* Santiago, 1940.

HAMILTON, EDUARDO. *Tienen Derecho a Vivir.* Santiago, 1938.

LABARCA, AMANDA. *Historia de la Enseñanza en Chile.* Santiago, 1939.

LATCHAM, RICARDO A. *Chuquicamata Estado Yankee.* Santiago, 1926.

ORREGO, ANTENOR. *El Pueblo Continente.* Santiago, 1939.

PICON-SALAS, MARIANO. *Intuición de Chile.* Santiago, 1935.

SIMON, RAÚL. *Determinación de la Entrada Nacional de Chile.* Santiago, 1937.

—— and others. *El Concepto de Industria Nacional y la Protección del Estado.* Santiago, 1939.

SUBERCASEAUX, BENJAMIN. *Chile o una loca geografía.* Santiago, 1940.

URUGUAY, PARAGUAY, PERU, AND ECUADOR

(In addition to general works cited.)

ELLIOTT, ARTHUR E. *Paraguay, Its Cultural Heritage, Social Conditions and Educational Problems.* New York, 1931.

FERNÁNDEZ ARTUCIO, HUGO. *Nazis en el Uruguay.* Buenos Aires, 1940.

FILES: *El Comercio.* Lima.

HANSON, SIMON G. *Utopia in Uruguay.* Oxford, 1938.

MARKHAM, CLEMENTS R. *History of Peru.* Chicago, 1892.

MARSH, MARGARET A. *The Bankers in Bolivia.* New York, 1928.

NILES, BLAIR. *Casual Wanderings in Ecuador and Peru.* New York, 1921.

POBLETE-TRONCOSO, MOISÉS. *Condiciones de Vida y de Trabajo de la Población Indigena del Peru.* Santiago, 1938.

SÁENZ, MOISÉS. *Sobre el Indio peruano.* Mexico, 1933.

—— *Sobre el Indio Ecuatoriano.* Mexico, 1933.

COLOMBIA AND VENEZUELA

(In addition to general works cited.)

FERGUSSON, ERNA. *Venezuela.* New York, 1939.

FILES: *El Tiempo.* Bogotá.

HENAO, JESÚS MARÍA, and ARRUBLA, GERARDO. *A History of Colombia.* Chapel Hill, 1918.

PARKS, E. TAYLOR. *Colombia and the United States.* Durham, 1935.

RIPPY, J. FRED. *The Capitalists in Colombia.* New York, 1936.

ROURKE, THOMAS. *Gómez, Tyrant of the Andes.* New York, 1936.

MIDDLE AMERICA

(In addition to general works cited.)

CHAPMAN, CHARLES E. *History of the Cuban Republic.* New York, 1927.

DAVIS, H. P. *Black Democracy: the Story of Haiti.* New York, 1928.

FERGUSSON, ERNA. *Guatemala.* New York, 1937.

JENKS, LELAND H. *Our Cuban Colony.* New York, 1926.

KEPNER, C. D., and SOOTHILL, J. H. *The Banana Empire.* New York, 1935.

KNIGHT, M. M. *The Americans in Santo Domingo.* New York, 1928.

LEGÉR, J. N. *Haiti: Her History and Her Detractors.* New York, 1928.

MUNRO, DANA G. *Five Republics of Central America.* New York, 1918.

NEARING, SCOTT, and FREEMAN, JOSEPH. *Dollar Diplomacy.* New York, 1925.

RIPPY, J. FRED. *Caribbean Danger Zone.* New York, 1940.

WELLES, SUMNER. *Naboth's Vineyard.* New York, 1928.

MEXICO

(In addition to general works cited.)

BRENNER, ANITA. *Idols Behind Altars.* New York, 1929.

CALLCOTT, W. H. *Church and State in Mexico.* Durham, 1926.

CHASE, STUART. *Mexico.* New York, 1935.

CLARK, MARJORIE. *Organized Labor in Mexico.* Chapel Hill, 1934.

DUNN, FREDERICK S. *Diplomatic Protection of Americans in Mexico.* New York, 1933.

GRUENING, ERNEST. *Mexico and Its Heritage.* New York, 1929.

HACKETT, CHARLES W. *The Mexican Revolution and the United States.* Boston, 1927.

HERRING, HUBERT, and TERRILL, KATHERINE (eds.). *The Genius of Mexico.* New York, 1931.

—— and Weinstock, Herbert (eds.). *Renascent Mexico*. New York, 1935.

Hübner, Manuel Eduardo. *México en Marcha*. Santiago, 1936.

Parkes, H. B. *A History of Mexico*. Boston, 1938.

Redfield, Robert E. *Tepoztlan*. Chicago, 1930.

Rippy, J. Fred. *The United States and Mexico*. New York, 1931.

Sáenz, Moisés. *México Integro*. Lima, 1939.

Senior, Clarence. *Democracy Comes to a Cotton Kingdom—the Story of Mexico's La Laguna*. Mexico, 1940.

Simpson, Eyler. *The Ejido*. Chapel Hill, 1937.

Tannenbaum, Frank. *Peace by Revolution*. New York, 1933.

INDEX